Middle East Conflict

Almanac

SECOND EDITION

Middle East Conflict

Almanac

SECOND EDITION

Sonia G. Benson
Jennifer Stock, Project Editor

U·X·L
A part of Gale, Cengage Learning

GALE
CENGAGE Learning®

Detroit • New York • San Francisco • New Haven, Conn • Waterville, Maine • London

GALE
CENGAGE Learning

**Middle East Conflict: Almanac,
2nd Edition**
Sonia G. Benson

Project Editor: Jennifer Stock

Rights Acquisition and Management:
   Christine Myaskvoksy

Composition: Evi Abou-El-Seoud

Manufacturing: Wendy Blurton

Imaging: John Watkins

Product Design: Kristine Julien

For product information and technology assistance, contact us at
Gale Customer Support, 1-800-877-4253.
For permission to use material from this text or product,
submit all requests online at **www.cengage.com/permissions.**
Further permissions questions can be emailed to
permissionrequest@cengage.com

Cover photographs reproduced by permission of LOOK Die Bildagentur
der Fotografen GmbH/Alamy (the Dome of the Rock and the Wailing Wall in
Jerusalem) and Mahmoudreza Kalari/Sygma/Corbis (Iranian soldiers during the
Iran-Iraq War). Cover art reproduced by permission of Shutterstock.com (border
image and arabic classical ornament).

While every effort has been made to ensure the reliability of the information
presented in this publication, Gale, a part of Cengage Learning, does not
guarantee the accuracy of the data contained herein. Gale accepts no payment
for listing; and inclusion in the publication of any organization, agency,
institution, publication, service, or individual does not imply endorsement of the
editors or publisher. Errors brought to the attention of the publisher and verified
to the satisfaction of the publisher will be corrected in future editions.

Library of Congress Cataloging-in-Publication Data

Middle East conflict reference library / [Jennifer Stock, project editor]. -- 2nd ed.
   v. cm.
   "U-X-L Reference Library".
   Includes bibliographical references and index.
   Contents: 1. Almanac / Sonia Benson -- 2. Biographies / Carol Brennan --
3. Primary sources / Terri Schell.
   ISBN 978-1-4144-8607-9 (set) -- ISBN 978-1-4144-8608-6 (almanac) --
ISBN 978-1-4144-8609-3 (biographies) -- ISBN 978-1-4144-8610-9
(primary sources)
   1. Arab-Israeli conflict--Sources--Juvenile literature. 2. Arab-Israeli conflict--
Juvenile literature. 3. Middle East--History--Juvenile literature. I. Stock, Jennifer
York, 1974- II. Benson, Sonia. Almanac. III. Brennan, Carol, 1966- Biographies.
IV. Schell, Terri, 1968- Primary sources.

DS119.7.M4713 2012
956.04--dc23   2011050994

Gale
27500 Drake Rd.
Farmington Hills, MI, 48331-3535

ISBN-13: 978-1-4144-8607-9 (set)   ISBN-10: 1-4144-8607-3 (set)
ISBN-13: 978-1-4144-8608-6   ISBN-10: 1-4144-8608-1
(Almanac)   (Almanac)
ISBN-13: 978-1-4144-8609-3   ISBN-10: 1-4144-8609-X
(Biographies)   (Biographies)
ISBN-13: 978-1-4144-8610-9   ISBN-10: 1-4144-8610-3
(Primary Sources)   (Primary Sources)
ISBN-13: 978-1-4144-8612-3   ISBN-10: 1-4144-8612-X
(Cumulative Index)   (Cumulative Index)

This title is also available as an e-book.
ISBN-13: 978-1-4144-9087-8 ISBN-10: 1-4144-9087-9
Contact your Gale, a part of Cengage Learning sales representative for
ordering information.

Printed in China
1 2 3 4 5 6 7 16 15 14 13 12

Table of Contents

Reader's Guide

From the early twentieth century to present times, no region in the world has been so badly torn by conflict as the Middle East and North Africa. What is most striking about the many conflicts that have occurred in the Middle East is their complexity. For many years differences over religion, cultural identity, and political philosophy have combined with tribal and ethnic biases to fan the flames of conflict. Western imperialism and influence, as well as the struggle between modernization and traditionalism, have also played important roles in Middle East conflict. Untangling these numerous and overlapping elements presents a challenge to even the most experienced scholars and diplomats.

Even the term "Middle East" is somewhat complicated. Because the region is not strictly defined by geography, culture, or language, its definition has never been precise. The term was originally coined by Europeans (for whom Asia lies to the east). In the nineteenth century Europeans used the term "Near East" to distinguish areas of western Asia that were closer to Europe than the "Far East," the area that includes Southeast Asia, China, Japan, and Korea. In the twentieth century, the newer term "Middle East" came to replace "Near East," denoting the same basic area of Western Asia.

The nations that are most often included as part of the Middle East in the twenty-first century are: Saudi Arabia, Yemen, Oman, Qatar, Kuwait, Bahrain, the United Arab Emirates, Israel, the Palestinian territories, Jordan, Lebanon, Syria, Iraq, and Iran. Turkey, which is located in western Asia and also in Europe, is considered part of the Middle East due to its location and its many cultural and historical connections to the region. Egypt, although geographically part of North Africa, is also considered a Middle Eastern nation. Other North African states, notably Libya, Algeria, Tunisia, Morocco, and sometimes Sudan, are included as part of the Middle East by many authorities.

To understand the conflicts that have shaped the Middle East, one must keep in mind a variety of important forces that have shaped the region. The oldest and most enduring force is that of religion. The Middle East is home to three of the world's great monotheistic (belief in one god) religions—Judaism, Christianity, and Islam. Each of these religions has deep roots in the Middle East and places great importance on religious shrines and temples that continue to exist in the region, especially in the fiercely contested city of Jerusalem, in present-day Israel. Religious differences, both those between the religions and those that arise among sects (groups) within the same religion, such as followers of the Sunni and Shiite branches of Islam, continue to play an important role in the Middle East.

Other sources of conflict are based in the Middle East's long political history. The region's ancient cultures were shaped and influenced by the rule of the Islamic empires, whose great caliphs were the spiritual, political, and military leaders of the world's Muslims from the seventh to the thirteenth century, and then by the Ottoman Empire, whose sultans ruled over an area encompassing most of the Middle East and North Africa and a large part of southeastern Europe for six hundred years, from 1299 to 1923. After the relatively stable rule of these great Muslim empires, many Middle East countries came under the rule of Western governments in the early twentieth century. Foreigners divided the Middle East into separate countries without regard to the cultures and politics of the inhabitants. The internal politics of the new nations often arose in opposition to foreign rule. After gaining independence from Western rule, many of the countries of the Middle East fell under the power of authoritarian leaders with powerful security forces.

In addition to the enduring influence of religion and Western power, other hostilities have contributed to conflict in the Middle East. Ethnic differences have often resulted in wars among groups such as the Arabs, Persians, and Turks, to name a few. Armenians and Kurds (a non-Arab ethnic group) struggled to establish self-rule over their own territories. The Armenians have been successful, but the Kurds remain the largest ethnic group in the world without a country of their own.

The flashpoint for much of the conflict in the Middle East has been the area of present-day Israel and the Palestinian territories. This region, known historically as Palestine, was home to the ancient Jewish kingdom. The Jews were expelled from Palestine as other ancient empires took control of the region, especially the Romans. As the centuries passed they faced anti-Semitism (prejudice against Jews) throughout the world. Then, in the nineteenth century, the Zionist movement arose calling for the creation of an independent Jewish state in Palestine. By this time Palestine had been home to Arabs for hundreds of years, and both groups pressed their claim to this land. The Jews were better organized, both politically and militarily, and in 1948 they declared the creation of the state of Israel. In the mid–twentieth century, Arabs fought against the Jewish state of Israel in a series of Arab-Israeli Wars. Arab Palestinians continue to claim the land that they believe was stolen from them, and they have sought various means—ranging from terrorism to political negotiation—to express their political will.

One of the driving forces of the conflicts in the Middle East since the mid–twentieth century has been oil. Oil has dramatically increased the wealth of those countries that produce it—especially Iran, Iraq, Kuwait, and Saudi Arabia—but it has not brought those countries peace, democracy, or political stability. In each of these countries, oil wealth has been controlled by a select few who hold power in the government. Foreign powers have worked aggressively to ensure that the oil-producing countries behave in ways that do not threaten foreign access to oil. Tensions created between various parties vying for control of oil in these countries causes ongoing conflict.

In 2011, the nature of Middle East conflict took a sudden, unexpected, and far-reaching turn when a series of prodemocracy uprisings rapidly spread throughout countries of the Middle East and North Africa that had long been suppressed by authoritarian rulers. Through their courageous efforts, the people of several Middle Eastern countries have overthrown their authoritarian leaders and worked create democratic governments. The place in history that this powerful prodemocracy movement, known as the Arab Spring, will take may be better understood in future times, but it has provided enormous insight into the causes and consequences of Middle East conflicts in modern times.

Coverage and features

Middle East Conflict: Almanac, 2nd Edition examines the historical events that have contributed to conflicts in the in the Middle East and North

Africa and traces developments to the present day. The volume's sixteen chapters cover the ancient Middle East, the rise and fall of the Ottoman Empire, the creation of Israel, the Palestinian Authority, the rise of Hezbollah in Lebanon, the Gulf Wars, terrorism, the Arab Spring uprisings, and more. Each chapter features informative sidebar boxes highlighting glossary terms and issues discussed in the text. Also included are more than one hundred photographs and illustrations, a timeline, a glossary, a list of research and activity ideas, sources for further reading, and an index providing easy access to subjects discussed throughout the volume.

Middle East Conflict Reference Library, 2nd Edition

Middle East Conflict: Biographies, 2nd Edition profiles thirty-five of the most influential figures from throughout the Middle East and North Africa. The volume profiles kings, presidents, and other political leaders, as well as activists and militants. Included are Iranian president Mahmoud Ahmadinejad, Lebanese politician Pierre Gemayel, Jewish author and activist Theodor Herzl, Libyan leader Mu'ammar al-Qaddaffi, Israeli prime minister Benjamin Netanyahu, and Egyptian president Anwar Sadat. Also included are prominent female leaders Golda Meir and Tzipporah Livni of Israel and Palestinian activist Hanan Ashrawi. The volume includes more than ninety photographs and illustrations, a timeline, sources for further reading, and an index.

Middle East Conflict: Primary Sources, 2nd Edition presents twenty-nine full or excerpted written works, poems, proclamations, or other documents relating to conflict in the Middle East and North Africa, divided into eight thematically organized chapters. Among the historic documents included are the Peel Commission Report of 1937, which recommended the division of Palestine into Arab and Jewish states; the 1948 declaration establishing the nation of Israel; and the 1968 Palestinian National Charter, which stated the goals of the Palestinian people. The volume also features personal accounts and artistic works, including an account by journalist Terry Anderson describing his time as a hostage in Lebanon and excerpts from the graphic novels *Palestine* and *Persepolis*. Also included are documents relating to the Arab Spring uprisings. More than eighty photographs and illustrations, a timeline, sources for further reading, and an index supplement the volume.

A cumulative index of all three volumes in *Middle East Conflict Reference Library, 2nd Edition* is also available.

Acknowledgements

The editors would like to thank the advisor for *Middle East Conflict Reference Library, 2nd Edition*, Michael R. Fischbach, PhD. Dr. Fischbach is a Professor of History at Randolph-Macon College, in Ashland, Virginia. He specializes in the history of the modern Middle East, especially Palestine, Israel, Jordan, and the Arab-Israeli conflict.

The editors also would like to acknowledge Tom and Sara Pendergast, authors of the first edition of *Middle East Conflict Reference Library*.

Comments and suggestions

We welcome your comments on *Middle East Conflict: Almanac, 2nd Edition* and suggestions for other topics to consider. Please write: Editors, *Middle East Conflict: Almanac, 2nd Edition*, Gale Cengage Learning, 27500 Drake Road, Farmington Hills, Michigan 48331-3535; call toll free: 1-800-877-4253; fax to 248-699-8097; or send e-mail via http:// www.gale.cengage.com.

Timeline of Events

7000 BCE: The first-known human civilizations begin to form in Mesopotamia, the site of present-day Iraq and parts of Syria, Turkey, and Iran.

2700 BCE: Egyptian society has developed into a sophisticated civilization.

c. 1030 BCE: Israelites, descendants of the Hebrew patriarch Abraham and ancestors of the Jews, take control of Canaan and call their kingdom Eretz Yisrael.

970–931 BCE: The First Temple of Solomon, which will become the center of the Jewish faith, is built in Jerusalem.

587–518 BCE: The First Temple of Solomon is destroyed by Babylonians and a second temple is built on the site.

146 BCE–**476** CE: Most of the Mediterranean region comes under the control of the Roman Empire.

66–73 CE: In the Great Revolt, the Jews rise up against Roman rule; the Romans, in return, destroy the Second Temple.

c. 312: Constantine I, emperor of the Eastern Roman (later Byzantine) Empire, embraces Christianity and proclaims it the official religion of the empire.

632: The Muslim prophet Muhammad dies.

635–750: Muslims create the caliphate, the entire community of Muslims under the leadership of the caliph. The Islamic Empire spreads to Damascus, Syria, Mesopotamia, Palestine, and Egypt, and then on to North Africa, across Persia toward India and China, and westward beyond present-day Turkey, toward Italy, and Spain.

750–1050: The Islamic empire experiences a golden age in the arts and sciences.

1095–1291: The Crusades begin when the pope urges thousands of Roman Catholic men to join military campaigns to take control of the Holy Land from Muslims.

1204: The crusaders conquer the Christian Byzantine capital city of Constantinople, sharpening divisions between the Eastern Orthodox Church and the Roman Catholic Church.

1243: Mongol armies led by Genghis Khan conquer much of central Asia and the Middle East, including Anatolia.

1299: Turkish leader Osman I begins to conquer new territories around Anatolia, establishing the Ottoman Empire.

1453: Constantinople is conquered by the Ottoman Empire, which has grown to include the Balkan Peninsula, as well as Albania, Greece, and Hungary.

1500s: Under Ottoman sultans Selim I and his son Süleyman I, the Ottoman Empire attains worldwide supremacy, expanding from its base in Anatolia and Europe to include Syria, Egypt, and the western Arabian Peninsula, as well as North Africa.

1744: Wahhabi religious leader Muhammad ibn Abd al-Wahhab allies with Arab leader Mohammad ibn Saud and together they take power in the southern Arabian Peninsula. Though eventually forced to retreat by the Ottomans, Ibn Saud and his family maintain control in the desert regions of Arabia.

1768–1774: The Russo-Ottoman War results in Russia gaining control of the Crimea and other Ottoman territory.

1785: The Qahar dynasty begins in Iran.

1798–1801: The French invade and occupy Egypt.

1805–1848: Reign of Muhammad Ali in Egypt.

1839: A series of reforms known as Tanzimat, based mainly on the European style of government, are instituted in the Ottoman Empire.

1858–1860: Civil unrest in Lebanon and Syria leads to European intervention.

1869: Construction is completed on Egypt's Suez Canal, linking the Mediterranean Sea to the Red Sea.

1878: European powers convene the Congress of Berlin to settle territorial questions of the weakening Ottoman Empire; they grant independence to several Balkan countries, humiliating the fiercely proud Ottomans.

1881: France declares Tunisia a protectorate.

1881–1884: A vicious series of pogroms directed against Jews sweeps through Russia.

1882–1922: Great Britain invades and occupies Egypt.

1896: Theodor Herzl publishes *The Jewish State*, drawing attention to the ideas of Zionism, and promoting the immigration of Jews to Palestine. By the twentieth century, thousands of Jews had moved to the region.

1908–1909: The Young Turks overthrow the Ottoman sultan, announcing their intentions to separate government from religion and to make the Turkish language the official language of the empire.

1912: Italy begins its rule of Libya. Most of Morocco becomes a French protectorate, while a small part goes to Spain.

1914–1918: World War I; the Ottoman Empire joins the Central Powers of Germany and Austria-Hungary against the Allies: Great Britain, France, Russia, and the United States. Defeated, the Ottoman Empire collapses at war's end.

1914: At the outbreak of World War I, Great Britain declares Egypt to be a protectorate of the British Empire.

1915–1923: The Turkish leaders of the Ottoman Empire order the mass killing and displacement of the Armenians living in the empire; between 600,000 and 1.5 million Armenians die.

1916–1918: Arabs revolt against the Ottomans under an agreement with the British, hoping for Arab independence after World War I.

1917: The Balfour Declaration is approved by the British war cabinet, promising British support for the Zionist cause in Palestine.

1919: Iran becomes a British protectorate when it signs the Anglo-Persian Agreement of 1919.

1919–1922: Under several international treaties, a large portion of former Ottoman lands are divided up into mandates, to be administered by European nations under the supervision of the League of Nations. France receives control of Syria and Lebanon, and Great Britain receives control of Palestine and Iraq.

1922: Great Britain declares Egypt a constitutional monarchy.

1923: The independent Republic of Turkey is recognized by the international community.

1925: Reza Khan establishes the Pahlavi dynasty in Iran.

1928: The Muslim Brotherhood, an Islamist group that seeks to promote Islam and rid Egypt of foreign influence, is established in Egypt.

1931: Zionists in the mandate of Palestine form one of the first contemporary terrorist groups in the Middle East: Irgun Zvai Leumi, better known as Irgun, which attacks Arab civilians and British authorities.

1932: Iraq gains independence from Great Britain.

1932: Ibn Saud unites large portions of the Arabian Peninsula under his rule and calls his kingdom Saudi Arabia.

1935: The German government under the Nazis passes the Nuremberg Laws, which take away the civil rights of German Jews.

1935–1939: Thousands of Zionist immigrants pour into Palestine.

1936–1939: The Arab Revolt in Palestine is organized to protest British rule and Jewish immigration.

1938: Vast quantities of oil are discovered in Saudi Arabia.

1939–1945: During World War II, the German Nazis initiate the systematic murder of Jewish people and several other groups, an act of genocide that will become known as the Holocaust.

1943: As France withdraws from Lebanon, it frames the National Pact, a sectarian system of government that calls for a ratio of six Christians to every five Muslims in the Lebanese government.

1945: The leaders of Egypt, Iraq, Lebanon, Transjordan, Saudi Arabia, Syria, and Yemen join to form the Arab League to promote cooperation within the Arab world. In the initial agreement, members pledge to preserve the rights of the Palestinians.

1946: France withdraws from its mandatory rule of Syria after decades of bitter resistance to its rule. With France gone, Syria faces many internal divisions.

1947: The United Nations Special Committee on Palestine (UNSCOP) calls for the partition of Palestine into two separate states, a Jewish one and an Arab one. The Palestinians reject this plan.

1947: The Ba'ath Party is founded with the objective of bringing about a rebirth of Arab power. It is popular in Syria and Iraq.

1947–1948: Civil war breaks out between the Palestinians and the Jews in the British Mandate of Palestine.

May 14, 1948: Jewish leader David Ben-Gurion announces the establishment of the independent state of Israel.

May 15, 1948: The armies of Egypt, Iraq, Lebanon, Syria, and Transjordan invade the former mandate of Palestine in an attempt to stop the creation of the new state of Israel, beginning the 1948 Arab-Israeli War.

August 1948: The 1948 Arab-Israeli War concludes with the defeat of the Arab forces. Israeli forces significantly expand their territory and ensure Israeli independence. An estimated 750,000 Palestinians are either forced to, or willingly, leave their homes and become refugees. Arabs refer to the events of 1948 as *al-Nakba* ("the catastrophe").

1952–1953: The Free Officers launch a military coup that overthrows the Egyptian monarchy.

1954: The United States helps Iranians stage a coup to return the ousted Mohammad Reza Pahlavi to power as shah of Iran.

1954–1962: In the eight-year Algerian war for independence from France nearly one million people are killed. Algeria declares its independence in 1962.

1956: Gamal Abdel Nasser becomes president of Egypt; he soon announces the nationalization of the Suez Canal, resulting in the Suez Crisis, a brief armed conflict with Great Britain, France, and Israel.

1956: France grants Tunisia independence.

1958–1961: In an attempt at creating a pan-Arab state, Gamal Abdel Nasser organizes the United Arab Republic (UAR), initially a political union between Egypt and Syria. Problems arise immediately, and a military coup in 1961 restores Syria's independence and disbands the UAR.

1959: Fatah, a Palestinian militant group dedicated to the establishment of an independent Palestinian state, is founded.

1964: The Palestine Liberation Organization (PLO) is founded.

1967: The 1967 Arab-Israeli War begins when Israel, fearing an attack from the Arab countries, attacks first, striking Egypt, Syria, and Jordan decisively. Israel nearly triples its size by taking the Golan

Heights, the West Bank, the Gaza Strip, and the Sinai Peninsula. Israel establishes military rule in the captured regions, which come to be known as the occupied territories.

1968: The Popular Front for the Liberation of Palestine (PFLP) hijacks an Israeli jetliner and diverts it to Algeria. The international attention gained by the hijacking encourages the PFLP and similar groups to continue to stage terrorist acts.

1969: Yasser Arafat becomes the chairman of the PLO, which has grown increasingly radical and violent. Palestinian militants launch constant guerrilla attacks against Israel in order to retake Palestinian land and return refugees to their homes.

1969: A group of military officers headed by Colonel Mu'ammar al-Qaddafi overthrows the Libyan king; al-Qaddafi establishes the Libyan Arab Republic and becomes its leader.

1970: The king of Jordan expels the PLO from his country in a bloody event known as Black September, in which three thousand Palestinians are killed. PLO leadership, forced out of the country, relocates to southern Lebanon.

1970: Syria's Ba'athist Party places Hafez Assad in power.

1972: At the Olympic Games in Munich, Germany, eight armed members of a Palestinian group calling itself Black September storm the apartments of the Israeli Olympic team, killing two team members and taking nine others hostage. During a rescue attempt, Black September murders the hostages.

1973: The brief 1973 Arab-Israeli War is launched by Egypt and Syria-led Arab forces against Israel. Arabs experience some initial success, although Israel successfully defends itself.

1973: Arabs and Arab members of the Organization of Petroleum Exporting Countries (OPEC), furious at U.S. interference in the 1973 Arab-Israel War, organize an embargo of oil shipments to the United States, effectively cutting off the majority of the U.S. oil supply.

1975: The fifteen-year Civil War in Lebanon begins.

1975: The Iraqi government tries to evict the Kurds from the country, forcing residents out of eight hundred Kurdish villages near the Iran-Iraq border.

1976: The Arab League grants Syria permission to station forty thousand Syrian troops in Lebanon as part of a peace agreement.

1978: The Camp David Accords are signed by Egyptian President Anwar Sadat and Israeli Prime Minister Menachem Begin at Camp David, setting the framework for Egypt to become the first Arab nation to recognize Israel as a state. Sadat and Begin are awarded Nobel Peace Prizes for their contributions to peace in the Middle East.

1978: Fatah members hijack an Israeli tourist bus, resulting in the deaths of thirty-eight Israelis. Outraged Israeli leaders launch Operation Litani, sending more than twenty thousand troops into southern Lebanon in an attempt to destroy the PLO.

1979: The Iranian Revolution (also known as the Islamic Revolution) transforms Iran from a secular (nonreligious) country into an Islamic country, in which the social, political, and economic institutions of the country are based on Islamic holy law.

1979: Saddam Hussein becomes president of Iraq and begins immediately to use his power to destroy opponents and establish an authoritarian government.

1979: The U.S. embassy in Iran is overtaken by a group of Iranian students. Fifty-two Americans are held hostage for 444 days.

September 1980: Iraq invades Iran, beginning the brutal, eight-year Iran-Iraq War.

1981: Egyptian president Anwar Sadat is assassinated; the militant group Egyptian Islamic Jihad is responsible.

1982: Israel launches an attack on Lebanon called Operation Peace for Galilee to push the PLO in southern Lebanon back from the Israeli borders. With international intervention, the fighting is stopped; the PLO leadership moves to Tunisia.

1982: The the Phalangists militia enter the Sabra and Shatila Palestinian refugee camps outside Beirut and massacre approximately one thousand Palestinian men, women, and children. During the massacre, Israeli troops surround the camps, doing little to stop the massacre.

1982: Syrian president Hafez Assad orders a brutal attack on the city of Hama, where the Muslim Brotherhood is headquartered. His forces kill more than ten thousand innocent inhabitants of the city.

1983: Small, militant Shiite Lebanese groups protesting the 1982 Israeli invasion of Lebanon launch a deadly series of suicide bombings: the first at the Beirut airport, which kills 241 U.S. Marines; a second that kills 58 French paratroopers; and a third that strikes an Israeli headquarters in southern Lebanon, killing 29 Israeli troops.

1985: Lebanese Shiite militant groups merge into a new Islamist group called Hezbollah. Hezbollah's immediate purpose is to drive Israeli forces, and all Western influences, out of Lebanon.

1987: The Palestinians in the West Bank and the Gaza Strip launch the First Intifada, an extended protest against Israeli occupation.

1988: Yasser Arafat promises to recognize Israel and to renounce terrorism.

1988: Iraq launches Anfal, an operation designed to destroy the Kurdish population in Iraq that includes bombing Kurdish villages, destroying Kurdish homes and farmlands, and forcing tens of thousands of Kurds to flee. One of the Anfal attacks is on the Kurdish town of Halabja, and it makes use of poison gases, such as sarin and mustard gas, killing and wounding thousands of Kurds.

1988: A terrorist bomb blows up Pan Am Flight 103 from London to New York over Lockerbie, Scotland, killing 243 passengers and 16 crew members. Libya's leader al-Qaddafi is suspected of being responsible.

1989: Osama bin Laden establishes al-Qaeda headquarters in Sudan and begins to train warriors to carry out terrorist acts.

1989: Islamic Jihad, a militant Palestinian group, claims responsibility for the first known suicide bombing of the Israeli-Palestinian conflict.

1989: Lebanese lawmakers convene in Taif, Saudi Arabia, to restructure Lebanon's sectarian government, allowing for better representation for Muslims.

1990: The Lebanese Civil War ends, but Syria's forces remain in Lebanon. The Lebanese government grants Syria control of Lebanon's internal affairs and management of its foreign policy and security issues.

1990: North Yemen and South Yemen unify, becoming the Republic of Yemen.

1990–1991: The Persian Gulf War begins with Iraq's invasion of Kuwait. A U.S.-led coalition of more than thirty countries challenges and defeats Iraq but leaves Saddam Hussein in power. International sanctions on trade with Iraq cause great suffering in the country in the decade after the war.

1992: Lebanon holds its first parliamentary elections since 1972 and elects Rafiq Hariri as prime minister.

1993: The Oslo Accords, a set of agreements between the Israelis and the Palestinians, outlines a process in which Palestinians can achieve self-rule under an elected body called the Palestinian Authority (PA).

1993: Four radical Islamist conspirators explode a powerful bomb in the underground parking garage in one of the towers of New York City's World Trade Center, killing six and injuring more than one thousand people.

1998: Osama bin Laden publicly declares that it is the duty of all Muslims to kill Americans, both military and civilian.

2000: Yasser Arafat and Israeli Prime Minister Ehud Barak meet at Camp David to prepare for a Palestinian state, but the negotiations fail.

2000: The Second Intifada begins in the occupied Palestinian territories, with more violence than the first.

2000: The eighteen-year Israeli occupation of Lebanon ends with the withdrawal of Israeli soldiers, a huge victory for Hezbollah.

2001: Following the death of president Hafez Assad in 2000, a period called Damascus Spring begins in Syria. Assad's son, Bashar Assad, promises reforms and eventual democracy, but quickly breaks his word and crushes democratic movements.

September 11, 2001: Al-Qaeda terrorists use passenger jets to destroy the World Trade Center towers in New York and damage the Pentagon building in Virginia. Nearly three thousand people are killed in the attack. The United States declares a war on terror.

2002: Israel launches Operation Defensive Shield, a military offensive against several West Bank cities. Yasser Arafat's compound in Ramallah is surrounded and the city is devastated.

2002: The United States claims that Iraq is secretly manufacturing weapons of mass destruction.

March 2003: A U.S.-led coalition makes air strikes on Baghdad, Iraq, starting the Iraq War.

2004: Photos are released to the public showing Iraqi prisoners being beaten and sexually humiliated by U.S. soldiers at Abu Ghraib, a prison in Baghdad where the United States is holding its detainees.

2004: Yasser Arafat dies.

2005: Fatah leader Mahmoud Abbas is elected president of the Palestinian Authority.

2005: Israeli Prime Minister Ariel Sharon orders the evacuation all of Israel's twenty-one settlements in the Gaza Strip and four in the West Bank.

2005: Former Lebanese prime minister Rafiq Hariri is assassinated in Beirut. Blaming Syria for the murder, an estimated one million Lebanese people demonstrate against Syria's oppressive presence in their country. Syria is forced to end its twenty-nine-year occupation of Lebanon.

2006: The Palestinian Authority holds its first national legislative elections to choose members of the Palestinian Legislative Council. Hamas, a militant Islamist group, wins the majority of the seats in the council.

2006: War erupts between Israel and Hezbollah in Lebanon. Thirty-three days of fighting devastate Lebanon but the war also harms Israel.

2006: A group of al-Qaeda in Iraq and Sunni extremists bomb the Askariya Mosque in Samarra, Iraq. Outraged Shiites blamed the Sunnis and form militias that sweep into Sunni neighborhoods, beating and killing Sunnis. Sunnis bomb and attack Shiites in revenge. An estimated one thousand deaths ensue, and hundreds of thousands of Iraqis flee their homes as the sectarian violence escalates.

December 2006: Iraqi President Saddam Hussein is executed for crimes against humanity.

2007: Fighting breaks out between Hamas and Fatah. After a violent split, Hamas serves as the sole ruler of the Gaza Strip and Fatah rules in the West Bank for the next four years. Under Hamas, the Gaza Strip continues to be a site for launching rockets into Israel.

2007: Israel labels the Gaza Strip a hostile entity and establishes a blockade of the territory that causes great suffering among the Gaza Strip's inhabitants.

2007: Mahmoud Abbas declares a state of emergency in the Palestinian Authority and creates a new government with moderate economist Salam Fayyad as prime minister.

2008: In response to attacks from Hamas, Israel launches Operation Cast Lead, a strike against the Gaza Strip that leaves thirteen hundred people dead and causes massive destruction.

2008: Hezbollah achieves a majority in the Lebanese government.

2009: In large numbers, Iranians protest what appear to be rigged elections, demanding the resignation of the president and democratic reforms. A government crackdown ends the demonstrations that come to be known as the Green Movement.

August 19, 2010: U.S. president Barack Obama declares the U.S. combat mission in Iraq over. All troops are scheduled to leave Iraq by the end of 2011.

December 17, 2010: In Sidi Bouzid, Tunisia, Mohamed Bouazizi sets himself on fire to protest poor treatment at the hands of officials, igniting a revolt against the authoritarian government in Tunisia. The revolt quickly leads to the Arab Spring, a series of prodemocracy uprisings throughout the Middle East.

2011: Fatah and Hamas reach a reconciliation agreement under which they agree to form a coalition government for the Palestinian Authority and then hold new elections in the Gaza Strip and the West Bank.

2011: The United Nation's Special Tribunal for Lebanon officially indicts four Hezbollah members in the assassination of Rafik Hariri; Hezbollah will not allow them to be arrested.

January 25, 2011: Tens of thousands of protesters position themselves in Tahrir Square in Cairo, Egypt, denouncing police brutality and demanding an end to president Hosni Mubarak's rule.

May 2, 2011: Osama bin Laden is killed by a U.S. Navy SEAL team in Pakistan.

October 20, 2011: Mu'ammar al-Qaddafi is killed by rebel forces while fleeing. The Libyan civil war is over.

March 18, 2011: Syrian security forces arrest, beat, and torture fifteen teenagers for painting graffiti on a school wall in Dara'a, setting off a protest that soon spreads to other cities. Within weeks, the Syrian government launches a violent crackdown.

Words to Know

A

Alawis: Also spelled Alawites; followers of a sect of Shia Islam that live in Syria. Their belief system and practices vary from Shiites in several ways, particularly in the belief that Ali, the son-in-law of the prophet Muhammad, was the human form of Allah (the Arabic word for God).

aliyah: The immigration of Jews to the historic Eretz Yisrael (Land of Israel).

anti-Semitism: Prejudice against Jews.

Arab League: A regional political alliance of Arab nations formed in 1945 to promote political, military, and economic cooperation within the Arab world.

Arabs: People of the Middle East and North Africa who speak the Arabic language or who live in countries in which Arabic is the dominant language.

Arab Spring: A series of prodemocracy uprisings in the Middle East and North Africa.

authoritarianism: A type of leadership in which power is consolidated under one strong leader, or a small group of elite leaders, who do not answer to the will of the people.

ayatollah: A high-ranking Shiite religious leader.

B

Ba'ath Party: A secular (nonreligious) political party founded in the 1940s with the goal of uniting the Arab world and creating one powerful Arab state.

Byzantine Empire: The eastern part of the Roman Empire, which thrived for one thousand years after the collapse of Rome in 476.

C

caliph: The spiritual, political, and military leader of the world's Muslims from the death of Muhammad in 632 until the caliphate was abolished in 1924.

caliphate: The entire community of Muslims under the leadership of the caliph.

chemical weapons: Toxic chemical substances used during armed conflict to kill, injure, or incapacitate an enemy.

Christianity: A religion based on the teachings of Jesus Christ.

cleric: An ordained religious official.

Cold War: A period of intense political and economic rivalry between the United States and the Soviet Union that lasted from 1945 to 1991.

Communism: A system of government in which the state plans and controls the economy and a single political party holds power.

Crusades: A series of military campaigns ordered by the Roman Catholic Church between 1095 and 1291 with the main goal of taking the Holy Land from the Muslims.

crucifixion: A form of execution in which a person is nailed or bound to a cross and left to die.

D

Druze: Members of a small sect of Islam who believe that the ninth-century caliph Tariq al-Hakim was God.

dynasty: A series of rulers from the same family.

E

Eretz Yisrael: "Land of Israel" in Hebrew; the ancient kingdom of the Jews.

emir: A ruler, chief, or commander in some Islamic countries.

ethnicity: Groupings of people in a society according to their common racial, national, tribal, religious, language, or cultural backgrounds.

evangelist: A Christian follower dedicated to converting others to Christianity.

excommunication: The official exclusion of a person from membership in the church.

Fatah: A Palestinian militant group and political party dedicated to the establishment of an independent Palestinian state.

fatwa: A statement of religious law issued by Islamic clerics.

fedayeen: An Arabic term meaning one who sacrifices for a cause; used to describe several distinct militant groups that have formed in the Arab world at different times. Opponents of the fedayeen use the term to describe members of Arab terrorist groups.

fundamentalism: A movement stressing adherence to a strict or literal interpretation of religious principles.

G

Gaza Strip: A narrow strip of land along the eastern shore of the Mediterranean Sea, west of Israel and bordering Egypt in the southwest. The region was occupied by Israel after the 1967 Arab-Israeli War.

Geneva Conventions: A series of international agreements that establish how prisoners of war and civilians in wartime are to be treated.

genocide: The deliberate and systematic destruction of a group of people based on religion, ethnicity, or nationality.

Golan Heights: A mountainous region located on the border of Syria and Israel, northwest of the Sea of Galilee. The region was occupied by Israel after the 1967 Arab-Israeli War and annexed in 1981.

guerilla warfare: Combat tactics used by a smaller, less equipped fighting force against a more powerful foe.

H

Haganah: The underground defense force of Zionists in Palestine from 1920 to 1948. It became the basis for the Israeli army.

hajj: The annual Muslim pilgrimage to Mecca that takes place in the last month of the year, which every Muslim is expected to perform at least once during their lifetime if they are able.

Hamas: A Palestinian Islamic fundamentalist group and political party operating primarily in the West Bank and the Gaza Strip with the goal of establishing a Palestinian state and opposing the existence of Israel. It has been labeled a terrorist organization by several countries.

Hebrew: The ancient language of the Jewish people and the official language of present-day Israel.

Hejaz: A coastal region on the western Arabian Peninsula that includes the Muslim holy cities of Mecca and Medina.

heretic: Someone whose opinions or beliefs oppose official church doctrine.

heresy: Opinions or beliefs that oppose official church doctrine.

Hezbollah: A Shiite militant group and political party based in Lebanon.

Holocaust: The mass murder of European Jews and other groups by the Nazis during World War II.

Holy Land: Roughly the present-day territory of Israel, the Palestinian territories, and parts of Jordan and Lebanon. This area includes sacred sites for Jews, Christians, and Muslims.

I

insurgency: An uprising, or rebellion, against a political authority.

Intifada: The Palestinian uprising against Israeli occupation in the West Bank and the Gaza Strip.

Irgun Zvai Leumi: A militant underground group founded in 1931 that worked to secure Israeli independence by staging violent attacks on British and Arab targets. Also known simply as Irgun.

Islam: The religious faith followed by Muslims based on a belief in Allah as the sole god and in Muhammad as his prophet.

Islamism: A fundamentalist movement characterized by the belief that Islam should provide the basis for political, social, and cultural life in Muslim nations.

J

jihad: An armed struggle against unbelievers, in defense of Islam; often interpreted to mean holy war. The term also refers to the spiritual struggle of Muslims against sin.

Jews: People who practice the religion of Judaism.

Judaism: The religion of the Jewish people based on the belief in one god and the teachings the Talmud.

K

kibbutz: A Jewish communal farming settlement in Israel, where settlers share all property and work collaboratively together. Plural is kibbutzim.

Koran: Also spelled Qur'an or Quran; the holy book of Islam.

Kurds: A non-Arab ethnic group who live mainly in present-day Turkey, Iraq, and Iran.

L

League of Nations: An international organization of sovereign countries established after World War I to promote peace.

M

mandate: A commission granting one country the authority to administer the affairs of another country. Also describes the territory entrusted to foreign administration.

mandate system: The system established after World War I to administer former territories of Germany and the Ottoman Empire.

Maronites: Members of an Arabic-speaking group of Christians, living mainly in Lebanon, who are in communion (share essential doctrines) with the Roman Catholic Church.

martyr: A person who dies for his or her religion.

militia: Armed civilian military forces.

millet: A community for non-Muslims in the Ottoman Empire, organized by religious group and headed by a religious leader.

Muslim Brotherhood: An Islamic fundamentalist group organized in opposition to Western influence and in support of Islamic principles.

Muslims: People who practice the religion of Islam.

mosque: A Muslim place of worship.

N

nationalism: The belief that a people with shared ethnic, cultural, and/or religious identities have the right to form their own nation. In established nations nationalism is devotion and loyalty to the nation and its culture.

nationalization: The practice of bringing private industry under the ownership and control of the government.

North Atlantic Treaty Organization (NATO): An international organization created in 1949 for purposes of collective security.

O

occupation: The physical and political control of an area seized by a foreign military force.

occupied territories: The lands under the political and military control of Israel, especially the West Bank and the Gaza Strip.

Organization of Petroleum Exporting Countries (OPEC): An organization formed in 1960 by the world's major oil-producing nations to coordinate policies and ensure stable oil prices in world markets.

Ottoman Empire: The vast empire of the Ottoman Turks which included southwest Asia, northeast Africa, and southeast Europe, and lasted from the thirteenth century to the early twentieth century.

P

Palestine: A historical region in the Middle East on the eastern shore of the Mediterranean Sea, comprising parts of present-day Israel and Jordan.

Palestine Liberation Organization (PLO): A political and military organization formed to unite various Palestinian Arab groups with the goal of establishing an independent Palestinian state.

Palestinian Authority (PA): The recognized governing institution for Palestinians in the West Bank and the Gaza Strip, established in 1993. Also known as the Palestinian National Authority.

Palestinians: An Arab people whose ancestors lived in the historical region of Palestine and who continue to lay claim to that land.

Pan-Arabism: A movement for the unification of Arab peoples and the political alliance of Arab states.

Pan-Islamism: A movement for the unification of Muslims under a single Islamic state where Islam provides the basis for political, social, and cultural life.

pasha: A provincial governor or powerful official of the Ottoman Empire.

pilgrim: A person who travels to a sacred place for religious reasons.

pilgrimage: A journey to a sacred place for religious reasons.

pogrom: A racially-motivated riot in which mobs, usually organized and sanctioned by the state, attack a minority group, most often Jews.

R

rabbi: A Jewish scholar, teacher, and religious leader.

refugees: People who flee their country to escape violence or persecution.

right of return: The right, claimed by a dispossessed people, to return to their historic homeland.

S

sanctions: Punitive measures adopted by the international community against a nation that has violated international law, usually in the form of diplomatic, economic, or social restrictions.

sect: A social unit within a society that is defined by its distinct beliefs or customs.

sectarian government: A government that distributes political and institutional power among its various religious sects and ethnic communities on a proportional basis.

settlements: Communities established and inhabited in order to claim land.

sharia: A system of Islamic law based on the Koran and other sacred writings. Sharia attempts to create the perfect social order, based on God's will and justice, and covers a wide range of human activities, including acts of religious worship, the law of contracts and obligations, personal status law, and public law.

sharif: A nobleman and political leader chosen from among descendants of the Muslim prophet Muhammad.

sheikh: An Arab tribal leader.

Shiites: Followers of the Shia branch of Islam. Shiites believe that only direct descendants of the prophet Muhammad are qualified to lead the Islamic faith.

socialism: A system in which the government owns the means of production and controls the distribution of goods and services.

Suez Canal: A shipping canal that connects the Mediterranean Sea with the Red Sea.

suicide bombing: An attack intended to kill others and cause widespread damage, carried about by someone who does not hope to survive the attack.

sultan: A ruler of a Muslim state, especially the Ottoman Empire.

Sunnis: Followers of the Sunni branch of Islam. Sunnis believe that elected officials, regardless of their heritage, are qualified to lead the Islamic faith.

synagogue: A Jewish place of worship.

T

Taliban: An Islamic militant and political group that controlled Afghanistan from 1996 to 2001.

Talmud: The authoritative, ancient body of Jewish teachings and tradition.

Tanakh: The Jewish Bible.

Temple Mount: A contested religious site in Jerusalem. It is the holiest site in Judaism, the third holiest site in Islam, and also important to the Christian faith.

Torah: A Hebrew word meaning teaching or instruction, it literally refers to the first five books of the Jewish Bible. The term is often used to refer to the body of wisdom held in Jewish scriptures and sacred literature.

tribute: Payment from one ruler of a state to another, usually for protection or to acknowledge submission.

U

United Nations: An international organization of countries founded in 1945 to promote international peace, security, and cooperation.

W

weapons of mass destruction: Any nuclear, chemical, or biological weapons capable of killing or injuring large numbers of people.

West Bank: An area between Israel and Jordan on the west bank of the Jordan River, populated largely by Palestinians. The region was occupied by Israel after the 1967 Arab-Israeli War.

World War I: 1914–18; a global war between the Allies (Great Britain, France, and Russia, joined later by the United States) and the Central Powers (Germany, Austria-Hungary, and their allies).

World War II: 1939–45; a war in which the Allies (Great Britain, France, the Soviet Union, the United States, and China) defeated the Axis Powers (Germany, Italy, and Japan).

Z

Zionism: An international political movement originating in the late nineteenth century that called for the creation of an independent Jewish state in Palestine.

Zionists: Supporters of an international political movement that called for the creation of an independent Jewish state in Palestine.

Research and Activity Ideas

The following research and activity ideas complement classroom work on studies related to conflicts in the Middle East. These suggestions enhance learning and provide cross-disciplinary projects for classroom, library, and Internet use.

Activity: mapping Middle East conflicts

Some of the bitterest disputes in the Middle East have occurred over land, sometimes even small portions of land. For example, Arabs and Jews fought bitterly over control of the historic region of Palestine, and Iranians and Iraqis went to war in part over a dispute about the Shatt al Arab waterway. Yet looking at maps of the entire region provides little help in understanding why these particular physical features should be worth going to war for. To gain a better understanding, explore the geography and history of one of the Middle East's disputed regions—such as the Suez Canal or the city of Jerusalem—in order to discover why people are willing to fight over them. Create a detailed map that shows the physical features under dispute, and write a brief essay explaining the historic and cultural significance of key features on your map.

Research: bias in Internet sources on the Arab-Israeli conflict

When researching the Arab-Israeli conflict on the Internet, it is worthwhile to remember that both the Israelis and the Palestinians have devoted large amounts of time, energy, and money to arguing their cause before the global community. Many of the resources on the

Internet that may appear neutral are actually biased toward one side or another. At times, the same piece of history or news item may be described in such vastly different ways that they do not appear to portray the same event. To compare some of the Internet resources on the Arab-Israeli conflict, pick an issue or topic to research. Some suggestions for topics are: the Palestinian right of return, Jewish settlements, Hamas, the blockade on the Gaza Strip, Palestinian terrorism, and East Jerusalem. Conduct a general Internet search on this topic and scan through at least 25 sites that come up. Look for bias in the coverage by different sites and then list any differences in content and the perspective that you may find in your search.

Research: Islam

One of the difficulties facing many people from Western countries (such as Great Britain, France, Germany, Canada, and the United States) as they attempt to understand conflicts in the Middle East is a lack of understanding of Islam, the religion of the majority of people living in the region. Research the religion and prepare a fact sheet explaining some of the key elements of the Islamic faith, such as the five pillars of Islam. You may also want to discuss some of the elements of Islam that Westerns typically find so confusing, such as sharia (Islamic religious law) and some of its traditional perspectives on women.

Classroom discussion: Palestinian poetry

Members of a group or class will individually read the poem "Different Ways to Pray" by Palestinian-American poet Naomi Shihab Nye (available online at the *Poetry Foundation* Web site, http://www.poetryfoundation. org/poem/178315). Take notes as you read, and make note of any parts of the poem that you do not fully understand. Who do you think these different types of people Nye describes in her poem are? Try to describe them in your own words. Are they rich/poor, young/old, conventional/ modern, educated/uneducated, urban/rural? How much can you tell about the religious beliefs of these people from the poem? How do their lives reflect, or not reflect, their religious beliefs? Nye shows several different ways to pray, or not to pray. How different are they?

As a class or group, discuss the poem. Begin by sharing your questions or the parts of the poem you did not understand. See if you can puzzle these out together. Share your descriptions of the different groups of people described in the poem. Finally, share your thoughts on how Nye portrays the different ways to pray. Do they reflect different religious beliefs or just different circumstances? Many conflicts in the Middle East, as elsewhere throughout history, have been caused by religious differences, even those within the same religion. The differences can seem very complicated. Discuss how this poem treats these differences.

Research: monitor current events

The many conflicts in the Middle East make the news on a daily basis. You can get a good sense for the ongoing issues in the Middle East by reading a reputable newspaper or news Web site on a regular basis. For one week (or better, for one month), pay close attention to all the news stories relating to the Middle East. Keep a journal with your notes on what issues are discussed and what is happening in the Middle East.

Activity: comparing religions

Outside observers often note that Jews, Christians, and Muslims share many of the same religious ideals and even believe in some of the same religious figures. Yet these groups have engaged in deep and enduring conflict in the Middle East. Prepare a table that compares and contrasts the key religious beliefs of these three major religions. Your table might consider the nature of God, the main religious sites, the duty of followers, and other such issues. Based upon your work, why do you think religion has been a source of conflict in the Middle East?

Classroom debate: the Gulf Wars

In the Persian Gulf War (1990–91), the United States and coalition forces entered Iraq in order to restore the nation of Kuwait, which Iraq had invaded in a dispute over land and oil reserves. In the Iraq War (2003–11), the United States attacked Iraq, vowing to find an alleged stockpile of weapons of mass destruction and to overthrow Iraqi president Saddam Hussein in the process. The United States played vastly different roles in the two wars. In the Persian Gulf War it accomplished a successful but limited mission that left Saddam and his regime in power, while in Iraq War the United States led an all-out effort to eliminate Saddam and transform Iraq's government, leading to years of violence and chaos.

Divide the class into four groups. Group one and two will read several resources about the Persian Gulf War. Group one will prepare to defend the limited action taken in that war, which left Saddam in power; group two will argue that the government should have pressed further and removed Saddam. Groups three and four will read several resources about the Iraq War. Group three will prepare to defend the U.S. efforts to remove Saddam from power in the Iraq War; group four will argue that the United States should not have fought this war. In class, the four groups will debate their points. Together, the class will compare the two wars and discuss the lessons that each war may have taught us.

Research: terrorism

The groups that have been labeled as terrorist organizations by Western states have some elements in common but also some distinct differences. Terrorists create fear and chaos by striking at innocent civilians, and many people view all terrorist groups as evil. Some terrorism experts and historians, however, note that some groups are more moderate than others. They also note that those involved in terrorist activities usually believe themselves to be acting in a logical manner, using the tools that they have available to pursue their political goals.

Use your research skills to explore the ideology (political philosophy) of one Middle Eastern terrorist group. As objectively as you can, explain the key goals and ideas of this group. What do they hope to accomplish? Why have they chosen to use terrorist tactics to accomplish their goal? Do they hope to eventually use other means to gain their objectives?

Research: social media and the Arab Spring

Research the role that the social media, such as *Facebook*, *YouTube*, and *Twitter*, played in the 2011 prodemocracy movements in the Middle East known as the Arab Spring. How were social media used, and by whom? How much of an effect did they have? Provide examples of specific events in which they were used. Finally, discuss how significant a role social media played.

Text Credits

The following is a list of the copyright holders who have granted us permission to reproduce excerpts from primary source documents in *Middle East Conflict: Almanac, 2nd Edition*. Every effort has been made to trace copyright; if omissions have been made, please contact us.

Copyrighted excerpts reproduced from the following books:

- Unknown, *The Ottoman Centuries: The Rise and Fall of the Turkish Empire*, New York: Morrow Quill Paperbacks, 1979, p. 189.

Copyrighted excerpts reproduced from the following other sources:

- 'The Balfour Declaration', November 2, 1917. Letter by Arthur James Lord Balfour to Lord Rothschild, www.mfa.gov.il/MFA/Peace Process/Guide to the Peace Process/The Balfour Declaration.

The Ancient Middle East: From the First Civilizations to the Crusades

The Middle East is a vast region in western Asia composed of diverse nations and peoples. The area that is considered the Middle East has varied over the years and still differs among scholars and journalists in the twenty-first century. The countries of the Arabian Peninsula—Saudi Arabia, Yemen, Oman, Qatar, Kuwait, Bahrain, and the United Arab Emirates—are always included as part of the Middle East, as are Israel, the Palestinian territories, Jordan, Lebanon, Syria, Iraq, and Iran. Egypt, though geographically part of North Africa, is generally considered a major Middle Eastern nation. A few other North African countries, notably Libya, Algeria, Tunisia, Morocco, and sometimes Sudan, are included as part of the Middle East by some authorities. Even when they are viewed as being in a separate geographical region, these countries are often featured prominently in discussions of the Middle East, because of shared history and culture. Finally, Turkey, which is located in western Asia and Europe, is usually considered part of the Middle East due to its location and its many cultural and historical connections to the region.

The modern-day nations of the Middle East were created in the twentieth century, but the region's history is long and complex. It is the home of the world's first-known human civilizations, and three major religions—Judaism, Christianity, and Islam—originated there. (Judaism is the religion of the Jewish people, Christianity is a religion based on the teachings of Jesus Christ, and Islam is the religious faith followed by Muslims based on a belief in Allah as the sole god and in Muhammad as his prophet.) The diverse lands of the Middle East are grouped together as one region in the twenty-first century largely because of events that happened long ago, when the forces of some mighty empires and the religion of Islam drew the people of the region together. This unity, however, was frequently disrupted by religious disputes within the

WORDS TO KNOW

Arabs: People of the Middle East and North Africa who speak the Arabic language or who live in countries in which Arabic is the dominant language.

Byzantine Empire: The eastern part of the Roman Empire, which thrived for one thousand years after the collapse of Rome in 476.

caliph: The spiritual, political, and military leader of the world's Muslims from the death of Muhammad in 632 until 1924.

caliphate: The entire community of Muslims under the leadership of the caliph.

Christianity: A religion based on the teachings of Jesus Christ.

Crusades: A series of military campaigns ordered by the Roman Catholic Church between 1095 and 1291 with the main goal of taking the Holy Land from the Muslims.

crucifixion: A form of execution in which a person is nailed or bound to a cross and left to die.

dynasty: A series of rulers from the same family.

Eretz Yisrael: "Land of Israel" in Hebrew; the ancient kingdom of the Jews.

evangelist: A Christian follower dedicated to converting others to Christianity.

excommunication: The official exclusion of a person from membership in the church.

Hebrew: The ancient language of the Jewish people and the official language of present-day Israel.

heretic: Someone whose opinions or beliefs oppose official church doctrine.

heresy: Opinions or beliefs that oppose official church doctrine.

Holy Land: Roughly the present-day territory of Israel, the Palestinian territories, and parts of Jordan and Lebanon. This area includes sacred sites for Jews, Christians, and Muslims.

Islam: The religious faith followed by Muslims based on a belief in Allah as the sole god and in Muhammad as his prophet.

Judaism: The religion of the Jewish people based on the belief in one god and the teachings the Talmud.

Koran: Also spelled Qur'an or Quran; the holy book of Islam.

Muslims: People who practice the religion of Islam.

nomads: People who move from place to place, with no fixed home.

Palestine: A historical region in the Middle East on the eastern shore of the Mediterranean Sea, comprising parts of present-day Israel and Jordan.

pilgrim: A person who travels to a sacred place for religious reasons.

prophet: A person who speaks for God, by divine inspiration.

rabbi: A Jewish scholar, teacher, and religious leader.

Shiites: Followers of the Shia branch of Islam. Shiites believe that only direct descendants of the prophet Muhammad are qualified to lead the Islamic faith.

Sunnis: Followers of the Sunni branch of Islam. Sunnis believe that elected officials, regardless of their heritage, are qualified to lead the Islamic faith.

Talmud: The authoritative, ancient body of Jewish teachings and tradition.

Tanakh: The Jewish Bible.

Torah: A Hebrew word meaning teaching or instruction, it literally refers to the first five books of the Jewish Bible. The term is often used to refer to the body of wisdom held in Jewish scriptures and sacred literature.

sheikh: An Arab tribal leader.

synagogue: A Jewish place of worship.

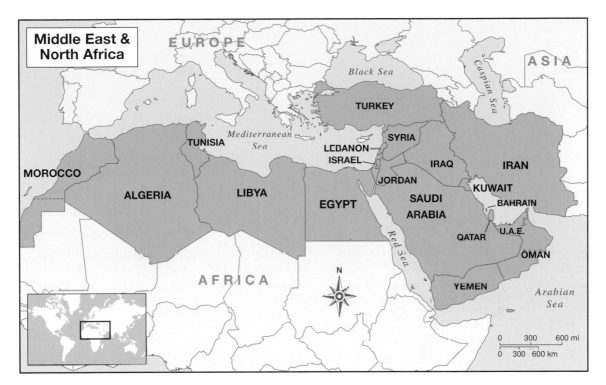

A map of the Middle East and North Africa. MAP BY XNR PRODUCTIONS, INC./CENGAGE LEARNING.

region and attacks from the outside world that led to a long history of conflict.

The Cradle of Civilization

As early as 7000 BCE, humans formed small settlements in Mesopotamia, a fertile region defined by the river valleys of the Tigris and Euphrates rivers. Mesopotamia, the site of present-day Iraq and parts of Syria, Turkey, and Iran, is called the Cradle of Civilization, because the first-known human civilizations developed there. These early organized civilizations included the Sumerians (3000–2300 BCE), the Akkadians (2350–2195 BCE), and the Babylonians (1894–1595 BCE), whose capital city, Babylon, was located south of the present-day city of Baghdad, Iraq. Other important historic civilizations in Mesopotamia were the Assyrians (1380–612 BCE) and the Persians (550–330 BCE).

Like the ancient Mesopotamian civilizations, ancient Egypt was also based in a fertile river valley. It developed along the banks of the Nile

River in northeastern Africa starting around 4000 BCE. By about 2700 BCE Egyptian society had become highly organized. At the top of Egyptian society was a powerful ruler called a pharaoh, who was revered as a god; at the bottom of society were thousands of slaves, many of them criminals or prisoners taken during various wars.

The great civilizations in Mesopotamia and Egypt developed independently of each other. They were separated by the great Arabian Peninsula, with its vast and hostile deserts. In remote areas of their realms, however, the Egyptians and the various Mesopotamian societies encountered a group of people called the Canaanites. These people were originally nomadic, meaning they moved from place to place, herding sheep or other livestock. But by the third millennium BCE the Canaanites had formed towns and settlements in areas lying between the Jordan River and the Mediterranean Sea, in the area that is present-day Lebanon, the Palestinian territories, Israel, and part of Jordan.

The origins of Judaism

The early societies of the Middle East, like most ancient societies, practiced polytheistic religions, which means that they worshipped many gods. Gradually several monotheistic religions (religions that worship only one god) emerged. Zoroastrianism, which many experts consider to be the world's first monotheistic religion, was founded by Zoroaster (c. 628–c. 551 BCE) in Persia (present-day Iran) about thirty-five hundred years ago. It later became the official religion of the Persians.

The most influential of the early monotheistic religions was Judaism, the religion of the Jewish people. The exact origins of the Jewish faith are hard to pinpoint. Most of what is known comes from the Torah, the first five books of the Tanakh (the Jewish Bible), which are also part of the Old Testament of the Christian Bible. According to the first book, the Book of Genesis, the father of Judaism was a man called Abraham, who lived between about 2000 and 1500 BCE (Christianity and Islam also claim Abraham as an important religious figure.)

Born in Mesopotamia and later living in Egypt, Abraham was the first person, according to Jewish religious texts, to worship one god, Yahweh. He soon spread this faith to others, who became his followers, and led them to settle in the land of Canaan, the site of the modern nation of Israel and the Palestinian territories. Abraham's grandson, Jacob (renamed Israel by Yahweh), fathered twelve sons who led what came to

Moses leading the Israelites out of Egypt. This major event in Jewish history is called the Exodus © NORTH WIND PICTURE ARCHIVES/ALAMY.

be known as the twelve tribes of Israel. Jacob's descendants, called the Israelites, are the ancestors of the Jewish people.

According to Jewish teachings, Jacob led his family out of Canaan to escape a time of drought and took them to Egypt. Over the centuries that followed, the Israelites did not fare well in Egypt, and they were enslaved by the Egyptians. After hundreds of years of slavery, one of the Israelites, Moses, led his people out of Egypt. This major event in Jewish history is called the Exodus. The Israelites, led by Moses, wandered through the desert of the

Arabian Peninsula for forty years. During that time, Yahweh spoke to Moses at Mount Sinai, providing the Israelites with the Ten Commandments and other wisdom that served as the basis for the Torah. After their journey, the Israelites settled in the land of Canaan sometime around 1200 BCE, where they battled for some time with the Canaanites for control.

The Land of Israel

The Israelites took control of Canaan in about 1030 BCE. They called their kingdom Eretz Yisrael, which means "Land of Israel" in Hebrew (the ancient language of the Jewish people and the official language of present-day Israel). One of their kings, Solomon, who is thought to have begun his rule around 967 BCE, built a great temple in the city of Jerusalem. The temple, called the Temple of Solomon (also known as the First Temple), became the center of the Jewish faith. In about 927 BCE Israel split into two kingdoms, the northern kingdom of Israel and the southern kingdom of Judah. Israel lasted until 722 BCE, when it was conquered by the Assyrians.

In 586 BCE Judah was conquered by the Babylonians, who destroyed Solomon's temple. The Babylonians moved most of the Jewish religious and civil leaders to Babylon, in what is known as the Babylonian Exile. The exile is a significant event in Jewish history, because it forced a large number of Jews to develop their life and culture outside of their homeland. After the Babylonian conquest of Judah, there were three distinct groups of Jews who, although separated from each other, carefully maintained their religion and traditions. One group was in Babylon and surrounding areas, one remained in Judah, and another group was in Egypt. The movement of many Jews from their homes in Eretz Yisrael is known as the Jewish Diaspora, which began with the Babylonian conquest of Judah and the destruction of Solomon's Temple and, by many definitions, continues into modern times.

Jews in Palestine

When the Israelites settled in Canaan, they displaced some of the people who lived there. One of these displaced groups was the Philistines. Little is known about them, except that they called their lands by the name Palestine. (Palestine is a historical region in the Middle East on the eastern shore of the Mediterranean Sea, comprising parts of present-day Israel and Jordan.) As early as the fall of Judah in 586 BCE, the name Palestine was frequently used by those who refused to recognize the Jewish claim to the area, although it was not yet an official name.

After the fall of the early Jewish kingdoms, many Jews continued to live in their homeland as a minority population, ruled by several different empires that came to control the region. Depending on which rulers were in control, Jews experienced varying levels of freedom and persecution. Under the rule of the Persian Empire (538–333 BCE), Jews were allowed to return to Jerusalem and practice their religion freely, and they were treated with respect. During this time, Jews built another temple on the site of the destroyed Temple of Solomon.

Under the rule of the Romans (63 BCE–330 CE), however, the Jews lived under a harsh and repressive government. In 66 CE they revolted against Roman rule in an event called the Great Revolt. Roman troops responded by ransacking the city of Jerusalem and destroying the Second Temple, the temple that was built to replace the Temple of Solomon. (The remains of that temple are called the Western Wall, or the Wailing Wall, an important Jewish holy site that still stands in the twenty-first century.) Sixty years later, the Jews mounted another major revolt, called the Bar Kokhba revolt (named after its leader Simon bar Kokhboa), which lasted from 132 to 135 CE. The Jews initially gained control over parts of their former kingdom of Judea, but the Roman troops retaliated fiercely. They killed or enslaved thousands of Jews, destroyed numerous Jewish villages, and forbade Jews from entering the holy city of Jerusalem. It was after the Bar Kokhba revolt that the Romans renamed the region Palestine, as a means of punishing the Jews for their revolt.

Jews adapt to the loss of their homeland

The destruction of the holy temple was a major disruption in Judaism as it was practiced at that time. The temple in Jerusalem had been the spiritual center for Jews, and many feared that Jewish traditions would be lost. At the time of the earlier Great Revolt, however, one man, Johanan ben Zakkai (c. 30–90 CE), had prepared the way for the Jews to survive as a people. Ben Zakkai had convinced the Romans to set aside the city of Jabneh (also spelled Yavneh; located about 15 miles [24 kilometers] south of present-day Tel Aviv, Israel) for the Jews. There he started a school, where he and other Jewish scholars studied the Torah. Over the years that followed, the scholarly rabbis composed a remarkable set of Jewish writings that would eventually become the Talmud, the authoritative, ancient body of Jewish teachings and tradition. The Jewish people used the Talmud for moral instruction and as the basis for their legal system.

The Jewish scholars, who were called rabbis, instructed the rest of the Jewish community about religious matters. The rituals that had once taken place at the temple in Jerusalem were replaced with regular services in synagogues, which are Jewish places of worship. This new form of worship, called Rabbinic Judaism, taught that the Jewish religion could remain vital among Jews no matter where they lived. For centuries after the destruction of their temple, Jews settled in a wide variety of locations worldwide. They accepted their separation from their homeland, but continued to cherish the Second Temple in Jerusalem as the holiest place on Earth.

The rise of Christianity

Christianity developed during the rule of the Roman Empire in Palestine. This religion is based on the teachings of Jesus Christ (c. 4 BCE–c. 29 CE), a man of the Jewish faith who offered new interpretations of the role of God and the need for individuals to devote themselves to God. His teachings challenged some of the Jewish beliefs and also, at times, challenged Roman rule. Around 29 CE, Jesus was arrested by Jewish religious leaders who charged that his teachings were disrespectful to God and often resulted in civil disobedience. Jesus was brought before Pontius Pilate, a Roman governor in Palestine, who ordered his crucifixion, a form of execution in which a person is nailed or bound to a cross and left to die. According to Christian religious teaching, Jesus later rose from the dead and ascended to heaven, taking his place as the son of God.

The followers of Jesus believed that he had been sent into the world to give a message to all mankind. They created a religion based on his teachings. Although it is based on the Jewish faith and claimed one god, Christianity differs from Judaism in that it stresses the role of personal salvation acquired through the acceptance of Jesus Christ as the son of God. It is, like Judaism, a monotheistic religion. Unlike Judaism, however, Christianity is an evangelistic faith, which means that its followers dedicate themselves to converting others to their faith.

Sometime around 312 CE Constantine I (272–337), emperor of the Eastern Roman Empire, which controlled over half of the Middle East and would later become known as the Byzantine Empire, embraced Christianity and proclaimed it as the official religion of the empire.

Christianity is based on the teachings of Jesus Christ (pictured). © DBIMAGES/ ALAMY.

In 326 Constantine ordered the construction of the Church of the Holy Sepulchre at a site in Jerusalem believed to be the location of Jesus's crucifixion and burial. Jerusalem had become the holy city of Christians as well as Jews.

The Jews and Christians did not always get along. According to Charles Smith, editor of *Palestine and the Arab-Israeli Conflict*, "Christians considered Jews to be rivals in Palestine, as well as a people who rejected Jesus as the savior sent by God." At first Jews were treated as citizens with some limited equality by the Byzantines. Although they did not accept the official religion, they were not considered heretics (people whose opinions or beliefs oppose official church doctrine), and they were not restricted in their religious practices. But by the fifth century, the Byzantines began to limit Jewish activities more rigorously and created new laws aimed at isolating the Jews.

Divisions among the Christians

When Constantine Christianized the Roman Empire in the fourth century, there was only one universal Christian (or Catholic) church. But differences in beliefs about Jesus's nature arose, causing divisions among Christians. One split occurred when a bishop from Constantinople (present-day Istanbul, Turkey) named Nestorius (died c. 451) professed his belief that Jesus was actually two separate beings: one divine and the other human. According to Nestorius, Jesus's mother, the Virgin Mary, gave birth to the human part. Therefore Mary, although revered, should not be granted the title Mother of God. Nestorius's understanding of Jesus's nature contradicted the Christian Church's view that Jesus was a single being that embodied two natures, the divine and the human. In 431 Nestorius's teachings were declared to be heresy (contrary to official church doctrine), and Nestorius was exiled to Egypt. The Nestorian Church later formed in the areas of the present-day nations of Syria, Iraq, and Iran.

Another split from the Christian Church occurred in 451, when the Christian Council of Chalcedon again declared that Jesus was one person uniting two natures, human and divine. A group of Christians called Monophysites, which held that Jesus had only one nature, divine, was thus deemed heretic. Egypt's Coptic Church was accused by the Christian Church of Monophysitism. Egypt was the home of a large population of Christians. Its Coptic Church dated back to the time of Jesus's death and had contributed greatly to the development of early Christianity. The Copts did not view themselves as Monophysites. They, too, believed that Jesus's human and divine natures were united. In their view, however, this union took place without any intermixing of the two natures. The accusations of heresy resulted in the Copts splitting off from the Christian Church. After the split, Copts were persecuted by other Christians.

Centuries later, in 1054, a huge split called the East-West Schism divided the Christian Church of the Byzantine Empire, based in Constantinople, from the Christian Church based in Rome, Italy. There had been a long history of dispute, both religious and political, between the churches of these two regions that had once formed the Roman Empire. Among other things, there was disagreement over the question of whether the Holy Spirit had descended from both God the Father and the Son, or solely from the Father. (In many Christian belief systems, God is defined as three distinct, coexisting entities: the Holy Spirit, God the Father, and the Son.) The Byzantine church also questioned the authority of the Roman pope (the leader of the Catholic Church) over the Christian churches of the east. In 1054 a spokesman for the pope excommunicated the patriarch of the church in Constantinople. (Excommunication is the official exclusion of a person from membership in the church.) Two separate Christian churches formed, the Eastern Orthodox Church and the Roman Catholic Church.

Arabs and the rise of Islam

The rulers of other parts of the Middle East rarely sent their forces into the Arabian Peninsula, a desert region populated by a people known as Arabs. (Arabs are people who speak the Arabic language or who live in countries in which Arabic is the dominant language.) To outsiders, Arabs seemed savage and hostile, and only the trade routes were of any interest in this loosely governed and sparsely populated region. The Arabs were related to the Canaanites and Jews, who had settled in Palestine prior to the rise of the Kingdom of Israel. Most Arabs were Bedouins, desert-dwelling nomads with no fixed home, who herded sheep, goats, and camels. They organized themselves into clans led by a sheikh (an Arab tribal leader), and violently resisted the influence of outsiders. Before the Muslim religion was founded, most Arabs worshipped local gods, as well as other gods that were worshipped widely throughout the region.

The religion of Islam, which arose in the sixth century CE, would eventually replace the various systems of belief in the Arab countries. Islam was founded by a man named Muhammad, who was born in the town of Mecca (in present-day Saudi Arabia) around 570. He was a member of the Quraysh tribe, which controlled trade in the coastal region known as the Hejaz. According to Islamic religious teachings, around the year 610 Muhammad was visited by the angel Gabriel, who told him that God had selected him to be a prophet, a person who speaks for God, by divine inspiration. As the angel continued to visit him, Muhammad became convinced that he was receiving God's messages. He began to memorize the angel's words so that he could later recite them to scribes, people who write documents by hand as a profession. (Like most Middle Easterners of his time, Muhammad

Source of Agreement: One True God

Most often when one religion is compared to another religion, it is the differences that are noted. These differences have often divided people. In the ancient Middle East, for example, members of the minority religious faith often faced restrictions on where they could live, whether and where they could build religious sites, and how fully they could participate in society. This was true when Jews ruled ancient Israel, when Christians controlled Palestine during the reign of the Byzantine Empire, and when Muslims controlled all or part of the Middle East. (Muslims are people who practice the religion of Islam.) These restrictions are apparent even in the twenty-first century in the holy city of Jerusalem, where strict limits exist on who has access to holy sites and when.

What is often left out of such discussions is that Jews, Christians, and Muslims share many of the same beliefs. Members of all three faiths believe in the dominance of one god, whether the word for that god is Yahweh, God, or Allah. Members of all three faiths claim Jerusalem as one of their most holy cities. Members of all three faiths believe that prophets (people who speak for God, by divine inspiration), such as Abraham, Moses, Jesus, and Muhammad, delivered messages from God to his people. Although these monotheistic religions differ on many issues, most religious scholars claim there are more similarities than differences among them.

had never learned to read or write.) These written messages eventually made up the Muslim holy book called the Koran (also spelled Qur'an or Quran). The Koran contains religious laws and instructions on how to live a moral life. After his visits from Gabriel, Muhammad began preaching to people in Mecca. He urged them to give up their false gods; to follow the path taught by the prophets of God, including Abraham, Moses, and Jesus; and to dedicate themselves to Allah, the one true god.

By 622 officials in Mecca were angry with Muhammad for preaching against the local gods. Soon Muhammad and his followers were forced to flee Mecca. Relocating in the town of Medina, Muhammad built a huge following. He acted as both a religious leader and a political one, bringing political order to Medina along with a new religious faith. He also took on the position of military leader. Fearing that forces from Mecca would attack his followers in Medina, Muhammad initiated an attack on Mecca with a small army and succeeded in taking the city by 630. The defeated Meccans allowed Muhammad's followers to mingle with the city's residents, and they quickly converted the majority to Islam. Soon the followers of Muhammad extended their control throughout the Arabian Peninsula. By the time of Muhammad's death in 632, most Arabs had converted to Islam. They accepted Muhammad as their prophet and viewed his teachings as the direct expressions of the will of Allah.

The city of Mecca in Saudi Arabia is the birthplace of the Muslim prophet Muhammad.
© TENGKU MOHD YUSOF/ ALAMY.

The first Islamic empire

When Muhammad died, his followers were determined to carry his message to the rest of the world. To do so they created the caliphate, the entire community of Muslims under the leadership of the caliph. The caliph was the powerful religious, political, and military leader whose realm was all of Islam. Under the caliphate, the new religion spread rapidly. Muslim armies captured Damascus, Syria, in 635; they took parts of Mesopotamia in 637 and Palestine by 638; and by 640 they controlled Egypt. From Egypt Muslim armies spread throughout North Africa, across Persia toward India and China, westward beyond present-day Turkey, toward the northern Mediterranean Sea region, including Italy and Greece, and as far west as Spain. The conquests of Muslim forces created an enormous realm, beginning a series of empires known as the Islamic empires. It is important to note, however, that the Muslim armies were tolerant of other religions and did not force their religion on the peoples they conquered. Many of the people in the empire chose to convert to Islam, and most of these people's descendants are Muslims in the twenty-first century.

Middle East historian Bernard Lewis describes the spectacular rise of the Islamic empire in *The Middle East: A Brief History of the Last 2,000 Years*: "Within little more than a century after the Prophet's death, the whole area had been transformed, in what was surely one of the swiftest and most dramatic changes in the whole of human history. . . . In this empire, Islam was the state religion, and the Arabic language was rapidly displacing others to become the principal medium of public life." In the centuries that followed, this great Islamic empire grew stronger under a variety of leaders and ruling family clans.

The Shiite-Sunni division

The rise and spread of Islam brought a unifying religious force to the Middle East. It did not, however, prevent conflicts in the region. One of the largest clashes struck within Islam itself. It involved the process of selecting a new caliph when the previous caliph died.

When Muhammad died, he had no sons, and he did not leave behind clear instructions about who should succeed him. Factions within the empire had differing ideas about how to choose a caliph. Some members of the Muslim community held that the new leader should be Ali (c. 598–661), Muhammad's cousin, who had been with him from his first days as prophet. Ali had married Muhammad's daughter, Fatima, and their sons were Muhammad's grandsons, creating a direct line of descent from the prophet from which succeeding caliphs could be chosen. Other members of the Muslim community, however, did not consider hereditary descent a deciding factor. They preferred instead to elect a caliph from among the leaders of their community.

When Muhammad died, the community of Muslim leaders chose his companion and father-in-law Abu Bakr (c. 573–634) to succeed him as the caliph. Abu Bakr died after only two years as caliph, and in the next few years two more caliphs, in turn, were chosen by the community and then passed away. Some Muslims disagreed with these first three choices, because the caliphs were not direct descendants of Muhammad. After the death of the third caliph in 656, Ali was selected as the fourth caliph of the Islamic empire. He served for only a few years, and his time as caliph was tumultuous, because he was strongly opposed by a rival, Muawiyah (c. 602–680), a powerful local governor who refused to recognize him as caliph.

Ali was assassinated in 661. His followers believed that only his direct descendant could lead the caliphate. These followers were called Shiites. (Their branch of Islam is known as Shia.) The majority of Muslims, however, continued to believe that the caliph of the Islamic empire could be elected. These followers (and their branch of Islam) were called Sunni. Divisions between Shiites and Sunnis deepened throughout Islam's history and continued into the twenty-first century.

Muslim dynasties

When Ali died, his son decided to acknowledge his rival, Muawiyah, as caliph rather than fight for the position. Muawiyah went on to establish the Umayyad dynasty. (A dynasty is a series of rulers from the same family.) Muawiyah moved the empire's capital to Damascus (in present-day Syria). The Umayyads were less religious in their rule than earlier caliphs and developed a reputation for corruption. Although the position of caliph was passed down among members of the Umayyad family for nearly a century, the Shiites refused to recognize these leaders as caliphs.

Nevertheless, under the Umayyads the caliphate went on to accomplish some of its greatest conquests. In the early eighth century the Islamic empire spread out over more than 5 million square miles (13 million square kilometers). It became the seventh-largest empire in world history,

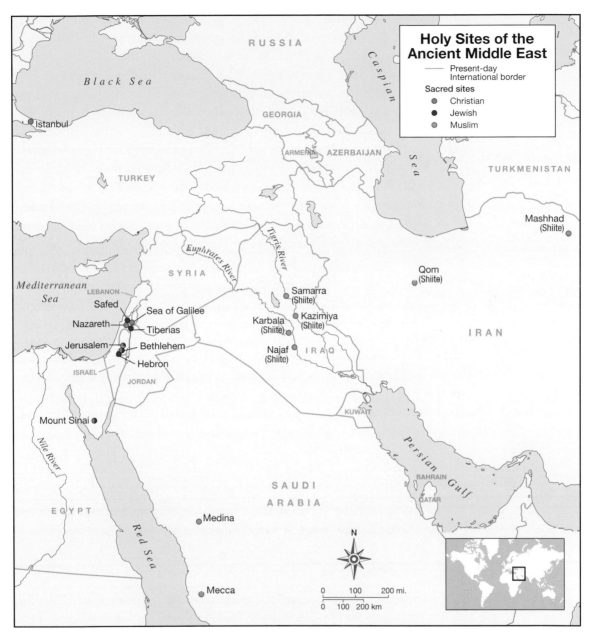

Holy Sites of the Ancient Middle East

— Present-day International border

Sacred sites
- Christian
- Jewish
- Muslim

A map showing the holy sites of the ancient Middle East, including which religions hold these sites sacred. MAP BY XNR PRODUCTIONS, INC./CENGAGE LEARNING.

with 62 million people, or about 30 percent of the world's population at the time, living within its rule. The Umayyad dynasty was the first Muslim dynasty to rule the Islamic empire.

A dynasty of rulers known as the Abbasids took over the caliphate in 750. The Umayyads, although no longer caliphs, established a powerful rule in Spain. The Abbasid dynasty received a great deal of support from the non-Arab region of Persia. They moved the capital of the empire to Baghdad (in present-day Iraq). Over the next three centuries, between 750 and 1050, the Islamic empire experienced a golden age in the arts and sciences. This period in history is known as the Middle Ages (c. 500–c. 1500) and at this time Europe was rejecting the classical learning that had been passed down from ancient Greece and Rome. However that knowledge was preserved and advanced in the Middle East. In areas such as math, science, medicine, architecture, and literature, the empire advanced well beyond Europe and was responsible for many aspects of learning and the arts that continue to influence the world in the twenty-first century.

The Abbasids were not as interested in conquest as earlier caliphs had been. Gradually during their rule, competing Muslim groups of the Islamic empire broke away from the empire to form their own governments. The Umayyads ruled in Spain. A group called the Fatimids, who led a sect (group) of Shiites, gained control over North Africa and Egypt, ruling from 909 to 1171. In the early eleventh century a group of nomadic warriors from central Asia called the Seljuk (also spelled Seljuq) Turks conquered most of the Middle East, except for Egypt and Syria. They ruled their vast empire from 1037 to 1194, although they remained loyal to the Abbasid caliph. Once they had established their dominance in the Middle East, the Seljuks began to invade regions of the Byzantine Empire. Emperor Alexius I (1048–1118), the Orthodox Christian ruler of the Byzantine Empire, was challenged by the expansion of Muslim rule. He called on Pope Urban II (1042–1099), the leader of the Roman Catholic Church, for help in fighting the Seljuks.

The Crusades

One of the places that had come under Seljuk control was Palestine, including the city of Jerusalem. Unlike other Muslim rulers before them, the Seljuks required Christian pilgrims to pay a tax to visit Jerusalem. (Pilgrims are people who travel to a sacred place for religious reasons.) Since Jerusalem is a holy site for Christians, as it is for Jews and Muslims, this treatment greatly angered the Roman Catholic pope. Beginning in 1095, the pope convinced thousands of Roman Catholic men to join the Crusades, a series of military campaigns to take control of the Holy Land (roughly the present-day territory of Israel, the Palestinian territories, and parts of Jordan and Lebanon) from Muslims. These crusaders, fueled by rumors about Muslim violence and heathen (non-Christian) religious practices, journeyed to the Middle East in organized armies. In 1099 they succeeded at capturing Jerusalem, killing much of the Muslim and what remained of the Jewish population. They held Jerusalem until 1187, when it was recaptured by a Muslim leader named Saladin (c. 1138–1193). In 1204 the crusaders invaded and conquered the Christian Byzantine capital city of Constantinople, sharpening divisions between the Eastern Orthodox Church and the Roman Catholic Church that would endure for many centuries.

The Crusades had a dramatic impact on relations between the Muslim and Christian worlds, fueling hatred and misunderstanding. While the Christians resented the Muslims' control over the holy city of Jerusalem, the Muslims viewed the crusaders as brutal invaders.

By the time the Crusades ended in the thirteenth century, the Islamic empire had disintegrated. The Arabian Peninsula returned to the control

Christian crusaders capturing Jerusalem in 1099. The Crusades had a dramatic impact on relations between the Muslim and Christian worlds. © THE ART GALLERY COLLECTION/ALAMY.

of minor sheikhs who claimed power over trade routes and desert villages. From 1250 to 1517, the dominant rulers of the Middle East were the Mamluks, who were mainly of Turkish origin. The Mamluks drove the Crusaders from the region and based their empire in Egypt and Syria. They brought little real organization to the Middle East, however, and regional political leaders were able to rule as they desired. It was this lack of organization that allowed the Mamluk dynasty to fall to the Ottoman Turks in the early sixteenth century.

For More Information

BOOKS

Drummond, Dorothy. *Holy Land Whose Land: Modern Dilemma Ancient Roots.* Seattle, WA: Educare Press, 2002.

Kort, Michael. *The Handbook of the Middle East.* Brookfield, CT: Twenty-First Century Books, 2002.

Lewis, Bernard. *The Middle East: A Brief History of the Last 2,000 Years.* New York: Scribner, 1995, p. 55.

Malam, John. *Mesopotamia and the Fertile Crescent, 10,000 to 539 B.C.* Austin, TX: Raintree Steck-Vaughn, 1999.

Nardo, Don. *The Islamic Empire.* Detroit, MI: Lucent Books, 2011.

Smith, Charles D., ed. *Palestine and the Arab-Israeli Conflict: A History with Documents,* 4th ed. Boston MA: Bedford/St. Martin's, 2001.

WEB SITES

Internet Islamic History Sourcebook. Fordham University, http://www.fordham.edu/halsall/islam/islamsbook.html#Islamic%20Nationalism (accessed on November 30, 2011).

The Islamic World to 1600. Applied History Research Group, University of Calgary. http://www.ucalgary.ca/applied_history/tutor/islam/ (accessed on November 30, 2011).

2

The Ottoman Empire: 1299 to 1923

The Ottoman Empire was one of the largest and most enduring empires in history. It existed for six hundred years, from 1299 to 1923, and at its height in the late sixteenth century, it spanned more than 8.5 million square miles (22 million square kilometers), encompassing most of the Middle East and North Africa and a large part of southeastern Europe. Although the ruling Ottoman family was Turkish and ruled under Islamic law, the empire came to encompass a highly diverse combination of cultures, religions, and languages and was influenced by Greek, Roman, Byzantine, Arab, and Persian traditions. At its peak, the empire was the strongest force in the world. In the nineteenth century, however, the Ottoman Empire began to decline, just as Europe began its gradual ascent to world dominance. During its long reign, the Ottoman Empire contributed greatly to the culture, religion, and politics of the Middle East, and in the twenty-first century its legacy is evident not only in Turkey, the homeland of the Ottoman rulers, but in the many other lands it ruled and in the diverse cultures it fostered.

A time of transition in Anatolia

In the thirteenth century the area that is known in the twenty-first century as the Middle East was fragmented, ruled mostly by weak local governments and what was left of earlier empires. Most regions were ruled by local leaders, but two regions were still ruled by powerful dynasties. (A dynasty is a series of rulers from the same family.) One was Egypt, which had come to be ruled by the Mamluk dynasty. The other was Anatolia, ruled by the Byzantine Empire and the Seljuk Turks. (The Byzantine Empire was the eastern part of the Roman Empire, which thrived for one thousand years after the collapse of Rome in 476.)

Anatolia, also called Asia Minor, is located where the continents of Asia and Europe meet. It lies on a peninsula on the western edge of Asia, where

WORDS TO KNOW

Byzantine Empire: The eastern part of the Roman Empire, which thrived for one thousand years after the collapse of Rome in 476.

caliph: The spiritual, political, and military leader of the world's Muslims from the death of Muhammad in 632 until the caliphate was abolished in 1924.

caliphate: The entire community of Muslims under the leadership of the caliph.

Crusades: A series of military campaigns ordered by the Roman Catholic Church between 1095 and 1291 with the main goal of taking the Holy Land from the Muslims.

dynasty: A series of rulers from the same family.

genocide: The deliberate and systematic destruction of a group of people based on religion, ethnicity, or nationality.

hajj: The annual Muslim pilgrimage to Mecca that takes place in the last month of the year, which every Muslim is expected to perform at least once during their lifetime if they are able.

Hejaz: A coastal region on the western Arabian Peninsula that includes the Muslim holy cities of Mecca and Medina.

Holy Land: Roughly the present-day territory of Israel, the Palestinian territories, and parts of Jordan and Lebanon. This area includes sacred sites for Jews, Christians, and Muslims.

Koran: Also spelled Qur'an or Quran; the holy book of Islam.

millet: A community for non-Muslims in the Ottoman Empire, organized by religious group and headed by a religious leader.

mosque: A Muslim place of worship.

nationalism: The belief that a people with shared ethnic, cultural, and/or religious identities have the right to form their own nation. In established nations nationalism is devotion and loyalty to the nation and its culture.

Ottoman Empire: The vast empire of the Ottoman Turks which included southwest Asia, northeast Africa, and southeast Europe, and lasted from the thirteenth century to the early twentieth century.

pilgrimage: A journey to a sacred place for religious reasons.

sharia: A system of Islamic law based on the Koran and other sacred writings. Sharia attempts to create the perfect social order, based on God's will and justice, and covers a wide range of human activities, including acts of religious worship, the law of contracts and obligations, personal status law, and public law.

sharif: A nobleman and political leader chosen from among descendants of the Muslim prophet Muhammad.

Shiites: Followers of the Shia branch of Islam. Shiites believe that only direct descendants of the prophet Muhammad are qualified to lead the Islamic faith.

sultan: A ruler of a Muslim state, especially the Ottoman Empire.

Sunnis: Followers of the Sunni branch of Islam. Sunnis believe that elected officials, regardless of their heritage, are qualified to lead the Islamic faith.

tribute: Payment from one ruler of a state to another, usually for protection or to acknowledge submission.

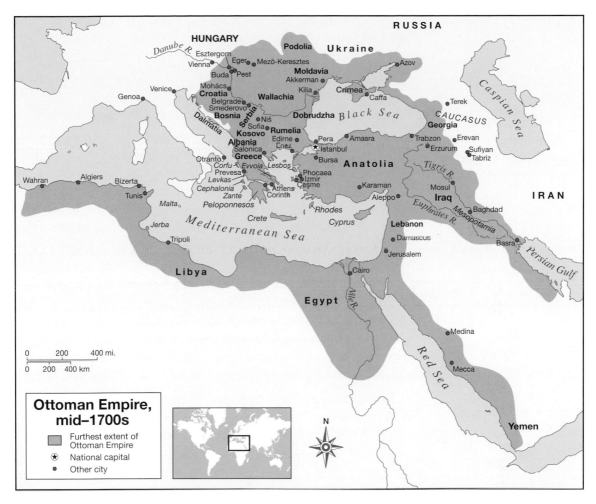

A map of the Ottoman Empire in the mid–1700s. The empire stretched across much of the Middle East and parts of Europe. MAP BY XNR PRODUCTIONS, INC./CENGAGE LEARNING.

the present-day Republic of Turkey is located. In the thirteenth century, parts of Anatolia were ruled by the Seljuks, a group of Turkish people with origins in central Asia who had conquered large areas of the Middle East in the early eleventh century. Anatolia was their permanent base.

The Seljuks were forced to share Anatolia with the Byzantines. The Byzantine Empire had ruled over eastern Europe for nine centuries from its capital of Constantinople (present-day Istanbul, Turkey) in the heart of Anatolia. When the western part of the Roman Empire collapsed in 476, the mainly Greek-speaking Byzantines continued to reign strong for centuries. In 1054 the Byzantine Christian Church split from the Roman Catholic Church over disagreements about doctrine and church politics. This separation is known as the Great Schism. From that time on, Christians in the Byzantine Empire were Eastern Orthodox (also known as Greek Orthodox) rather than Roman Catholics.

Anatolia experienced two major invasions in the thirteenth century that threw both the Byzantines and the Seljuks into turmoil. The first was one of the invasions of the Crusades, a series of military campaigns in which European invaders attacked the Middle East that occurred from 1095 until 1291. The Crusades had been ordered by the Roman Catholic Church with the main goal of capturing the city of Jerusalem. Jerusalem is a holy city to Christians, but since the seventh century, it had been ruled by the Islamic Empire, which ruled over much of the Middle East. The Crusades were mainly attacks on the Muslims and Jews living in the Holy Land (roughly the present-day territory of Israel, the Palestinian territories, and parts of Jordan and Lebanon). In 1204, however, the Roman Catholic crusaders attacked the Eastern Orthodox Christian capital of Constantinople, causing great devastation. The Roman Catholics would hold Constantinople for half a century before the Byzantines regained control.

The second major invasion of Anatolia in the thirteenth century occurred in 1243, when the powerful armies of Mongols (a people of present-day Mongolia), led by Mongol ruler Genghis Khan (c. 1162–1227), conquered much of central Asia and the Middle East, including Anatolia. Both the Byzantines and the Seljuks were forced to pay tribute and acknowledge the Mongols as their rulers, even though the Mongols moved on and allowed them to rule themselves. (Tribute is payment from one ruler of a state to another, usually for protection or to acknowledge submission.)

The rise of the Ottoman Empire

After the Crusades and the Mongol invasion, the Byzantine Empire and the Seljuks were too weak to prevent a large migration of Turks into their regions. Some of these migrants were Muslim warriors known as *ghazis*, who arrived ready to fight the Christians in the Byzantine Empire in the name of their religion. Most made their living by stealing goods from the Christian villages they raided. Anatolia became a kind of frontier country, without any strong central governing force. The ghazis, prosperous from their plunder, began to form small principalities, or states under the authority of a prince (or in the case of the ghazi principalities, a prince-like chief or leader), in Anatolia under the loose administration of the Mongols.

In the 1290s one of these Turkish principalities, which was located near Constantinople, came under the leadership of Osman I (1259–1326). Although little factual information is known about Osman I, it is clear that he enlisted the forces of the ghazi warriors to rapidly expand his realm, conquering rural towns and the countryside in nearby Byzantine areas. In 1299 Osman stopped paying tribute to the Mongols, thereby declaring his territory an independent state. This marked the beginning of the Ottoman

Osman I, the founder of the Ottoman Empire.
© INTERFOTO/ALAMY.

Empire. (Osman's name in the Arabic language is Uthman, and from this name comes "Ottoman.") From this time forward, Osman and his descendants would rule the Ottoman Empire.

After Osman died in 1326, his successors continued to expand the Ottoman Empire by acquiring more Byzantine territory. Osman's grandson, Murad I (c. 1326–1389) created the title of sultan for the leaders of the Ottoman dynasty. The sultan was the absolute ruler. He was the head of the government, military, and religion, and his right to rule was considered to be given by God. Second in power to the sultan in the Ottoman Empire was the grand vizier, the sultan's top minister. Murad greatly added to the territory of the Ottoman Empire in the 1360s, when his forces captured Adrianople (in the European part of modern-day Turkey), and a large portion of the Balkan Peninsula, including parts of Thrace, Bulgaria, Macedonia, and Serbia.

The early Ottoman Empire

By the time of Murad's reign, it was clear that the Ottoman Empire was to be dominated by its warriors. In the early empire, most Ottoman warriors were *sipahis*, warriors who fought on horseback. The sipahis received large plots of land, worked by local peasants, in return for their service. On the land they were given, the sipahis were the rulers over the local people. Murad changed the customs of the Ottoman military. He is believed by historians to be the creator of an elite wing of the Ottoman army made up of soldiers known as *janissaries*. The janissaries were boys taken from the conquered Christian towns. They were converted to Islam and then trained to become skilled and disciplined warriors. To ensure their complete loyalty to the sultan, they were separated from the rest of society and not allowed to marry while in service, but they were highly regarded and received many privileges. The janissaries took great pride in their skill as warriors. For many centuries they were vital to the expansion and security of the empire.

Historians have dated the establishment of other new Ottoman traditions to Murad's time, as well. The practice of religious tolerance thoughout the empire was one of these changes. In the territories Murad conquered, the residents were granted full citizenship in the Ottoman Empire. All non-Muslims, however, had to pay a special tax. Many Christian peasants converted to Islam in order to avoid the tax.

By the end of the fourteenth century, most of the Balkan Peninsula was under Ottoman rule. A milestone in the Ottoman rise to power came in 1453, when the Byzantine capital of Constantinople fell to the Ottomans. Its fall marked the end of the city's long history as a center of the Christian Church, as well as the end of both Roman and Byzantine rule. Ottoman sultan Mehmed II (432–1481) changed the name of the city to Istanbul and moved the Ottoman capital there. Appreciating the great cultural significance of the city, Mehmed brought in artists and scholars from other parts of the world.

Istanbul became the Ottoman capital just as the empire was reaching its peak as the world's major power. The Ottomans conquered vast areas, including Albania, Greece, and Hungary. As the empire grew, it was divided into *sanjaks*, or districts, which were administered by local governors called beys, who answered to the sultan or his grand vizier. Depending on the district's importance to the empire, the bey might be a local ruler or one sent by the sultan.

Conflict between the Persians and the Ottomans

In 1501 a powerful dynasty called the Safavid Empire rose to power in Persia (present-day Iran) and would flourish there until 1722. Established by Ismail I (1487–1524), the Safavid Empire was comprised mainly of Shiites, followers of the Shia branch of Islam who had separated from the majority over certain points of religious doctrine. Their primary disagreement was over the succession of the leader of Islam. The Shiites believed only the direct descendants of the Muslim prophet Muhammad (c. 570–632) could lead the Muslim people. The Ottomans, on the other hand, were Sunnis, followers of the Sunni branch of Islam. They believed that the leaders of Islam could be chosen by the Muslim people.

The Ottomans and the Safavids were frequently at war with each over who would rule the eastern Arabian Peninsula and particularly Mesopotamia (present-day Iraq and parts of Syria, Turkey, and Iran). Their battles, which would continue for well over a century, began in 1514 in eastern Anatolia with the Battle of Chaldiran. Ottoman forces under the newly enthroned sultan Selim I (c. 1465–1520) defeated the Safavids and secured Anatolia and northern Iraq. The Ottomans were never able to conquer Persia.

Ottomans fighting off Persian invaders. The Persians often invaded Ottoman territory, trying to gain control of the Middle East. © STAPLETON COLLECTION/CORBIS.

The empire reigns supreme

By the sixteenth century, the reigns of Selim I "the Grim" (1467–1520) and his son Süleyman I (1494–1566) marked the worldwide supremacy of the Ottomans. Selim greatly expanded the empire, adding Syria,

Egypt, and Hejaz (a coastal region on the western Arabian Peninsula that includes the Muslim holy cities of Mecca and Medina). These acquisitions brought great wealth to the empire, particularly because they brought control of the eastern shore of the Mediterranean Sea with its flourishing trade. Istanbul became a thriving administrative center, with a well-organized government, sophisticated systems of finance and tax collecting, and training centers for government officials and military leaders.

Selim was succeeded by his son, Süleyman, who is considered the greatest of the Ottoman sultans. He conquered the country of Hungary in 1526 and led his troops to Vienna, the capital of Austria, in 1529, although they did not succeed in conquering the city. He also led his forces east into Persia to secure the pirate-overrun North African ports of Tripoli, Algiers, and Tunis.

Süleyman is remembered for his conquests, and many other accomplishments. He was called "Süleyman the Lawgiver," because he established a new code of laws that governed the empire along with sharia, a system of Islamic religious law based on the Koran (also spelled Qur'an or Quran; the holy book of Islam). Most records show that his rule was viewed by the people of the empire as a time of justice and fairness. He was also known as as "Süleyman the Magnificent," because he greatly beautified Istanbul and contributed to its cultural progress. During his reign, the Ottoman capital became a center of art and architecture that encompassed classical Greek and Latin arts as well as the Turkish, Arab, and Persian art that had more recently emerged. Istanbul was noted throughout Europe for its textiles and carpets, its exquisite jewels, and particularly for its elegant mosques and buildings. (A mosque is a Muslim place of worship.) By the end of Süleyman's reign, the city had a population of about seven hundred thousand, making it larger than any European city, including Paris, France, and London, England, at the time. In addition to its cities' power and beauty, the Ottoman Empire in the sixteenth century was perhaps the most advanced civilization on Earth. Its political and economic policies brought stability to the Middle East.

A German Folk Song about the Ottomans

Ottoman sultan Süleyman's armies penetrated deeply into Europe during the sixteenth century, conquering vast lands (such as the areas of present-day Hungary, Austria, and Germany) and threatening the great cities. To many Europeans the Ottomans seemed to be an unstoppable force, as illustrated in this German folk song about Süleyman and the ever-approaching Turks:

> From Hungary he's soon away
> In Austria by break of day,
> Bavaria is just at hand,
> From there he'll reach another land,
> Soon to the Rhine perhaps he'll come.

KINROSS, LORD. *THE OTTOMAN CENTURIES: THE RISE AND FALL OF THE TURKISH EMPIRE.* NEW YORK: MORROW QUILL PAPERBACKS, 1979, P. 189.

Sülemaniye Mosque in Istanbul, Turkey. Süleyman I greatly beautified the city and it became noted throughout Europe, particularly for its elegant mosques and buildings.
© JEFF GREENBERG/ALAMY

Many languages and religions

Although the Ottoman Empire had been established through military means, Selim had wished to stress its Islamic basis. He proclaimed that Ottoman sultans would take the title of caliph, like the leaders of the earlier Islamic caliphates (the entire community of Muslims under the leadership of the caliphs), thus asserting the sultans' leadership of Muslims worldwide. (For more information on earlier caliphates, see **The Ancient Middle East: From the First Civilizations to the Crusades**.) A caliph was the spiritual, political, and military leader of the world's Muslims. As caliphs, the Ottoman sultans were, for the most part, revered by Muslims. For the many Arab Muslims in the Ottoman Empire, this strong basis in Islam helped to reconcile them with being led by Turks.

The acquisition of Hejaz also brought great religious prestige to the sultans. One of the most sacred events in Muslim life was the *hajj*, an annual pilgrimage (a journey to a sacred place for religious reasons) to the holy city of Mecca. All Muslims who are able are required to make this pilgrimage at least once during their lifetime. The less-frequent pilgrimages to sacred sites in Medina were revered as well. According to author Albert Hourani, in *A History of the Arab Peoples*, "to organize and lead the annual pilgrimage [to Mecca and Medina] was one of [the sultan's] main functions; conducted with great formality and as a major public act, the pilgrimage was an annual assertion of Ottoman sovereignty in the heart of the Muslim world." However, the sultans did not want to risk angering the Arab Muslims by failing to recognize their leaders. They granted part of the rule of the capital city of Mecca to the Sharif of Mecca. (A sharif is a nobleman and political leader chosen from among descendants of the Muslim prophet Muhammad.)

Although the Ottoman Empire was a Muslim state, its rapid expansion placed it in control of areas with large populations of Christians and smaller populations of Jews. The Muslims did not ask the people of their conquered lands to convert to Islam. Instead, they established *millets*, or communities for non-Muslims, organized by religious group. Christians and Jews each had their own millets, where they could freely practice their religions in churches or synagogues and teach their traditions in schools and seminaries. Each millet, headed by the community's religious leader, was responsible for maintaining its own infrastructure, such as roads, courts, police, education, and other public works. Although they did not receive all the rights of Muslims, religious minorities enjoyed a much greater quality of life under Muslim rule than did similar minorities in Europe at the time.

Decline of the empire

In 1683 the Ottomans mounted a second military campaign to conquer Vienna. A long siege, involving nearly twelve thousand Ottoman soldiers, failed to take the city. Finally, the Ottomans were defeated by a coalition of Austrian, German, and Polish-Lithuanian forces. By the terms of the 1699 Treaty of Karlowitz that followed, Austria was awarded the Ottoman territories of Hungary and Transylvania.

By the eighteenth century the Ottomans were experiencing significant problems within their own government. For one thing, the janissaries, who for several centuries had contributed greatly to the Ottomans' standing as a world superpower, had become so powerful that they were often able to threaten and even overthrow sultans who crossed them, as they did in revolts in 1622 and 1807. Blinded by their power and focusing on their own status, the elite military group failed to adequately modernize their techniques and military equipment to keep up with the empire's many enemies. Gradually the janissaries came to be seen as old-fashioned and ineffective. At the same time many of the agencies of the Ottoman government had grown corrupt, with their elite administrators growing rich and privileged at the expense of the welfare of the empire.

While the Ottoman government and military were beginning their decline, Europe was engaged in world exploration and economic advance. The European colonies had provided vast riches in gold and silver and profitable new trade routes. As European industry progressed, the colonies served as a market for its products and provided Europeans with the raw materials they needed to keep producing. The Ottoman economy lacked the type of innovations that could help it keep up with the Europeans. As it fell behind, the empire was forced to get loans from the Europeans to pay for maintaining the empire and conducting its many wars. The Ottomans soon found themselves unable to pay their debt, adding greatly to the empire's humiliation and general decline.

Losing territory

By the eighteenth century the Ottomans' main European foe was Russia. The Russo-Ottoman War of 1768–74 (also called the Russo-Turkish War) saw Russia gain control of the Crimea, a region located on the northern shores of the Black Sea. The Russians also won shipping rights through the straits (waterways) that connect the Black Sea to the Mediterranean Sea. There were several other wars between the Ottomans and Russia from 1828 to 1878. Other European powers, particularly Great Britain and France, did not wish to see Russia gain crucial territory and trade routes in the Ottoman Empire, fearing it would tip the balance of power in Europe against them. They often supported the Ottoman Empire in its wars for territorial control in order to maintain the balance of power.

More trouble came from Egypt. From the moment that Egypt was brought into the Ottoman Empire in 1517, it had proved a difficult region to control. Egyptians were proud of their distinctive cultural history, which dated back to ancient times, and as ethnic Arabs they disliked taking instructions from Turkish imperial leaders. They fought with their Ottoman rulers to keep control of the wealth produced by their advanced agriculture, and they sought to keep control of the trade routes that provided passage between the Mediterranean Sea and the Red Sea. Several Egyptian rulers had established Egypt's independence from the empire. Then, in 1798, French troops conquered Egypt. Great Britain helped the Ottomans remove the French by 1801. Although Ottoman rule was restored, Great Britain later established itself as the sole power in Egypt in 1882. In the meantime, more of North Africa was lost as Algeria and Tunisia came under French rule. In Europe, Greece and Albania won their independence from the Ottoman Empire.

The "sick man of Europe"

The continuing collapse of the Ottoman Empire began to pose a real problem for European powers, especially Great Britain, France, Russia, and Germany. None of them wanted to see their rivals take power in territory left by the Ottomans. The Bulgarians revolted in 1876 and two years later the Russians captured most of the Ottoman Empire's European territory. The greatly weakened Ottomans had no choice but to recognize the independence of their former European territories. In 1878 some of the European powers, including a representative of the Ottoman Empire, convened the Congress of Berlin in hopes of settling territorial questions of the Ottoman Empire without going to war. In this congress, Romania, Serbia, and Montenegro were declared independent, and Bosnia-Herzegovina was given to Austria-Hungary to administer. Though the Ottoman leaders could do nothing to stop them, these territorial losses were humiliating to the fiercely proud Ottomans.

From the early nineteenth century onward, the combined effects of the agricultural and industrial revolutions (a shift from hand tools and home manufacturing to power-driven tools and factory production) only

Delegates arrive at the Congress of Berlin in 1878. European powers convened the Congress of Berlin in hopes of settling territorial questions of the Ottoman Empire without going to war. © DIZ MUENCHEN GMBH, SUEDDEUTSCHE ZEITUNG PHOTO/ALAMY.

heightened the differences between the two cultures. In the West, farmers learned to dramatically increase the amount of food they could produce, and manufacturers used modern power sources and production techniques to expand the number of goods they could produce while reducing their cost. As a result, the standard of living increased for people throughout the West, increasing the economic advantage of Western countries. Similar revolutions did not reach the Middle East until well into the twentieth century. Middle Eastern farmers still tilled their land using hand tools, and most household goods—clothes, food, and blankets—were handmade and locally produced. As a result, the Middle East fell behind the West technologically, and the majority of the people experienced a far lower standard of living than was known in the West. In a world where money was increasingly equated with power, the Middle East grew weaker as the West continued to gain power.

Just as the Ottomans had viewed the Europeans as their inferiors during their prosperous times, by the nineteenth century, the Europeans had come to view the Turks as barbarians, or people who lacked civilization. Leaders of countries such as Russia, who wanted to have more access to the Ottoman lands, spread fears that the Ottomans were likely to inflict harm on the Christians within their realm. Through various treaties, Europeans arranged a right of protection for non-Islamic people in the Ottoman Empire. The protected Christians and Jews were granted trade privileges that allowed them to prosper. The arrangement created economic inequality and increased resentment between Muslims and non-Muslims. Other treaties gave Europe highly favorable trade privileges that were disastrous for the empire's own economy. Weakened, losing territory, economically ailing, and constantly at war on all fronts, the empire became known in the European press as the "sick man of Europe."

The Young Turks

In the mid–nineteenth century, two Ottoman sultans, Abdülmecid I (1823–1861) and Abdülaziz (1830–1876) began to institute a series of reforms known as Tanzimat, based mainly on the European style of government. They hope to secularize the Ottoman Empire and pave the way for a more modern government. The reforms were an effort to secure basic human rights for all the subjects of the empire. Among the reforms were efforts to modernize the system of taxation, as well as the courts, schools, and the military. The reforms required a stronger central government, though, and by the 1870s the position of the Ottoman sultan had gained exorbitant powers. Most of the sultans that followed abused this power. Many of the younger generation of Turks in the Anatolia region, however, continued to seek a more modern government and society. One such group, called the Young Ottomans, emerged in the 1860s. They promoted, among other things, an ideology called Ottomanism, which was a blend of ideas that included modernizing the Ottoman Empire while at the same time preserving its devout Islamic basis and Turkish identity.

Toward the end of the nineteenth century, a group of military officers called the Young Turks emerged in the Ottoman Empire. The Young Turks hoped to keep the empire safe from foreign control. While some wanted to achieve this through democracy, equal rights for everyone, and

A Westerner's Portrait of the Turks in the Nineteenth Century

Italian writer Edmondo de Amicis (1846–1908) published a travel book called *Constantinople* in 1878. In it he describes the Ottomans as he had seen them, in what he calls their "act of transformation" from earlier times of strong Islamic and Turkish tradition to modern times when Western influences were taking hold. According to de Amicis, the Turks were deeply divided in the late nineteenth century, and it was easy to distinguish between traditionalists and modernists by the way they dressed. "The inflexible old Turk," he wrote, "still wears the turban, the caftan [a full-length garment with long sleeves], and the traditional slippers of yellow morocco [goatskin leather]; and the more obstinate [stubborn] the man, the bigger his turban." But de Amicis noted a great difference in the dress of the younger Turkish men that he called "reforming Turks," who sought to modernize their country. "The reforming Turk," according to de Amicis, "wears a long black frock coat buttoned to the chin, trousers with straps, and nothing Turkish but the fez [hat]...."

De Amicis noted that these two groups, the "inflexible old Turk" in his turban, caftan, and slippers, and the "reforming Turk" in frock coat and fez, not only looked entirely different, but had almost nothing in common. The old-fashioned Turk believed without question in traditions, and felt that there was no room to change them. De Amicis noted that the traditional Turk carefully followed many time-honored rituals, such as washing as part of a religious rite at certain times of the day and always being home by sunset. On the other hand, according to de Amicis, the young reformers scorned the religious traditions and rituals and adopted many Western manners. "The Turk of the black frock coat laughs at the Prophet [Muhammad], gets himself photographed, speaks French, and passes his evening at the theatre"

De Amicis concluded that the time had come when the older, traditional Turks were dying off, and the younger, secular, and Westernized Turks were taking over. "Every year sees the fall of thousands of caftans, and the rise of thousands of frock coats; every day dies an old Turk and a reformed Turk is born."

DE AMICIS, EDMONDO.
CONSTANTINOPLE. TRANSLATED
BY CAROLINE TILTON. NEW YORK:
G.P. PUTNAM'S SONS, 1872, P. 104.

modernization, other Young Turks were intent on creating a more unified Turkish state with a Turkish national identity and a unified Turkish language and culture. By 1908, the Young Turks and other reform groups had formed a political organization called the Committee of Union and Progress (CUP). The CUP forced the Ottoman sultan to declare a constitutional government. The constitution offered equal rights to everyone in the empire. Within a year the sultan was deposed and another, far weaker, sultan took his place.

In 1912 Bulgaria, Greece, Serbia, and Montenegro declared war on the Ottoman Empire. The empire was defeated, resulting in the permanent loss of nearly all of the Balkan Peninsula. The empire's European territories had dwindled down to the city of Istanbul and a small section of Thrace, a region encompassing parts of present-day Greece, Bulgaria, and Turkey. During this period, Italy defeated the Ottomans in a brief battle and took over the island of Rhodes and the area of present-day Libya. The emotional effect of the loss of life, territory, property, and status was overwhelming for the Ottomans.

Still hoping to reverse the mismanagement that they believed had ruined their empire, the Young Turks overthrew the sultan and took power in a violent coup (overthrow of the government) in 1912. It became clear almost at once that the Young Turks were divided in ideology. While some sought democracy, others favored a strong central state. After a power struggle, the latter group established a dictatorship that would rule what was left of the empire from 1913 to 1918. (The empire at that time was comprised mainly of the Turkish region of Anatolia; a small part of Thrace, in Europe; and much of the Arab regions of the Middle East.) The Young Turks were strongly secular, meaning they kept the government separate from religion. They wanted to extend Turkish rule and to make the Turkish language the official language of the entire empire.

These new policies offended many Arabs, who had initially supported the Young Turks. In 1913 a group of young Arab men, who later called themselves the Young Arab Society, held a conference in Paris, France. They resolved to take back local power and to make Arabic the official language in the Arab countries of the empire.

The Young Turks had taken power just in time to see the Ottoman Empire thrown into the greatest conflict the world had ever seen. World War I (1914–18) pitted the Allies (Great Britain, France, and Russia, joined later by the United States) against the Central Powers (Germany, Austria-Hungary, and their allies). The Ottoman Empire, headed by the Young Turks, joined the Central Powers, glad to fight against their old foe, Russia.

The Armenian massacre

As World War I began, the Young Turks made a cruel and deadly decision in regard to one of the culture groups in their realm: the Armenians.

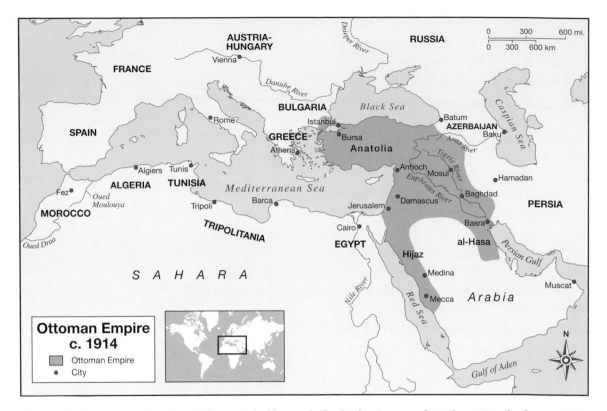

A map of the Ottoman Empire, c. 1914. The empire had lost much of its land in Europe and Asia by 1914, and only controlled present-day Turkey and part of the Middle East. MAP BY XNR PRODUCTIONS, INC./CENGAGE LEARNING.

Ethnic Armenians had lived in the Middle East region since 3500 BCE. The Armenian culture has ancient roots in the mountainous region near Mount Ararat, and as the population increased over the centuries, Armenians came to live in portions of the present-day nations of Armenia, Azerbaijan, Iran, Syria, Turkey, and the Republic of Georgia. The Armenians became Christians in the early third century CE and have their own language and alphabet. As part of the Ottoman Empire, the Armenians, like other minorities, were allowed to practice their religion and traditions with little interference. In the nineteenth century, a movement of nationalism (the belief that a people with shared ethnic, cultural, and/or religious identities have the right to form their own nation) arose among Armenians. They staged protests and armed uprisings, and the Ottomans retaliated. In the 1890s the Ottomans ordered the killing of tens of thousands of Armenians within Ottoman-ruled regions. They also took away the surviving Armenians' rights as citizens of the Ottoman Empire and confiscated much of their property.

When the Young Turks took over the Ottoman government, they restricted the use of the Armenian language and the practice of Armenian cultural and religious celebrations. The Armenians refused to give up their culture, leading to frequent clashes with the new Turkish government. Unable to absorb Armenians into Turkish society and fearing that the Armenians might give support to the Russians if an invasion occurred, the Turkish government authorized the extermination of its Armenian population starting in 1914. An official notice from Minister of the Interior Talaat Pasha sent on September 16, 1916, to the government of the Turkish province of Aleppo clearly detailed the plan: "It was at first communicated to you that the government, by order of the Jemiet [Young Turk Committee], had decided to destroy completely all the Armenians living in Turkey. . . . An end must be put to their existence, however criminal the measures taken may be, and no regard must be paid to either age or sex nor to conscientious scruples," as quoted by David Kherdian in *The Road from Home: The Story of an Armenian Girl.* Turkish soldiers rounded up Armenians and shot them; gathered them into churches that were then burned to the ground; or forced Armenian men, women, and children to march across the desert to Syria, a journey that killed many.

Historians estimate that between 600,000 and 1.5 million Armenians were killed. Many experts consider the massacre to be one of history's worst genocides. (Genocide is the deliberate and systematic destruction of a group of people based on religion, ethnicity, or nationality.) After the war, the Armenians eventually obtained land that had once belonged to the Ottoman Empire and they were able to establish an independent country. (It is worthwhile to note, however, that in the twenty-first century, the government of Turkey still denies that the killing of the Armenians was genocide.)

The Ottomans were defeated along with the other Central Powers in World War I. The victorious Allies carved what was left of the empire into small states, leaving only a region in Anatolia for the Turks. (For more information, see **Forging New Nations from the Ottoman Empire: 1914 to 1950**.) One last Ottoman sultan, who was virtually powerless, served until 1923. After centuries in power, the Ottoman Empire had come to an end.

This memorial in Yerevan, Armenia, commemorates the mass killing of Armenians in 1915. Historians estimate that between 600,000 and 1.5 million Armenians were killed by the Turks. © STRINGER/RUSSIA/X01235/REUTERS/CORBIS.

For More Information

BOOKS

Braude, Benjamin, and Bernard Lewis, eds. *The Central Lands*, vol. 1 of *Christians and Jews in the Ottoman Empire: The Functioning of a Plural Society*. New York: Holmes & Meier, 1982.

De Amicis, Edmondo. *Constantinople*. Translated by Caroline Tilton. New York: G.P. Putnam's Sons, 1872, p. 104.

Hourani, Albert. *A History of the Arab Peoples*. Cambridge, MA: Belknap, 1991, p. 222.

Kherdian, David. *The Road from Home: The Story of an Armenian Girl*. New York: Greenwillow Books, 1979, p. vii.

Kinross, Lord. *The Ottoman Centuries: The Rise and Fall of the Turkish Empire*. New York: Morrow Quill Paperbacks, 1979, p. 189.

Kort, Michael. *The Handbook of the Middle East*. Brookfield, CT: Twenty-First Century Books, 2002.

Lewis, Bernard. *The Middle East: A Brief History of the Last 2,000 Years.* New York: Scribner, 1995.

Pope, Nicole and Hugh Pope. *Turkey Unveiled: A History of Modern Turkey.* Woodstock, NY: Overlook Press, 1997, p. 38.

Smith, Charles D., ed. *Palestine and the Arab-Israeli Conflict: A History with Documents*, 4th ed. Boston, MA: Bedford/St. Martin's, 2001.

WEB SITES

Internet Islamic History Sourcebook. Fordham University, http://www.fordham.edu/halsall/islam/islamsbook.html#Islamic%20Nationalism (accessed on November 30, 2011).

The Islamic World to 1600. Applied History Research Group, University of Calgary. http://www.ucalgary.ca/applied_history/tutor/islam/ (accessed on November 30, 2011).

The Ottomans.org. http://www.theottomans.org/english/history/index.asp (accessed on November 30, 2011).

3

Forging New Nations from the Ottoman Empire: 1914 to 1950

World War I (1914–18; a global war between the Allies [Great Britain, France, and Russia, joined later by the United States] and the Central Powers [Germany, Austria-Hungary, and their allies]) dramatically reshaped the Middle East. The Ottoman Empire, the vast empire of the Ottoman Turks which included southwest Asia, northeast Africa, and southeast Europe, and lasted from the thirteenth century to the early twentieth century, fought alongside the Central Powers and collapsed at the end of the war. (For more information, see **The Ottoman Empire: 1299 to 1923**.) Afterward, its lands in the Middle East fell under the rule of the Allies. At that time the United States had little interest in the Middle East, and Russia had withdrawn its involvement in the region after experiencing a revolution in 1917. Great Britain and France thus found themselves in control of large parts of the Middle East. The decisions that these two countries made in the aftermath of World War I shaped politics in the region well into the twenty-first century.

Plans for the reshaping of the Middle East actually began well before the war ended. Great Britain was the most involved. It already controlled Egypt and had economic interests in what would become Iraq. It had promised its support to a variety of groups that were competing for local control, including an Arab independence movement centered in Mecca (in present-day Saudi Arabia) and the supporters of a cause known as Zionism, an international political movement originating in the late nineteenth century that called for the creation of an independent Jewish state in Palestine (a historical region in the Middle East on the eastern shore of the Mediterranean Sea, comprising parts of present-day Israel and Jordan). France had similar, although more limited, commitments in the region of present-day Lebanon and Syria. Within the Middle East itself, some powerful leaders were also

WORDS TO KNOW

Alawis: Also spelled Alawites; followers of a sect of Shia Islam that live in Syria. Their belief system and practices vary from Shiites in several ways, particularly in the belief that Ali, the son-in-law of the prophet Muhammad, was the human form of Allah (the Arabic word for God).

anti-Semitism: Prejudice against Jews.

Arabs: People of the Middle East and North Africa who speak the Arabic language or who live in countries in which Arabic is the dominant language.

Ba'ath Party: A secular (nonreligious) political party founded in the 1940s with the goal of uniting the Arab world and creating one powerful Arab state.

caliph: The spiritual, political, and military leader of the world's Muslims from the death of Muhammad in 632 until the caliphate was abolished in 1924.

caliphate: The entire community of Muslims under the leadership of the caliph.

Druze: Members of a small sect of Islam who believe that the ninth-century caliph Tariq al-Hakim was God.

Hejaz: A coastal region on the western Arabian Peninsula that includes the Muslim holy cities of Mecca and Medina.

kibbutz: A Jewish communal farming settlement in Israel, where settlers share all property and work collaboratively together. Plural is kibbutzim.

Kurds: A non-Arab ethnic group who live mainly in present-day Turkey, Iraq, and Iran.

mandate: A commission granting one country the authority to administer the affairs of another country. Also describes the territory entrusted to foreign administration.

Maronites: Members of an Arabic-speaking group of Christians, living mainly in Lebanon, who are in communion (share essential doctrines) with the Roman Catholic Church.

nationalism: The belief that a people with shared ethnic, cultural, and/or religious identities have the right to form their own nation. In established nations nationalism is devotion and loyalty to the nation and its culture.

Ottoman Empire: The vast empire of the Ottoman Turks which included southwest Asia, northeast Africa, and southeast Europe, and lasted from the thirteenth century to the early twentieth century.

Palestine: A historical region in the Middle East on the eastern shore of the Mediterranean Sea, comprising parts of present-day Israel and Jordan.

Pan-Arabism: A movement for the unification of Arab peoples and the political alliance of Arab states.

pogrom: A racially-motivated riot in which mobs, usually organized and sanctioned by the state, attack a minority group, most often Jews.

sharif: A nobleman and political leader chosen from among descendants of the Muslim prophet Muhammad.

Shiites: Followers of the Shia branch of Islam. Shiites believe that only direct descendants of the prophet Muhammad are qualified to lead the Islamic faith.

socialism: A system in which the government owns the means of production and controls the distribution of goods and services.

sultan: A ruler of a Muslim state, especially the Ottoman Empire.

Sunnis: Followers of the Sunni branch of Islam. Sunnis believe that elected officials, regardless of their heritage, are qualified to lead the Islamic faith.

Zionism: An international political movement originating in the late nineteenth century that called for the creation of an independent Jewish state in Palestine.

preparing for the approaching collapse of the Ottoman Empire, some in collaboration with the Allies.

After the war, the Allies partitioned (divided up) many lands of the Middle East that had been under the rule of the Ottoman Empire at the time of World War I—a region that includes the present-day states and regions of Jordan, Israel, the Palestinian territories, Iraq, Lebanon, and Syria—and formed other decisions regarding Egypt, Turkey, and the Kurdish population. (The Kurds are a non-Arab ethnic group who live mainly in present-day Turkey, Iraq, and Iran. They are the largest ethnic group in the world that does not have an independent country.) Some countries, such as Iran, the countries of the Arabian Peninsula, and North Africa, escaped the post–World War I partition. (For more information on the counties that were not partitioned, see **Other Rising Middle East Nations in the Twentieth Century**.)

The Arab Revolt of 1916

Although the Ottoman Empire had lost most of its European and North African territory prior to World War I, it still ruled the vast Arabic-speaking regions of Syria, Palestine, and Iraq, as well as the Arabian Peninsula when the war began in 1914. The Arabs (people who speak the Arabic language) had generally been supportive of Ottoman rule. The Ottoman sultan (ruler) was considered the caliph, or the spiritual, political, and military leader of the world's Muslims, and was revered by many Arabs. The Ottoman sultans had wisely promoted Arab political, business, and religious leaders into high positions in the government. They also allowed Arabs to speak their own language and practice their own customs. The Ottomans contributed generously to the upkeep of the holy cities of Mecca and Medina. But conditions for Arabs changed when a a group of young reformers overthrew the Ottoman sultan in 1908. By the time of World War I, a group of military officers known as the Young Turks had taken control of the Ottoman Empire. An Ottoman sultan still reigned, but with very little power. The Young Turks secularized the government (made it nonreligious) and began to exalt the Turkish identity over the Arab. Opposition to the new government quickly spread through the Arab regions of the empire. When the Young Turks took measures to repress Arab independence movements, it only intensified the opposition.

One of the foremost Arab opposition leaders was Husayn ibn 'Ali (also spelled Hussein bin Ali; c. 1854–1931), the sharif of Mecca.

(A sharif is a Muslim nobleman and political leader chosen from among the descendants of of the prophet Muhammad [(c. 570–632)].) As relations between the Arab provinces and the Turkish government of the Ottoman Empire deteriorated during the early years of World War I, Husayn sought an alliance with the British. In an exchange of letters with Sir Henry McMahon (1862–1949), the British high commissioner in Egypt, Husayn pledged to stage a large Arab uprising against the Turks, as the Ottoman rulers were increasingly known, if Great Britain would promise to recognize the independence of the Arab lands at the end of the war. In his response McMahon seemed to promise this independence, although he was vague about which areas of the Middle East the British would agree to support in their independence movements.

The Turkish government learned of the Husayn-McMahon correspondence, and in May 1916 twenty-one leading Arabs suspected of taking part in the plan were arrested and executed. Outrage at the crackdown sparked widespread Arab support for an uprising against the Turks. Under orders from Husayn, Arab forces, some led by the sharif's third son, Faisal (1885–1933), attacked Turkish garrisons in the Hejaz (a coastal region on the western Arabian Peninsula that includes the Muslim holy cities of Mecca and Medina). In time the British provided military supplies and military advisers for the endeavor. British colonel T.E. Lawrence (1888–1935) joined the Arab forces led by Faisal and helped put the Turkish forces on the defensive. Lawrence later wrote what is considered a romanticized version of his collaboration with Faisal in his memoirs, *Seven Pillars of Wisdom* (1922), and his exploits are the subject of the award-winning 1962 British film *Lawrence of Arabia*. The Arab revolt against the Turks ended in October 1918 when Arab armies captured the city of Damascus, in present-day Syria. Faisal established Damascus as the capital of the new independent Arab state, the Arab Kingdom of Syria. In Hejaz, his father Husayn proclaimed himself the king of Hejaz and of all Arabs.

Changes in plans and broken promises

While McMahon was negotiating with Husayn about the fate of Arab regions of the Middle East, Great Britain began making separate plans for the Middle East with its main wartime ally, France. In 1916, after secret negotiations, an agreement was reached between British diplomat Sir Mark Sykes (1879–1919) and French diplomat François Georges-Picot

Husayn ibn 'Ali, the sharif of Mecca. In correspondence with British official Sir Henry McMahon, Husayn pledged to stage a large Arab uprising against the Ottomans if Great Britain would promise to recognize the independence of the Arab lands. © THE PRINT COLLECTOR/ALAMY.

(1870–1951). Under the Sykes-Picot Agreement, the British would control an area roughly comprised of present-day Jordan and Iraq, Palestine would be governed by an international administration, and the French would control Syria and Lebanon.

Most historians consider the Sykes-Picot Agreement a contradiction of the agreement made in the Husayn-McMahon correspondence, because the Arabs had been led to believe they would be free to rule their own lands after helping the British. On the other hand, all parties, Arab and European, shared an interest in filling the power vacuum (the lack of a central government in a region) that would almost certainly follow the Ottoman Empire's collapse. Of the lands that had until then been ruled by the Ottomans, only a few had developed into political entities that had readily available resources to govern themselves.

The Zionists' plan for a Palestinian home

Plans for the Middle East were ongoing in other parts of Europe as well. Long before World War I, the Zionist movement had developed in eastern Europe. Jews there faced anti-Semitism, prejudice against Jews. The discrimination often included violence and restrictions on resources, jobs, and places to live. During the nineteenth century, anti-Semitism in Poland, Russia, and other parts of Europe resulted in pogroms, racially-motivated riots in which mobs, usually organized and sanctioned by the state, attack a minority group, most often Jews. Hoping to escape the persecution and make a better life for themselves and their descendants, Jews began seeking a place where they could establish their own self-governed community. Most early Zionists were drawn to the idea of returning to the site of the ancient Jewish Kingdom of Israel in Palestine.

A vicious series of pogroms that swept through Russia from 1881 to 1884 inspired Jewish author Leo Pinsker (1821–1891) to write *Auto-emancipation*, a pamphlet promoting the idea of Jewish self-rule. Pinsker argued that the only way for Jews to save themselves from persecution was to form their own community and govern themselves. Although his pamphlet was not widely read, it did prompt a group of European Jews to immigrate to Palestine. In 1896 a Hungarian Jew named Theodor Herzl (1860–1904) published a popular exploration of the same idea. His book *The Jewish State* drew widespread attention to the ideas of Zionism, and Herzl founded the World Zionist Organization to promote and fund

Theodor Herzl, author of The Jewish State. *Herzl's book drew widespread attention to the ideas of Zionism.*
© BETTMANN/CORBIS.

the immigration of Jews to Palestine. By the twentieth century, thousands of Jews had moved to the region.

Zionism initially promoted the idea that Jews would thrive if they could form a separate community of their own, but it developed into a complex plan for building a Jewish state. Zionist organizations formed in many countries in Europe and in the United States. They collected money and helped organize the migration of Jews from anti-Semitic communities to Palestine. Once Jews reached Palestine, Zionist agencies helped the immigrants settle in, finding them jobs or places in the kibbutzim that they had established there. (A kibbutz is a Jewish communal farming settlement, where settlers share all property and work collaboratively together.)

The Balfour Declaration

During World War I, a group of British Zionists, including influential lobbyist Chaim Weizmann (1874–1952), who would later become the first president of Israel, convinced British government authorities to support the cause of a Jewish homeland in Palestine. On November 2, 1917, the Balfour Declaration, a short paragraph written by leaders of the Zionist movement, was approved by the British war cabinet. The declaration, which was sent by the British foreign secretary Lord Arthur Balfour (1848–1930) to Zionist leader Walter Rothschild (1868–1937), reads:

> His Majesty's Government view with favor the establishment in Palestine of a national home for the Jewish people, and will use their best endeavors to facilitate the achievement of this object, it being understood that nothing shall be done which may prejudice the civil and religious rights of the existing non-Jewish communities in Palestine, or the rights and political status enjoyed by Jews in any other country.

The declaration is deliberately vague. It does not, for example, specify whether the Jewish people in Palestine would establish a state, using the phrase *national home* instead. The declaration also does not mention Arabs living in Palestine by any other identity than "non-Jewish communities," although the Arabs made up 90 percent of the Palestinian population at the time. Under the Husayn-McMahon correspondence, the Arabs believed they had negotiated independence for an area that included Palestine. The Balfour Declaration, despite its promise to uphold the civil and religious rights of "non-Jewish communities," was viewed with grave concern by the Arabs in the region.

The League of Nations and the mandate system

World War I ended on November 11, 1918. The fate of the collapsed Ottoman Empire was determined by the Treaty of Sevres (1920) after fifteen months of deliberation by the Allied powers. Even before the negotiating had started, however, European countries had started to occupy the region that is present-day Turkey. The British occupied the capital of Istanbul, the French occupied Cilicia (a region that extends inland from the southeastern coast of modern Turkey), and the Italians had troops on the southern coast. Great Britain had also promised Turkish lands to Greece in exchange for its support in the war.

The formal deliberations about the Ottoman Empire began in January 1919 when representatives from thirty Allied countries met at the Paris Peace Conference in France to negotiate a peace treaty and to resolve financial and territorial matters related to the war. One of the accomplishments of the yearlong conference was the creation of the League of Nations, an international organization of sovereign countries established after World War I to promote peace. The League's purpose was to settle disputes between countries through negotiation, and improve relations between nations. One of the League's powers was to establish mandates for regions such as the Ottoman Empire, where the government had collapsed. (Mandates are territories entrusted to foreign administration.) The mandates were to be administered by one of the Allied nations in an attempt to guide them toward independence and statehood.

Negotiations about the fate of the Ottoman Empire continued at the San Remo Conference in April 1920, in San Remo, Italy where Great Britain, France, Italy, and Japan attempted to determine the boundaries of the mandates that were being considered for the Ottoman Empire. By August, significant agreement had been reached and the Treaty of Sevres was signed. Under the treaty, the land that is the present-day nation of Turkey was to be split up among various countries (but not under the mandate system). The Turks were to keep the area known as Anatolia, with its capital of Istanbul, but other portions of the region were set aside for an independent Armenian state and an independent state for the Kurdish people. Large parts of the region were to be granted to Greece for administration, and both France and Italy were granted small regions.

Under the Treaty of Sevres, Great Britain and France received responsibility for the postwar government administration of several Middle Eastern mandates. Their rule was to be supervised and approved by the League of Nations to ensure that they guided the mandates to future independence and did not attempt to take over the new nations. Great Britain was granted two mandates. The first was known as Mesopotamia, but its name was soon changed to Iraq. The second, the British Mandate of Palestine, was not established until two years later by the League of Nations, because its boundaries had not been settled in the earlier treaty.

The British Mandate of Palestine included present-day Jordan, Israel, and the Palestinian territories.

The central and northern parts of the Ottoman Empire were assigned to France, which subdivided them into two republics: Lebanon, a small state on the coast of the Mediterranean; and Syria, a larger territory that stretched eastward toward Iraq. Great Britain had sidestepped the mandate process with Egypt, which it had taken control of at the start of World War I. Although their negotiations for an independent Arab world had failed, the Arabs of the Arabian Peninsula maintained their independence and were not partitioned by the Europeans. (For more information, see **Other Rising Middle East Nations in the Twentieth Century**.)

Most of the Middle East that had been under the rule of the Ottoman Empire until 1920 had never before been divided by Western-style borders. The Middle East had many distinct regions and communities that had formed under tribal and family interests. Most had long histories of local customs and had usually operated under the rule of larger empires. According to many historians, the negotiations that led to the Treaty of Sevres, which were heavily influenced by Great Britain and France, ignored the history and cultures of these regions when they created new borders.

The Republic of Turkey

Turkey was the seat of the Ottoman Empire's government for over six hundred years. At the end of World War I, however, the country was in danger of disappearing. The Turks, however, refused to let their country be divided. They joined together in a new spirit of Turkish nationalism, the belief that a people with shared ethnic, cultural, and/or religious identities have the right to form their own nation. Led by General Mustafa Kemal Atatürk (1881–1938), the Turks fought off the Greek and Italian armies and reclaimed control of their eastern lands. In 1923 the independent Republic of Turkey was recognized by the international community, including the Allies. Atatürk took his place as the nation's first president.

Atatürk chose to model Turkey's new economic and political systems on those in the Western world. He believed this was necessary for Turkey's survival. Among the first steps he took in establishing the new republic was to abolish the Ottoman Empire and the caliphate. The caliphate was the community of the world's Muslims, which, since the death of Muhammad in 632 had been led by a spiritual, political, and

Turkish citizens walk past a banner of Mustafa Kemal Atatürk, the first president of the Republic of Turkey.
© CHRIS HELLIER/CORBIS.

military leader called a caliph. During the Ottoman era, the Ottoman sultan had served as the caliph, but Atatürk eliminated the role of the caliph. Under Atatürk, Islam was no longer the state religion, and the Ottoman legal system, which was based on sharia (Islamic religious law) was dismantled. Atatürk wanted a legal system based on secular (non-religious) laws and a separation between church and state, as in most Western countries. He pursued many programs to make his country more like those in the West. He granted women equal status with men, including the right to vote and hold office; he enforced the use of the Latin alphabet, rather than Arabic script; and he demanded that the Turkish people wear Western-style clothes. Although Atatürk's reforms often focused on restricting the cultural traits associated with the Muslim Middle East, he also encouraged his people to identify with their Turkish heritage, inspiring great pride throughout Turkey.

Atatürk achieved significant economic progress in Turkey and steered the country clear of some of the wars that erupted in Europe and the Middle East, remaining officially neutral most of the time. But Turkey was not a democracy. During his lifetime, Atatürk's rule was absolute;

the elected parliament served to approve his policies without question, and he used the military to enforce unpopular programs.

The British mandate of Palestine

When Great Britain was granted the mandate for Palestine by the League of Nations in 1922, it had already promised Jewish Zionists, who wanted to create a Jewish homeland in Palestine, the right to settle in Palestine. However, it had also promised Arab Palestinians that they would lose none of their rights and privileges to the Jewish immigrants. From the beginning, control of the mandate of Palestine was hotly disputed between native Arab Palestinians and Jewish immigrants. Because of this conflict, the British placed the mandate under its direct control, rather than selecting a leader whose rule they would supervise, as they did in Iraq and Jordan. Palestine was supervised by Sir Herbert Samuel (1870–1963), an experienced British politician. The British mandate seemed to be structured to favor the Zionists. Samuel was Jewish as well as a supporter of Zionism, and the documents authorizing the British mandate included the text of the Balfour Declaration and declared that there would be three official languages in Palestine: English, Arabic, and Hebrew, the ancient language of the Jewish people, which had been revived in the nineteenth century to unite Jews scattered across the globe.

However, the British, and Samuel, had pledged to cooperate with Arab leaders to develop the economy of Palestine. Samuel also publicly proclaimed Great Britain's duty to live up to its promises to uphold the rights of Arab Palestinians. But the promises the British had made to both sides of the emerging conflict for control of Palestine made it very difficult for them to commit their resources to the support of either side. As a result, Great Britain's support continued to shift, favoring first one group, then the other. In the meantime, the Zionists, one of the most organized and outspoken groups in Palestine, slowly gained power with every passing year.

Arabs who had lived in Palestine before the war had long opposed European Jewish immigration and were suspicious of Zionist intentions. But after the war, the massive postwar Jewish immigration increasingly angered the Palestinians. Zionists were buying land in Palestine that they restricted for use and resale only to Jews. During the mandate period, the Jews built schools, universities, courts, hospitals, and military defense systems, preparing themselves for nationhood. The Arab Palestinians protested, sometimes violently, against the British administration and the Jewish community. Both Jews and Palestinians were killed in the angry clashes, but the Palestinians lacked the organization to effectively stop the progress of the Jewish state. (For more information, see **Palestine and Zionist Settlement: Nineteenth Century to 1948**.)

Jordan: stability amid turmoil

The country of Jordan was not an individual political entity prior to the twentieth century. Throughout history the area that is present-day Jordan was part of some larger state or empire. It was previously considered part of Palestine (to the west), part of greater Syria (to the north), or part of the unmapped deserts of Arabia (to the south).

The Emirate of Transjordan was established in 1921, to be ruled under British supervision by Abdullah bin Husayn (1882–1951), an Arab leader who had helped the British defeat the Ottoman Empire during World War I. Transjordan had a population of just four hundred thousand people, and the majority of these people were Bedouins (nomadic Arab tribes who lived in the desert). It was in the handful of larger towns and villages that Abdullah established his base of power. With British assistance he trained an effective army called the Arab Legion, built roads and schools, and established an efficient government. Through the 1920s and 1930s, Great Britain transferred more administrative duties to Abdullah. During World War II (1939–45; a war in which the Allies [Great Britain, France, the Soviet Union, the United States, and China] defeated the Axis Powers [Germany, Italy, and Japan]), Abdullah remained a faithful ally of the British, supplying one of the more accomplished Arab regiments to the British war effort. After the war, in 1946, Transjordan gained its full independence and changed its name to the Hashemite Kingdom of Jordan, often referred to simply as Jordan. Abdullah became king of Jordan.

Like most nations of the Middle East, the course of Jordan's history was changed profoundly by the 1948 declaration of the Zionists that they had formed an independent nation called Israel in Palestine. Abdullah had originally cooperated with the British in their efforts to build a multiethnic state in Palestine between 1920 and 1947. But when Great Britain withdrew from the region in 1948 and the Jews in Palestine declared their independence it forced thousands of Arab Palestinians from their homes into neighboring Arab countries. The Jordanians, along with several other

Abdullah bin Husayn became emir of Transjordan in 1923, then king of Jordan in 1946.
POPPERFOTO/GETTY IMAGES.

Arab nations, felt compelled to help Palestinians regain their land and Abdullah sent the Arab Legion to fight against Israel in the 1948 Arab-Israeli War, along with the forces of Egypt, Syria, Lebanon, and Iraq. (For more information, see **The Arab-Israeli Conflict: 1948 to 1973**.)

Although the general Arab military effort to get rid of Israel after it declared independence was a failure, Abdullah's Arab Legion fought well. After the war, Jordan acquired a significant amount of territory in the West Bank (an area between Israel and Jordan on the west bank of the Jordan River), as well as in the eastern half of the city of Jerusalem. With these victories came a new set of problems for Jordan. By taking over the West Bank, Jordan became responsible for its five hundred thousand inhabitants. During the 1948 Arab-Israeli War and again later in the 1967 Arab-Israeli War (in which the victorious Israel captured more Arab territory, including the Sinai Peninsula and the Gaza Strip from Egypt, the West Bank from Jordan, and the Golan Heights from Syria) an estimated 750,000 Palestinians fled from the hostile conditions within Israel and moved into refugee camps inside the borders of Arab nations including Jordan. Since Jordan's 1948 conflict with Israel, Arab Palestinians have become a majority of the population of Jordan. The Palestinians caused significant political problems within Jordan, not the least of which was their open commitment to wage war on Israel. Navigating this conflict fell to Abdullah's successor, his grandson Hussein ibn Talal (1935–1999), who ruled beginning in 1953 as King Hussein I.

Iraq

Until it gained its independence in 1932, the present-day country of Iraq was controlled by a series of empires and nations. It is the site of ancient Mesopotamia, one of the oldest civilizations in history. It has been ruled by the ancient Greeks, the Romans, and the Persians, among others. At the beginning of the twentieth century, Iraq was part of the Ottoman Empire. After World War I the League of Nations made Iraq a British mandate.

Iraq is home to several populations that have clashed at times throughout its history. It has a large Kurdish population. This Kurdish minority has long hoped for an independent country of its own. The majority of the population is Shiite. Shiites are followers of the Shia branch of Islam. They believe that only direct descendants of the prophet Muhammad are qualified to lead the Islamic faith. Many of Iraq's Shiites feel an allegiance to neighboring Iran, which has an overwhelming Shiite majority. Iraq also has a sizable number of Sunnis, followers of the Sunni branch of Islam. Sunnis believe that elected officials, regardless of their heritage, are qualified to lead the Islamic faith. Sunnis are in the majority in every Arab nation except Iran and Iraq.

When Great Britain took over the mandate of Iraq after World War I, it installed Faisal, the son of Husayn (the leader of the Arab Revolt) and the brother of Abdullah, the king of Transjordan, as king of Iraq in 1921. Most of the people of Iraq opposed British rule and because of this they welcomed King Faisal I. Nevertheless, the king still had to contend with an ethnically divided population. After 1927, when oil was discovered in Iraq, European countries began to fight for control of this precious resource. Faisal may have been king, but the real power in Iraq lay in oil wealth, and ownership of oil rights in Iraq was split between Great Britain, France, the Netherlands, and the United States. Iraq thus began its modern history as a nation divided along ethnic and religious lines and without access to its main source of wealth.

Despite these problems, Faisal used the small funds that Iraq received from the oil business to improve the country. This created a sense of pride and a national identity in the Iraqi people. By earlier agreement, the British mandate ended in 1932, but British influence remained strong in the country. The Iraqi royal family remained loyal to Great Britain, and payments from foreign oil interests helped build the Iraqi economy. Increasingly, however, a growing group of Iraqi nationalists promoted rejecting British and Western interference and claiming control of Iraq's oil wealth. The nationalists sided with the Germans during World War II, prompting temporary British occupation of the country.

In the post–World War II years, Iraqi nationalists were vocal in their call for the destruction of Israel and later supported the call for Pan-Arabism, a movement for the unification of Arab peoples and the political alliance of Arab states. In 1958 General Abdul Karim Qassem (1914–1963), leader of a group of Iraqi military officers called the Free Officers, killed King Faisal II (1935–1958) and installed himself as ruler of Iraq. For the next ten years, bloody feuds between rival nationalist groups made Iraqi politics highly unstable. Finally, the Ba'ath Party, a Pan-Arab group that combined nationalism with socialism (a system in which the government owns the means of production and controls the distribution of goods and services), took full control of Iraq in 1968 and remained in power until president Saddam Hussein (1937–2006) was removed from power in 2003. Under the Ba'ath Party, Iraq was often at odds with other Arab nations, especially its rival Syria, and was an enemy of Israel for many years.

Faisal I was installed as king of Iraq when Great Britain took over the mandate of Iraq after World War I.
© HULTON-DEUTSCH COLLECTION/CORBIS.

The division of Syria and Lebanon

Throughout history the region that became present-day Syria was almost continuously occupied by a larger foreign powers. Like most of its Arab neighbors, Syria fell under Ottoman rule in the period between 1516 and

1517 and remained part of the empire until the end of World War I. In the Arab Revolt of 1916, Arab nationalists attempted to declare independence in a region that included modern-day Syria and Lebanon. But French forces defeated the Arab uprising and, in 1920 France was granted control over the region under the mandate system of the League of Nations.

Early French plans were to establish separate states for each population group in the ethnically and religiously diverse region. Sunnis, Shiites, Alawis, Druze, and Maronites would all be allotted their own territory. The Alawis are followers of a sect of Shia Islam that live mainly along the Turkish border of Syria. Their belief system and practices vary from Shiites, particularly in the belief that Ali, the son-in-law of the prophet Muhammad, was the human form of the god Allah. The Druze are members of a small sect of Islam who believe that the ninth-century caliph Tariq al-Hakim was God. The Maronites are Arabic-speaking Christians living mainly in Lebanon, who are in communion (share essential doctrines) with the Roman Catholic Church.

In order to defeat Arab Muslim resistance to its rule, France divided Syria and Lebanon into two countries. What was then called Lebanon was the small Ottoman province of Mount Lebanon. Mount Lebanon's most powerful group was the Maronites, who, as Catholic Christians, tended to favor French interests. (France is a predominantly Catholic nation.) As Catholics, the French had been the self-appointed protectors of Maronite interests in Lebanon since Ottoman times. The French decided to annex some of the Muslim-majority cities and coastal ports from Syria to the new mandate of Lebanon. This made Lebanon more religiously diverse and weakened Syria by diluting its Muslim population. The legacy of this division can be seen in the nearly continuous conflict that Syria and especially Lebanon have suffered ever since.

Lebanon France had manipulated the borders of Lebanon in such a way that Christians of all denominations comprised a majority. Although not all Christians in Lebanon were Maronite Catholics, the Maronites formed a large portion of the Christian population and held many positions of power within the Lebanese government in the 1930s and 1940s. When the French mandate ended, the National Pact of 1943 created a sectarian system of government, one that divided the people by their religious groups. It was based on the results of a 1932 census in which Christians outnumbered Muslims by a ratio of six to five. The National Pact favored the Maronites and the Sunnis, the two largest groups in Lebanon in 1932. Under the pact, the Lebanese government would consist of six Christians to every five Muslims. The Lebanese president had to be a Maronite and the prime minister a Sunni. The speaker of the house was to be a Shiite and the chief of staff a Druze. This plan remained in place until 1989, when the Taif agreement restructured the National Pact to reduce the privileged status of the Maronites and more accurately reflect the religious groups of Lebanon's population.

Lebanon achieved its official independence from France in 1943, but real independence did not occur until French troops left the country in 1946, at the end of World War II. Deprived of the stabilizing influence of France, Lebanon soon faced internal conflict, including decades of civil war between the Christians, the Muslims, and various other religious groups in the country, and a lengthy military occupation by neighboring Syria, as well as a military occupation by Israel in southern Lebanon from 1982 to 2000.

A Maronite monastery in Lebanon. Due to their large numbers, Maronites held many positions of power within the Lebanese government during the French mandate. © ROGER WOOD/CORBIS.

Syria Under French control, instability and disunity reigned in Syria. France had imagined Syria run by a federal system (a union of states under a central government). Arab nationalists wanted to unify control of the country, but Druze, Sunni, and Shiite factions fought bitterly over who would wield the most power. Several political parties formed during the 1930s, as French diplomats sought ways to withdraw their military presence. Finally, during World War II, international pressure forced France to withdraw its presence from Syria, although it demanded that its economic interests be protected. Syria immediately elected a pro-Arab leader, joined the Arab League, and declared its independence on April 17, 1946. (The Arab League is a regional political alliance of Arab nations formed in 1945 to promote political, military, and economic cooperation within the Arab world.)

After World War II Syria alternated between military and civilian governments, with a series of violent coups (overthrows of the government). Ever since declaring independence, Syria has played a dominant role in regional conflict. It has been one of Israel's greatest enemies since it declared war on that country in 1948. It has been an instigator of civil unrest in Lebanon, using its power to undermine stable governments in that country. The Syrian Ba'ath Party, which is distinct from the Iraqi Ba'ath Party, emerged in the early 1950s as the dominant political influence in the country. It led Syria into a brief political union with Egypt from 1958 to 1961 as a member of the United Arab Republic and encouraged Syrian alliances with the Soviet Union, Iran, and with terrorist groups. The Assad family, which came to power in 1970, brought Syria's factions together under its strong government, but it also brutally suppressed any opposition.

The end of the mandates

Of the mandates, Iraq was the first to achieve independence in 1932. When World War II began, the French mandates, Lebanon and Syria, fell under the temporary control of the Vichy government (the government of German-occupied France). The Vichy forces in Lebanon and Syria were overthrown by the Allies in 1941, and the two countries were granted independence, although this did not become official until 1943. Jordan's independence was recognized in 1946. The only mandate that did not achieve independence in 1946 was Palestine. Great Britain, weary of the struggle between the Arabs and the Jews, sought help from the United Nations in 1947 and began to withdraw its forces. (The United Nations is an international organization of countries founded in 1945 to promote international peace, security, and cooperation.)

Two other populations that were part of the Ottoman Empire when World War I began, the Egyptians and the Kurds, never participated in the mandate system and did not achieve independence as quickly, or in the Kurds' case, at all.

Egypt

Egypt was officially part of the Ottoman Empire at the beginning of World War I, although Great Britain had controlled it since 1882. When the war started, Great Britain declared Egypt a protectorate and then used it as a base for British troops fighting against the Ottoman Empire. Not long after the war, in 1922, Great Britain declared Egypt a constitutional monarchy (in which the powers of the monarch are granted by the nation's constitution), led by King Fuad (1868–1936) and with an elected parliament. Still, British forces remained strong in Egypt.

Fuad and his successor, his son Farouk (1920–1965), who took power in 1936, were opposed by an emerging Egyptian nationalist movement called the Wafd al Misri, or simply the Wafd. The Wafd's members were educated, middle-class Egyptians, who wanted a constitutional monarchy with an elected parliament and strove to rid Egypt of British intervention in its affairs. From 1922 on, the king and the Wafd fought for control of Egyptian politics. In 1936 the Wafd negotiated a smaller British military presence in Egypt, but the events of World War II saw Great Britain again exercising its control of the country.

In the years following World War II, Egypt became increasingly unstable. Corruption and incompetence led to a widespread lack of confidence in the government, and popular uprisings emerged to challenge both the king and the Wafd. The most powerful radical group was the Muslim Brotherhood, an organization established in 1928 that pressed for Egypt to become an Islamic state (one in which Islam provides the basis for the political, social, and cultural life). The Muslim Brotherhood was one of several groups leading riots against Western influence in the country and protesting Egypt's failure to deny the Jewish state of Israel its independence in 1948. But neither the monarchy or the Muslim Brotherhood was to prevail; on July 23, 1952, a group of military men led by Gamal

Abdel Nasser (1918–1970) took power. They forced the king into exile and crushed the Muslim Brotherhood.

Nasser eventually became president of Egypt and proved to be a strong, authoritarian leader. Under Nasser, Egypt rose to be a powerful nation. Nasser is remembered especially for his attempt to create a Pan-Arab movement, which aspired to unify all the Arab countries into a single, powerful entity that would be able to defend itself from Western powers.

The Kurds struggle for independence from Iraq

The Kurds are the largest ethnic group in the world that does not have an independent country. Kurds speak Kurdish, a non-Arab language. The Kurdish culture, which dates back to the world's first civilizations in 3500 BCE, existed originally among people living in a region called Kurdistan, a 200,000-square-mile (517,998-square-kilometer) area that encompasses parts of the present-day Iraq, Iran, Turkey, and Syria. Under the Ottoman Empire, the Kurdish people were governed by their own tribal leaders in Kurdistan. These Kurdish leaders had an arrangement with the Ottoman rulers allowing them to maintain order within their own population.

After World War I, the League of Nations promised the Kurds their own country. The promise was never fulfilled, however, mainly because the new Turkish republic, along with Iran and Iraq, refused to recognize an independent Kurdish state. Those states were awarded the Kurdish land instead. The Kurdish population was separated as the borders of Iraq, Turkey, Syria, and Iran cut through the former land of Kurdistan and the Kurds came under the control of whichever country they happened to reside within.

Despite being separated, the Kurds maintained a strong sense of national identity. Kurds living in each of the countries that formally made up Kurdistan formed nationalist movements over the years to fight for the rights of Kurds to have their own independent country and to maintain the Kurdish way of life. In the Saadabad Treaty of 1937, however, the governments of Turkey, Iran, and Iraq agreed to use force if necessary to stop Kurdish nationalist movements, and long after the treaty expired these sentiments remained firm into the twenty-first century.

For More Information

BOOKS

Cleveland, William L. *A History of the Modern Middle East.* Boulder, CO: Westview Press, 2004.

Encyclopedia of the Modern Middle East, 4 vols. New York: Macmillan Reference USA, 1996.

Gilbert, Martin. *The Arab-Israeli Conflict: Its History in Maps*, 5th ed. London: Weidenfeld and Nicolson, 1992.

Hourani, Albert Habib. *The Emergence of the Modern Middle East.* Berkeley: University of California Press, 1981.

Kort, Michael. *The Handbook of the Middle East.* Brookfield, CT: Twenty-First Century Books, 2002.

Lewis, Bernard. *The Middle East: A Brief History of the Last 2,000 Years.* New York: Scribner, 1995.

Lewis, Bernard. *What Went Wrong? The Clash between Islam and Modernity in the Middle East.* New York: Perennial, 2003.

Schneer, Jonathan. *The Balfour Declaration: The Origins of the Arab-Israeli Conflict.* New York: Random House, 2010, p. 341.

WEB SITES

"The Balfour Declaration." *Israel Ministry of Foreign Affairs.* http://www.mfa.gov.il/MFA/Peace%20Process/Guide%20to%20the%20Peace%20Process/The%20Balfour%20Declaration (accessed on November 30, 2011).

"The Great Arab Revolt." *The Hashemite Kingdom of Jordan History.* http://www.kinghussein.gov.jo/his_arabrevolt.html (accessed on November 30, 2011).

"A History of Conflict—Israel and the Palestinians: A Timeline." *BBC News.* http://news.bbc.co.uk/2/shared/spl/hi/middle_east/03/v3_ip_timeline/html/ (accessed on November 30, 2011).

Internet Islamic History Sourcebook. Fordham University. http://www.fordham.edu/halsall/islam/islamsbook.asp (accessed on November 30, 2011).

The Question of Palestine and the United Nations. United Nations Department of Public Information (March 2003). http://www.un.org/Depts/dpi/palestine/ (accessed on November 30, 2011).

4

Other Rising Middle East Nations in the Twentieth Century

For hundreds of years the vast Ottoman Empire was the main power in the Middle East, ruling much of southwest Asia, northeast Africa, and southeast Europe, from the thirteenth century to the early twentieth century. However, the empire began to decline in eighteenth century, finally coming to an end after fighting on the losing side in World War I (1914–18; a global war between the Allies [Great Britain, France, and Russia, joined later by the United States] and the Central Powers [Germany, Austria-Hungary, and their allies]). After the war Western powers partitioned (divided up) the Ottoman Empire, establishing new political entities that would be administered by European countries. These included Palestine, Jordan, Iraq, Lebanon, and Syria. (For more information, see **Forging New Nations from the Ottoman Empire: 1914 to 1950**.)

But not all countries in the Middle East were part of the Ottoman Empire at the time of its collapse. Iran, the countries of the Arabian Peninsula (present-day Saudi Arabia, Kuwait, Bahrain, the United Arab Emirates, Qatar, Oman, and Yemen) and the Arabic-speaking countries of North Africa (Algeria, Tunisia, Libya, and Morocco) were not partitioned. The history of these nations reflects the remarkable diversity of the Middle East, as well as the variety of conflicts that have beset the region.

Iran

Iran has played a special role in the history of the Middle East. Known to Westerners for thousands of years as Persia, it came to be known as Iran in 1935, when the Iranian ruler asked that foreigners call the nation by the historic name used by its inhabitants. Iran has always been physically, ethnically, and religiously different from most other Middle Eastern

WORDS TO KNOW

Arabs: People of the Middle East and North Africa who speak the Arabic language or who live in countries in which Arabic is the dominant language.

ayatollah: A high-ranking Shiite religious leader.

caliph: The spiritual, political, and military leader of the world's Muslims from the death of Muhammad in 632 until the caliphate was abolished in 1924.

caliphate: The entire community of Muslims under the leadership of the caliph.

cleric: An ordained religious official.

Communism: A system of government in which the state plans and controls the economy and a single political party holds power.

dynasty: A series of rulers from the same family.

emir: A ruler, chief, or commander in some Islamic countries.

fundamentalism: A movement stressing adherence to a strict or literal interpretation of religious principles.

Hejaz: A coastal region on the western Arabian Peninsula that includes the Muslim holy cities of Mecca and Medina.

Hezbollah: A Shiite militant group and political party based in Lebanon.

Islamism: A fundamentalist movement characterized by the belief that Islam should provide the basis for the political, social, and cultural life in Muslim nations.

Koran: Also spelled Qur'an or Quran; the holy book of Islam.

Muslim Brotherhood: An Islamic fundamentalist group organized in opposition to Western influence and in support of Islamic principles.

nationalism: The belief that a people with shared ethnic, cultural, and/or religious identities have the right to form their own nation. In established nations nationalism is devotion and loyalty to the nation and its culture.

occupation: The physical and political control of an area seized by a foreign military force.

Organization of Petroleum Exporting Countries (OPEC): An organization formed in 1960 by the world's major oil-producing nations to coordinate policies and ensure stable oil prices in world markets.

Ottoman Empire: The vast empire of the Ottoman Turks which included southwest Asia, northeast Africa, and southeast Europe, and lasted from the thirteenth century to the early twentieth century.

Pan-Arabism: A movement for the unification of Arab peoples and the political alliance of Arab states.

pasha: A provincial governor or powerful official of the Ottoman Empire.

sanctions: Punitive measures adopted by the international community against a nation that has violated international law, usually in the form of diplomatic, economic, or social restrictions.

sharia: A system of Islamic law based on the Koran and other sacred writings. Sharia attempts to create the perfect social order, based on God's will and justice, and covers a wide range of human activities, including acts of religious worship, the law of contracts and obligations, personal status law, and public law.

sharif: A nobleman and political leader chosen from among descendants of the Muslim prophet Muhammad.

sheikh: An Arab tribal leader.

socialism: A system in which the government owns the means of production and controls the distribution of goods and services.

Suez Canal: A shipping canal that connects the Mediterranean Sea with the Red Sea.

countries, yet its stance on issues central to the conflicts in the Middle East have made it an important participant.

Iran straddles the boundary between the Middle East and southern Asia. A majority of Iran's people are ethnically Indo-European, while the majority of the population in the other Middle Eastern countries (except Turkey and Israel) is Arab. (Arabs are people who speak the Arabic language or who live in countries in which Arabic is the dominant language.) Few Iranians speak Arabic outside of religious ceremonies. Instead they speak a form of Persian called Farsi. Nearly 90 percent of Iran's population is Shiite. Shiites are followers of the Shia branch of Islam. They believe that only direct descendants of the prophet Muhammad (c. 570–632) are qualified to lead the Islamic faith. Sunnis, followers of the Sunni branch of Islam, dominate in the rest of the Middle East. Sunnis believe that elected officials, regardless of their heritage, are qualified to lead the Islamic faith.

These differences, combined with the fact that Persia maintained its own empire distinct from the Ottoman Empire for most of the nation's history, have made Iran an outsider to the exclusively Arab components of regional conflict. Yet Iran's difficult relationship with the West gives it much in common with other Middle East nations. Since its 1979 revolution, in which it adopted an Islamic republican government (one that is based on Islamic laws and a constitution), Iran has refused to even recognize the Jewish state of Israel, calling it only "the Zionist regime." (Zionism is the political movement originating in the late nineteenth century that called for the creation of an independent Jewish state in Palestine.) Despite hostilities with the West, Israel, and other Middle Eastern nations, Iran has gradually risen to become one of the most powerful nations in the Middle East.

The unique Iranian culture Iran is home to some of the oldest civilizations in the world. The Elamite Empire, for example, began to develop thousands of years ago in the region of the present-day southwestern Iranian province of Khuzestan. Around 3200 BCE, Elam was home to increasingly sophisticated cities where trade was conducted; agriculture had advanced forms of irrigation; and the people had developed a form of writing. The ancient Medes, a people with roots in Iran dating back to the second millennium BCE became one of the most powerful states in the Middle East. The Medians were overthrown by the Achaemenid Empire, also known as the first Persian Empire, around 500 BCE. The Achaemenid

Empire grew to be the world's largest empire up to its time, and was known for its accommodation of diverse peoples and its well-developed central government. From these and other ancient civilizations the strong Persian culture arose, with its distinctive art and philosophy, as well as the world's first known monotheistic religion, Zoroastrianism. (A monotheistic religion is one that worships only one god.) Around 640 CE, Persia was conquered by the Islamic empire that arose after the death of Muhammad in 632. The Persians accepted the religion of Islam, but they maintained a strong sense of their own identity.

For centuries, the Persian people were ruled by one invader after another: first the Arabs, then the Turks and Mongols. Finally in 1502 the Safavid dynasty came to power and restored Persia to its own leadership and culture. (A dynasty is a series of rulers from the same family.) Under the Safavid dynasty, the Shiite branch of Islam became the majority

A Zoroastrian temple in Iran. Zoroastrianism, the world's first known monotheistic religion, developed in ancient Iran.
© WOLFGANG KAEHLER/CORBIS.

religion in Iran, and it remained so into the twenty-first century. The Safavids were constantly threatened by the Ottoman Empire but managed to remain independent until the decline of the dynasty in the early eighteenth century. Over the next few centuries, several other Persian dynasties, such as the Afsharid, Zand, and Qajar dynasties, ruled Iran.

In 1905 the Iranians rose up against their shah (king) in an uprising, called the Persian Constitutional Revolution. At that time, Iran established an elected parliament (legislature). The new government was a constitutional monarchy, in which the powers of the monarch are granted by the nation's constitution. It allowed for some elected representation but left the shah in power as the leader of Iran.

By the early twentieth century, however, Great Britain had become heavily involved in Iran's affairs. In 1908 British interests had discovered oil on Iranian land, and thereafter the development of the oil industry played a large role in the area. Iran remained neutral during World War I, but its land provided a route for combatants between Asia and the Middle East. Consequently, many battles between foreign powers occurred on Iranian land. At the end of the war, the British persuaded the Iranian prime minister to sign the Anglo-Persian Agreement of 1919, which made Iran a British protectorate, or a state that is controlled and protected by another, stronger country. Most Iranians hated this arrangement and felt that the shah's regime was too heavily influenced by the British and other Western nations.

In 1921 a military commander named Reza Khan (1878–1944) rose to power as an opponent of the shah's rule. By 1923 Reza Khan had forced the shah from power and claimed that office for himself. In 1925 the Majlis, the Iranian parliament, gave him the title of Reza Shah, after which he became known as Reza Shah Pahlavi. Reza Shah quickly began to modernize Iran. He built roads and railways, reformed the educational system, supported the growth of industry, and offered greater rights to women. But the shah was an authoritarian ruler. He ruled with absolute authority and the people of Iran had no voice in their own government. The shah's administration did not allow for basic political freedoms, such as freedom of speech, and he used harsh methods to oppress any opposition that arose. He clashed greatly with Iran's religious leaders, and most Iranians resented his policy of limiting the role of religion in government as well as his inflexible style of ruling.

Reza Shah Pahlavi became ruler of Iran in 1923 and worked to modernize the nation. © BETTMANN/ CORBIS.

Reza Shah allied himself with Germany in the 1930s and sympathized with the Axis Powers during World War II (1939–45; a war in which the Allies [Great Britain, France, the Soviet Union, the United States, and China] defeated the Axis Powers [Germany, Italy, and Japan]). Although Reza Shah never actually joined the war on the side of the Axis powers and Iran remained neutral, Allied troops occupied Iran and forced Reza Shah from power in 1941. In his place they installed his son, Mohammad Reza Pahlavi (1919–1980), as shah.

Mohammad Reza Pahlavi The years following World War II saw major conflicts within Iranian society and politics. The Soviet Union began to support Communist groups that were trying to overthrow the shah. (Communists are advocates of Communism, a system of government in which the state plans and controls the economy and a single political party holds power.) Many Iranians disliked the control that foreign powers had over Mohammad Reza Pahlavi. Prime Minister Mohammad Mosaddeq (also spelled Mossadegh; 1880–1967) helped lead an uprising to assert Iranian power over the government. Mosaddeq seized control of Iran's oil industry, which had been controlled by British and American companies. He also tried to increase the power of the legislature, and in 1953 he forced the shah into exile. The United States, however, was unwilling to lose control in Iran, particularly given the Soviet Union's interest in the country. The United States helped Iranians stage a coup (overthrow of the government) and returned Mohammad Reza Pahlavi to power in 1954. The shah continued to favor the United States, while expanding the modernization process begun by his father. Over the years, however, it became apparent that the wealthy, educated, and secular (nonreligious) governing minority was out of touch with the overwhelmingly poor and devoutly religious Muslim population.

The 1979 Iranian Revolution By the late 1970s, public discontent became so strong in Iran that the shah's regime began to collapse, and he fled the country in January 1979. Two weeks later, the popular and charismatic Muslim religious leader, Ayatollah Ruhollah Khomeini (c. 1900–1989), returned to Iran. (An ayatollah is a high-ranking Shiite religious leader.) Khomeini had been in exile in Iraq for fifteen years because, after relentlessly criticizing the shah, he had been expelled from Iran in 1964. On his arrival in Iran's capital of Tehran in 1979, millions of Iranians took to the streets to joyously greet him.

Khomeini, an outspoken opponent of the shah's regime, was traditional in his religious values and strongly anti-Western. He and his followers created a new constitution for Iran that was based on both Islamic law and some democratic principles. The constitution created a government maintained by clerics (ordained religious officials). In this government, the ayatollah would rule as the Supreme Leader, a position involving almost full control of the country. The nation would also have an elected president and legislative assembly, but both institutions were restricted in their powers by the Supreme Leader and his appointed

Army soldiers holding posters of Ayatollah Ruhollah Khomeini join other protestors in the street during the Islamic Revolution in Iran. This popular revolt changed the country's government from secular to one based on Islamic law. KEYSTONE/GETTY IMAGES.

clerics. Presented with this constitution, the people of Iran were allowed a yes or no vote. The result was a resounding 99 percent approval. With that, the 1979 Iranian Revolution (also known as the Islamic Revolution) was over and the new Islamic Republic of Iran was formed.

Iran was the first nation in the world to undergo an Islamic revolution, a change in government that allowed the Islamic religion to govern all matters in the country, including laws, foreign policy, and economics. As Supreme Leader, Khomeini oversaw the revolutionary reforms. He imposed new laws, such as mandating that women wear head scarves and banning Western movies. He also closed down the universities for three years in order to rid them of non-Islamic influences. In the new Iran opposition to the Supreme Leader and his government was not tolerated. Nearly one thousand of the shah's officials were executed when Khomeini took power, and by the mid–1990s it was estimated that nearly five thousand dissenters (people who express disagreement with the government) had been killed and forty-five thousand more imprisoned.

Aside from Iran's regular military, Khomeini created an elite security group known as the Revolutionary Guard in 1979. The Revolutionary Guard's role was to protect the revolutionary movement and its ideals. It was loyal to the Supreme Leader and his clerical leaders. Among the Guard's functions was the spread of the Islamic revolution throughout the Middle East. It was the Revolutionary Guard that set up camps in Lebanon in the early 1980s that helped to establish Hezbollah, a Shiite militant group based in Lebanon. Over the years, the Revolutionary Guard grew to approximately 125,000 troops who serve in the group's ground force, navy, and air force.

In 1979 shortly after the revolution, the U.S. embassy in Iran was overtaken by a group of Iranian students, who took the entire U.S. staff hostage. They demanded that the shah, who was receiving medical treatment in the United States, be returned to Iran to face trial. Khomeini supported the militants' actions, although his prime minister resigned in disapproval. Some of the hostages were initially released, but fifty-two Americans were held hostage for 444 days. With an act of terrorism as its first international act, the new Islamic Republic of Iran immediately established a hostile and defiant relationship with the West.

The Islamic Republic At this early stage in the new republic's history, Iraqi president Saddam Hussein (1937–2006) invaded Iran, thinking that the country would be too weak to resist attack. Iran was forced to enter the brutal and destructive Iran-Iraq War (1980–88), and it defended itself far more successfully than Hussein had anticipated. In the end, however, Iran suffered five hundred thousand deaths in the war by some estimates. Syria supported Iran in the war, starting a long-term alliance between the two countries. While Iran was fighting Iraq, its Kurdish population demanded independence. (About four million Kurds lived along Iran's western frontiers with Turkey and Iraq.) Khomeini sent troops to crush the Kurdish rebellion in 1979, and a violent war between the Iranian forces and the Kurdish guerilla fighters raged until the Kurds were suppressed in 1982. Khomeini died soon after the Iran-Iraq War ended. He was succeeded by Ayatollah Ali Khamenei (also

Islamism

Islamism is a fundamentalist movement characterized by the belief that Islam should provide the basis for the political, social, and cultural life in Muslim nations. Using the holy texts of Islam as their guide, Islamists seek to build ideal Muslim societies. They reject the Western notion that religion should be set apart from social institutions, such as government, justice systems, and the economy.

From the time of its founding in the seventh century, Islam has been a political as well as a religious philosophy. It prophet, Muhammad (c. 570–632), led Muslims in both spheres. The leaders of Islam who succeeded Muhammad, called caliphs, created a powerful Islamist empire that lasted until about 1258 and spread Islam throughout the Middle East. (For more information, see **The Ancient Middle East: From the First Civilizations to the Crusades**.) Since then, Islamism has influenced the Middle East.

Two Middle East nations practice Islamism, although in different forms. In the 1930s when Saudi Arabia became a nation, it based its government on a political and religious form of Sunni Islam called Wahhabism. Wahhabism promotes strict observance of sharia, a system of Islamic religious law based on the teachings of the Koran (also spelled Qur'an or Quran; the holy book of Islam) and other sacred writings. In 1979 Iran became the first nation in the world to undergo an Islamic revolution. Saudi Arabia is Sunni while Iran is Shiite, and the relations between these two countries have frequently been hostile due to the theological differences between these two sects.

One of the first and most enduring Islamist groups is the Muslim Brotherhood, which was founded in Egypt in 1928 by Hasan al-Banna (1906–1949). In its early form, the group worked to spread Islam and to conduct social aid programs that would improve Egyptian society. Opposition to Great Britain's financial and military presence in Egypt at the time, however, motivated the Brotherhood's leaders to become politically active. The Muslim Brotherhood went through a period, from the 1940s to the 1970s, when some of its leaders used violent methods to oppose the Egyptian government and Western influences. During these years, some of its members began to follow a more radical or extremist philosophy. Many left Egypt and started up organizations based on the Muslim Brotherhood's model in other countries of the Middle East and beyond. By the 1970s, the Muslim Brotherhood in Egypt formally renounced violence and was increasingly viewed as a moderate Islamist organization. Some of the branches that grew out of the original movement, however, such as Islamic Jihad and Hamas in Palestine, the Islamic Action Front in Jordan, and the National Islamic Front in Sudan, are militant groups that openly advocate using violence to attain their political goals. The late 1980s saw the formation of extremist groups, such as al-Qaeda, that have developed rigid interpretations of the holy texts and advocate terrorism and global war to defend Islam.

Most scholars are careful to distinguish between Islamists and Islamic extremists. The extremists are a small minority of Islamists and represent only the political fringe of the broad-based, popular Islamist movement.

spelled Khāmene'i; 1939–). (For more information, see **The Iran-Iraq War: 1980 to 1988**.)

Under Ayatollah Khamenei, Iran continued to provoke most Western countries. Its leaders took a strong anti-Israel stance. This especially concerned the United States, because of growing suspicions that Iran was developing nuclear weapons, and that the result could be a nuclear attack on Israel. Iran, both openly and secretly, also contributed money and soldiers to Islamic revolutionary groups, such as Hezbollah, in other countries. The United States had placed sanctions on Iran as far back as the 1979 hostage crisis. (Sanctions are punitive measures adopted by the international community against a nation that has violated international law, usually in the form of diplomatic, economic, or social restrictions.) In 1984 the U.S. embassy and Marine barracks in Lebanon was bombed, killing sixty-three people. The act was linked to Iran, and the United States labeled Iran a sponsor (a provider of financial support) of international terrorism. Sanctions and unfriendly relations between Iran and the West continued into the twenty-first century.

Feelings about Iran varied in the Middle East. The Iranian revolution convinced Islamists that it was possible to bring about a revolution that would make Islam the focus of national life, just as it was the focus of personal life for so many Muslims. But there were also fears that Iran was getting too powerful and had ambitions to take over or manipulate other Middle Eastern countries.

Within Iran, citizens have at times voted reformers into elected office, hoping to restore some individual rights and democratic practices in their country. Most experts note that well into the twenty-first century, there was great support for the Islamist government in Iran, but many Iranians opposed some of their government's authoritarian methods.

The Arabian Peninsula

The largest physical landmass in the Middle East is the Arabian Peninsula. At 1 million square miles (2.6 million square kilometers), it is about one-third the size of the continental United States and home to seven countries: Saudi Arabia, Kuwait, Bahrain, the United Arab Emirates (UAE), Qatar, Oman, and Yemen. The Arabian Peninsula is a forbidding desert region with deadly heat, a lack of water, and fierce Bedouin tribes (people who live and raise animals in the desert with no permanent homes). Only the seventh-century rise of Islam, based in the holy Arab cities of Mecca and Medina in the Hejaz region (the western coastal region of the peninsula), brought real unity to the land, but even that unity lasted only a couple of centuries. In the sixteenth century the Ottoman Empire claimed to control the Arabian Peninsula, but in fact large sections remained independent, including the lands of present-day Yemen and Oman, and the Nejd region (the central area of the peninsula).

Saudi Arabia

The first Saudi state came about in the eighteenth century, primarily as the result of an Arab religious movement that arose in the Nejd known as Wahhabism (wuh-HAH-biz-uhm). Wahhabism is named after its founder, Muhammad ibn Abd al-Wahhab (1703–1792). Ibn Abd al-Wahhab and his followers preached a conservative version of Islam: They wanted Muslims to revere only the prophet Muhammad and to follow sharia closely. Wahhabis believe in the strict observance of daily prayers and the exclusion of women from employment, leadership positions, land ownership, and other areas of life considered by Wahhabis to be reserved for men only.

In 1744 Ibn Abd al-Wahhab allied himself with a sheikh (tribal leader) named Mohammad ibn Saud (1710–1765), who ruled in the Nejd. Together, Ibn Saud and Ibn Abd al-Wahhab built a following and an army, and began to take power in the southern Arabian Peninsula. By the end of the century they controlled Mecca and Medina, and had advanced troops as far north as Syria. This rapid expansion worried the Ottoman Empire. In 1818 the Ottomans sent their Egyptian governor, Muhammad Ali (1769–1849), to the peninsula to attack the Saud family. Defeated, the Sauds moved their capital to Riyadh. While Egyptian forces were able to limit the spread of the Wahhabi movement, Ibn Saud and his family maintained control in the desert regions of Arabia.

Ibn Saud In the late 1800s, a feud with a rival family forced the Saud family to flee to Kuwait. They took with them a fourteen-year-old boy named Abd al-Aziz ibn Abd al-Rahman (1876–1953), more commonly known as Ibn Saud. In 1902 he returned and reclaimed the family base of power at Riyadh. Ibn Saud went on to conquer great portions of the Nejd and parts of the east coast of the Arabian Peninsula. He revived the family alliance with the Wahhabis and Wahhabism spread rapidly.

During World War I, Ibn Saud's rising influence in the Nejd and the eastern Arabian Peninsula came into conflict with the power of Husayn ibn 'Ali (also spelled Hussein bin Ali; c. 1854–1931), the sharif of Mecca, who held control in the Hejaz. (A sharif is a nobleman and political leader chosen from among descendants of the Muslim prophet Muhammad.) As a Wahhabi, Ibn Saud was a strict and conservative follower of Islam. He believed that the religion had been corrupted, and he disapproved of Husayn's worldly ways. Thus, in 1924, when the sharif of Mecca proclaimed himself caliph, Ibn Saud gathered his forces and attacked Mecca, forcing Husayn into exile. Ibn Saud took the title of king of Hejaz. In 1932 he united the Nejd with the Hejaz and named the new kingdom Saudi Arabia after his family. The Saud family continued to rule Saudi Arabia into the twenty-first century.

Saudi Oil wealth In 1938 great change came to Saudi Arabia when vast quantities of oil were discovered there. The country's oil fields contain an estimated one-quarter of the world's oil reserves, and it is the largest producer and exporter of oil in the world. This brought vast wealth to the previously poor country. The Saudi government, with its oil funds, provides its citizens with free medical care and university education as well as generous housing subsidies and a high standard of living. The Saudi royal family itself is exceedingly wealthy. For many years, Saudi Arabia's isolation from other countries, as well as its great oil wealth, made it one of the most stable Islamic powers in the Middle East.

Throughout most of the twentieth century, Saudi Arabia maintained good foreign relations with Western countries. It was a close ally of the United States starting in the 1970s. The United States purchased the majority of Saudi oil and provided the kingdom with military protection. In 1990, when Iraq invaded Saudi Arabia's neighbor, Kuwait, the Saudi government asked the United States to provide military forces to help stop Iraq's invasion. The United States began a military build-up in Saudi Arabia and led a coalition of nations in a defense of Kuwait. As a result, 500,000 coalition troops, including about 200,000 Americans, were based in Saudi Arabia.

Islamic rule in Saudi Arabia Saudi Arabia's Islamic government is extremely conservative. It is a monarchy, and the king has control over all aspects of the government. He consults only with members of the royal family and a few advisers. The only other power in the country lies in its Islamic clerics, who ensure that the government and its people follow the principles of Wahhabism. Sharia is generally followed literally. Mutaween

Ibn Saud was the founder of Saudi Arabia and his family continues to rule the country in modern times. © ART DIRECTORS & TRIP/ALAMY.

(government-authorized religious police) make sure that the religious codes are being followed by all. It is illegal to publicly practice any religion but Islam. Public entertainment, such as movies and concerts, are banned. Alcoholic beverages are not allowed. Women and men are separated in

The 1973 Oil Embargo

Although not as strong militarily as Western nations, the countries of the Middle East have had one global advantage since the 1930s. They own the world's greatest oil reserves and control their fuel production. Only once, during the 1973 Arab-Israeli War, have the Arab nations of the Middle East used their control over oil production as a decisive strategic weapon. In that war, Egypt and Syria attacked Israel in an attempt to win back territory lost during the 1967 Arab-Israeli War. Israel gained the advantage in the conflict, however, and captured even more territory. During the war, the United States flew military supplies to Israel and promised more than two billion dollars in military aid. Arabs were furious at the U.S. interference, and Arab members of the Organization of Petroleum Exporting Countries (OPEC), an organization of oil-producing nations, responded by organizing an embargo

(stoppage) of oil shipments to the United States, effectively cutting off the majority of the U.S. oil supply. At the same time, OPEC took actions to quadruple the price of oil.

The impact of the oil embargo was enormous in the United States. Gas prices skyrocketed, huge lines formed at gas stations, speed limits were decreased to save fuel, and governments and car manufacturers sought ways to conserve energy. Within a short time, the embargo's economic impact was felt throughout much of the world. After five months, the embargo was lifted, but the effects on U.S. policy in the region were substantial. The embargo had successfully pressured the United States to negotiate more openly with Arab countries. U.S. diplomats negotiated Israeli withdrawal from parts of the Egyptian territory of Sinai, and paved the way for a settlement between Israel and Syria regarding the Golan Heights.

public places, and in public places all females must wear an *abaya*, a loose robe that covers the body from head to toe, except for the face, hands, and feet.

Although the Saudi regime has always been strict about its religious laws, it has long been resisted by fundamentalist groups. One devastating instance of extremism in the twentieth century occurred in November 1979 at the Grand Mosque in Mecca. An estimated one hundred thousand worshippers had gathered at the mosque for prayer, when a group of about five hundred Islamic radicals pulled out machine guns and announced that the Mahdi (messiah, or savior) had arrived. They denounced the House of Saud, saying that it had yielded to Western influences, corrupting Islam and betraying its principles. They held the worshippers hostage for two weeks, and hundreds were killed.

In the 1990s Islamist groups increasingly criticized the Saudi relationship with the West, especially when U.S. troops entered the country during the Persian Gulf War (1991–91). Saudi terrorist Osama bin Laden (1957–2011), for example, was a follower of Wahhabism who began to call for an Islamic revolution within Saudi Arabia, claiming that the royal family had perverted Islam to support its own wealthy and lavish lifestyle, and to maintain its political alliances. In the twenty-first century the Saudi government struggled to contain unrest among Islamic activists who wanted more religious purity, while at the same time trying to accommodate Arab reformers who pressed for the easing of religious restrictions and democratic reform.

Kuwait

Kuwait is a small desert country on the Persian Gulf that shares borders with Saudi Arabia and Iraq, and it has one of the world's largest oil fields. For most of history, Kuwait's population consisted mainly of nomads (people who move from place to place, with no fixed home) and some traders passing through its ports. In the eighteenth and nineteenth centuries, two clans, the Al Sabahs and the Utabs, settled in present-day Kuwait City. The Al Sabah family was chosen by the Kuwaitis to represent the region in its relations with the Ottoman Empire. Under Al Sabah rule, which has continued into the twenty-first century, Kuwait City was transformed into a major trading port, and Kuwait's pearl and boat-building industries thrived. In 1899 Kuwait agreed to become a British protectorate, in part, at least, to avoid being taken over by the Ottomans or other Arab neighbors.

The country remained a British protectorate until 1961. When British forces withdrew, however, Iraq claimed that the newly independent country was under its rule, because Kuwait had been under Iraqi rule at times during the Ottoman Empire era. With Iraqi forces approaching, Kuwait asked for military help and British forces returned. They successfully defended Kuwait from an Iraqi invasion and in 1963 Iraq recognized Kuwait as an independent nation.

Under its constitution, Kuwait established an elected body of legislators, but for decades the real power of the Kuwaiti government lay with the country's emir (ruler). During the 1990s, however, the elected body, the National Assembly (or parliament) became more powerful and in 2009 Kuwait opened up its democracy to women when it elected four women to its National Assembly.

An oil refinery in Kuwait.
The nation is one of the world's
top-ten largest oil exporters.
© HEINI SCHNEEBELI;
EDIFICE/CORBIS.

Kuwait has been one of the world's top-ten largest oil exporters since World War II. The emir receives half of the country's oil profits and distributes most of it to be used for education and welfare. The native Kuwaiti people have prospered from the oil money, enjoying a high standard of living. Like other oil-rich states of the Arabian Peninsula, however, Kuwait suffered from a lack of laborers. Foreigners from all over the world migrated to Kuwait to take the jobs the wealthy Kuwaitis did not want. The foreigners were not given the privileges of citizens or a path to citizenship. In 2008 a government census estimated that 2,289,538 of

Kuwait's population of 3,328,136 people were non-Kuwaitis, making native Kuwaitis a minority in their own country.

In 1990, Iraqi President Saddam Hussein (1937–2006) intiated hostilities with Kuwait. The trouble started over disputes about oil production in the region, but also at issue was the large debt to Kuwait that Iraq had incurred during the Iraq-Iran War. Saddam also had ambitions to lead a united Arab state. Kuwait, which had been connected with Iraq in the Ottoman era, was a likely starting point for these ambitions. Thus, in 1990 Iraq invaded Kuwait and annexed it as part of Iraq. A U.S.-led coalition evicted the Iraqis in 1991, but only after a six-month occupation in which the Iraqis destroyed Kuwait's cities, burned its oil wells, and brutalized its population. (For more information, see **The Gulf Wars: 1991 to 2011**.) At great cost, Kuwait rebuilt its devastated nation after the war.

Yemen and Oman

Civilizations have existed in Yemen and Oman, the two countries at the southern end of the Arabian Peninsula, since ancient times. The ancient societies were centered around Yemen's port of Aden on the Red Sea and Oman's ports on the Gulf of Oman, which permit entry to the Persian Gulf. Both Yemen and Oman engaged in a profitable trade in myrrh and frankincense (fragrant products from the local trees). Many empires tried to control these countries, but none succeeded until the Islamic caliphate invaded in the seventh century.

Yemen When Yemen became part of the Islamic caliphate, most Yeminis converted to Islam as Sunnis, but divisions began three centuries later, in the tenth century, when Yemen came under the rule of a Shiite dynasty. Many centuries later, in 1728, a Sunni dynasty gained control of the southern part of Yemen. In 1839 Great Britain took control of Aden, and South Yemen became a British protectorate.

North Yemen established a monarchy in 1918 and for nearly fifty years was ruled by a series of Shiite imams (Muslim leaders). North Yemen's monarchy ended in 1962, when a military group overthrew the imam and created the Yemen Arab Republic (YAR). A civil war followed. The revolutionaries were backed by Egypt and the Soviet Union; Saudi Arabia and Jordan supported the imam and his followers, who were defeated in 1969.

South Yemen remained a British protectorate until 1962, when the Yemenis revolted against the British. In 1967 the independent People's

Republic of Southern Yemen was established. South Yemen was strongly influenced by the Soviet Union in the 1970s, and in 1979, it became the only Marxist state (a state with a society that does not have social classes, or divisions between rich and poor) in the Middle East.

In 1990 the two countries of Yemen unified as one, becoming the Republic of Yemen. Ali Abdullah Saleh (1942–), the president of the YAR, became the new nation's first president. The people of South Yemen resented the new government and unsuccessfully revolted against Saleh's rule in the 1994, resulting in a civil war. North Yemen won the battle and took over the south, but South Yemen continued to accuse the Saleh administration of corruption and discrimination against southerners and threatened to secede (withdraw) from Yemen. Yemen remained a very poor country, without the great oil wealth of the other countries of the Arabian Peninsula. It has garnered attention from the Western world in the twenty-first century, mainly because of its connections to terrorist plots and its increasingly powerful extremists groups.

Oman Neighboring Oman was occupied by the Portuguese in the sixteenth century, who used its ports to establish a trade route through the Persian Gulf. After the Portuguese were expelled in the seventeenth century, Oman was never again ruled by a foreign power. It developed a prosperous trade because of its ports on the gulf and became a power in the Arab world. In the late nineteenth century, however, the opening of the Suez Canal (a shipping canal that connects the Mediterranean Sea with the Red Sea) diminished the need for merchant ships to stop in Oman, and the country became impoverished and weak, relying on the British for aid. The sultan of Oman, Said ibn Taimur (1910–1972), was a fundamentalist who kept Oman isolated from the world. In 1970 he was sent into exile by his son, Qaboos ibn Said Al Said (1940–). After initiating oil production, Qaboos modernized Oman, using oil profits to build the infrastructure for electricity and running water, and to provide Omanis with free education and medicine.

Bahrain, Qatar, and the United Arab Emirates

The present-day countries of Bahrain, Qatar, and the United Arab Emirates (UAE) are located between Kuwait and Oman on the Persian Gulf. All three of these nations established a relationship with Great Britain in the nineteenth century in which Britain was allowed to sail safely in the gulf

Ali Abdullah Saleh became the first president of the Republic of Yemen after the new nation was formed in 1990. © WILL MOODY/ALAMY.

in exchange for its protection of each of the states. In 1968 Great Britain decided to withdraw its forces. Its plan was to establish a federation that would unite the UAE, Bahrain, and Qatar, but differences between the states made such a federation impossible.

Bahrain, an archipelago (group of islands) situated off the shores of Saudi Arabia in the Persian Gulf, declared itself an independent state in 1971. It has been ruled by the al-Khalifa dynasty since the eighteenth century. The al-Khalifas are Sunni, while about two-thirds of Bahrain's population is Shiite. Bahrain discovered oil on its lands in 1931, but the resource has not been as abundant as in neighboring countries, and Bahrain remains relatively poor. The Shiites have generally been the most impoverished, and they claim to have faced discrimination by the Sunni rulers. Hamad bin Isa Al Khalifa (1950–), who became emir of Bahrain in 1999, declared himself king in 2002 and introduced a new constitution with democratic elections for representatives in one house of its National Assembly (parliament). Shiites won a majority of legislative seats but discontent continued to simmer, and during the Arab Spring of 2011, a series of prodemocracy uprisings in the Middle East and North Africa, the Shiites in Bahrain rose up against the king, resulting in brutal reprisals. (For more information, see **The Arab Spring: 2011**.)

Throughout the second half of the twentieth century, the citizens of Qatar and the UAE enjoyed some of the highest living standards in the world due to their oil revenue. Qatar has been ruled by the al-Thani family since the mid–nineteenth century. Hamad bin Khalifa Al Thani (1952–), emir since 1995, is considered a progressive ruler in many ways. One of his accomplishments is the creation of the news station Al Jazeera, which was the only station in the Arabian Peninsula to broadcast uncensored news at the time.

The UAE is made up of seven states: Abu Dhabi, Dubai, Sharjah, Ra's al Khaymah, Fujairah, Umm al Qaywayn, and 'Ajman. Abu Dhabi, which has most of the nation's oil, is the richest and most powerful of the states, followed by Dubai and Sharjah. The country's leaders have poured oil revenue into health care and education and toward developing the country's enormous economy. The government is liberal and tolerant of other religions and cultures but remains a monarchy without a constitution.

As in Kuwait, foreign workers have been drawn to the UAE and Qatar in large numbers to work in the oil industry and other jobs. The result is that Qataris and UAE natives are privileged minorities in their own countries. Natives make up only 25 percent of the population of Qatar and less than 20 percent of the population of the UAE in the early twenty-first century.

North Africa: the Maghreb

Arabs have lived in North Africa, the portion of the African continent that is located north of the Sahara Desert, since the seventh century, when the armies of the Islamic empire conquered Egypt and Libya. In time the Arabs came to control the Maghreb, an area that also includes present-day Tunisia, Libya, Algeria, and Morocco. This area was the home of a group of people known as the Berbers. Over time, many of the people of the Maghreb converted to Islam and came to speak the Arabic language.

In the sixteenth century, the Maghreb had little central government. Spain and the Ottomans both threatened to take it over, but for a time neither major power could succeed. Instead, in the early years of the century, the Maghreb became the headquarters for pirates. In the first years of the century, brothers Aruj (also known as Barbarossa; c. 1474–1518) and Hizir (c. 1478–1546) established pirate communities in the Maghreb. Aruj took over the city of Algiers in 1516. He was killed two years later. Hizir took the name Barbarossa, in honor of his brother, and became even more famous as he raided Western ships. Barbarossa worked closely with the Ottoman Empire, becoming the recognized ruler of Algiers and an Ottoman commander at sea. With Algiers as a base and Barbarossa securing the area, the Ottoman forces went on to conquer Libya in 1551. In 1574 the Ottoman Empire established rule over Tunis. The Turkish sultan appointed a series of rulers called pashas to govern the North African provinces.

Piracy at sea remained one of the main sources of income for the Maghreb, and over the next centuries, lawlessness reigned in many areas. The Barbary corsairs, pirates based in the Mahgreb, preyed upon ships until the nineteenth century. Great Britain and the United States both tried, and failed, to eliminate the pirates from their Maghreb havens. Finally France sent in massive forces that occupied Algeria in 1834. Nearly fifty years later, when the economy of Tunisia began to falter, the French established a protectorate there in 1881. In 1911 Italy invaded Libya. The Ottomans ceded Libya to Italy in 1912, even though Libyans resisted the Italian rule. In 1912 most of Morocco became a French protectorate, while a small part went to Spain.

Libya When Italy was defeated in World War II, France and Great Britain took control of Libya, but they granted it independence in 1951. Libya became a kingdom, and Muhammad Idris (1889–1983), hero of the resistance against the Italians, became king. In the following years, oil was discovered in the once impoverished country. In 1969 a group of military officers headed by Colonel Mu'ammar al-Qaddafi (also spelled Moammar al-Gaddafi; 1942–2011) overthrew the king in a coup. Al-Qaddafi established the Libyan Arab Republic and became its leader.

Al-Qaddafi instituted a wide range of new policies, such as forms of socialism (a system in which the government owns the means of production and controls the distribution of goods and services), Pan-Arabism (a movement for the unification of Arab peoples), Islamism, and later, a Pan-Africanism movement designed to unite Africans in the United States of Africa, a federation of African states, through which al-Qaddafi hoped to unify the Africa people in a manner similar to earlier attempts at a Pan-Arab movement. In the 1970s and 1980s, al-Qaddafi supported anti-West terrorist groups, causing great alarm in Western countries. The United States bombed Libya in 1986 in an unsuccessful attempt to kill al-Qaddafi. Then, in 1988 Pan Am Flight 103 exploded in the sky over Lockerbie, Scotland, due to a terrorist's bomb, killing all 243 passengers and 16 crew, as well as 11 people on the ground. Libya, and al-Qaddafi in particular, were suspected of being involved in the bombing and faced heavy sanctions.

In the 1990s al-Qaddafi renounced terrorism and tried to establish better relations with the West. Nevertheless, on February 15, 2011, during the Arab spring uprisings that year, rebels in Libya mounted a furious battle to rid their country of its leader of forty-one years. North Atlantic Treaty Organization (NATO; an international organization created in 1949 for purposes of collective security) forces aided the rebels in their fight. On September 16, 2011, the rebels' temporary governing organization, the National Transitional Council, was recognized as the legitimate government of Libya by the United Nations. On October 20, 2011, al-Qaddafi was killed as he fled from Sirte, Libya, the place of his birth and his last base of operations. (For more information, see **The Arab Spring: 2011**.)

Tunisia, Algeria, and Morocco The French granted Tunisia independence in 1956, after a long independence movement. Under the government of Habib Bourguiba (1903–2000) and his Neo-Destour (New Constitution) Party, Tunisia became a socialist state. In 1987 Bourguiba was declared incompetent, and his prime minister, Zine el Abidine Ben Ali (1936–) was elected president in 1989. Ben Ali continued to rule until

Libyan leader Mu'ammar al-Qaddafi arrives at the United Nations headquarters in New York City, in 2009. RICK GERSHON/GETTY IMAGES.

2011, when an uprising in Tunisia forced him to flee the country. (For more information, see **The Arab Spring: 2011**.)

The Algerians rose up against the French in 1954. The Algerian war for independence was devastating, with nearly one million people killed—one-tenth of the country's population—in six years. At last France withdrew its forces, and Algeria declared its independence in 1962. In 1965 Algeria's military took over the government and maintained its rule into the twenty-first century. In the late 1980s in an effort at reform, the military rulers decided they would permit new political parties to form and participate in elections. One of the parties was the Islamic Salvation Front, known by its French acronym FIS (Front Islamique du Salut), a conservative group that sought a return to traditional Islamic values. FIS was unexpectedly popular, and in 1991 the Algerian government cancelled scheduled elections, out of fear that the FIS would win. It also sent an estimated ten thousand members of FIS into exile. Civil war erupted. Some experts estimate that thirty thousand people were killed. The rulers endured, but violent clashes continued into the twenty-first century.

Moroccans rebelled against French and Spanish rule until achieving independence in 1956. The largest opposition party was the nationalist Istiqlal Party. After independence, the country became a constitutional monarchy, and Sultan Muhammad V (1909–1961) took the title of king. When he died in 1961, his son, King Hassan II (1929–1999) took the throne. He began democratic reforms, which continued into the twenty-first century, but Morocco's monarchy remained the ultimate authority. As the Arab Spring uprisings of 2011 arose in other parts of the Middle East and North Africa, Morocco experienced some protests of its own. (For more information, see **The Arab Spring: 2011.**)

For More Information

BOOKS

Cleveland, William L. *A History of the Modern Middle East.* Boulder, CO: Westview Press, 2004.

Encyclopedia of the Modern Middle East, 4 vols. New York: Macmillan Reference USA, 1996.

Etheredge, Laura S., ed. *Persian Gulf States: Kuwait, Qatar, Bahrain, Oman, and the United Arab Emirates.* New York: Rosen/Britannica Educational Publishing, 2011.

Hourani, Albert Habib. *The Emergence of the Modern Middle East.* Berkeley: University of California Press, 1981.

Kort, Michael. *The Handbook of the Middle East.* Brookfield, CT: Twenty-First Century Books, 2002, p. 192.

Lewis, Bernard. *The Middle East: A Brief History of the Last 2,000 Years.* New York: Scribner, 1995.

Long, David E, Bernard Reich, and Mark Gasiorowski, eds. *The Government and Politics of the Middle East and North Africa,* 6th edition. Boulder, CO: Westview Press, 2010.

Taheri, Amir. *The Persian Night: Iran Under the Khomeinist Revolution.* New York: Encounter Books, 2010.

WEB SITES

Internet Islamic History Sourcebook. Fordham University. http://www.fordham.edu/halsall/islam/islamsbook.asp (accessed on November 30, 2011).

"Profile: Egypt's Muslim Brotherhood." *BBC News.* http://www.bbc.co.uk/news/world-middle-east-12313405 (accessed on November 30, 2011).

"Iran: A Brief History." *MidEast Web.* http://www.mideastweb.org/iranhistory.htm (accessed on November 30, 2011).

5

Palestine and Zionist Settlement: Nineteenth Century to 1948

Palestine, a historical region in the Middle East on the eastern shore of the Mediterranean Sea, comprising parts of present-day Israel and Jordan, is an area claimed by two determined peoples, the Jews and the Arabs. (Arabs are people who speak the Arabic language or who live in countries in which Arabic is the dominant language.) Each of these groups has distinct religious and cultural traditions, and can point to a long history of occupying this land. Both have physical landmarks, such as ancient holy temples, rural villages, and groves of olive trees, that prove their claim. And both the Jews and the Arabs feel that they were promised access to and control of this land by the foreign powers that governed Palestine during the 1800s and 1900s.

For hundreds of years Palestine was a peaceful outpost of the Ottoman Empire, the vast empire of the Ottoman Turks which included southwest Asia, northeast Africa, and southeast Europe, and lasted from the thirteenth century to the early twentieth century. It was noted for its coastal agricultural areas, its tranquil lake and river valley in an area called the Galilee, and a seemingly unlivable desert area called the Negev. Palestine is also the site of the ancient Jewish kingdom of Eretz Yisrael, where the Jewish people had been united and powerful. Beginning in the late nineteenth century, Jews began to migrate to Palestine, hoping to create a community free from the persecution they had encountered throughout the centuries in many other places in the world.

To the Jews who looked to Palestine as a potential home, the land seemed mostly unused and barely populated, and thus perfect for developing into a Jewish state. But to the Arabs who farmed and traded there, Palestine was home. After the fall of the Ottoman Empire, they hoped for independent Arab rule over the region. Thus, the movement by Jews to create a national home in Palestine, called Zionism, brought them

WORDS TO KNOW

aliyah: The immigration of Jews to the historic Eretz Yisrael (Land of Israel).

anti-Semitism: Prejudice against Jews.

Arab League: A regional political alliance of Arab nations formed in 1945 to promote political, military, and economic cooperation within the Arab world.

Arabs: People of the Middle East and North Africa who speak the Arabic language or who live in countries in which Arabic is the dominant language.

Eretz Yisrael: "Land of Israel" in Hebrew; the ancient kingdom of the Jews.

Haganah: The underground defense force of Zionists in Palestine from 1920 to 1948. It became the basis for the Israeli army.

Hebrew: The ancient language of the Jewish people and the official language of present-day Israel.

Holocaust: The mass murder of European Jews and other groups by the Nazis during World War II.

Irgun Zvai Leumi: A militant underground group founded in 1931 that worked to secure Israeli independence by staging violent attacks on British and Arab targets. Also known simply as Irgun.

kibbutz: A Jewish communal farming settlement in Israel, where settlers share all property and work collaboratively together. Plural is kibbutzim.

mandate: A commission granting one country the authority to administer the affairs of another country. Also describes the territory entrusted to foreign administration.

Ottoman Empire: The vast empire of the Ottoman Turks which included southwest Asia, northeast Africa, and southeast Europe, and lasted from the thirteenth century to the early twentieth century.

Palestine: A historical region in the Middle East on the eastern shore of the Mediterranean Sea, comprising parts of present-day Israel and Jordan.

Palestinians: An Arab people whose ancestors lived in the historical region of Palestine and who continue to lay claim to that land.

pogrom: A racially-motivated riot in which mobs, usually organized and sanctioned by the state, attack a minority group, most often Jews.

refugees: People who flee their country to escape violence or persecution.

Temple Mount: A contested religious site in Jerusalem. It is the holiest site in Judaism, the third holiest site in Islam, and also important to the Christian faith.

Zionism: An international political movement originating in the late nineteenth century that called for the creation of an independent Jewish state in Palestine.

---

immediately into conflict with the existing Arab population. In years to follow, the conflict would be greatly changed by the formation of the Jewish nation of Israel in 1948, and Israel's subsequent military occupation of the lands on which the Arab Palestinians had been living for many years. (For more information on the founding of Israel and the conflicts between Israel, the Palestinians, and the surrounding Arab countries, see **Arab-Israeli Conflict: 1948 to 1973** and **Israeli-Palestinian Relations: 1973 to 2011**.) It was during the period between the beginning of Jewish settlements in the nineteenth century to the establishment of Israel in 1948, however, that the Jews and the Arabs first became locked into the conflict that continues to divide the Middle East.

The rise of Zionism

Around 1030 BCE an ancient Hebrew-speaking people, known as the Israelites, took control of the land of Canaan, the site of the modern nation of Israel and the Palestinian territories. The Israelites, whose descendants came to be known as the Jews a few centuries later, called their land Eretz Yisrael (Land of Israel), and established a powerful kingdom with a capital in the city of Jerusalem. In Jerusalem, under the supervision of the tenth-century BCE Jewish king Solomon, the Israelites built the Temple of Solomon (also called the First Temple), which became one of the main holy sites for Jews to practice their religion, Judaism. The Jews remained the dominant force in the region for hundreds of years, but eventually the lands came to be repeatedly conquered by other powers. By 135 CE the Jews had been driven from Eretz Yisrael, which was then named Palestine. A strong Jewish presence would not control in the region again for more than eighteen hundred years. (For more information, see **The Ancient Middle East: From the First Civilizations to the Crusades**.)

Over the centuries Jews settled in small communities throughout the Middle East. They also settled in larger numbers in both western and eastern Europe. From the moment Jews formed communities in Christian-dominated European countries, they faced discrimination due to widespread anti-Semitism (prejudice against Jews). Anti-Semitism kept Jews from access to certain jobs, education, and from political representation. At times, anti-Semitism also led to brutal physical attacks on Jews. In the nineteenth century, discrimination against Jews grew worse in eastern Europe. In Russia and Poland, areas with some of the highest Jewish populations, Jews faced terrible levels of harassment, intimidation, and oppression.

In the late nineteenth century Jews in Russia were the frequent target of pogroms (racially-motivated riots in which mobs, usually organized and sanctioned by the state, attack a minority group). Russian Jews began to leave the country to settle in Palestine. The first such groups formed an organization called Lovers of Zion. (Zion is an ancient name for Eretz Yisrael.) In 1881 a Russian named Leo Pinsker (1821–1891) wrote a pamphlet called *Autoemancipation*, in which he argues that Jews would continue to face discrimination as long as they lived under the rule of non-Jews in Western society. In order to free themselves of persecution, according to Pinsker, Jews needed to govern themselves in a Jewish state. Pinsker's pamphlet led to the first aliyah (immigration of Jews to the historic Eretz Yisrael), which lasted from 1882 to 1903. The movement brought thousands of Jews to Palestine, but it was not well organized and many of the immigrants returned to Europe. The Arabs living in Palestine remained largely undisturbed.

The second wave of immigration was far more organized. A Hungarian Jew named Theodor Herzl (1860–1904) independently came to many of the same conclusions as Pinsker, and in 1896 he published a book called *The Jewish State*, which drew mass attention to the Zionist cause. Herzl argues convincingly that Jews living throughout Europe had all the characteristics of a nation, such as a shared religion, history, and culture, but that they lacked a state in which they could live out their hopes and dreams for the future. The book inspired many eastern European Jews to join the Zionist movement, and from 1896 on, Zionists grew ever more focused on creating a national home for Jews in Palestine. Herzl organized the world's first Zionist Congress in 1897, and he enlisted the support of prominent Jews from across Europe.

The surge of Zionist organizing led to the second aliyah, which brought approximately forty thousand Jews to Palestine, mostly from Russia, between 1904 and 1914. This influx of settlers helped to establish some of the first stable and permanent Jewish social institutions in Palestine. Settlers built the foundations for the city of Tel Aviv, the first all-Jewish city. They joined together to create farms that would allow Jews to be self-sufficient, meaning that they could provide all of their own food. In 1909 they established the first kibbutz, a Jewish communal farming settlement, where settlers share all property and work collaboratively together. They also began to form Jewish newspapers, published in Hebrew, the ancient language of the Jewish people. The Jews were building an independent Jewish society alongside, but independent of, the Arab society that already existed in the area. The Jews, however, wanted more than this society within Palestine; they wanted to form an independent Jewish state.

A group of early Jewish settlers on a kibbutz in Palestine.
© EVERETT COLLECTION INC./ALAMY.

A change in world powers

Under Ottoman rule, the populations of the regions of Palestine, present-day Syria and Lebanon, and Mesopotamia (present-day Iraq) were left under the control of leading Arab families. As long as the families paid taxes to the empire, the empire generally did not interfere in their affairs, including the affairs of Jews who began to represent a significant minority population in Palestine. But the coming of World War I (1914–18; a global war between the Allies [Great Britain, France, and Russia, joined later by the United States] and the Central Powers [Germany, Austria-Hungary, and their allies]) brought immense change to the region. The Allies, in their plans to defeat the Ottoman Empire, recognized that the Arab populations in the region had legitimate claims to self-rule. In order to encourage Arab assistance in the war, Great Britain and France, the Allies that were most involved in the affairs of the region, promised that they would help the Arabs build independent nations. But Great Britain was also interested in gaining cooperation from the Jewish community in Palestine. High-placed Jews in London, England, especially Chaim

Weizmann (1874–1952), a spokesman for the Zionists, convinced British diplomats that they could win the support of Russia (which encouraged Jewish immigration to Palestine) in the war if they offered support for a Jewish homeland in Palestine. Great Britain and France also wanted to maintain access to financial interests they had developed in the Middle East at the end of the war.

In order to secure all of its many interests, including its humanitarian interest in providing Jews a safe haven from the worst aspects of anti-Semitism, in 1917 the British government issued a brief statement known as the Balfour Declaration, which stated that Britain favored "the establishment in Palestine of a national home for the Jewish people, and will use their best endeavours to facilitate the achievement of this object," while at the same time qualifying this statement by saying "that nothing shall be done which may prejudice the civil and religious rights of the existing non-Jewish communities in Palestine." Great Britain had committed itself to what would soon prove to be a nearly impossible task, creating an independent Jewish state in Palestine without taking away the rights or the privileges of the Arabs already there, called the "non-Jewish community" in the Balfour Declaration, even though they made up 90 percent of the country. (For more information, see **Forging New Nations from the Ottoman Empire: 1918 to 1950**.)

After World War I, the victorious Allies devised a plan for dividing up the lands of the defeated Ottoman Empire with help from the League of Nations, an international organization of sovereign countries established after World War I to promote peace. The plan put establish mandates, territories entrusted to foreign administration. The region was divided into territories that would be administered by Western nations and were expected to eventually become independent nations. Great Britain and France would provide different levels of guidance and support for those countries, depending on how well developed the political systems of those territories were. Great Britain's most difficult assignment was Palestine, which soon became deeply divided between the Jewish and Arab populations.

Under the supervision of the British High Commissioner of Palestine, Sir Herbert Samuel (1870–1963), the British Mandate of Palestine initially favored the Zionists. The British leaders attempted to uphold the rights of Arab Palestinians, but the conflicting promises the British had made to both sides meant that its support frequently shifted. This gave the Zionists, the most organized and outspoken group in Palestine, the

Sir Herbert Samuel, the British High Commissioner of Palestine. © LEBRECHT MUSIC AND ARTS PHOTO LIBRARY/ ALAMY.

opportunity to slowly gain power. (For more information, see **Forging New Nations from the Ottoman Empire: 1918 to 1950**.)

Zionist resolve

From the beginning of the mandate period, Jews were a distinct minority of the population of Palestine. Estimates indicate that they represented around 14 percent of the population in 1920, growing to 16 percent according to the first reliable census taken in 1931. What they lacked in numbers, however, they made up for in motivation, funding, and organization. Many Jewish settlers had come from horrific conditions in eastern Europe. They had left their homes and everything they owned to start a new life in Palestine. Most believed passionately that the creation of an independent Jewish state was the only way for Jews to be safe from persecution. This resolve and determination was important to the survival of the idea of Zionism, especially when obstacles such as Arab resistance and a lack of support from British policies threatened Zionist goals.

Zionist dedication was reflected in the organizations the Jews built in their new home. The World Zionist Organization, founded in 1897, helped to fund immigration to Palestine. It also helped to establish the Palestine Zionist Executive (later renamed the Jewish Agency), which acted as a form of government for Jews in Palestine. The Jewish Agency helped to build banks, health-care systems, schools, and other institutions that aided the steadily growing Jewish population in the region. As president of the World Zionist Organization and later the Jewish Agency, Weizmann, back in England, spoke for the Jewish community in its interaction with the British.

The Histadrut, or Federation of Jewish Labor, began as a trade union but eventually became much more, as it started to develop a wide range of Jewish businesses and to encourage the growth of kibbutzim, the collectively owned and operated farms that provided the base for Jewish agriculture. The Histadrut also developed the first Jewish defense force, called the Haganah, which developed over the years into a well-trained, well-armed military. By 1930 the Histadrut dominated the Mapai Party, under the leadership of David Ben-Gurion (1886–1973). The Mapai Party became the leading Jewish political party in Palestine. (Later, when the state of Israel was founded in 1948, Ben-Gurion, as the leader of the Mapai Party, became Israel's first prime minister.)

Jews were not completely united in their views of how their life in Palestine should be organized. A small group that came to be known as Revisionist Zionists opposed cooperation with Great Britain, which they felt was slowing the pace at which Zionists could gain political control in Palestine. Led by a radical Russian Zionist named Vladimir Jabotinsky (1880–1940), the Revisionists called for massive Jewish immigration to Palestine and Transjordan (present-day Jordan). The Revisionists dropped out of the World Zionist Organization and established their own underground, or secret, political party. In 1936 they also took over Irgun Zvai

A Haganah fighter dashes across a human bridge formed by two comrades laying on top of a barbed wire obstacle during a training exercise in 1948. Haganah was a defense force established by Jewish settlers, which developed over the years into a well-trained, well-armed military.
© EVERETT COLLECTION INC./ALAMY.

Leumi, a militant underground group founded in 1931, as an alternative to the Haganah. Irgun worked to secure Israeli independence, frequently by staging violent acts British and Arab targets. The militia took the lead in instigating conflicts with Arabs in the region with its violence. Two of the more prominent politicians in Israel's history, Menachem Begin (1913–1992) and Yitzhak Shamir (1915–), got their political start with the Revisionists.

Arab dissension

For a variety of reasons, the Arab Palestinians never had the political unity or organization that the Jewish population developed. The reasons are, in part, historic. For hundreds of years Palestine had been a territory of the Ottoman Empire, and governance of the region was entrusted to several powerful, established families who maintained peaceful, stable order. Arabs in Palestine had never needed to organize themselves to compete in politics in the region, and their defense had been entrusted to Ottoman soldiers. Because of this, Palestinians had no single representative to defend their interests when Great Britain took over the area after World War I.

In 1921 Amin al-Husayni (also called Haj Āmin al-Husayni; 1893–1974), a member of a prominent Palestinian family, was appointed as the grand mufti of Jerusalem, a title that recognized al-Husayni as the leader of Muslim religious and political life in the largest city in Palestine and by extension in all of Palestine. Al-Husayni felt that Zionism posed a threat to Palestinians, but he pledged that he would cooperate with the British as

Amin al-Husyani, the Grand Mufti of Jerusalem. © DIZ MUENCHEN GMBH, SUEDDEUTSCHE ZEITUNG PHOTO/ALAMY.

long as they protected the rights of Palestinians. This plan to continue to work with the British divided the Palestinians. While some felt that the British would help to maintain Arab rights in Palestine, many more felt that it was the British who were giving away Arab land to Jewish settlers.

Al-Husayni worked to build institutions to serve the Arab population in Palestine, and many Arabs accepted him as their leader, but he faced obstacles that kept him from advancing the Palestinian cause during the mandate years. He was opposed in his leadership by another prominent family in Palestine, the Nashashibis. Their constant challenges to his rule undermined his authority and convinced other factions to go their own way. The Palestinian community also lacked the wealth it would need for developing schools, businesses, and other social institutions. Unlike Zionists, who received much of their funding from foreign countries, the Palestinians were not supported by other Arab nations and were not able to make their communities as stable or as prosperous as the Jewish communities in the region. In the late 1930s, the Zionists became more forceful in their demands for control and, despite British laws limiting Jewish immigration, thousands of Zionist immigrants poured into Palestine, revealing the inability of Great Britain to stop Zionist expansion. At that time, al-Husayni took a committed stand against the Jews, but by then it was too late for a peaceful solution.

Zionists and Arabs clash in Palestine

Throughout the early 1920s, a Jewish society developed in Palestine with no organized Arab resistance. Using their superior wealth, Jews purchased land from Arab landowners, who often did not occupy their land and thus had little interest in the local community. The Jews created towns under Jewish control and developed a social system that was largely independent of Arab society. Before long, however, a growing number of Arabs were displaced when the land they had been farming was sold by distant Arab landlords. They began to express anger at the way Jews were buying up the best farmland and forcing them to move. They also resented the demands of Jews for access to holy sites in the city of Jerusalem. It was in regard to one such site, the Western Wall (also known as the Wailing Wall), that the first serious outbreak of violence between Jews and Arabs occurred.

The Western Wall is located on the western side of the Temple Mount, the holiest site in Judaism, the third holiest site in Islam, and also important to the Christian faith. The Western Wall is all that remains of the Temple of Solomon. According to Muslim teachings, the site of the Temple of Solomon was part of a holy compound that the prophet Muhammad (c. 570–632) had visited on his journey to heaven. Muslims worship at the Dome of the Rock and the Al-Aqsa Mosque, also located on that site. In the early twentieth century, Muslims controlled the site, but they granted Jews access to it. However, they did not allow Jews to place seating at the site, nor did they allow them to put up screens to divide men and women, as the Jewish religion prefers. A series of clashes between Jews and Arabs over access to the site became violent in August 1929. Jewish and Arab mobs fought in the streets of Jerusalem, Hebron, and Safad. By the time the riots were over, 133 Jews and 116 Arabs had been killed.

The Dome of the Rock is seen behind the Western Wall in Jerusalem. This place is holy to both Jewish and Muslim religions, and a series of clashes between Jews and Arabs over access to the site became violent in 1929. © LOOK DIE BILDAGENTUR DER FOTOGRAFEN GMBH/ALAMY.

During the 1920s and 1930s, the Arab inhabitants of Palestine directed several violent uprisings against the Jews and against the British administration of the mandate. In response to the uprisings, Great Britain appointed a commission to study the issues. The commission proposed to limit the sale of land to Jews and to limit Jewish immigration. The proposal so angered Zionists that it was quickly discarded. This in turn so angered the Arab population that they began to push more strongly for limits to be placed on the rights of Jews.

Elsewhere in the world, Jews were beginning to face dire circumstances. The Jews of Germany faced increasing persecution under Nazi leader Adolf Hitler (1889–1945). By 1933, Nazi soldiers had begun their increasingly anti-Semititic campaign with attacks on Jewish businesses. In 1935 the German government passed the Nuremberg Laws, which took away the civil rights of German Jews and forced them to wear yellow stars to show that they were Jewish. These acts were just the beginning of Nazi policies that would lead eventually to the Holocaust, the mass murder of European Jews and other groups by the Nazis during World War II (1939–45; a war in which the Allies [Great Britain, France, the Soviet Union, the United States, and China] defeated the Axis Powers [Germany, Italy, and Japan]). Frightened Jews fled the violence in increasing numbers. Many of them sought a new home in Palestine, just as conflicts in Palestine began to increase.

From 1936 to 1939, the Palestinians protested against British rule and Jewish immigration to the mandate. The Arab revolt in Palestine began with a series of strikes (work stoppages) and demonstrations for a Palestine independent of British rule. The British administrators of the mandate were able to stop the peaceful protests, but by 1937, Palestinian insurgents (rebels) in growing numbers began to target the British forces in Palestine with increasing violence. The British used extremely harsh measures to suppress the Arabs. The uprising continued until 1939, interrupted by periodic cease-fires, as the opposing sides considered and rejected plans to end the violence. By the time the revolt ended in 1939, approximately three thousand Arabs, two thousand Jews, and six hundred British had been killed.

The revolt of 1936–39, also called the Great Uprising, was in many ways a disaster for the Palestinians. Their political leadership was splintered by disagreement, and al-Husayni fled the country after clashing with British officials. Many Palestinians were killed or driven from their land. In addition, the revolt increased Palestinian hostility toward the Jews.

The Population of Palestine

Determining the population of Palestine during the British mandate years (1920–48) is not a simple matter. Prior to British rule, Ottoman census takers made no real effort to determine the population of what was then just a region. Civil unrest in Palestine and the events of World War II (1939–45) made the population difficult to determine in later years. The best early data comes from a 1931 British census. In that year, the Arab population numbered 864,806, which was 82 percent of the population. There were 174,139 Jews, who were only 16 percent of the population. Five years later, the Jewish population had swelled to 382,857, which was 28 percent of the population, almost double the percentage of 1931. By 1941 the number of Jews totaled 489,830, which was 30 percent of Palestine; the number of Arabs had grown to 1,123,168, or 68 percent of the population. The last British census, taken in 1946, showed that Jews were 31 percent of the population in Palestine, and the Arab population accounted for 67 percent.

Arabs were still in the majority in 1948. In that year, a major war broke out between the Arabs and the Jews when the Zionist leaders announced the establishments of the independent Jewish nation of Israel in Palestine. Approximately 750,000 Arabs were either forced to leave Palestine as Jewish forces took control of the areas in which they lived or chose to flee the violence and chaos of war. This massive flight of the Palestinians during the war, which later became known as the 1948 Arab-Israeli War, completely transformed the makeup of the population.

Despite the cost in lives and the disruption to the economy, the revolt may have strengthened the Jewish position. Both the Haganah and the Irgun gained new weapons from the British and others, as well as valuable military experience as they fought the Palestinians. More Jews began to express their willingness to fight in order to build a stable national home. Despite the efforts of the British to slow immigration, nearly 250,000 Jews moved to Palestine between 1929 and 1939, effectively doubling the Jewish population.

Britain's slow withdrawal from Palestine

British policy makers were confounded by events in Palestine. They entered the region in 1920 hoping to pave the way for an independent nation jointly ruled by Jews and Arabs, but by the late 1930s it had become apparent to all that the Jews and Arabs were not willing to live together in Palestine. In 1936 a British commission headed by William Robert Wellesley (1867–1937), the first Earl Peel, began an investigation into the causes of the Great Uprising in an effort to make reforms to the management of the mandate. The resulting British Peel Commission Report of 1937 called for Palestine to be partitioned (divided) into independent Arab and Jewish states. Jews considered this solution, but wanted to modify it. Arabs rejected it outright, declaring that giving land to an outside minority was an unjust solution. Increasingly, neighboring Arab countries began to express sympathy with the Palestinians.

In 1939 the British tried again, issuing a policy paper, called the White Paper, which tried to satisfy the demands of Palestinians and neighboring countries. The White Paper proclaimed that Great Britain no longer planned for Palestine to become a Jewish state and announced further limits on Jewish immigration to Palestine. By this time, gaining Arab support had become crucial. World War II was beginning in Europe. Britain knew that it must gain allies against Germany and Italy in the war, and it wanted the Arab nations on its side.

The coming of World War II also posed a dilemma for Jews in Palestine. They could not support Germany, which was openly anti-Semitic, yet they could not support the British White Paper, because it threatened Jews who wanted desperately to escape from Germany by limiting Jewish immigration to Palestine. Ben-Gurion expressed his people's difficult position when he said, as quoted by author William L. Cleveland in *A History of the Modern Middle East,* "We shall fight with Great Britain in this war as if there was no White Paper, and we shall fight the White Paper as if there was no war."

The UN partition of Palestine

The events of World War II brought about major shifts in power, both in the Middle East and in the rest of the world. Three of these shifts were particularly important regarding the politics in Palestine. First, the war had exhausted Great Britain, severely depleting its soldiers, supplies, financial reserves, and spirit. As the war came to an end, the British looked for ways to withdraw from its commitment to administer Palestine. Second, world opinion after the war was in favor of granting independence to the Arab nations of the Middle East. The Arab League, a regional political alliance of Arab nations formed in 1945, was especially sympathetic to the desire of Palestinians for their own nation. Finally, the world was horrified at Hitler's Final Solution, his attempt to exterminate all European Jews. The Nazis had systematically killed an estimated six million

Jews. Sympathy for the plight of the Jews inspired great support, especially in the United States, for the creation of a Jewish state in Palestine. These conflicting forces all contributed to the attempt to force a solution to the long stalemate in Palestine.

In February 1947 Great Britain announced that it planned to end its administration of the mandate of Palestine and requested the United Nations (UN; an international organization of countries founded in 1945 to promote international peace, security, and cooperation) to provide assistance with Palestine. By August of that year the United Nations Special Committee on Palestine (UNSCOP) called for the partition of Palestine into two separate states, a Jewish one and an Arab one. Under this plan, the Jews would receive about 56 percent of Palestine and the Arabs would receive about 43 percent; the rest would be considered an international zone. This would give the Jews, who only owned about 7 percent of the Palestinian land at the time, a great deal of land and power over hundreds of thousands of Arabs living on the lands they acquired. The UN plan also provided for the *corpus serparatum* (meaning "separated body" in Latin) of Jerusalem, and internationally administered zone that guaranteed that Christians, Jews, and Muslims could access their holy sites in the city.

The partition plan passed in the UN on November 29, 1947, marking the first time that the international community publicly endorsed the idea of a Jewish state. The Arabs rejected the proposal. Arabs, who comprised more than 67 percent of the population of Palestine at the time, believed the 43 percent they were to receive under the UN plan stole land from them. The proposal was never put into effect, largely because of the increasingly violent conflict that was taking place between Jews and Arabs in Palestine.

The Intercommunal War and the 1948 Arab-Israeli War

From the moment that UNSCOP announced its two-state plan for Palestine in 1947, the situation in Palestine changed from a political conflict with politicians lobbying to win support for their land claims to a military conflict with armed groups fighting one another to secure land. This scramble to claim land and define boundaries occurred in two distinct phases. The first was the Intercommunal War, when Jews and Palestinians fought among themselves, and the second was the

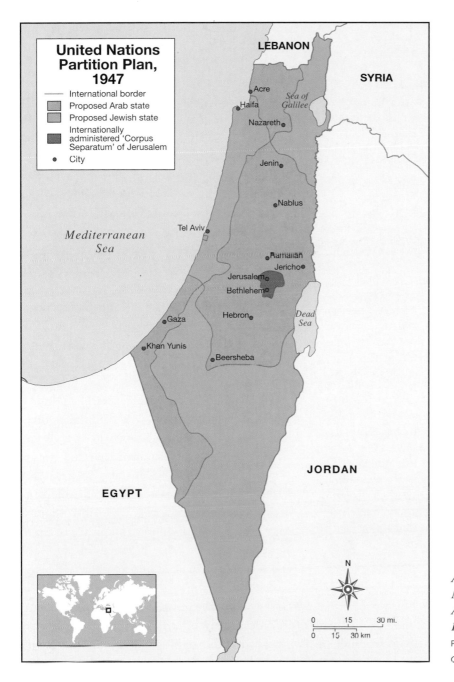

A map showing the United Nations plan to create separate Arab and Jewish states in Palestine. MAP BY XNR PRODUCTIONS, INC./ CENGAGE LEARNING.

1948 Arab-Israeli War (known in Israel as the War for Independence) in which the neighboring Arab nations fought to deny Israel its independence.

The United States and Zionism

For most of its history, Israel has had a close relationship with the United States. Although there are no formal treaties or alliances between the two countries, the United States has long been one of Israel's greatest supporters in its many struggles with the Arab world. The relationship has roots that go back to the administration of U.S. president Woodrow Wilson (1856–1924), who in 1917 urged Great Britain to offer its support to the Zionist cause as a key strategic step in winning World War I. As Great Britain's role in administering the mandate became increasingly complicated, and as Zionists came to believe that they could not rely on Britain to protect their interests, the center of support for Zionism shifted to the United States, which has a sizable and prosperous Jewish population.

In 1942 some six hundred American Zionists met at the Biltmore Hotel in New York City to announce their support for a Jewish state and call on all democratic nations to offer their support. The United States embraced this role and became a vocal leader in building support for the United Nations' partitioning of Palestine. The well-known U.S. support for Israel angers Arab leaders and contributes greatly to the negative image of the United States in the Middle East.

The Intercommunal War was, literally, a war between two communities that began in November 1947, when well-organized Jewish troops of the Haganah forcibly moved into some of the lands that were promised to them under the UN partition plan. The Arabs who lived there were ill-prepared to deal with these invasions. Former Palestinian leader al-Husayni tried to organize resistance from his base in Egypt, and other Palestinian groups also formed small bands of fighters to attempt to stop the Jewish forces. The Palestinians were lightly armed and poorly funded and organized; they proved better at harassing Jewish settlers with sneak attacks and destruction of property than at competing in armed battles. Slowly, Jewish forces gained control of strategic areas. Their victories forced as many as four hundred thousand Palestinians to flee their homes and villages and take refuge in areas under Arab control.

A pivotal moment occurred in the midst of a Jewish offensive in April 1948. Palestinian forces had offered extreme resistance in the villages around the city of Jerusalem, but the nearby Arab village of Deir Yassin (also spelled Dayr Yâsîn) had remained peaceful. On the morning of April 9, 1948, however, Irgun forces joined with another radical militia group called Lehi to attack the village. What began as an organized attack soon degenerated into a reckless massacre; Jewish soldiers moved from house to house, robbing people and murdering many who resisted. Accounts of the events of the Deir Yassin massacre differ greatly, often depending on whether the witness was Arab or Jewish. The number of those killed is also uncertain. Some sources say that around 250 men, women, and children were slaughtered; other sources place the number closer to 100. The incident was widely reported by Arab radio stations, and it terrified surrounding Arab communities. Jewish forces played up this terror with radio announcements telling the Arabs to leave Palestine if they wanted to avoid such a fate. This atrocity moved many Arab nations to enter the growing conflict.

On May 14, 1948, British forces departed from Palestine. They had earlier announced the end of the mandate and prepared to leave by this date. On the same day that they British left, Ben-Gurion proclaimed the establishment of the independent state of Israel. The next day, the armies of Egypt, Iraq, Lebanon, Syria, and Transjordan invaded the region of the former mandate. These states, acting through the Arab League, had denied the legitimacy of the partition plan, and now they would use their combined armies in an attempt to stop the creation of this new state of Israel.

From the very beginning, the Arab armies faced serious problems. First, they were outnumbered. Their combined forces totaled 21,500, while the Israeli's totaled 30,000. Second, they were poorly organized. There was no central leader coordinating the attacks, and thus each Arab

David Ben-Gurion declared the establishment of the independent state of Israel on Mary 14, 1948. FRANK SCHERSCHEL/TIME LIFE PICTURES/GETTY IMAGES.

army acted alone. Only the army from Transjordan, the Arab Legion under the command of King Abdullah I (1882–1921), fought well. Third, they faced well-prepared Israeli forces, which had been trained to fight on Palestinian terrain. Funds from the foreign countries that supported Zionism, including the United States, had been used to arm Israeli soldiers.

The fighting was largely over by August 1948. Israeli forces not only secured the areas granted by the UN partition, but they also significantly expanded their territory in the north, capturing the entire northern quarter of Palestine all the way to the Lebanese border and making real gains on both the northern and southern edges of the West Bank, an area between Israel and Jordan on the west bank of the Jordan River. Transjordan was the only Arab country that experienced any lasting success in the war. It had entered the war hoping to claim all or part of the West Bank as part of Transjordan, and by the war's end it had gained control of the West Bank and East Jerusalem. Had it not been for effectiveness of the Transjordanian army, it is possible that Israel might have captured the entire West Bank. By the middle of 1949, Israel had negotiated cease-fire agreements with all its neighboring countries and considered its borders secure and established. The state of Israel was now a reality, recognized by the United Nations and welcomed by many in the international community.

Lasting effects on the Middle East and the world

The creation of the independent state of Israel caused significant regional problems. The first and largest problem was that of Palestinian refugees. (Refugees are people who flee their country to escape violence or persecution.) An estimated 750,000 Palestinians were either forced to leave their homes or willingly fled during the 1948 Arab-Israeli War. Arabs refer to the events of 1948 as *al-Nakba* (an Arab word meaning "the catastrophe"). The refugees fled primarily to the West Bank and the Gaza Strip (a narrow strip of land along the eastern shore of the Mediterranean Sea, west of Israel and bordering Egypt in the southwest), occupied by Transjordan and Egypt, respectively, but also to other neighboring countries. Many Palestinians lost everything they owned as they moved, and others became sick and died in refugee camps, where conditions were poor and medical supplies were scarce. The large numbers of Palestinian refugees, in turn, created economic problems for the nations in which they took refuge, as they entered their new homes without jobs or means of supporting their community and began to compete with locals for limited resources.

Israel's rise to independence and the 1948 Arab-Israeli War created lasting ill will and anger among the nations of the Middle East. Arab nations would fight a series of wars with Israel over the years to come, and they consistently denied Israel's right to exist. Most Arab nations sided with Palestinians in believing that Palestine had been stolen from its rightful owners, and they blamed the Western countries that had supported Israel, especially Great Britain and the United States, for this crime. Israel thus became a symbol for the great cultural clash between the West and the Arab countries of the Middle East. All of these issues, the Palestinian refugee problem, Arab anger toward Israel, and the cultural divide between the Arab and Western worlds, continued to be the focus of conflict in the region into the twenty-first century.

For More Information

BOOKS

Cleveland, William L. *A History of the Modern Middle East*, 3rd ed. Boulder, CO: Westview Press, 2004, p. 260.

Encyclopedia of the Modern Middle East, 4 vols. New York: Macmillan Reference USA, 1996.

Farsoun, Samih K., with Christina E. Zacharia. *Palestine and the Palestinians*. Boulder, CO: Westview Press, 1997.

Karsh, Efraim. *The Arab-Israeli Conflict: The 1948 War*. New York: Rosen Publishing, 2008.

McCarthy, Justin. *The Population of Palestine: Population History and Statistics of the Late Ottoman Period and the Mandate*. New York: Columbia University Press, 1990.

Miller, Debra A. *The Arab-Israeli Conflict*. San Diego, CA: Lucent Books, 2005.

Shlaim, Avi. *Israel and Palestine: Reappraisals, Revisions, Refutations*. London and New York: Verso, 2010.

Smith, Charles D., ed. *Palestine and the Arab-Israeli Conflict: A History with Documents*, 4th ed. Boston, MA: Bedford/St. Martin's, 2001.

Wagner, Heather Lehr. *Israel and the Arab World*. Philadelphia, PA: Chelsea House, 2002.

PERIODICALS

Hogan, Matthew. "The 1948 Massacre at Deir Yassin Revisited." *Historian* 63, no. 2 (Winter 2001): 309.

WEB SITES

"The Balfour Declaration." *Israel Ministry of Foreign Affairs.* http://www.mfa.gov.il/ MFA/Peace%20Process/Guide%20to%20the%20Peace%20Process/The%20 Balfour%20Declaration (accessed on November 30, 2011).

"The British Mandate for Palestine." April 24, 1920. http://www.mtholyoke. edu/acad/intrel/britman.htm (accessed on November 6, 2011).

The Question of Palestine and the United Nations. United Nations Department of Public Information (March 2003). http://www.un.org/Depts/dpi/palestine/ (accessed on November 30, 2011).

"Palestine." *The Map Room: The British Empire.* http://www.britishempire.co.uk/ maproom/palestine.htm (accessed on November 30, 2011).

"Timeline: Palestine since 1915." *Aljazeera.* http://english.aljazeera.net/focus/ arabunity/2008/02/20085251908164329.html (accessed on November 30, 2011).

6

The Arab-Israeli Conflict: 1948 to 1973

On May 14, 1948, the state of Israel was established. Zionists, supporters of an international political movement that called for the creation of an independent Jewish state in Palestine, had achieved their ultimate goal. (Palestine is a historical region in the Middle East on the eastern shore of the Mediterranean Sea, comprising parts of present-day Israel and Jordan.) Arab countries (countries where Arabic is the dominant language) in the Middle East felt that the Israelis had stolen land from Palestinians (the Arab people whose ancestors lived in the historical region of Palestine) to create their country. The nations of Transjordan (present-day Jordan), Syria, and Egypt, along with other countries in the Arab League (a political alliance of Arab nations formed in 1945 to promote political, military, and economic cooperation within the Arab world) attacked Israel in late May 1948, starting the 1948 Arab-Israeli War (known in Israel as the War for Independence). Israel was the victor in the war, but the conflict between Israel and the Arab countries of the Middle East would continue to plague the region for decades.

The competition between two peoples, the Israelis and the Palestinians, for the same territory is at the root of the Arab-Israeli conflict, and it affects the entire Middle East. Nearly every Arab country went through a period of significant political change after Israel was founded. The governments of Egypt, Iraq, and Syria, for example, were humiliated by their military defeat to Israel in the 1948 Arab-Israeli War, and their citizens began to seek new leaders. Several Arab countries were also transformed by the huge influx of Palestinian refugees (people who flee their country to escape violence or persecution), who fled Israel during the war. Influencing all of these factors was the Cold War (1945–91; a period of intense political and economic rivalry between the United States and the Soviet Union), as both Israel and its Arab neighbors sought alliances that would help them in the constant struggle to maintain or regain cultural dominance and territory.

WORDS TO KNOW

Arab League: A regional political alliance of Arab nations formed in 1945 to promote political, military, and economic cooperation within the Arab world.

Arabs: People of the Middle East and North Africa who speak the Arabic language or who live in countries in which Arabic is the dominant language.

Ba'ath Party: A secular (nonreligious) political party founded in the 1940s with the goal of uniting the Arab world and creating one powerful Arab state.

capitalism: An economic system in which the means of production and distribution are privately owned.

Cold War: A period of intense political and economic rivalry between the United States and the Soviet Union that lasted from 1945 to 1991.

Communism: A system of government in which the state plans and controls the economy and a single political party holds power.

Fatah: A Palestinian militant group and political party dedicated to the establishment of an independent Palestinian state.

fedayeen: An Arabic term meaning one who sacrifices for a cause; used to describe several distinct militant groups that have formed in the Arab world at different times. Opponents of the fedayeen use the term to describe members of Arab terrorist groups.

guerilla warfare: Combat tactics used by a smaller, less equipped fighting force against a more powerful foe.

Haganah: The underground defense force of Zionists in Palestine from 1920 to 1948. It became the basis for the Israeli army.

Irgun Zvai Leumi: A militant underground group founded in 1931 that worked to secure Israeli independence by staging violent attacks on British and Arab targets. Also known simply as Irgun.

kibbutz: A Jewish communal farming settlement in Israel, where settlers share all property and work collaboratively together. Plural is kibbutzim.

militia: Armed civilian military forces.

nationalism: The belief that a people with shared ethnic, cultural, and/or religious identities have the right to form their own nation. In established nations nationalism is devotion and loyalty to the nation and its culture.

nationalization: The practice of bringing private industry under the ownership and control of the government.

occupied territories: The lands under the political and military control of Israel, especially the West Bank and Gaza Strip.

Palestine: A historical region in the Middle East on the eastern shore of the Mediterranean Sea, comprising parts of present-day Israel and Jordan.

Palestine Liberation Organization (PLO): A political and military organization formed to unite various Palestinian Arab groups with the goal of establishing an independent Palestinian state.

Palestinians: An Arab people whose ancestors lived in the historical region of Palestine and who continue to lay claim to that land.

Pan-Arabism: A movement for the unification of Arab peoples and the political alliance of Arab states.

refugees: People who flee their country to escape violence or persecution.

socialism: A system in which the government owns the means of production and controls the distribution of goods and services.

Suez Canal: A shipping canal that connects the Mediterranean Sea with the Red Sea.

Zionists: Supporters of an international political movement that called for the creation of an independent Jewish state in Palestine.

Building a Jewish nation

When Jews began immigrating to Palestine in the 1880s to fulfill the Zionist goal of creating a Jewish national home, they were prepared from the start to build the solid social institutions they would need to look after their interests. Although at the turn of the twentieth century there were only a few thousand Jews in Palestine, they had already succeeded in developing kibbutzim (Jewish communal farming settlements, where settlers share all property and work collaboratively together) that were capable of providing nearly all needed food. They formed a workers' union that soon developed into a political party, called the Mapai Party, and its elected leaders became spokespeople for Jewish political issues. They also established several militias (armed civilian military forces) most notably the Haganah, the underground defense force of Zionists in Palestine from 1920 to 1948 which became the basis for the Israel army, and the Irgun Zvai Leumi (also known simply as Irgun), a militant underground group founded in 1931 that worked to secure Israeli independence by staging violent attacks on British and Arab targets. All of these groups were in place when Israel declared its independence in 1948, and they contributed to the new country's success in defeating the combined, though poorly coordinated, forces of the Arab countries who sought to deny that independence in the 1948 Arab-Israeli War.

Israelis received a psychological lift from their military victory, which solidified the nation of Israel. From its beginnings in the late nineteenth century, the Zionist movement had proclaimed that Jews could only live peaceably in the world if they had an independent state of their own. After the horrors faced by Jews during World War II (1939–45), when German leader Adolf Hitler (1889–1945) ordered the murder of millions of European Jews, most Western countries, including Great Britain, France, Canada, and the United States, supported Zionist goals. Soon after Israel declared its independence, many nations welcomed Israel into the world community. Jewish immigrants poured into Israel in large numbers. By 1948 there were an estimated 650,000 Jews in Palestine. Between 1948 and 1951 the population of Israel doubled, as approximately 684,000 Jews moved from countries where they had been persecuted to a nation where their Jewish identity formed the basis of the state.

Jewish immigrants arriving in Tel Aviv, in 1948. Soon after Israel declared its independence, Jewish immigrants poured into Israel in large numbers. © BETTMANN/CORBIS.

Israelis soon created unique political, social, and cultural traditions. Their political system, finalized by 1949, allowed all Jewish citizens to vote. Most Palestinians living in Israel were granted citizenship and could vote, but for the first years, citizenship came with some major limitations for Arab Israelis, such as curfews (regulations about what time each day one needed to be off the streets) and travel restrictions. In Israel, voters cast their ballots for a political party, and the parties name members to the 120-seat, single-house legislature called the Knesset, based on the proportion of the votes received by the party. From 1949 to 1977 the Mapai Party (later called the Labor Party) dominated Israel's politics. The Mapai formed a coalition (political alliance) with other parties to name the prime minister and the cabinet, a body of high-ranking officials who advise the prime minister. The Knesset also chooses the president, whose role is largely ceremonial. Israel's first prime minister was David Ben-Gurion (1886–1973).

Ben-Gurion had risen to power in Jewish politics in part because of his success in creating the Haganah. One of Ben-Gurion's first acts following Israeli independence was to bring competing militia groups, especially the Irgun, headed by political rival Menachem Begin (1913–1992), under IDF control. Soon, the IDF became an important shaper of Israeli identity. All Jewish Israeli males, with the exception of those with disabilities and those who studied in religious seminaries, were required to complete three years of military training; single Jewish Israeli females without children were required to serve for two years. Thereafter, they became part of the military reserve. In the event of war the entire population (between the ages of eighteen and fifty) could be called to fight. Because the majority of Israeli citizens shared the common bond of military service, the population was unusually united in its determination to defend Israel.

Ben-Gurion and other important Israeli politicians promoted the idea that because Israel was a newly created country, it was weak and constantly in danger from Arab countries that wanted to destroy it. Ben-Gurion hoped to convince Israelis as well as foreign allies that it was proper for Israel to continue to build its army but also to extend its borders when possible in order to create a buffer zone, or neutral area, between Israel and the Arab countries that sought to cause it harm. He promoted a doctrine that declared that any attack on Israel must be met with a counterattack of disproportionately greater force. Only by being aggressive in its own defense, according to Ben-Gurion, could Israel ensure its security. This way of thinking was due in large part to Israel's small size, the history of Jewish persecution in Europe and the Middle East, and being surrounded on all sides by Arab countries that opposed its existence. Fortunately for Israel, the countries surrounding it were going through their own political changes and were not able to coordinate an attack against Israel throughout most of the 1950s.

The Arab League

On March 22, 1945, the leaders of Egypt, Iraq, Lebanon, Transjordan, Saudi Arabia, Syria, and Yemen joined together to form the League of Arab States, better known as the Arab League. They formed the league to promote political, military, and economic cooperation within the Arab world and to ensure a unified response to conflicts in the region. As part of its initial agreement, the league members pledged to preserve the rights of the Palestinians.

To Palestinians the 1948 Arab-Israeli War and the refugee crisis that followed seemed such a disaster that it became known as *al-Nakba* (an Arab word meaning "the catastrophe"). It was also a crisis to the neighboring countries that had to absorb the displaced Palestinians and endure the humiliation of defeat to the Israeli forces. Throughout the 1950s, many individual Arab countries offered support for Palestinian refugees, but they could seldom agree on a shared solution to the problem.

Egypt's rise to Arab leadership

The effects of Israel's defeat of the Arab countries in the 1948 Arab-Israeli War was dramatic in Egypt, one of the Middle East's most powerful countries since ancient times. At the time of the war, Egypt was led by King Farouk I (1920–1965), who, to many Egyptians, seemed to be more responsive to British demands than to those of the Egyptian people. After the 1948 Arab-Israeli War, increasing numbers of Egyptians were dissatisfied with Farouk's rule. Poor peasants were unhappy with their lack of political representation. Also, a five-hundred-thousand-member religious faction called the Muslim Brotherhood demanded greater loyalty to Islamic values and an end to Western influences in the country. (The Muslim Brotherhood is an Islamic fundamentalist group organized in opposition to Western influence and in support of Islamic principles.) Finally, powerful officers in the country's military were outraged at the way Egypt's military was being run and how it had failed in battle against the Israeli forces.

In 1952 an Egyptian military group calling itself the Free Officers staged a coup, or overthrow of the government, forcing Farouk to leave the country. Leading the group was a young officer named Gamal Abdel Nasser (1918–1970), who would become the most powerful man in the Arab world in the 1950s and 1960s.

In 1956 Nasser became president of Egypt, and he proved to be a strong, authoritarian leader. He allowed only one political party and suppressed any opposition that arose. Nasser developed a socialist system, or a system in which the government owns the means of production and controls the distribution of goods and services. He also began a program of nationalization, the practice of bringing private industry under the ownership and control of the government.

Gamal Abdul Nasser in 1953. After Nasser became president of Egypt in 1956, he made Egypt a leader in the Arab world by promoting Arab nationalism. BENTLEY ARCHIVE/POPPERFOTO/ GETTY IMAGES.

Nasser wanted more than the leadership of Egypt, however. He wanted to work with other Arab countries in the Middle East to create a large Arab alliance that would combine the resources of Arabs in the Middle East and become a powerful entity in the region. His movement for the unification of Arab peoples and the political alliance of Arab states, which is called Pan-Arabism, stressed the importance of Arab nationalism. (Nationalism is devotion and loyalty to a nation and its culture, in this case the entire Arab world.)

One of the rallying points of Nasser's Pan-Arabism, which is sometimes called Nasserism, was his opposition to Israel. For Muslims like Nasser, opposition to Israel was not a matter of anti-Semitism, or prejudice against Jews. In fact, Muslims had always respected the Jewish faith as an ancestor to Islam. Rather, Nasser and other Arabs resented the way that Jews had claimed what they considered to be Arab land. Pan-Arabists also thought that Western countries used Israel as a means to spread their influence in the Middle East and to attack Arab and Islamic culture. Nasser encouraged Arabs to unite in opposition to Israel.

Nasser's hope for the pan-Arab movement was to eventually create one large Arab state, ridding the Arab countries of the borders between them, which they viewed as the artificial creation of Western powers. Nasser led the first real attempt to bring about Arab unification in 1958, when he organized the formation of the United Arab Republic (UAR), a political union between Egypt and Syria. Although Egypt and Syria did not share a border, they began to merge their economic and political systems. Nasser was named the UAR's president. Most Syrians initially favored the union, but problems arose immediately because Egypt was much more powerful than Syria. Once the UAR had been established, Syria began to feel that it had invited an Egyptian takeover. Popular resistance to the union led to a military coup in 1961 that restored Syria's independence and effectively disbanded the UAR.

Shifts in the Arab world

As in Egypt, political change was occurring in nearly every other Arab country in the 1950s, in varying degrees. In Syria the leaders who had ordered the failed military effort against Israel were discredited and driven from office. Between 1949 and 1971, several groups fought for leadership of Syria, each with support from some element of the military. In the

Pan-Arabism

Pan-Arabism is a movement for the unification of Arab peoples and the political alliance of Arab states. In its simplest form, Pan-Arabism holds that two unifying forces form the basis for national identity: Arab ethnicity and Islam. In the late nineteenth century, when the Ottoman Empire was in a state of decline, political thinkers in the Arab world began to suggest that Arabs should unite to form a powerful, unified nation. With the strength of this unity, Arab leaders hoped to reclaim the former glory that the region had enjoyed before the Western powers of Europe had begun to militarily overpower the empire's forces and expand into the Middle East, interfering in the region's economy and politics. When the Ottoman Empire collapsed, however, the Arab leaders in the former empire were not in a position of power. Instead, an alliance of mainly Western nations led by Great Britain and France chose to divide the Arab world into individual nations, defining its borders as they saw fit.

Some of those who resented the Europeans' interference in the region contended that the answer to the troubles plaguing the Middle East could be found in Pan-Arabism, the unification of the people of the Arab world. The Middle East moved toward pan-Arab unification in 1945, when seven Arab countries formed the Arab League, a regional political alliance of Arab nations formed to promote political, military, and economic cooperation within the Arab world. In the 1950s, Egyptian president Gamal Abdel Nasser (1918–1970) became the foremost leader of the movement. In 1958 he attempted to take the first step in building a pan-Arab state when he united Egypt and Syria as the United Arab Republic (UAR). This experiment soon failed. It seemed that the one thing that unified the Arab states was their mutual support for Palestinians, who were struggling with Israelis for control of Palestine. But the continued failure of Arab nations to defeat Israel and rid themselves of the influence of Western countries led to disillusionment with Pan-Arabism, while the tendency of individual leaders to try to gain power splintered the various groups that had supported it. By the mid–twentieth century most Arab countries had developed different goals.

country's first government, Communists (advocates of Communism, a system of government in which the state plans and controls the economy and a single political party holds power) who were allied with the Soviet Union played an important political role. Fear of Communism contributed to the Syrian decision to merge with Egypt and create the UAR in 1958. When this pan-Arab experiment failed in the 1960s, the Ba'ath Party took control of the Syrian government. (The Ba'ath Party is a secular [nonreligious] political party founded in the 1940s with the goal of uniting the Arab world and creating one powerful Arab state.) The Ba'ath Party was a socialist group that originally supported a democratic style of government and Arab unity as a way to strengthen all Arab countries in the region. In 1970 Hafez Assad (also spelled al-Assad;

1930–2000) took power of the Ba'ath Party as the leader of a nonviolent coup, or overthrow of the leaders of the party (who were also the leaders of the government). Assad called this coup the Corrective Movement. After placing people loyal to him in the top positions of the party, Assad assumed the position of president of Syria. He quickly transformed the representative government into an authoritarian regime in which power is consolidated under one strong leader, Assad himself, who does not answer to the will of the people.

The situation was similar in Iraq. The Iraqi royal family maintained control of the country after the 1948 Arab-Israeli War, thanks largely to British support. During these years, an Iraqi Ba'ath Party (similar though distinct from Syria's Ba'ath Party) emerged in Iraq. After a military coup against the king in 1958, Iraqi politics were unstable for a period of about ten years, with ethnic and religious groups fighting for power. By 1968, however, the Ba'ath Party gained control of the military, and a Ba'ath leader, Ahmad Hassan al-Bakr (1914–1982), became president of Iraq. Although they shared origins, the Ba'ath parties in Syria and Iraq were not allies; in fact, they fought bitterly over whose vision of Arab unity was best.

Transjordan, which changed its name to Jordan in 1949, and Lebanon, both of which share a border with Israel, took more complicated positions with regard to Israel. Both countries had a tradition of good relations with Western countries and neither was eager to engage in open military conflict with Israel. Yet both Jordan and Lebanon were forced to absorb large numbers of Palestinian refugees, and the political activism of those refugees pressured them to join Arab actions against Israel in the 1960s.

Egypt supports Palestinian fedayeen

By 1949, some of the border issues between Israel and its Arab neighbors Lebanon, Syria, Jordan, and Egypt had been resolved, at least temporarily. Israel had agreed to borders in some areas, and in others to cease-fire lines (lines at which disputing forces stop firing and withdraw according to a cease fire agreement) in others. Refugee camps existed along the borders of Jordan, Syria, Egypt, and Lebanon, as well as in the West Bank (an area between Israel and Jordan on the west bank of the Jordan River), and the Gaza Strip (a narrow strip of land along the eastern shore of the Mediterranean Sea, west of Israel and bordering Egypt in the southwest), where Palestinians endured terrible conditions, living in tents or poorly made shelters with little sanitation. The Palestinians did not need much encouragement to launch attacks across the border on Israel. Most of the Arab nations that had taken the Palestinians in after the 1948 Arab-Israeli War did not wish to renew conflict with a nation that had recently defeated them. Egypt, however, began to provide secret funding and training to the Palestinian fighters, who called themselves fedayeen (an Arabic term meaning one who sacrifices for a cause; used to describe several distinct militant groups that have formed in the Arab world at different times).

Small fedayeen attacks on Israeli citizens from refugee camps in the Gaza Strip and from the West Bank began in the early 1950s. By 1955 with Nasser's encouragement, these attacks grew larger and more concentrated.

The Suez Crisis

Nasser was antagonizing Israel and the West in other ways, as well. The Suez Canal was a major part of this. In the mid–1850s, the Ottoman governor of Egypt, Said Pasha (1822–1863), had commissioned French diplomat Ferdinand de Lesseps (1805–1894) to develop a 100-mile-long (161-kilometer-long) shipping canal across the Isthmus of Suez, the narrow strip of land in Egypt between the Mediterranean Sea and the Red Sea that links the continents of Africa and Asia. De Lesseps created the Suez Canal Company, the shares of which were jointly owned by a group of private investors De Lesseps had gathered from France and by the Egyptian government. The Suez Canal Company was officially an Egyptian company, but Said Pasha granted the company a 99-year lease on the tolls that would be charged on the canal. The company built the canal between 1856 and 1869, using the labor and resources of the Egyptian people.

In 1875, Said Pasha was in financial trouble. He sold his share of the company, and the British government purchased it. Great Britain took advantage of Egypt's financial crisis in other ways, as well, gaining increasing power in the nation. For a time, the British government and French stockholders owned majority interests in the canal. By 1882, Great Britain had come to rule Egypt in a protectorate relationship that would last until 1922. At that time, Egypt became an independent constitutional monarchy, but Great Britain's military forces remained, and its interference in Egypt's affairs continued.

Egypt also faced a new enemy at home in 1948, when it joined other Arab nations in the war against the nation of Israel. After defeat in Israel's war of independence, Egypt had closed the Suez Canal to Israeli ships, making it nearly impossible for Israel to conduct trade with other countries. In 1949 Israel complained to the United Nations (UN; an international organization of countries founded in 1945 to promote international peace, security, and cooperation) about Egypt's blockade against Israeli ships. The United Nations ordered Egypt to open the canal to Israel, but Egypt refused to change its policy.

By the mid–1950s, Nasser was Egypt's leader. Hostilities arose between Nasser and the Western powers on many fronts, including his involvement in attacks on Israel and his increasing relations with the Soviet Union. Great Britain and the United States reacted to these actions by withdrawing their financial assistance in his pet project of building the Aswan Dam across the Nile River in the Egyptian desert. Then, in July 1956, in a long public speech, Nasser announced that he was nationalizing the Suez Canal (bringing it under government ownership and control). He noted that 120,000 Egyptians had died building the canal, and that the Egyptian people received very little benefit from it. Nasser claimed he would use the canal to fund the construction of the Aswan Dam. He ordered Egyptian troops to take over control of the canal's operations from the British and French.

Great Britain, France, and Israel saw this action as an aggressive move. British and French troops gathered on the islands of Cyprus and Malta, preparing to attack, and Nasser prepared his troops for battle. By arrangement with Great Britain and France, Israeli troops entered the Sinai Peninsula on October 29. Thanks largely to their strong tank divisions and well-trained army, the Israelis quickly captured the Gaza Strip and much of the Sinai Peninsula. Great Britain and France offered to stop the fighting if given possession of the canal, hoping to protect Western interests in the region. Egypt refused, and British and French troops entered the conflict. The Egyptian forces took heavy losses.

It seemed that the Egyptian army was on the verge of defeat when the United States forced a diplomatic solution to the crisis. It pressured Great Britain and France to remove their troops, replacing them with troops from a United Nations emergency force. It also used its influence to force Israeli troops to withdraw from captured territory in the Sinai Peninsula. Egypt regained that territory as long as it pledged to keep the

British troops on patrol in Egypt during the Suez Crisis. WALTER BELLAMY/DAILY EXPRESS/HULTON ARCHIVE/ GETTY IMAGES.

canal open to all shipping. Despite being overpowered militarily, Egyptians celebrated the crisis as a victory. Nasser had proved that Arab countries could stand up to foreign powers; Israel was forced to give up captured Egyptian territory, and Great Britain and France were reduced to minor powers in the region and replaced by the United States as the main foreign influence. The Suez Crisis established a troubled peace in the region that would last until the late 1960s.

Palestinians organize

After the 1948 Arab-Israeli War, Palestinians had few resources. Forced to abruptly leave their homeland, hundreds of thousands of Palestinians had become refugees, living in temporary homes in Arab countries. The largest groups of Palestinians gathered in the Egyptian-held Gaza Strip and in the Jordan-held West Bank. While many middle- and upper-class Palestinians were able to secure housing and jobs in Arab nations, the refugee camps were filled with uneducated and unskilled workers, most of whom had fled their homes without any of their possessions. Life in the camps was miserable, as they lacked proper sanitary conditions, education systems for children, any security, or a governing system.

By the mid–1950s many young Palestinian men who had fought against Israel with the Egypt-supported fedayeen were determined to use force to reclaim Palestine, and they began to organize. They established a group called Fatah, a Palestinian militant group (and later political party) dedicated to the establishment of an independent Palestinian state. Fatah soon came under the leadership of a passionate, college-educated Palestinian named Yasser Arafat (1929–2004). Other groups willing to use force to achieve Palestinian goals also emerged in Egypt, Jordan, and Syria, most notably the Popular Front for the Liberation of Palestine (PFLP), led by George Habash (1926–2008), and the Democratic Front for the Liberation of Palestine (DFLP).

At the Arab League summit in Cairo, Egypt, in 1964, the Arab League decided to sponsor (provide financial and administrative support for) the formation of the Palestine Liberation Organization (PLO), a political and military organization formed to unite various Palestinian Arab groups with the goal of establishing an independent Palestinian state. The PLO was led by Ahmad Shuqayri (1908–1980), a moderate Palestinian. Shuqayri called for Palestinian unity, but he did not openly endorse Palestinian attacks and raids on Israel. For many young Palestinians growing up in refugee camps, Shuqayri's leadership was too focused on pleasing Arab leaders and not nearly effective enough in restoring their former home. From the early 1960s onward, Palestinian groups, especially Fatah, obtained weapons and began to launch attacks on Israel from within Arab nations.

The refugee situation caused a conflict between Jordanians and other Arabs. In the years since the 1948 Arab-Israeli War, Jordan had absorbed huge numbers of Palestinians, both poor refugees of the war who mainly lived in the camps and nonrefugees (people who had migrated to Jordan for reasons other than the 1948 Arab-Israeli War) who lived and worked in Jordan's existing communities. By some estimates, in the years immediately following the war with Israel, nearly one million Palestinians had come to reside in Jordan, and they outnumbered the native Jordanians. By the 1960s Arafat and his Fatah fighters had moved into the Palestinian refugee areas of Jordan, trying to escape from the Israeli forces that were tracking them down. Their violent campaigns against Israel threatened Jordan's stability.

By 1966 Palestinian militants had also built up a following in Syria and were attacking the northeast corner of Israel, near the Golan Heights, a mountainous region located on the border of Syria and Israel, northwest

A Palestinian girl receiving food at a refugee camp run by the United Nations Relief And Works Agency (UNRWA) in Jordan. After the 1948 Arab-Israeli War, Jordan absorbed huge numbers of Palestinian refugees. THREE LIONS/GETTY IMAGES.

of the Sea of Galilee. The Syrian government encouraged Palestinians to attack Israel from the West Bank as well, in an attempt to draw Jordan into the conflict. By early 1967 there were frequent battles between IDF soldiers and Syrian and Palestinian fighters along the borders of Syria and, to a more limited extent, Jordan.

The 1967 Arab-Israeli War

By May 1967 Palestinian attacks on Israel from Syria were so persistent that many of the countries in the region began to prepare for war. Egypt, hoping to prove its leadership among Arab countries, pledged to support Syria in the event of an Israeli attack. Pressured by pro-Palestinian factions in his country, Jordan's King Hussein I (1935–1999) signed a mutual defense pact with Egypt in which Jordan and Egypt agreed to protect one another in the event of an attack on either country. It soon appeared to Israel that some of the Arab countries in the Middle East were planning to wage war on Israel.

Israel determined that war with the Arabs had become impossible to avoid. Many of the country's leaders contended that if Israel wished to win this unavoidable war, it must be the first to attack, catching the Arab countries unprepared. Therefore the Israeli government ordered the Israeli Air Force (IAF) to attack Egyptian airfields on the morning of June 5, 1967. The IAF attack succeeded in surprising Egypt, destroying nearly every Egyptian warplane before the Egyptians could them off the ground to counterattack. Encouraged by the success of this first strike, Israeli ground forces began to cross the Sinai desert into Egyptian territory, defeating a large number of Egyptian forces and establishing control in the Gaza Strip and the entire Sinai Peninsula within three days.

Israel's battles against Syria and Jordan were equally decisive. On the evening of June 5, 1967, the IAF destroyed two-thirds of Syria's air force. Unwilling to advance ground troops into Israel, Syria instead began striking Israeli targets with rocket attacks launched from towns from mountain bases in the Golan Heights, which towered some 1,700 feet (518 meters) above the Israeli valley below. Despite the overwhelming difficulty of climbing the mountains on narrow roads, the Israelis used a combination of aerial bombing and ground assault to capture the Golan Heights over the next several days. By June 9, they had pushed the Syrians from their mountain bases and established a cease-fire line along a border that came to be known as the Purple Line. The new border marked Israel's control of the Golan Heights.

Reluctant Jordanian forces attacked Israel from the West Bank on June 5, 1967, and faced similar resistance from the Israelis. With their few planes destroyed by the IAF, and their ground troops defeated by the well-trained IDF troops, Jordanian fighters were quickly pushed out of the West Bank and across the Jordan River. By June 10, 1967, each of the Arab countries had accepted a cease-fire agreement and the 1967 Arab-Israeli War (known in Israel as the Six-Day War) was over.

New borders, new tensions

Israel's victory in the 1967 Arab-Israeli War reshaped the Middle East. Israel, a country established on only a portion of the original land of Palestine, had nearly tripled its size when it took the Golan Heights, the West Bank, the Gaza Strip, and the Sinai Peninsula. These acquisitions

Israeli tanks advance into Syria during the 1967 Arab-Israeli War. © VITTORIANO RASTELLI/CORBIS.

greatly increased the Palestinian refugee problem. When Israel captured the West Bank and the Gaza Strip, another 300,000 Palestinians were prompted to flee into neighboring Arab countries. After the war, Israel found itself in control of territories containing an Arab population estimated at 1.5 million people. Recognizing that it could not simply absorb this population, Israel established military rule in these regions, which came to be known as the occupied territories. After 1967, a majority of Palestinian protests and military action against Israel would come from within the occupied territories as well as refugee camps along Israeli borders.

For the Arab nations, a new defeat by the Israelis came as a profound shock. Since their first war with Israel in 1948, many of the Arab nations in the Middle East (excluding Jordan) had formed new governments and built larger armies. They fully expected to defeat the Israelis. No group was more disappointed with the leadership of the Arab nations than the Palestinians. They began to increasingly look to the leadership of the

The Cold War in the Middle East

At the close of World War II (1939–45), a period of intense political and economic rivalry between the United States and the Soviet Union began. This rivalry was called the Cold War (1945–91). Although these two major world powers had fought alongside each other in the war, in 1945 they found themselves pitted against one another, each believing that the principles that governed its society were best. The Soviet Union wanted to spread Communism (a system of government in which the state plans and controls the means of production and distribution and a single political party holds power) to other nations in the world, while the United States supported democracy (a government in which the people exercise their voice in the government through free elections) and capitalism (an economic system in which the means of production and distribution are privately owned). The Cold War was a not a traditional war in which troops fought directly on a battlefield. Instead, the superpowers sought to influence other nations to align with them. In the immediate aftermath of World War II, the Soviet Union had quickly persuaded nations in Eastern Europe to adopt Communism and become its allies, creating a group of closely allied communist nations called the Soviet Bloc. The United States was convinced that the Soviets' expansion would create what it called the "domino effect," meaning that if one nation in a region fell to Communism, others would surely follow. Thus, the United States devoted immense resources to limiting Soviet expansion.

In the postwar years the Soviets funded Communist groups attempting to overthrow the neighboring governments of Turkey and Iran. Reacting against Soviet involvement in the region, the United States provided money and weapons to the existing governments of the two countries, overlooking the antidemocratic nature of these governments in the interest of resisting Soviet influence.

PLO, which by 1968 was headed by Arafat. The PLO and its activities had become radical and increasingly violent.

Having the PLO headquartered in his country became a great concern for Jordan's King Hussein, who wished to maintain peace. In September 1970, after learning of several violent PLO terrorist acts, the king ordered his soldiers to drive the PLO out of Jordan. The PLO then moved to Lebanon, a country that openly supported the group's actions against Israel.

From the War of Attrition to the 1973 Arab-Israeli War

In the aftermath of the 1967 Arab-Israeli War, the United Nations passed Security Council Resolution 242, which held that no countries should acquire territory by war, and that all countries had the right to live in

In the 1960s Iraq and Syria saw the emergence of the Ba'ath Party as a dominant political force. The Ba'ath Party seemed a natural ally to the Soviets as it promoted socialism and secular (nonreligious) rule. Thus, the Soviet Union channeled money and arms to the Ba'ath Party in both countries. The aid was gladly accepted, but in the end neither Iraq nor Syria was willing to accept direct orders from the Soviet Union. Nevertheless, the Soviets had given Syria and Iraq much stronger militaries, and they would go on to use them in attempts to dominate their neighbors in the Middle East.

The Cold War played a large role in the 1967 Arab-Israeli War. Early that year, Arab countries began to mass forces along their borders with Israel, with Egyptian president Gamal Abdel Nasser (1918–1970) publicly vowing to bring about the destruction of Israel. Because the Soviet Union supported Egypt, Syria, and other Arab nations, U.S. president Lyndon B. Johnson (1908–1973) thought the Soviets might be behind the Arab preparations for war. He announced that the United States would lend its support to maintaining the existing borders of Middle Eastern nations and protect any nation from attack. With this statement, he opened the way for the United States to protect Israel if it was attacked by its Arab neighbors. It was Israel that attacked first, however. Despite its promise to help any Middle East nation against attack, the United States threw its support behind Israel, which within a few days captured substantial territories from its Arab neighbors and shifted the balance of power in the region.

For several tense days, observers around the world feared that the United States and the Soviet Union would become actively involved in the war. Since the two superpowers possessed nuclear weapons, the possibility of war between them was especially frightening. In the end, the superpowers negotiated an end to the fighting. After the war, the United States continued to be Israel's biggest supporter in the region, while the Soviet Union supported the Palestinians. Until the collapse of the Soviet Union in 1991, relations between Israel, the Palestinians, and neighboring Arab nations were influenced by their relations with the two superpowers.

peace within secure and recognized boundaries, free from threats or acts of force. The UN hoped that Resolution 242 would provide a framework by which Israel and its Arab neighbors could work out their differences peacefully, but it did little to resolve the disputes in the region. Arab nations seized upon the prohibition against acquiring land through war to strengthen their case that Israel should give back the Sinai Peninsula, the West Bank, the Gaza Strip, and the Golan Heights. Israel, however, argued that it could only secure its right to live in peace through the acquisition of territory by war. Conflict between the Arabs and Israelis continued on a smaller scale.

After the 1967 Arab-Israeli War, Egypt tried to win back the Sinai Peninsula by launching small attacks on the Israelis stationed along the cease fire line at the Suez Canal, in the occupied Sinai Peninsula. In what

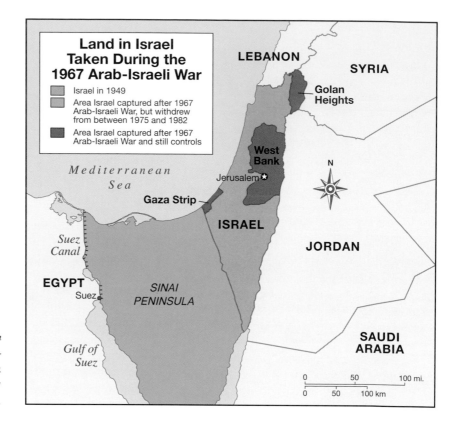

Land in Israel Taken During the 1967 Arab-Israeli War

- Israel in 1949
- Area Israel captured after 1967 Arab-Israeli War, but withdrew from between 1975 and 1982
- Area Israel captured after 1967 Arab-Israeli War and still controls

LEBANON

SYRIA

Golan Heights

Mediterranean Sea

West Bank

Jerusalem

Gaza Strip

ISRAEL

JORDAN

Suez Canal

EGYPT

Suez

SINAI PENINSULA

Gulf of Suez

SAUDI ARABIA

N

0   50   100 mi.

0   50   100 km

A map showing the land taken by Israel during the 1967 Arab-Israeli War. MAP BY XNR PRODUCTIONS, INC./ CENGAGE LEARNING.

has become known as the War of Attrition (1968–70), Egypt attempted to wear down Israel's border troops with constant artillery attacks and limited troop engagements. Israel fought back fiercely, at one point penetrating deep into Egypt. For several years, there was a stalemate, as Arab countries demanded the return of their land and Israel demanded guarantees of peace, and neither party was willing to compromise.

In 1973 conflict between Israel and numerous Arab countries resumed on a large scale. Israel was surprised on October 6, 1973 (the first day of the Jewish Yom Kippur holiday, during which Jews pray for the forgiveness of sins), when Egyptian troops attacked Israeli positions along the Suez Canal and in the Sinai Peninsula, and Syrian troops assaulted Israeli targets from the Golan Heights. Israeli military intelligence had not predicted these attacks, and in the first hours and days of the 1973 Arab-Israeli War (known in Israel as the Yom Kippur War), Israel lost ground steadily to Arab troops. Once Israel recovered from the surprise and rushed more troops to both battle sites, however, the IDF once again proved its superior military force and effectively won back much of the territory lost in the first few days of the war. In Syria IDF forces advanced so far that they were able to bomb the capital, Damascus. In Egypt the IDF captured the Suez Canal and threatened to penetrate further into Egypt. By October 22, however, pressure from countries outside of the Middle East forced the end of the war and, eventually, the return to borders similar to those determined by the 1967 Arab-Israeli War.

Although the Yom Kippur War did not significantly change the borders, about eighty-five hundred Arabs and twenty-eight hundred Israelis were killed in the brief conflict. Israel was deeply shaken by the way its military had been caught by surprise. The Arab countries, too, were discouraged by yet another defeat, but soon after the war, they discovered a new weapon: oil. Late in 1973 the Arab countries announced an embargo (ban) on the sale of oil to the West, causing a huge disruption in Western economies. (For more information, see **Other Rising Middle East Nations in the Twentieth Century**.) Countries outside of the Middle East were deeply disturbed by the conflict, not only because of the oil embargo but also because the Soviet Union and the United States had nearly gone to war against each other as a result of events in the Middle East.

Although the 1973 Arab-Israeli War had largely put an end to the armed hostilities between Israel and neighboring Arab countries, the Arab nations strongly resisted the idea of negotiating with Israel. They refused

The Israeli army firing artillery shells on the Syrian border during the 1973 Arab-Israeli War. Israel was surprised when Arab forces attacked on October 6, 1973, but successfully defended its borders. © BETTMANN/ CORBIS.

to recognize Israel's right to exist and denounced its denial of the rights of the Palestinians. Peace talks began shortly after the end of the 1973 Arab-Israeli War, but the Arab refusal to recognize Israel was a major obstacle.

Since 1948, Egypt had been a leading force against Israel, but by the mid–1970s Egyptian president Anwar Sadat (also spelled al-Sadat; 1918–1981) realized that his country lacked the resources to continue with nearly constant armed conflict. Sadat flew to the city of Jerusalem, which was under Israeli control, and gave a speech expressing his desire for peace. He was the first Arab leader to set foot on Israeli soil. Israeli prime minister Begin responded that he, too, desired peace. Peace talks soon followed. In September 13, 1978, U.S. president Jimmy Carter (1924–) met with the two sides at the U.S. presidential retreat at Camp David in the state of Maryland in the United States. Over a period of thirteen days the three leaders forged an agreement called the Camp David Accords. They shook hands and signed the agreement in Washington, D.C., on September 17, 1978. The Camp David Accords set the framework for the groundbreaking 1979 Egypt-Israel Peace Treaty, in which Egypt became the first Arab nation to recognize Israel as a state, and as a result, it regained the Sinai Peninsula and the Suez Canal. Sadat and Begin were both awarded Nobel Peace Prizes and were praised worldwide for their contributions to peace in the Middle East. Despite the gains made by his efforts, Sadat was condemned by many Egyptians for recognizing Israel, and Egypt was expelled from the Arab League for a decade. The Arab nations of the Middle East were never again as unified as they had been before the 1970s.

For More Information

BOOKS

Cleveland, William L. *A History of the Modern Middle East*, 3rd ed. Boulder, CO: Westview Press, 2004.

Farsoun, Samih K., with Christina E. Zacharia. *Palestine and the Palestinians.* Boulder, CO: Westview Press, 1997.

Gunderson, Cory Gideon. *The Israeli-Palestinian Conflict.* Edina, MN: Abdo, 2004.

Kort, Michael. *The Handbook of the Middle East.* Brookfield, CT: Twenty-First Century Books, 2002.

Miller, Debra A. *The Arab-Israeli Conflict.* San Diego, CA: Lucent Books, 2005.

Rabinovich, Itamar. *The Lingering Conflict: Israel, Arabs, and the Middle East, 1948–2011.* Washington, DC: Brookings Institution Press, 2011.

Shlaim, Avi. *Israel and Palestine: Reappraisals, Revisions, Refutations.* London: Verso, 2009.

Smith, Charles D., ed. *Palestine and the Arab-Israeli Conflict: A History with Documents*, 4th ed. Boston, MA: Bedford/St. Martin's, 2001.

"The Suez Crisis: An Affair to Remember." *The Economist* (July 27, 2006). Available online at http://www.economist.com/node/7218678 (accessed on November 30, 2011).

WEB SITES

"Middle East: History in Maps." *BBC News.* http://news.bbc.co.uk/2/hi/middle_east/7380642.stm (accessed on November 30, 2011).

"Israel and the 1948 War." *The History Learning Site.* http://www.historylearningsite.co.uk/israel_and_the_1948_war.htm (accessed on November 30, 2011).

"The Six-Day War." *Six-Day War.co.* http://www.sixdaywar.co.uk/ (accessed on November 30, 2011).

7

Israeli-Palestinian Relations: 1973 to 2011

In 1948 the country of Israel was established, and it almost immediately went to war with neighboring Arab countries who did not recognize the legitimacy of the Jewish nation. (Arabs are people who speak the Arabic language or who live in countries in which Arabic is the dominant language.) During the 1948 Arab-Israeli War, many Palestinians (an Arab people whose ancestors lived in the historical region of Palestine, comprising parts of present-day Israel and Jordan, and who continue to lay claim to that land) who were living on the land that became Israel became refugees. (Refugees are people who flee their country to escape violence or persecution.) More than twenty years later, Israel went to war with its Arab neighbors again in the 1967 Arab-Israeli War, this time seizing land from some of those neighbors. The Israelis began establishing Jewish settlements (communities established and inhabited in order to claim land) on the lands they now occupied.

The Palestinians not only felt that their homes and livelihoods had been stolen from them by the Israelis, but they also felt increasingly abandoned by the Arab nations that had once promised to protect them. They wanted to fight against the Israeli occupation of their lands, but unlike Israel, they were poor and unorganized and had few resources to build any kind of defense force. The Palestinians eventually organized and began to fight the large and powerful military forces of Israel with whatever means they could find, from throwing stones to guerrilla warfare (combat tactics used by a smaller, less equipped fighting force against a more powerful foe) and terrorist acts, such as hijacking planes and kidnapping people. They also gathered in peaceful protest movements and waged campaigns to alert the world of their plight. Despite grave disagreements and frequent incidents of violence, the Israelis and the Palestinians began a slow movement toward peace by the end of the twentieth century. In the early twenty-first century, however, relations deteriorated, and the result was a series of violent uprisings and small wars, with little or no progress toward a peaceful solution.

WORDS TO KNOW

Arab League: A regional political alliance of Arab nations formed in 1945 to promote political, military, and economic cooperation within the Arab world.

Arabs: People of the Middle East and North Africa who speak the Arabic language or who live in countries in which Arabic is the dominant language.

Fatah: A Palestinian militant group and political party dedicated to the establishment of an independent Palestinian state.

Geneva Conventions: A series of international agreements that establish how prisoners of war and civilians in wartime are to be treated.

guerilla warfare: Combat tactics used by a smaller, less equipped fighting force against a more powerful foe.

Hamas: A Palestinian Islamic fundamentalist group and political party operating primarily in the West Bank and the Gaza Strip with the goal of establishing a Palestinian state and opposing the existence of Israel. It has been labeled a terrorist organization by several countries.

Holocaust: The mass murder of European Jews and other groups by the Nazis during World War II.

Intifada: The Palestinian uprising against Israeli occupation in the West Bank and the Gaza Strip.

Irgun Zvai Leumi: A militant underground group founded in 1931 that worked to secure Israeli independence by staging violent attacks on British and Arab targets. Also known simply as Irgun.

mandate: A commission granting one country the authority to administer the affairs of another country. Also describes the territory entrusted to foreign administration.

martyr: A person who dies for his or her religion.

militia: Armed civilian military forces.

Muslim Brotherhood: An Islamic fundamentalist group organized in opposition to Western influence and in support of Islamic principles.

occupation: The physical and political control of an area seized by a foreign military force.

occupied territories: The lands under the political and military control of Israel, especially the West Bank and Gaza Strip.

Palestine: A historical region in the Middle East on the eastern shore of the Mediterranean Sea, comprising parts of present-day Israel and Jordan.

Palestine Liberation Organization (PLO): A political and military organization formed to unite various Palestinian Arab groups with the goal of establishing an independent Palestinian state.

Palestinian Authority (PA): The recognized governing institution for Palestinians in the West Bank and the Gaza Strip, established in 1993. Also known as the Palestinian National Authority.

Palestinians: An Arab people whose ancestors lived in the historical region of Palestine and who continue to lay claim to that land.

pogrom: A racially-motivated riot in which mobs, usually organized and sanctioned by the state, attack a minority group, most often Jews.

refugees: People who flee their country to escape violence or persecution.

right of return: The right, claimed by a dispossessed people, to return to their historic homeland.

settlements: Communities established and inhabited in order to claim land.

suicide bombing: An attack intended to kill others and cause widespread damage, carried about by someone who does not hope to survive the attack.

Shifting tides in Israeli politics

For the first twenty-five years of their country's existence, the people of Israel enjoyed an unusual level of agreement on key political issues. They agreed that Israel had the right to exist in its current borders; they agreed that all Israeli citizens had the right to vote; and most embraced the idea that they were a tolerant nation that valued basic human and civil rights. Many Israelis had fled persecution, whether from the Holocaust (the mass murder of European Jews and other groups by the Nazis during World War II [1939–45]) or from anti-Semitic (prejudice against Jews) discrimination in eastern Europe, where pogroms and other abusive treatment frequently occurred. (A pogrom is a racially-motivated riot in which mobs, usually organized and sanctioned by the state, attack a minority group, most often Jews.) In their new nation, Israelis established a law of return, whereby anyone of Jewish ancestry could immigrate to Israel and become a citizen there. In founding a Jewish nation, Israelis strove to establish a democratic nation free of the discrimination and persecution that Jews had endured for centuries.

In 1967 Israel's victory in the 1967 Arab-Israeli War changed the way Israelis and the rest of the world perceived the young country. Tensions between Israel and its Arab neighbors, mainly due to Palestinian attacks being launched against Israel by Palestinians in those countries, had increased to the point that Israel felt war was inevitable. To gain military advantage, Israel attacked first, and by the end of the brief war had seized the West Bank (an area between Israel and Jordan on the west bank of the Jordan River) from Jordan, the Golan Heights (a mountainous region located northwest of the Sea of Galilee) from Syria, and the entire Sinai Peninsula from Egypt. While Israel had hoped to expand its borders slightly to improve its security, capturing this much territory was an unexpected event. Moderate Israelis believed that Israel should use the seized territory to negotiate for peace with its Arab neighbors. They envisioned an exchange of land for peace. However, to some of Israel's deeply religious conservatives, many of whom were in the military, the capture of these lands fulfilled a dream that Israel would one day dominate on both sides of the Jordan River. From 1967 on, the question of what Israel should do with the captured land became a disruptive issue among Israelis.

The Israeli government originally decided to govern the newly acquired territory with military troops. Thus these lands, particularly the

West Bank and the Gaza Strip (a narrow strip of land along the Mediterranean Sea on the Sinai Peninsula), became known as the occupied territories (lands under the political and military control of Israel). From the very beginning of the occupation, Israel restricted the rights of the Arab residents of these areas. They were unable to travel freely, some were harassed or arrested by soldiers, and they were not allowed to cross the border into Jordan. At first, Palestinians living in the occupied territories had little contact with the outside world and lacked political organization. As the occupation stretched into the 1970s and early 1980s, however, small militant groups united and organized Palestinians to fight back.

The Palestinians organize

Palestinians refused to submit to life ruled by Israel in the occupied territories. They sought their own state in their former lands and held two objectives they considered vital to peace: the right of return (the right, claimed by a dispossessed people, to return to their historic homeland) and control of the holy city of Jerusalem. Both goals were unacceptable to Israel.

By the 1960s, the scattered Palestinians began to form structures to represent themselves. The Palestine Liberation Organization (PLO), a political and military organization formed to unite various Palestinian Arab groups with the goal of establishing an independent Palestinian state, was established in 1964 by the Arab League (a regional political alliance of Arab nations formed in 1945 to promote political, military, and economic cooperation within the Arab world). The Arab League appointed a moderate Palestinian, Ahmad Shuqayri (1908–1980), to lead the group. By 1968 Shuqayri's policies were deemed too moderate for many Palestinians who were unhappy about being unable to return to their homes in Palestine, and he was removed from power.

Leaders, such as Yasser Arafat (1929–2004) of the group Fatah (a Palestinian militant group and political party dedicated to the establishment of an independent Palestinian state) and George Habash (1926–2008) of the Popular Front for the Liberation of Palestine (PFLP), battled for control over the PLO after Shuqayri's removal. Although these groups differed on other matters, both believed in launching constant guerrilla attacks against Israel in order to retake Palestinian land and return refugees to their homes. In 1969 Arafat was named chairman of the PLO, a role he held until his death in 2004.

The Right of Return

During the 1948 Arab-Israeli War, an estimated 750,000 Palestinians who lived in the area of conflict either fled from the violence or were driven from their homes by the powerful Jewish militias. (A militia is an armed civilian military force.) Entire villages were emptied. The Palestinians referred to the war and the refugee crisis that followed as *al-Nakba* (an Arab word meaning "the catastrophe"). Most of the refugees went to the Gaza Strip in Egypt and the West Bank in Jordan; others went to Syria and Lebanon. Two decades later, the 1967 Arab-Israeli War forced an estimated 300,000 more Palestinians to flee their homes as Israeli forces seized the Sinai Peninsula, including the Gaza Strip, from Egypt; the West Bank from Jordan, and the Golan Heights from Syria.

As of the early twenty-first century, many of the refugees of the two wars remained in overcrowded refugee camps in Jordan, Syria, Lebanon, the West Bank, and the Gaza Strip. Their descendants are also considered refugees, and the total number of refugees has multiplied to an estimated 4.8 million people.

Since their flight or forced removal from what is now Israel, Palestinians have consistently called for the right of return; that is, they contend that they have the legal and moral right to return to their old homes and villages in present-day Israel and to take possession of what was once theirs. Many Palestinians still have the deeds (proof of ownership) to the houses they left behind. Some even keep the keys to their houses, even though half a century has passed and the houses are probably gone now. The Palestinians cite as a legal basis for the right of return the 1948 United Nations Resolution 194, which states that Palestinian "refugees wishing to return to their homes and live at peace with their neighbours should be permitted to do so at the earliest practicable date, and that compensation should be paid for the property of those choosing not to return," as quoted by Ami Isseroff on the *MidEastWeb Gateway* Web site. (The United Nations is an international organization of countries founded in 1945 to promote international peace, security, and cooperation.)

Most Israelis—both those who favor peaceful negotiations with the Palestinians and those who favor military solutions—steadfastly deny the Palestinian concept of right of return. There are practical reasons for this. Arabs greatly outnumber Jews in the region, and on all sides of Israel, Arab countries have openly called for the new nation's destruction. The early borders established by Israel left it exposed to attack. As the borders were set in 1949, Israel was only about 14 miles (22.5 kilometers) wide at its narrowest point, making security efforts difficult. In 2011 there were 5.8 million Jews compared to 1.6 million Arabs in Israel. If 4.8 million Palestinian refugees were to take up residence in Israel through a right of return, they would form the majority, and the Israeli dream of a Jewish state would be lost.

ISSEROFF, AMI. "MIDEASTWEB HISTORICAL DOCUMENTS UNITED NATIONS GENERAL ASSEMBLY RESOLUTION 194." *MIDEASTWEB GATEWAY.* HTTP://WWW.MIDEASTWEB.ORG/194.HTM (ACCESSED ON NOVEMBER 30, 2011).

Black September

After 1967, when the Israeli occupation of the West Bank and the Gaza Strip made it too dangerous for PLO leaders to live in the occupied territories, the PLO established a large base in Jordan. There, the PLO brought together a wide range of militants who were willing to use extreme measures to regain land from Israel. They launched persistent guerrilla attacks on Israel from within Jordanian borders. As actions against Israel increased, the PLO became a major problem for Jordan's leaders, particularly King Hussein I (1935–1999), who did not want another war with Israel. PLO leaders ignored most of Jordan's laws and rejected Hussein's request that they stop launching attacks on Israel from Jordan.

In September 1970 the PFLP hijacked four airliners full of passengers and diverted them to Jordanian airstrips. While many in Jordan supported the right of the Palestinians to fight for their land, most did not like the idea of Jordan being connected with acts of terrorism, such as hijacking. King Hussein used this event to gain public support for driving the PLO out of Jordan. Over the next several weeks the Jordanian army attacked Palestinian refugee camps, killing civilians and PLO leaders alike. Between September 15 and September 25, three thousand Palestinians were killed and the leadership of the PLO was forced out of the country, eventually relocating in Lebanon and Syria. This event came to be known among Palestinians as Black September. Jordan's expulsion of the PLO brought greater stability to its relations with Israel, but it drove some Palestinians to more extreme ways of drawing attention to their cause.

One of the most notorious examples of Palestinian terrorism of this era occurred at the Olympic Games in Munich, Germany, in September 1972. It was carried out by eight armed members of a Palestinian group calling itself Black September, named after the events that forced the PLO out of Jordan. The members of Black September stormed the apartments of the Israeli Olympic team. They shot and killed two team members and took nine hostages. The group demanded the release of more than two hundred Palestinians held in Israeli jails in exchange for the release of its hostages. Israeli officials refused to negotiate with Black September, fearing that giving in to the group's demands would encourage more violent acts. During a rescue attempt by German police, Black September murdered the hostages, and the police killed five of the Black September members. Israel retaliated by bombing PLO headquarters in Syria and Lebanon and by authorizing its secret service, Mossad, to assassinate key Palestinian political figures.

After the PLO was expelled from Jordan in 1970, a Palestinian militant and member of Fatah known as Abu Nidal (also known as Sabri al-Banna; 1937–2002) began to lead attacks on Israel, which became so disruptive that he brought more contempt than sympathy to the Palestinians and their cause. By 1974 he was expelled from the PLO (to which Fatah belonged). Thereafter he and the operatives who worked with him in his own organization, which came to be known as the Abu Nidal Organization (ANO), attacked the PLO, as well as Israel. Authorities believe that Abu Nidal masterminded the murder or wounding of over nine hundred people in twenty countries from the 1970s to the 1990s.

The rise of settlements

In 1977 Israeli politics shifted dramatically when the Labor Party, a liberal political party that had dominated Israel since its creation, was voted out of power. At this time the conservative Likud Party allied with the ultraconservative Herut Party to form a new government. They chose Menachem Begin (1913–1992) as their prime minister, a controversial choice considering that Begin had been a part of Irgun Zvai Leumi, a military group that used violence in the 1940s to promote the creation of an independent Jewish nation.

Begin called for the annexation (addition) of the occupied territories to the country of Israel, but he knew there was not enough support in Israel for this goal. Annexation was further complicated by other countries that wanted Israel to return the land it had taken in the 1967 Arab-Israeli War for the sake of peace in the region. Begin decided to try another tactic: the building of Jewish settlements in the occupied territories. Begin hoped that over time, with enough Jewish settlements, he could make a case for annexing the territories to protect the interests of the Jewish settlers living there. His plan became one of the most controversial issues in Israeli history.

Jewish settlers soon began to move onto lands in the West Bank, East Jerusalem, the Gaza Strip, and the Golan Heights, where they created self-sustaining communities where only Jews had jobs and access to services. One settlement was also established in the occupied Sinai Peninsula. The Israeli government invested heavily in the construction, maintenance, and military protection of the settlements. Under this plan, the Jewish population in the occupied territories increased dramatically, rising from about 3,200 in 1977 to about 28,400 by 1983.

A Jewish settlement in the West Bank, seen through the barbed wire barrier of a security fence. © ANDY AITCHISON/IN PICTURES/CORBIS.

Jews living in the occupied territories had all the same rights as citizens of Israel, while the Palestinians living there had few rights. Many Israelis wondered how Israel could promote itself as a tolerant democracy, yet deny basic citizenship rights to Palestinians under its control. Palestinians living in the occupied territories were segregated, or separated, from Jewish residents in nearby settlements. They were often prohibited from using the settlements' roads and other assets, such as schools, medical clinics, roads, electricity grids, and water pipes. The Palestinians' travel was restricted. They were frequently denied building permits by the Israeli administration, which resulted in their inability to build or repair their own homes, schools, and roads. To ensure that the Jewish settlements were secure, Palestinians were required to arrange for military coordination (ask the military to watch over them) in order to go to their own farmlands if those lands were near a Jewish settlement.

When the Israeli administrators denied this coordination, it often meant that the Palestinians lost crops.

Jewish settlements in the occupied territories changed the relationship between Israelis and Palestinians dramatically. Resenting the presence of Jewish settlers on their land, Palestinians attacked them, which in turn brought retaliation from Israeli soldiers. Jewish settlers were also allowed by the Israeli government to take aggressive actions against Palestinians; in numerous cases, settlers shot at or bombed Palestinians. The Israeli military increased its presence to protect the Jewish settlers, creating harsh and oppressive conditions for Palestinians. Because Palestinians did not have the same rights as citizens, the military could detain Palestinians for months without charging them with a crime, and it often deported them from the territories. Israel also built roads to connect the Jewish settlements to Israel but did not let Palestinians use these roads.

Other countries around the world never accepted Israel's settlements in the occupied territories, because they violate the Geneva Conventions, a series of international agreements that establish how prisoners of war and civilians in wartime are to be treated. Article 49 of the Geneva Conventions prohibits an occupying power from moving its own civilian population onto occupied lands as permanent residents. Israel is one of the many countries that signed and agreed to abide by the Geneva Conventions. In 1997 the United Nations General Assembly stated in Resolution 52/66 that "Israeli settlements in the Palestinian territory, including Jerusalem, and in the occupied Syrian Golan are illegal and an obstacle to peace and economic and social development." (The United Nations is an international organization of countries founded in 1945 to promote international peace, security, and cooperation.)

War in Lebanon

After being evicted from Jordan, the PLO leadership relocated to southern Lebanon in the 1970s. Lebanon was home to some three hundred thousand Palestinian refugees, most of whom lived in camps in Beirut and in the south of the country, along its border with Israel. Lebanon seemed at first to be the perfect place for the PLO, because the Lebanese government granted the PLO almost complete control over governance in the refugee camps. In return, the Lebanese government asked the PLO to seek its consent for raids into Israel. The PLO, however, rarely consulted with the Lebanese government before firing artillery shells

Jerusalem

Jerusalem, in present-day Israel, is cherished as a holy city by three major religions: Judaism, Christianity, and Islam. In the tenth century BCE, Solomon, king of the ancient Jewish kingdom, built a temple in Jerusalem. It was later destroyed and a second temple was built on the same site. This site remained the center of Judaism even after the second temple was destroyed and the Jewish people were driven from the land. Jerusalem became a center of Christianity after Jesus Christ was crucified in Jerusalem around 33 CE. The Church of the Holy Sepulchre was built in Jerusalem in 330 at the site of the crucifixion and may also be Christ's burial place. When the Muslims conquered Palestine in the seventh century, they too revered Jerusalem as a holy place. This was partly because they viewed the prophets of Judaism and Christianity as important prophets of Islam. Also, according to Muslim holy texts, the prophet Muhammad (c. 570–632) began his ascent to heaven from Jerusalem. The Muslims built Al-Aqsa Mosque and the Dome of the Rock at the site of the Jewish temple ruins on Temple Mount and consider Jerusalem the third-holiest Muslim city. (The Temple Mount is a contested religious site in Jerusalem. It is the holiest site in Judaism, the third holiest site in Islam, and also important to the Christian faith.)

Jerusalem was not a large city throughout most of its long history. By the last quarter of the nineteenth century, its population was only about ten thousand people. At that time, Jews following the dream of establishing a Jewish community began to arrive in the city. They built neighborhoods outside the walls of the part of Jerusalem known as the Old City, where the population was mainly Arab. Under the British mandate (administrative authority) of Palestine, the Jewish population continued to grow.

In 1947 the United Nations (UN) proposed that Palestine be divided into Jewish and Arab states. The city of Jerusalem, because it was so cherished by the various religions and groups, was to be placed under special international protection and administered by the UN.

In the 1948 Arab-Israeli War, Israel gained control of the western part of Jerusalem. Jordan maintained control of the Old City and other East Jerusalem neighborhoods, as well as the West Bank. Eighteen years later during the 1967 Arab-Israeli War, Jerusalem fell entirely under Israeli control. At the time, there were twenty-eight Arab towns and villages in East Jerusalem but only a few hundred Jews lived there. Nevertheless, after gaining control of the whole city, Israel moved its capital from Tel Aviv to Jerusalem and in 1980 declared Jerusalem its

across the border into Israel or sending armed groups to attack military targets and civilians.

The Israeli military responded to these attacks by striking back against PLO targets in southern Lebanon and by sending assassins to kill Palestinian leaders in the Lebanese capital of Beirut, well north of the Lebanese-Israeli border. By the mid–1970s the nearly constant battles along the Lebanese-Israeli border had become extremely disruptive to politics in Lebanon, a country that was already dealing with religious and capital. However, most other countries, including the United States, do not recognize Jerusalem as Israel's capital and continue to operate their embassies in Tel Aviv.

Jewish settlers have been moving into East Jerusalem since it was occupied by Israel in 1967. The number of Jews living on that land almost quadrupled between 1993 and 2010. In the first decade of the twenty-first century, East Jerusalem was approximately 43 percent Jewish and 57 percent Arab.

While Israel has remained firm about keeping all of Jerusalem as its capital, the Palestinians are equally resolved that East Jerusalem must be returned to the Arabs. Their plans for a Palestinian state in the West Bank and the Gaza Strip always feature East Jerusalem as its capital.

The city of Jerusalem cherished as a holy city by the three major monotheistic religions, Judaism, Christianity, and Islam.
© LANCE NELSON/CORBIS.

cultural problems. The large population of Palestinian refugees was one of the conflicts that led to the Lebanese civil war in 1975. The war would last for fifteen years and cost hundreds of thousands of lives. (For more on the Lebanese civil war, see **Syria and Lebanon: 1936 to 1990.**)

The PLO continued to use southern Lebanon as a base for its attacks on Israel even during Lebanon's civil war. In 1978 members of Fatah hijacked an Israeli tourist bus. The violent hijacking, one of the worst up to that time, resulted in the deaths of thirty-eight Israelis, including thirteen children. Outraged Israeli leaders launched Operation Litani, sending more than twenty thousand troops into southern Lebanon in an attempt to destroy the PLO. In the attack Israel Defense Forces (IDF) troops killed several thousand Palestinians, but most were civilians, and the PLO leadership remained intact. The violent attack accomplished little and led to increased Arab support for the PLO. Despite international calls for Israel to withdraw its troops from Lebanon, the Israeli forces evicted both Palestinians and Lebanese Muslims from villages along the southern border in order to establish a buffer zone (a neutral area separating two hostile countries) for their troops to occupy between Lebanon and Israel. Lebanon, engulfed in civil war at this time, was powerless to change the actions of the Israelis or the Palestinians.

PLO leader Yasser Arafat (left) walks with an aide in Beirut, Lebanon, in 1982.
© BETTMANN/CORBIS.

In 1982 Begin's government launched another attack on Lebanon called Operation Peace for Galilee. Its objective was to push the PLO in southern Lebanon back far enough from the Israeli borders so its rockets would no longer threaten Israeli settlements near the border. Forces overseen by Israel's then–defense minister Ariel Sharon (1928–) advanced quickly across the southern third of Lebanon and then ranged well beyond the area needed to ensure Israel's security. They advanced to Beirut, where an estimated fifteen thousand PLO troops were assembled in fortified areas. For ten weeks, the Israelis subjected the Palestinian portions of West Beirut to bombings launched by land, air, and sea. The bombings took the lives of many civilians and ended only when France, United States, and Italy intervened. Under an agreement arranged with international peacekeeping forces, about fourteen thousand PLO fighters left Lebanon. Tunisia became the new PLO headquarters. Israel then withdrew the majority of its troops into its buffer zone in the south of Lebanon.

The war, however, was not yet over. When Lebanese president elect Bashir Gemayel (1947–1982) was assassinated in 1982, Israel sent its armies back into West Beirut. Gemayel had been a leader of the Lebanese Front, a powerful Christian Lebanese militia group that had become allied with Israel in its quest for power in Lebanon. (A militia is an armed civilian military force.) Initially seeking Gemayel's killer, on September 16, 1982, units of the Lebanese Front militia entered the Sabra and Shatila refugee camps outside Beirut. There, over a period of three days, they brutally massacred approximately one thousand Palestinian men, women, and children. During the massacre, Israeli troops surrounded the camps. While it is uncertain how much the Israeli military participated in the massacre, it is clear that they did little to stop it. An Israeli investigation later found Sharon indirectly responsible for the killings. He was forced to resign his commission as minister of defense, but he remained in the government and in 2000 would become Israel's prime minister.

When news of the massacre reached Israeli civilians, public support for Israel's war in Lebanon disappeared. By 1983 Begin was forced to withdraw the majority of Israeli troops from Lebanon, although a security force remained in the southern half of the country until 2000. Israel's war in Lebanon had been a disaster. It failed to destroy the PLO; Lebanon remained politically unstable and eventually fell under the strong influence of Syria (one of Israel's enemies); and Israel was criticized by other nations for its cruelty and excessive violence. In Israel, popular outrage at the military and public relations disaster forced Begin from office.

The First Intifada

By the mid–1980s two decades of continual small conflicts, protests, attacks, and retaliations had left Israelis and Palestinians locked in a dispute that had no clear solution. Both sides were deeply troubled. The PLO leadership was mainly stationed at new headquarters in Tunisia, hundreds of miles away from the Palestinian people. In Israel divided support for the major parties forced the Labor and Likud parties to form a National Unity government that was unable to agree on political issues. Both the Palestinians and the Israelis sought to present themselves to the world as victims of wrongdoing by the other. A war of words emerged, in which any event that took place between the two countries would be described entirely differently by each side. Tensions grew and by the fall of 1987 violence between Israelis and Palestinians in the West bank and the Gaza Strip had increased.

An incident occurred in early December 1987 that at first did not stand out as unusual. In a traffic accident in a refugee camp in the Gaza Strip, an Israeli vehicle killed four Palestinian laborers. Rumors began to spread among Palestinians that the Israelis had planned the killings. At the laborers' funeral on December 9, built-up emotions erupted. A massive Palestinian protest demonstration spontaneously formed, directed at the Israeli security post in the camp. The Israeli troops reacted harshly, firing live ammunition and tear gas into the crowd, killing a young Palestinian man.

As word spread of the killing of the young man, thousands of Palestinians poured into the streets of the Gaza Strip to protest, and within days, similar protests erupted in the West Bank. Protestors were of all ages and both genders. Many threw rocks or used slingshots to hurl debris at Israeli soldiers to show their dissatisfaction with the military occupation. They called their movement the Intifada, an Arabic term meaning "a shaking off." After a later uprising, this event became known as the First Intifada.

The PLO, although not involved in starting the protest, began organizing it. Under the banner of the Unified National Leadership (UNL), the PLO published a fourteen-point description of the goals of the First Intifada. It called on Israel to stop stealing Arab land and building settlements in the occupied territories and to lift the restrictions and taxes that

A group of Palestinian boys throws stones to protest Israeli occupation of the occupied territories during the First Intifada.
© PATRICK ROBERT/SYGMA/CORBIS.

made life so difficult for Palestinians. (The Israeli military administration required its subjects to pay income, property, and consumer taxes.) Its most controversial goal, however, was the demand that Israel recognize the Palestinians' right to self-government in their own state.

Over the next several years, local leaders and distant PLO officials based in Tunisia worked together to draw the world's attention to their goal of self-government and to the conditions to which they were being subjected by the Israelis. Early in the uprising, Palestinian protesters had made the choice not to use military weapons against the Israelis; instead, they stood against their enemy with sticks, stones, and homemade weapons, such as Molotov cocktails (bottles filled with gasoline and stuffed with rags that are lit on fire and thrown at a target). The televised images of the First Intifada, especially a photo of a young Palestinian boy

The Intifada and Islamic Conservatism

Up until the First Intifada (a Palestinian uprising against Israeli occupation in the West Bank and the Gaza Strip) in 1987, conservative Islamic religious opinion played a small role in Palestinian politics. Since 1948, both religious and secular (nonreligious) Palestinians had been united in their desire to reclaim their homeland. The Palestine Liberation Organization (PLO), which served as the main leadership of the Palestinians, was a secular political organization.

In 1988, when PLO leader Yasser Arafat recognized Israel's right to exist and renounced the use of violence and terrorism, the PLO gained credibility in the international community and improved its bargaining position with Israel. To conservative Islamic groups, however, Arafat's new position seemed a betrayal of everything the Palestinian organizations were fighting for. These groups, most notably Hamas and Islamic Jihad, decided to pursue their own course apart from the PLO and to continue to use violence in their mission: the destruction of Israel.

Hamas was created in 1987 as an outgrowth of an Egyptian group called the Muslim Brotherhood, an Islamic fundamentalist group organized in opposition to Western influence and in support of Islamic principles. Hamas's leader, Sheikh Ahmed Yassin (c. 1937–2004), wanted Palestinians to have an alternative to the secular leadership of Arafat. The Hamas charter, which circulated in the Middle East in 1988, announced that it wanted to establish an Islamic state in the former Palestine and would not recognize any

Israeli claim to territory. Since its founding, Hamas has killed and injured hundreds of Israelis. Even though most world governments consider Hamas to be a terrorist organization, it continues to have many followers in the Middle East.

Islamic Jihad, the other main Palestinian Islamic conservative group that emerged during the years of the First Intifada, is smaller, poorly organized, and has less support from the Palestinian population than Hamas. The Syrian-supported Islamic Jihad has conducted several successful raids over the years. Its goals are virtually the same as those of Hamas.

These militant groups adhere to the idea that their religious mission is to destroy Israel and reclaim Palestine for Muslims. They are ready both to kill and to die as martyrs (people who die for their religion) for this mission. Until 1989, suicide bombings had not existed in the Israeli-Palestinian conflict. (A suicide bombing is an attack intended to kill others and cause widespread damage, carried about by someone who does not hope to survive the attack.) In 1989 Islamic Jihad claimed responsibility for a suicide bombing. The next known suicide bombing, in 1993, was attributed to Hamas and may have been that organization's first. This tactic, which would become common among militant Palestinians in the twenty-first century, allowed the bombers to penetrate deep into Israel to create havoc and murder in places once considered secure.

throwing a stone at a huge Israel tank, highlighted the drama of impoverished Palestinians fighting against well-armed IDF troops, helping to shift world public opinion to sympathize with the Palestinians. Alongside the protests, Palestinian leaders, especially Arafat, called repeatedly for the creation of a Palestinian state in the occupied territories. By the early 1990s Israeli officials, pressured by their own people, by world leaders, and by Palestinians protesting in the streets, began to consider this once-radical idea.

Negotiations begin

The First Intifada lingered on in protests, worker strikes, and refusals (refusing to pay taxes required by the Israeli government) into the early 1990s, but the pressure produced by the uprising began to reshape conditions between Israel and the Palestinians as early as 1988. That year, Arafat took a significant step toward negotiating with Israel: He stated that the PLO recognized the right of Israel to exist, and that the PLO renounced (gave up) terrorism. The PLO did not immediately act on these announcements, but this was a milestone in the organization's policy and tactics.

In return for his concessions, Arafat asked Israel to recognize the right of Palestinians to establish an independent state in the West Bank and the Gaza Strip. Israel refused, but it promised to engage in direct negotiations with the Palestinians for a peaceful solution to the conflict. These negotiations, it was agreed, should take place within a framework established by the United Nations in Security Council resolutions 242 and 338. These resolutions, issued in 1967 and 1973, respectively, recognized the right of people "to live in peace within secure and recognized boundaries free from threats or acts of force." They called for the removal of Israeli troops from the occupied territories and a resolution of the refugee problem and implored both sides to work for a "just and lasting peace."

Negotiations began in 1991 and continuing into 1993. Representatives of Israel and the Palestinians as well as other interested nations began to meet for discussions in Madrid, Spain, and elsewhere, including Washington, D.C. Little progress was made between Israel and the PLO, but the meetings led to a peace agreement between Israel and Jordan in 1994.

The Oslo Accords

Meanwhile, the Israelis, exhausted from years of war, elected Labor Party leader Yitzhak Rabin (1922–1995) as prime minister in 1992. His campaign platform was a pledge to strive for peace with the Palestinians, and he was willing to do what no Israeli leader had done in the past: to negotiate directly with representatives of the PLO. Secret high-level negotiations between the PLO and Israel began in Oslo, Norway, in early 1993.

The negotiators in Oslo reached a broad and unexpected set of agreements, called the Oslo Accords. First, the accords provided for mutual recognition. Israel recognized that the PLO was the representative of the Palestinian people, and the PLO formally agreed to Arafat's 1988 promise to recognize Israel and renounce terrorism. Second, a document known as the Declaration of Principles on Palestinian Self-Rule outlined a gradual process by which Israeli troops would withdraw from certain areas of the occupied territories and Palestinians would be granted self-rule under a temporary elected body called the Palestinian Authority (PA). The Gaza Strip and the West Bank, even though they are 25 miles (40 kilometers) apart, were recognized as a single territorial unit. Israeli troops would be stationed outside Palestinian population centers and would be allowed to maintain security for Jewish settlements. Several issues were not resolved, particularly the issue of who would control the city of Jerusalem or how it could be partitioned between interested parties. The negotiators of the Oslo Accords postponed that and other issues until later. Final talks were set for 1999, when it was hoped that the temporary self-government provisions could be made permanent.

Israeli prime minister Yitzhak Rabin and Shimon Peres at the signing of the Oslo Peace Accords. © PETER TURNLEY/ CORBIS.

On September 13, 1993, Arafat and Rabin shook hands to seal the Oslo Accords. The event took place on the lawn of the White House in Washington, D.C., orchestrated by U.S. president Bill Clinton (1946–). For their part in this historic agreement, Rabin, Arafat, and Israel's foreign minister Shimon Peres (1923–) were awarded the 1994 Nobel Peace Prize.

The Palestinian Authority

The Palestinian Authority (PA) was founded as a temporary elected body representing the stateless Palestinians. The Palestinians held a democratic election for the presidency of the PA in January 1996, and Arafat won easily. As agreed in the Oslo Accords, Israel pulled its troops out of specified areas in the West Bank and the Gaza Strip. By 1997 the PA controlled all of the Gaza Strip except for the Israeli settlements. The West Bank, however, had been divided into districts. In some districts the PA governed, in some Israel governed, and in others the PA had only limited authority. The PA established a court system; post office; military, intelligence, and police forces; and even a small Olympic team. Arafat ruled with a large council, but he never shared authority well and frequently ignored the decisions of his courts. By 1997 other Palestinian leaders called for reform.

The peace process did not advance as hoped. In 1995 Rabin was assassinated by a conservative Jewish man who believed that giving up Israeli land was a betrayal of the Jewish religion. Religious zealots on both sides used violence to disrupt progress toward peace. In 1994, for example, an Israeli settler named Baruch Goldstein (1956–1994) fired a gun at Palestinians praying in a mosque near the city of Hebron in the West Bank, killing twenty-nine people. Early in 1996, four suicide bombings in Israel, attributed to the Palestinian group Hamas, killed dozens and injured hundreds. (A suicide bombing is an attack intended to kill others and cause widespread damage, carried about by someone who does not hope to survive the attack.)

Frightened Israelis elected as prime minister Benjamin Netanyahu (1949–), a conservative Likud leader who promised that the security of Israel would be a top priority. During his term in office, Netanyahu did little to further the peace initiatives, although in 1998 Israel and the Palestinians signed the Wye River Memorandum, which resulted in another small withdrawal of Israeli troops from the West Bank and the

Gaza Strip. Netanyahu was defeated in the 1999 elections by Ehud Barak (1942–), who promised to restart the peace initiative.

At this point, the Palestinians were divided about the peace process and their leadership. Older and wealthier Palestinians supported Arafat, mainly because he used his power to provide them with privileges. But more conservative Islamic organizations criticized Arafat for negotiating with Israel, and younger Palestinians accused him of heading a corrupt organization that was out of touch with the needs of the people. Groups like Hamas and Islamic Jihad continued to conduct violent actions against Israeli targets, undermining Arafat's promises to stop Palestinian violence against Israelis. Although Arafat controlled the PA, he was unable to control the divided Palestinian people.

The Second Intifada

In July 2000 Arafat and Barak met with Clinton at Camp David, the American presidential retreat in Maryland, to address the unresolved issues from the Oslo Accords and prepare for a Palestinian state. Expectations for success were high on both sides. Barak agreed to a Palestinian state in the Gaza Strip and part of the West Bank, but he insisted that Israel remain in control of Jerusalem, offering the Palestinians only guardianship of some of the holy Muslim sites. This was unacceptable to the Palestinians, who wanted Jerusalem as their capital as well as recognition of the Palestinian refugees' right of return. The two sides could not agree, and to the dismay of Palestinians and Israelis alike, the negotiations failed.

One of the most hotly contested items in the Camp David talks was control over the Temple Mount, a holy site in Jerusalem. On September 28, 2000, Sharon led a group of security forces to the Temple Mount. Sharon was the leader of Israel's Likud Party at that time and well-known for his unbending dedication to Israeli security and his battlefield successes against Palestinian groups. In front of a crowd of reporters, Sharon claimed the Temple Mount as Israeli territory for eternity. Whether in response to this event or to the failure of the negotiations at Camp David, by the next day Palestinians were protesting and fighting with Israeli forces in the streets of Jerusalem. This was the beginning of the uprising called the Second Intifada.

The Second Intifada differed from the First Intifada in that the protesters used violent methods, and they were organized by Palestinian groups, like Hamas and Islamic Jihad, as well as by Arafat's original group, Fatah. The Palestinian groups used rocket attacks and suicide bombers to strike at Israeli targets. The IDF responded by using tanks, helicopters, and warplanes to strike at Palestinian targets. Israeli citizens responded to Palestinian violence and threats to their security at the polls by electing Sharon as prime minister in 2001.

Operation Defensive Shield

Sharon's election was viewed with concern by other countries around the world. Many observers and diplomats worried that Sharon and Arafat would not be able to stop the Second Intifada. Representatives of the United States, Russia, the European Union (EU; an economic and political association of European countries), and the United Nations created a plan they called "A Performance-Based Roadmap to a Permanent Two-State Solution to the Israeli-Palestinian Conflict" (which quickly gained the short name, Roadmap to Peace). The Roadmap to Peace proposed international support for ending violence, removing Israeli troops, and moving toward Palestinian statehood in the occupied territories. Although widely supported by Western nations, the plan was virtually ignored in Israel and among the Palestinians.

On March 27, 2002, Jewish guests, many of them elderly, at the Park Hotel in Netanya, Israel, were celebrating the Jewish holiday of Passover when a member of Hamas entered the room and detonated a bomb he was carrying. The explosion killed thirty Israelis and wounded more than one hundred others. Sharon ordered his troops to strike back against Palestinians, starting a massive initiative called Operation Defensive Shield.

Beginning on March 29, 2002, the IDF stormed into seven West Bank cities. It was the largest military offensive against Palestinians since the 1948 Arab-Israeli War. Israel used tanks, Apache attack helicopters, fighter jets, and well-armed ground troops. By April 21, much of the West Bank lay in ruins. An estimated 220 Palestinians had been killed, hundreds were wounded, and thousands had been arrested by the Israelis. Israeli tanks had entered the West Bank city of Ramallah in the early stages of the incursion and surrounded Arafat's compound there. He was not allowed to leave his compound until October 2004, when he flew to Paris, France, for medical treatment of an illness that has never been publicly identified. He died in a Paris hospital on November 11, 2004.

In June 2002, during Operation Defensive Shield, Israel began construction of a barrier between Israel and the West Bank in order to protect Israelis from suicide attacks and rockets. Much of the barrier consists of an electric fence surrounded by a patrol path and barbed wire. Where the barrier enters into cities or more populated areas, however, it consists of a tall concrete wall. According to Israel's plans, the barrier was scheduled to be between 450 and 500 feet (724 to 805 kilometers) long on completion. The barrier was still under construction when the International Court of Justice (a judicial court of the United Nations) ruled in 2004 that it violated the Geneva Conventions and infringed on Palestinians' human rights. For example, in some places the barrier displaced Palestinians from their homes, and/or required the destruction of Palestinian property. It created checkpoints that made travel difficult, and major parts of the wall were actually

The separation barrier between Israel and the West Bank. Israel began building this wall in 2002 as part of Operation Defensive Shield. ©MAHMOUD ILLEAN/DEMOTIX/DEMOTIX/CORBIS.

within the Palestinians' territory. The route of the barrier was designed to encompass areas in which Israel had built Jewish settlements in the West Bank since the 1970s. Despite the court ruling, Israel continued to build the wall, although it rerouted several areas in response to Palestinian complaints. In 2010 the barrier was about 65 percent completed, at about 320 miles (515 kilometers) long.

Unexpected changes

In 2004 Sharon surprised the world when he announced his disengagement plan, under which Israel would withdraw completely from the Gaza Strip, and partially from the West Bank. No one knows for certain why Sharon made this startling change from being one of the leading promoters of Jewish settlements in the occupied territories to ordering their dismantlement (destruction) in the Gaza Strip. One likely reason was that it was highly dangerous and difficult for Israeli security forces to protect the twenty-one scattered settlements in Gaza. The settlements in the West Bank and East Jerusalem were more valued by Israel, and the security forces could be put to better use there. Also, with mounting pressure from the international community to make even larger changes to Israel's policies, according to many authorities Sharon probably felt the loss of the Gaza Strip settlements was a small price to pay. Other experts believe he made the order strictly in the interest of Israeli security, which was always his primary goal. Despite an uproar from the conservatives in his own party who were furious at the idea of giving up any land, Sharon evacuated all of Israel's twenty-one settlements in the Gaza Strip and four in the West Bank. Some 9,480 Jewish settlers were expelled from the settlements, and their homes and businesses were destroyed.

In 2006 Sharon suffered a stroke that left him in a permanent coma. He was succeeded by Ehud Olmert (1945–). Meanwhile, Mahmoud Abbas (1935–), one of the cofounders of Fatah, had been elected president of the PA to replace Arafat. Abbas was elected on a moderate platform that promised to bring about Palestinian self-rule, reform the PA, and bring under control Palestinian groups that used violence against Israel. In 2006 the PA held long-postponed legislative elections (to elect their council, or parliament). Quite unexpectedly, Hamas, the Islamist organization that had long refused to recognize Israel or renounce violence against it, won an overwhelming majority of council seats, giving it the right to form the next government under Abbas.

Fatah and Hamas had never had friendly relations. For a time, the two parties attempted to work together, but less than a year after the election, violent fighting broke out between them. After a violent split, Hamas served as the sole ruler of the Gaza Strip and Fatah ruled in the West Bank for the next four years. The split in the PA changed the nature of relations between Israel and Palestine considerably. Israel's leaders refused to deal with Hamas and, for the most part, they supported the moderate Abbas.

A time of war

From the Gaza Strip, Hamas persistently launched across-the-border attacks on Israel. In September 2007 Israel labeled the Gaza Strip a hostile entity and began a blockade of the territory, restricting goods from going in or coming out. Israel controlled the ports and all other routes of entry and exit except for a 9-mile (14.5-kilometer) section of border that the Gaza Strip shares with Egypt. Egypt and Israel agreed that Egypt would only allow humanitarian supplies into the Gaza Strip, in an effort that Israel claimed was for the purpose of making sure the Palestinians did not acquire the materials needed to launch rocket attacks on Israel. Many analysts around the world theorized that Israel's real motive was to create problems between Hamas and the people of the Gaza Strip. Under the blockade, the Gaza Strip received only about one quarter of the goods it usually consumed, and the already frail economy of the territory deteriorated. Its unemployment rate became one of the highest in the world. Many observers claimed that the blockade created a humanitarian crisis (presented a critical threat to the health, safety, security, or well-being of a community).

Using secret tunnels between the Gaza Strip and Egypt, Hamas and other militants managed to get materials to make rockets and their strikes continued. In late December 2008 Israel launched an all-out air attack on Hamas facilities in the Gaza Strip, in a mission called Operation Cast Lead. Its air strikes destroyed government buildings, schools, hospitals, factories, and homes. This was followed by a ground attack in January. By the time a cease-fire was declared on January 18, the twenty-two-day assault had killed more than thirteen hundred people, and thousands more lost their homes. The strikes also destroyed 96 percent of the industry of the Gaza Strip; an estimated six hundred to seven hundred factories were destroyed. An estimated $1.9 billion worth of damage,

Smoke rises from the Gaza Strip after an Israeli air strike in January 2009. The strike was part of Israeli Operation Cast Lead.
PATRICK BAZ/AFP/GETTY IMAGES).

including homes, factories, businesses, mosques, roads, bridges, health facilities, water pipes, and much more, had occurred.

With its blockade and military campaign against the Gaza Strip, Israel drew increasing criticism from human-rights organizations and other observers worldwide. On May 31, 2010, a group of six hundred pro-Palestinian activists traveled aboard a flotilla (small fleet) of ships from Turkey to the Gaza Strip to deliver goods to the people there, defying the blockade. About 8 miles (12.9 kilometers) off the Israeli coast, the flotilla was stopped by Israeli commandos, who boarded the largest ship, the *Mavi Marmara*, from helicopters. The activists aboard the ship said the commandos began shooting as soon as they were aboard. The commandos, however, said the activists attacked them with clubs, knives, and even guns, forcing them to fire back in self-defense. Nine of the activists were killed, and thirty more wounded. Israel denied that any law was broken by its commandos but eased some of the restrictions of the blockade a month later. After Egypt overthrew its longtime leader, Hosni Mubarak (1928–) in 2011, it opened its border crossing with the Gaza Strip.

In April 2011 the two divisions of the PA, Fatah and Hamas, reached a reconciliation agreement, under which they would form a coalition government and then hold new elections in the Gaza Strip and the West Bank. (A coalition government is one in which political parties cooperate with each other, because no party holds the majority.) Israeli prime minister Netanyahu, who had begun his second term as prime minister in 2009, immediately announced that Israel would not

A map showing the location of Israeli settlements in the occupied territories, in 2011. MAP BY XNR PRODUCTIONS, INC./CENGAGE LEARNING.

negotiate with the PA as long as it included Hamas. Several weeks later, U.S. president Barack Obama (1961–) called for a new peace process. According to Obama, Israel must take the first steps toward peace by withdrawing to the borders it had prior to the 1967 Arab-Israeli War, using land swaps to make the new borders more acceptable to both parties. Netanyahu quickly rejected the idea, claiming that the 1967 borders were indefensible for Israel. He affirmed his long-held position: Israel would not consider allowing the return of the millions of Palestinians who were forced to flee their homes in Israel during the wars of the twentieth century, and it would never allow Jerusalem to be divided.

In 2011 the PA began work on a new quest for statehood, omitting Israel from the negotiations and instead applying directly to the United Nations for membership as a state. In September 2011 Abbas appeared before the United Nations Security Council to request recognition of a Palestinian state with pre-1967 borders. Although the Palestinians had the sympathy of many nations, the United States held that only negotiations between Israel and the Palestinians can bring about a Palestinian state and vowed to veto the Palestinian application. Most European nations planned to abstain if the vote made it to the Security Council, and most authorities predicted that the bid for membership in the UN as a state would soon fail. The bid stalled in November when the Security Council admissions committee failed to reach an agreement on the request. The UN appeal revealed increasing international support for the Palestinians, but according to many commentators, it provided no real answers to the problems that have beset Israeli-Palestinian relations over the last six decades.

For More Information

BOOKS

Cleveland, William L. *A History of the Modern Middle East.* 3rd ed. Boulder, CO: Westview Press, 2004.

Farsoun, Samih K., with Christina E. Zacharia. *Palestine and the Palestinians.* Boulder, CO: Westview Press, 1997.

Gunderson, Cory Gideon. *The Israeli-Palestinian Conflict.* Edina, MN: Abdo, 2004.

Journalists of Reuters. *The Israeli-Palestinian Conflict: Crisis in the Middle East.* Upper Saddle River, NJ: Prentice Hall, 2003.

Katz, Samuel M. *Jerusalem or Death: Palestinian Terrorism.* Minneapolis, MN: Lerner, 2004.

Kort, Michael. *The Handbook of the Middle East.* Brookfield, CT: Twenty-First Century Books, 2002.

Myre, Greg, and Jennifer Griffin. *This Burning Land: Lessons from the Front Lines of the Transformed Israeli-Palestinian Conflict.* Hoboken, NJ: Wiley, 2010.

Smith, Charles D., ed. *Palestine and the Arab-Israeli Conflict: A History with Documents.* 7th ed. Boston: Bedford/St. Martin's Press, 2009.

Wingate, Katherine. *The Intifadas.* New York: Rosen, 2004.

WEB SITES

Beinin, Joel, and Lisa Jajjar. "Palestine, Israel and the Arab-Israeli Conflict: A Primer." *Middle East Research and Information Project.* http://www.merip. org/palestine-israel_primer/intro-pal-isr-primer.html (accessed on November 30, 2011).

Grace, Francie. "Munich Massacre Remembered." *CBS News.* (February 11, 2009). http://www.cbsnews.com/stories/2002/09/05/world/main 520865.shtml (accessed on November 30, 2011).

Isseroff, Ami. "MidEastWeb Historical Documents United Nations General Assembly Resolution 194." *MidEastWeb Gateway.* http:// www.mideastweb. org/194.htm (accessed on November 30, 2011).

"Operation Cast Lead." *Global Security.org.* http://www.globalsecurity.org/military/ world/war/operation-cast-lead.htm (accessed on November 30, 2011).

"United Nations General Assembly Resolution 52/66: Israeli Settlements in the Territories, December 10, 1997." *Israel Ministry of Foreign Affairs.* http:// www.mfa.gov.il/MFA/Foreign+Relations/Israels+Foreign+Relations+since+ 1947/1996-1997/177+United+Nations+General+Assembly+Resolution+ 52-.htm?DisplayMode=print (accessed on November 30, 2011).

"United Nations Security Council Resolution 242, November 22, 1967." *MidEast Web Historical Documents.* http://www.mideastweb.org/242.htm (accessed on November 30, 2011).

"United Nations Security Council Resolution 338, October 22, 1973." *MidEast Web Historical Documents.* http://www.mideastweb.org/338.htm (accessed on November 30, 2011).

8

The Palestinian Authority: 2004 to 2011

By the end of the 1948 Arab-Israeli War, many Palestinians (an Arab people whose ancestors lived in the historical region of Palestine, comprising parts of present-day Israel and Jordan, and who continue to lay claim to that land) had become refugees. (Refugees are people who flee their country to escape violence or persecution.) To assist them with basic needs, such as shelter and food, the United Nations (UN) established the United Nations Relief and Works Agency for Palestine Refugees in the Near East (UNRWA) in 1949. (The UN is an association of countries formed in 1945 to promote peace, security, and cooperation between nations.) UNRWA, according to the organization's Web site, defines Palestinian refugees as "people whose normal place of residence was Palestine between June 1946 and May 1948, who lost both their homes and means of livelihood as a result of the 1948 Arab-Israeli conflict." By 1950, UNRWA was providing aid to 750,000 Palestinian refugees. After the Arab-Israeli War of 1967, in which Israel captured and then established a military occupation in the West Bank (an area between Israel and Jordan on the west bank of the Jordan River) and the Gaza Strip (a narrow strip of land along the eastern shore of the Mediterranean Sea, west of Israel and bordering Egypt in the southwest), a large wave of Palestinians fled or were expelled from their homes, and UNRWA set up ten more refugee camps to accommodate them.

Over time, fifty-eight recognized Palestinian refugee camps were established in Jordan, Syria, Lebanon, the West Bank, and the Gaza Strip. The camps generally separated the refugees from the rest of each country's population. The hosting Arab (Arabic-speaking) countries and the Palestinians themselves agreed that Palestinians should not permanently settle anywhere but their former homes in Palestine. Most Palestinians believe that they have the right to return to the land from which they or their ancestors fled. Israel has refused to repatriate the refugees

WORDS TO KNOW

Arabs: People of the Middle East and North Africa who speak the Arabic language or who live in countries in which Arabic is the dominant language.

Arab Spring: A series of prodemocracy uprisings in the Middle East and North Africa.

authoritarianism: A type of leadership in which power is consolidated under one strong leader, or a small group of elite leaders, who do not answer to the will of the people.

Fatah: A Palestinian militant group and political party dedicated to the establishment of an independent Palestinian state.

Gaza Strip: A narrow strip of land along the eastern shore of the Mediterranean Sea, west of Israel and bordering Egypt in the southwest.

guerilla warfare: Combat tactics used by a smaller, less equipped fighting force against a more powerful foe.

Hamas: A Palestinian Islamic fundamentalist group and political party operating primarily in the West Bank and the Gaza Strip with the goal of establishing a Palestinian state and opposing the existence of Israel. It has been labeled a terrorist organization by several countries.

Hebrew: The ancient language of the Jewish people and the official language of present-day Israel.

Intifada: The Palestinian uprising against Israeli occupation in the West Bank and the Gaza Strip.

Islamism: A fundamentalist movement characterized by the belief that Islam should provide the basis for the political, social, and cultural life in Muslim nations.

mandate: A commission granting one country the authority to administer the affairs of another country. Also describes the territory entrusted to foreign administration.

Muslim Brotherhood: An Islamic fundamentalist group organized in opposition to Western influence and in support of Islamic principles.

occupation: The physical and political control of an area seized by a foreign military force.

occupied territories: The lands under the political and military control of Israel, especially the West Bank and Gaza Strip.

Palestine: A historical region in the Middle East on the eastern shore of the Mediterranean Sea, comprising parts of present-day Israel and Jordan.

Palestine Liberation Organization (PLO): A political and military organization formed to unite various Palestinian Arab groups with the goal of establishing an independent Palestinian state.

Palestinian Authority (PA): The recognized governing institution for Palestinians in the West Bank and the Gaza Strip, established in 1993. Also known as the Palestinian National Authority.

Palestinians: An Arab people whose ancestors lived in the historical region of Palestine and who continue to lay claim to that land.

refugees: People who flee their country to escape violence or persecution.

settlements: Communities established and inhabited in order to claim land.

suicide bombing: An attack intended to kill others and cause widespread damage, carried about by someone who does not hope to survive the attack.

West Bank: An area between Israel and Jordan on the west bank of the Jordan River.

(let them come back to their land), largely because there are so many of them. If all Palestinian refugees returned to their former homes, then the majority of the population in Israel would be Muslims. Most Israelis believed that this would put Israel's identity in peril, since it was specifically created to be the home of Jews.

The UNRWA definition of refugees also includes the descendants of the original Palestinian refugees who fled or were expelled from Palestine in the Arab-Israeli wars of 1948 and 1967. By 2011 more than 4.8 million Palestinians were considered refugees by UNRWA. According to the agency, about one third, or 1.4 million, of the Palestinian refugees live in refugee camps. The remaining two thirds live in and around the cities and towns of the host countries or regions. Scattered throughout the world, there are about 9 million people, both refugees and non-refugees, who consider themselves Palestinians.

Palestinians have been a people without their own country for well over half a century, but over the course of that time they formed a governmental body called the Palestinian Authority (PA), and they have acquired some, but not full, control of the Gaza Strip and the West Bank. In the twenty-first century, the PA became one of the first Arab governments to change its leadership through democratic processes.

The Palestinian Authority

In the first decades after the formation of Israel in 1948, the Palestinian refugees had little political organization or representation. Gradually they organized under the leadership of the Palestinian Liberation Organization (PLO), a political and military organization formed to unite various Palestinian Arab groups with the goal of establishing an independent Palestinian state. The PLO is an umbrella organization (one that brings together many smaller organizations with similar goals, so that they can share their skills and resources) founded in 1964 to coordinate the efforts of the different Palestinian groups that arose over the years to represent the Palestinian people and to fight Israel. One of the groups within the PLO was Fatah, a Palestinian militant group and political party. Fatah's leader, Yasser Arafat (1929–2004), became head of the PLO in 1969.

Shortly before Arafat became the leader of the PLO, Palestinians underwent a traumatic change. In the 1967 Arab-Israeli War (a short war fought between Israel and the Arab countries of Egypt, Jordan, and

Syria), Israel seized the West Bank from Jordan, the Golan Heights (a mountainous region located on the border of Syria and Israel, northwest of the Sea of Galilee) from Syria, and the entire Sinai Peninsula (including the Gaza Strip) from Egypt. These areas became known as the occupied territories, lands under the political and military control of Israel. The war caused an estimated three hundred thousand Arabs to flee from their homes in the occupied territories.

The 1967 Arab-Israeli War enraged Palestinians, and, Arafat, based at that time in Jordan, tried to organize a retaliatory guerrilla attack. (Guerrilla warfare is combat tactics used by a smaller, less equipped fighting force against a more powerful foe.) His effort failed, but angry young Palestinian men began signing up in large numbers to fight with the PLO. Guerrilla attacks launched against Israel from Jordan increased. As actions against Israel increased, the PLO became a major problem for Jordan's leaders, particularly King Hussein I (1935–1999), who did not want another war with Israel. PLO leaders ignored most of Jordan's laws and rejected Hussein's request that they stop launching attacks on Israel from Jordan. After a militant Palestinian group hijacked four airliners full of passengers and diverted them to Jordanian airstrips in September 1970, King Hussein gave orders to the Jordanian army to drive the PLO out of Jordan. Over the next several weeks the army attacked Palestinian refugee camps, killing civilians and PLO leaders alike. Between September 15 and September 25, three thousand Palestinians were killed and the leadership of the PLO was forced out of the country, eventually relocating in Lebanon and Syria. This event came to be known among Palestinians as Black September.

After being expelled from Jordan, Arafat moved the PLO headquarters to Lebanon, and then, in 1982, to Tunisia. From these bases, the PLO organized guerrilla attacks on Israel, as well as kidnappings, plane hijackings, and other violent crimes, causing many Western nations to label it a terrorist organization.

With the PLO leadership located so away from the occupied territories and the Israeli military rulers interested mainly in borders and security, the Palestinians living in the West Bank and the Gaza Strip began to carry out their own local rule. Without a real government, they created grassroots organizations (groups established and managed by citizens rather than a government). These organizations handled such things as charity, sports, student unions, and trade unions, and they were largely based on democratic principles.

In 1987, when tensions between the Palestinians and the Israeli occupying forces were high, the First Intifada, a largely nonviolent Palestinian uprising against Israeli occupation (the physical and political control of an area seized by a foreign military force), broke out throughout the West Bank and the Gaza Strip. Since Arafat and other PLO leaders were in Tunisia, most of the initial organizing of the uprising fell to local groups.

Arafat gathered his resources to regain his leadership of the Palestinians. From Tunisia, he inserted himself into the press coverage of the uprising. Despite being far away, he gradually gained some control over the Palestinians uprising Then, in 1988, after years of directing violence and terrorism at Israel, he made a historic about-face. In the name of the PLO, he recognized the right of Israel to exist and renounced (gave up) terrorism as a means of reaching a solution to the conflict. This led to the first real negotiations between Israelis and Palestinians.

The West Bank and the Gaza Strip

In 1993 the Oslo Accords, a broad set of agreements reached by Palestinian and Israeli negotiators, provided for mutual recognition between Israel and the Palestinian people and outlined a gradual process by which Israeli troops would withdraw from certain areas of the occupied territories and Palestinians would be granted self-rule under a temporary elected body called the Palestinian Authority (PA). The PA was to have authority over matters of security and police in the Gaza Strip and in about one third of the West Bank. Designed only as an interim (temporary) government, the PA was not a sovereign (self-governing) state. However, it was one of the stated goals of the Oslo Accords that the PA would achieve full statehood in the West Bank and the Gaza Strip by the end of 1999. Although the Oslo Accords were never fully realized and the PA did not achieve statehood, the PA became the acting government for the Palestinians in two geographically unconnected and culturally different areas: the West Bank and the Gaza Strip.

The West Bank is an area of about 2,300 square miles (5,957 square kilometers) lying to the west of Jordan across the Jordan River. It is otherwise surrounded by Israel, with coastline along the Dead Sea. In 2010 its population was 2,568,555. Like the rest of Palestine, the West Bank was part of the British mandate (territory entrusted to foreign administration) of Palestine from 1920 to 1948. In the 1948 Arab-Israeli War, Jordan captured the West Bank and annexed it (made it a permanent part of Jordan), ruling there for nearly two decades. When Israel captured the West Bank in the 1967 Arab-Israeli War, it opted not to annex it. Instead, Israel set up a military government there. One area of the West Bank that Israel did annex was East Jerusalem, and, despite the strong protest of the Palestinians who viewed East Jerusalem as their capital and a holy Muslim center, Jerusalem soon became Israel's national capital. However, most other countries, including the United States, do not recognize Jerusalem as Israel's capital and continue to operate their embassies in Tel Aviv.

The Gaza Strip is much smaller than the West Bank at 140 square miles (363 square kilometers). Twenty-six miles (41.8 kilometers) long and 7 miles (11.2 kilometers) wide, it is surrounded by Israel, Egypt, and the Mediterranean Sea. With a population of 1,657,155, it is one of the most densely populated places on Earth and has only one-fifteenth the area of the West Bank. Until 1967, the Gaza Strip was under Egyptian control, and Egypt had ruled it through a military governor. After the 1967 Arab-Israeli War, an Israeli military government was established there.

Under the Oslo Accords, the Gaza Strip and the West Bank were brought together in 1994 under the PA. The two regions, separated by 25 miles (40.2 kilometers) of land, were to be treated as a single entity, even though their histories and their cultures differ greatly. The West Bank had a healthy economy, a secular (nonreligious) local government, a well-educated middle class, and far fewer residents in refugee camps than the Gaza Strip. The West Bank also had universities, museums, and other sophisticated cultural institutions. Palestinian refugees who moved to the West Bank while it was under Jordan's control were offered citizenship and certain citizenship rights. Egypt had not offered similar rights to the refugees in the Gaza Strip. The Gaza Strip's economy was meager and a far larger proportion of its residents lived in refugee camps. There was a much stronger leaning toward Islamism (the belief that Islam should provide the basis for the political, social, and cultural life in Muslim nations) in the Gaza Strip than in the West Bank. Even though the outlook and customs of the people of these two regions differed in many ways, most people of both lands sought to be part of the new Palestinian state.

The PA under Arafat

After the Oslo Accords were signed in 1994, Arafat returned from Tunisia. In 1996 he was elected president of the PA, ruling the West Bank and the Gaza Strip from his headquarters in the city of Ramallah in the West Bank.

Arafat was popular for two seemingly contradictory reasons. He was one of the first and fiercest organizers of the armed struggle against Israel, and yet in later times he proved that he was able to negotiate with Israel. The Palestinians assumed their best hope was in a negotiated agreement in which they attained statehood, but at the same time, many Palestinians favored the use of whatever means of force was available to them to fight Israeli occupation. Arafat was seen by them as both freedom fighter and diplomat.

Under the Oslo Accords, the PA was designed to be a democracy. The president and the eighty-eight member Palestinian Legislative Council, Palestinians' parliament (legislature), had been elected by popular vote. However, it was not long before Arafat came to be seen by many as authoritarian (with power consolidated under one strong leader, or a small group of elite leaders, who do not answer to the will of the people) rather than a democratic leader. He gave important jobs to friends and family, arrested his opponents, and overruled the courts' decisions. His government was also suspected of corruption, with funds that were badly needed by the Palestinian people stolen by dishonest leaders. Arafat had long enjoyed widespread support, but within a few years of his return, many Palestinians were becoming disillusioned with him.

With Arafat back in the region, negotiations continued between the Israelis and Palestinians with the goal of creating an independent Palestinian state. Among the many areas of contention was the question of who would control East Jerusalem, which both sides refused to give up, as well as the steadily growing Jewish settlements, communities that were rapidly being built on the occupied territories, where the Palestinians hoped to build their new state.

In 2000 eagerly awaited negotiations between Israel and the PA unexpectedly broke down. A large Palestinian uprising, called the Second Intifada, followed. The protesters of the Second Intifada used violent methods. They were organized by Palestinian groups, like Hamas and Islamic Jihad, two militant Palestinian Islamist organizations that have been designated as terrorist groups by Western countries, as well as by the Al-Aqsa Brigade, a growing militia that claimed to be Fatah's military wing. These groups launched rocket attacks on Israeli targets, and expanded their operations with increasing use of suicide bombers. These individuals volunteered or were persuaded to strap bombs onto their bodies or vehicles. They then went into crowded public places in

Israel and detonated the bombs, killing themselves as well as the innocent Israeli bystanders around them. Suicide bombers created havoc and great fear in Israel's cities and countryside.

A Palestinian man uses a slingshot to hurl stones at Israeli police during the Second Intifada. The protestors of the Second Intifada used violent methods. DAVID SILVERMAN/ NEWMAKERS/GETTY IMAGES.

The Israel Defense Forces (IDF) responded to the Second Intifada violence with force. In a 2002 military raid known as Operation Defensive Shield, Israeli forces invaded the West Bank and the Gaza Strip and reoccupied the Palestinian cities and towns from which they had recently withdrawn under provisions of the Oslo Accords. More than two hundred Palestinians were killed in the invasion, and there was widespread destruction of buildings and homes. The IDF remained in the West Bank and the Gaza Strip, and they harshly restricted the daily lives of Palestinians, including Arafat, whose headquarters in Ramallah was surrounded by tanks.

In addition to blaming Israel for its fierce invasion, many Palestinians blamed the PA. They were frustrated that their government lacked the democracy they had expected, that their leaders were corrupt, and most of all, that they could not effectively stop Israel's occupation of the West Bank and the Gaza Strip.

Amid this chaos, Arafat died from an unknown illness in 2004. Although they mourned their leader, many Palestinians had been ready for a change even before Arafat's death. According to a 2004 public opinion poll cited by Robin Wright in *Dreams and Shadows: The Future of the Middle East*, "Eighty-seven percent of Palestinians surveyed believed that Arafat's government was corrupt and that its leaders were opportunists who became rich off their powers. Ninety-two percent wanted sweeping political reform of the Palestinian government."

Palestinians had looked forward to the prospect of democracy that had been established in the Oslo Accords and many took the promise of democracy very seriously. By the early twenty-first century, Palestinians tended to be better educated than many of their Middle Eastern counterparts, and they were familiar with the different forms of government and economic systems that could benefit their newly forming country. Furthermore, many Palestinians had worked or lived in Israel and, although they did not receive equal benefits under its laws, they witnessed Israel's democracy and its stable economy. Many young Palestinians wished for a similar government and economy for themselves. But these wishes had been delayed. Presidential and parliamentary elections had been scheduled for 2001 but the Second Intifada had interfered. It was not until March 2005, after Arafat's death, that representatives of several Palestinian groups met in Cairo, Egypt, to establish an election system.

The presidential election of 2005

In 2005 the long-delayed election was held to determine the next president of the PA. Arafat's political party, Fatah, presented two potential candidates: Marwan Barghouti (1959–) and Mahmoud Abbas (1935–). Barghouti was the most popular candidate for president, but there was one problem—he was in prison. Barghouti had been given to five life sentences by Israeli courts and ran his campaign from a jail in Israel. Barghouti had long been an activist. He had been exiled by the Israelis in the 1980s but returned to the West Bank in 1994. He strongly promoted the peace process, even going so far as learning to speak Hebrew (the ancient language of the Jewish people and the official language of present-day Israel) to converse better with the Israelis. He was also a highly successful local politician. Unlike many Fatah leaders, who isolated themselves from the Palestinian people, Barghouti worked among the people and was a skilled grassroots organizer. When the Second Intifada broke out in 2000, he joined the militant youth in the streets and quickly became a leader of the uprising. Arrested during the intifada by the Israelis, he was found guilty of having ordered the killings of Jewish settlers in the West Bank and condemned to five life sentences. While Israel viewed him as a militant and a murderer, most Palestinians viewed him as a hero. Even though he was a strong advocate of the peace negotiations with Israel, Barghouti always contended that the Palestinians had a right to resist, or use violent force against, the Israelis who occupied their territories. Barghouti's mixed message of both peacemaking and armed resistance made him very popular.

The other Fatah candidate, Abbas, was a founding member of Fatah and a longtime associate of Arafat's. He had been one of the chief Palestinian negotiators in talks that led to the Oslo Accords and had served briefly as prime minister of the PA in 2003. Upon Arafat's death, Abbas took over the leadership of the PLO. He was nearly seventy years old when he ran for president of the PA in 2005, and many observers noted that he did not connect with the younger generation of Palestinians as well as Barghouti did. Abbas denounced violence and was considered a moderate voice. Israel and the Western nations favored him, and many Palestinians placed their hope in his plans to continue negotiations with Israel while building up the institutions of a Palestinian state. In time Barghouti decided to endorse Abbas and withdrew from the election.

The Palestinians had another prominent political group: Hamas. The word *Hamas* is an acronym for Harakat al-Muqawama al-Islamiya,

(Islamic Resistance Movement), but the word also means "enthusiasm," or "zeal" in Arabic. Hamas modeled itself after the Muslim Brotherhood, an Islamic fundamentalist group organized in opposition to Western influence and in support of Islamic principles. The people of the Gaza Strip, in particular, were greatly influenced by the Muslim Brotherhood during the years that Egypt ruled there.

Hamas came into being during the First Intifada in 1987, and its activities intensified greatly during the Second Intifada of 2000. In its covenant, or founding document, Hamas pledges to make Islam the law of all of Palestine. It also vows to fight Israel and rejects all forms of negotiation. Article thirteen of the Hamas covenant states, "There is no solution for the Palestinian question except through Jihad [armed struggle]. Initiatives, proposals and international conferences are all a waste of time and vain endeavors. The Palestinian people know better than to consent to having their future, rights and fate toyed with."

From the time of the First Intifada, Hamas was committed to the destruction of Israel; Israel, in turn, was committed to the destruction of Hamas. During the 1990s, Hamas was responsible for many of the gruesome and deadly suicide bombings that terrorized Israeli civilians. The group's violence escalated in the Second Intifada, when they were responsible for large suicide bombings that killed dozens of Israeli civilians. Still, many Palestinians supported the group, probably due to their feeling of powerlessness against Israel. In 2004 Palestinians were outraged when Israeli forces in helicopters fired missiles at the wheelchair-bound Hamas spiritual leader Ahmed Yassin (1937–2004), killing him instantly. He was one of several Hamas leaders the Israelis targeted for assassination at the time.

Although Hamas's violent attacks on Israeli targets were what made the organization known in the West, armed resistance was only a small part of Hamas's mission. Hamas has a huge nonmilitary wing that has provided critical social services in hard-hit refugee camps for many years. According to Beverly Milton-Edwards and Stephen Farrell in *Hamas*:

> In these sinks of poverty Hamas's non-military wings provide the food, medical services, clothing, books, schooling, orphanages, kindergartens, summer camps and other social services which are the bedrock of its success. . . . It eventually grew into a shadow state which supplemented—and in many cases rivaled—the services provided by the official PA, the United Nations and humanitarian organizations.

Hamas was established as an organization of armed resistance and social aid, not as a political party. Hamas chose not to field a candidate for the presidential election of 2005 and called for a boycott of the election (meaning that Hamas supporters should not vote).

With Barghouti in jail and no members of Hamas running, it was no surprise that Abbas won the 2005 presidential election by a wide margin. But even with this election victory, the new president did not have enough support among the Palestinians to rule effectively. Arafat had feared the power of Hamas and restricted their activities, but Abbas knew he would need to come to some kind of an arrangement with the militant group to keep order. Abbas's need for Hamas support became even more pronounced in 2005, when Israeli prime minister Ariel Sharon (1928–) enacted his disengagement plan, completely evacuating Israeli settlements in the Gaza Strip and withdrawing troops from the area. The Gaza Strip's residents, most of whom lived in eight refugee camps, were poor, and many were unemployed. They celebrated the Israeli withdrawal as a day of liberation, but with the military government gone the territory was virtually lawless. Although Arafat, as the PA president, had ruled the West Bank and the Gaza Strip, both he and his Fatah party had much less control in Gaza than on the West Bank. With the Israel forces gone, the Gazans sought leadership, and Hamas, with a strong presence on Gaza already and a reputation for providing badly needed services that the PA had neglected, appealed to many Palestinians.

The legislative elections of 2006

In late 2005 Hamas decided to enter politics. The organization had always been very effective at the local level, so when local elections were held throughout the West Bank and the Gaza Strip in December 2005, Hamas candidates ran in most of them. They fared well; through these elections, Hamas gained control of town councils almost everywhere except the city of Ramallah, where Fatah had the majority support.

National legislative elections (electing members of the Palestinian National Council) were held in January 2006. In these elections, Hamas promoted itself simply, promising to end corruption and lawlessness in the territories. The group did not retract its pledge to destroy Israel, although many people believed it would consider a truce (a halt in the fighting) in order to achieve the creation of a Palestinian state. Fatah's campaign, on the other hand, was poorly run. The party allowed many of its candidates to run for the same positions, which divided the party's supporters.

A Palestinian woman casts her vote during the Palestinian presidential election in 2005. PLO leader Mahmoud Abbas won the election by a wide margin. DAVID SILVERMAN/ GETTY IMAGES.

It was a shock to observers throughout the world, including Hamas itself, when the votes were tallied and it was announced that Hamas had won the majority of the seats in the council. With those seats, Hamas, a

Hamas supporters celebrate their victory in the 2006 Palestinian legislative elections. Hamas won a majority of seats, as well as the right to form a majority government in the Palestinian Authority. © SHAWN BALDWIN/CORBIS.

militant, Islamist group that had been labeled a terrorist organization by many Western nations, had won the right to form a majority government in the PA. Throughout the world, questions mounted about what would come next. But many also hailed the milestone that had just occurred. Wright notes, "After half a century of dominating Palestinian politics, Fatah's monopoly had ended. It was the first time an Arab electorate ousted autocratic [ruling with absolute power] leadership in free and fair elections—a message that resonated throughout the region."

Divisions within the PA

In March 2006 Hamas formed a new PA government, naming a veteran Hamas leader, Ismail Haniyeh (1963–), as prime minister. Abbas continued to serve as president of the PA, but Hamas leaders ran the government ministries. The new government was soon faced with overwhelming obstacles. As soon as Haniyeh was sworn in, an international group called the Quartet, made up of the United States, the European Union (EU; an economic and political association of European countries), the UN, and Russia, all of which contributed large amounts of financial aid to the Palestinians every year, announced that they would stop their support unless Hamas recognized Israel, accepted the agreements that had been signed in the past by the PLO and the PA, and renounced violence. Hamas refused. The United States and the EU immediately stopped financial support. Israel swore it would never deal with Hamas, and it withheld the tax revenue collected on behalf of the PA in the amount of about fifty-five million dollars per month, more than half of the PA's normal domestic income. Thus, from the start Hamas was unable to pay the salaries of government workers. Within a year, the majority of Palestinians in the Gaza Strip and the West Bank were living in poverty.

During this time of political and economic challenges, a group of Palestinian militants raided an Israeli army post across the border from the Gaza Strip. During the raid, the Palestinians killed two Israeli soldiers and wounded three. They then took nineteen-year old IDF corporal Gilad Shalit (1986–) prisoner. He was the first Israeli soldier since the early 1990s to be captured by the Palestinians. In exchange for Shalit, Hamas demanded that Israel release one thousand Palestinian prisoners, including Marwan Barghouti, plus all females and prisoners under the age of eighteen. Instead, Israel launched a large military attack on the Gaza Strip in which several hundred Palestinians were killed. The Israeli attack failed to rescue Shalit, however, and Hamas refused to allow him the normal privileges of a prisoner of war required by international law. Shalit was finally released in October 2011, in exchange for 1,027 Palestinian prisoners.

Without sufficient funding, under attack from Israel, and with the Palestinian economy deteriorating rapidly, Hamas was unable to govern effectively. Under this pressure, in March 2007 Abbas and representatives of Hamas agreed to form a unity government, with members of both Hamas and Fatah in the cabinet. The new unity government adopted moderate positions and avoided controversial issues, such as recognizing Israel. Its key financial leader was moderate economist Salam Fayyad (1952–), who had many strong connections in the Western world. Once Fayyad was in a leadership position and the PA had adopted the new moderate tone, the United States and several other countries renewed a portion of their former funding of the PA.

Hamas and Fatah, however, were unable to work together. Despite the formation of a unity government in March 2007, violence between members of the two groups had been escalating in the Gaza Strip since late 2006, and more fighting between the two groups erupted in May 2007, during which thirty Palestinians were killed. Israel joined these skirmishes by launching air strikes against Hamas. Israel claimed to be retaliating for Hamas strikes against Israel, but many Palestinians believed that Israel was trying to help Fatah eliminate Hamas.

On June 10 the violence between Fatah and Hamas exploded in the Gaza Strip. The worst fighting began when Hamas forces threw one of Abbas's guards off the roof of a tall building, killing him. Fatah forces responded with revenge deaths throughout the Gaza Strip. Hamas, in turn, attacked Fatah military posts, police stations, government buildings, and hospitals. By June 14, after a vicious battle, Hamas had gained control of all Fatah posts in the Gaza Strip. On that same day, Abbas declared a national emergency, dissolved the unity government, and formed an interim (temporary) government, which took over rule in the West Bank. Hamas took control of the Gaza Strip, and the PA was split in two.

Palestinian women attend a protest calling for an end to the internal fighting between Hamas and Fatah in February 2007. Violence between the two groups would continue to escalate, with the worst fighting erupting in June 2007.
© IBRAHEEM ABU MUSTAFA/ REUTERS/CORBIS.

More turmoil in the Gaza Strip

The rise of Hamas in the Gaza Strip posed enormous problems for Israel. Militants in the Gaza Strip had been launching rockets into Israel on a regular basis. With Hamas in control, it seemed likely the attacks would increase. In September 2007 Israel declared Hamas a terrorist organization and the Gaza Strip hostile territory. Israel had long exercised control over the Gaza Strip's borders, but after 2007, it imposed a tight blockade, stopping the movement of people through its borders and preventing many supplies from entering or leaving the territory. In addition to depriving the residents of the Gaza Strip of needed supplies, the blockade closed down most industries due to lack of materials. It greatly harmed the economy and, according to many international organizations, caused great suffering among the people.

The United States and many European countries supported the blockade, isolating Hamas while at the same time supporting Abbas's government. Israeli spokespeople claimed that the blockade was its only means of preventing materials used to make rockets and bombs from entering the Gaza Strip. Many people worldwide, however, said that the harsh tactics against the whole community were motivated by Israel's desire to turn the people of the Gaza Strip against Hamas. Most of the Western world hoped that the moderate Abbas could regain power in the Gaza Strip. Hamas leader Khalid Mashaal (1956–) believed that some powers were actively working to eliminate Hamas. He accused the United States of trying to arm Fatah troops in the Gaza Strip just prior to the split in the PA. Its intent, according to Mashaal, was to overturn the democratic election. Whether or not this is true, the United States, Canada, many EU countries, Japan, and Israel all designated Hamas as a terrorist organization. Australia and the United Kingdom labeled just Hamas's armed military wing as terrorist. Most nations in the Arab and Muslim world, however, do not view Hamas as a terrorist organization, and terrorist groups, like al-Qaeda, consistently criticized Hamas for participating in a government established under the Oslo Accords and other agreements that al-Qaeda scorned.

Israel's blockade of the Gaza Strip increased resentment among Palestinians toward Israel. Militants in the Gaza Strip continued to launch thousands of small rockets into Israel, killing Israeli civilians. In response, in December 2008, Israel launched a fierce twenty-two-day military campaign called Operation Cast Lead. Israeli air strikes destroyed the Gaza Strip's government buildings, schools, hospitals, factories, and

Khaled Mashaal

Khaled Mashaal, the leader of Hamas, was born in the West Bank village of Silwad, near Ramallah, in 1956. Israel occupied the West Bank after the 1967 Arab-Israeli War, and Mashaal and his family moved to Kuwait. In his early teens, Mashaal became active in the Muslim Brotherhood, an Islamic fundamentalist group organized in opposition to Western influence and in support of Islamic principles. Mashaal went on to study physics at Kuwait University and later taught in Kuwait, but he never lost his interest in Islamist politics. In 1987, during the First Intifada, the Muslim Brotherhood created a new organization, Hamas, in the Gaza Strip. Mashaal became active in the Kuwait chapter of Hamas and eventually became the chapter's leader. In 1990 Mashaal moved to Amman, Jordan, where he led Hamas's efforts in international fund-raising and foreign relations.

In 1997 Israeli prime minister Benjamin Netanyahu (1949–) authorized Mossad, Israel's chief intelligence and secret-service agency, to assassinate several Hamas leaders, including Mashaal. Two Mossad agents, posing as Canadian tourists, accosted Mashaal outside his Amman office and injected a deadly nerve toxin into his ear. The agents then fled, but Mashaal's bodyguard gave chase and held them for the Jordanian police. Under pressure, the agents admitted to poisoning Mashaal. By the next day, Mashaal was unconscious and extremely ill. Jordan's King Hussein I (1935–1999), infuriated by Israel's disregard for its alliance with Jordan, demanded that Netanyahu deliver the antidote to the poison before Mashaal died. When Netanyahu refused, King Hussein called U.S. president Bill Clinton (1946–), who exerted pressure on Netanyahu. The Israeli prime minister finally sent a Mossad agent with the antidote, and Mashaal survived.

In 1999 King Hussein's son, King Abdullah II (1962–), allied Jordan with Abbas and the Palestinian Authority. Although his father had supported Hamas, in 1999 King Abdullah shut down Hamas's base in Amman and expelled Mashaal and other leaders from Jordan. Mashaal

homes. They were followed by a ground attack in January 2009. When the military campaign was over on January 21, more than thirteen hundred Gazans had been killed and thousands had lost their homes. The air strikes destroyed 96 percent of the industry of the Gaza Strip. Many people there now relied on humanitarian aid to survive.

The West Bank

When Abbas was faced with the split between Hamas and his party, Fatah, in June 2007, he had declared a state of emergency, which he claimed gave him the authority to create a new government. He asked established a new base in Damascus, Syria, in 2001. He could not return to the West Bank for fear of being assassinated or arrested by Israel. In 2004 Israel assassinated Hamas leaders Ahmed Yassin (1937–2004) and Abdel-Aziz Al-Rantissi (1947–2004) in the Gaza Strip. Many authorities believe that Mashaal took the lead position in Hamas at that time.

As leader of Hamas, Mashaal consistently held that Palestinians have the right to armed resistance against Israel, and he denies the right of Israel to exist as a Jewish state on the lands that the Palestinians claim as theirs. But he has also raised the prospect of "peace based on justice." In a letter published in the British newspaper the *Guardian* not long after Hamas won the 2006 elections, Mashaal wrote:

> We shall never recognise the right of any power to rob us of our land and deny us our national rights. We shall never recognise the legitimacy of a [Jewish country] created on our soil in order to atone for somebody else's sins or solve somebody else's problem. But if you are willing to accept the principle of a long-term truce, we are prepared to negotiate the terms. Hamas is extending a hand of peace to

Hamas leader Khaled Mashaal. © ITAR-TASS PHOTO AGENCY/ALAMY.

those who are truly interested in a peace based on justice.

MASHAAL, KHALED. "WE WILL NOT SELL OUR PEOPLE OR PRINCIPLES FOR FOREIGN AID." *GUARDIAN* (JANUARY 31, 2006).

Fayyad to head the government as prime minister. Fayyad, who was born in the West Bank, held a Ph.D. from the University of Texas. He had worked as an economist in the United States and for the World Bank (an international banking organization) and the International Monetary Fund (a UN agency promoting trade and monetary cooperation) before returning to the West Bank as a finance minister under Arafat. He had formed a political party called the Third Way, which, as an alternative to Fatah and Hamas, promised to root out corruption, reform the government, and stabilize the Palestinian economy. But in the January 2006 legislative elections, the Third Way only won 2.4 percent of the votes.

Originally the temporary government under Fayyad had representatives of many Palestinian political parties and factions. After many false starts and resignations, however, on May 29, 2009, Abbas asked Fayyad to create a new government. Its representatives in the council were almost entirely technocrats, technical experts in leading governmental positions. Within a couple of months, Fayyad presented a plan to establish a democratic Palestinian state within two years. His approach was to build a country rather than to declare one. He figured that if the Palestinians built governmental, legal, security, and economic institutions in the West Bank, the rest of the world would be forced to accept a Palestinian state as a reality. Fayyad's moderation and his many links to the United States appealed greatly to Israel, many Arab states, and the West, and his new government received financial support from around the world. Fayyad's government of technocrats oversaw thousands of new development projects in the West Bank, including schools, hospitals, roads, new companies, and housing projects. The economy of the West Bank improved as a result.

One of the main changes under the new West Bank government was its crackdown on all types of armed groups, such as criminal gangs, drug smugglers, and militias and other armed resistance groups, including Hamas. Despite the fact that Hamas had been elected into the national council by a majority of voters, Fayyad held that Hamas members were to be treated as criminals. Mohsen Mohammad Saleh, director of the Al-Zaytouna Centre for Studies and Consultations in Beirut, Lebanon, quotes Fayyad on his policy toward Hamas in an article on the *Middle East Monitor* Web site: "As long as the status quo remains [the current situation stays the same] in Gaza, Hamas will remain an organisation that is an adversary [opponent] to the [Palestinian] Authority, and the government shall deal with it in light of this reality." To this end, the PA began a program of training security forces in Jordan under an American program developed by Lieutenant General Keith Dayton (1949–), the U.S. security coordinator for Israel and the PA. The PA's new security forces were successful in eliminating many armed groups and in dismantling almost all of Hamas's activities in the West Bank. Palestinian attacks on Israel decreased significantly. Hamas claims that 2,921 Hamas members were arrested for political reasons in the West Bank in the five-month period between June 10, 2007, and November 11, 2008.

Members of the Palestinian security force march at Palestinian Authority (PA) headquarters in the West Bank, in June 2007. The PA's new security forces were successful in eliminating many armed groups and in dismantling almost all of Hamas's activities in the West Bank. © ELIANA APONTE/REUTERS/CORBIS.

Although Western countries and Israel supported Fayyad, many Palestinians did not. During Israel's 2008–09 war on the Gaza Strip, many West Bank residents were outraged at Israel's behavior and took to the streets to demonstrate against it. The PA harshly suppressed the demonstrations, in just one example of what many international observers considered an increasingly authoritarian government. The new government relied mainly on the decrees of President Abbas and Prime Minister Fayyad rather than democratic decisions that included the council. Many Palestinians were scornful of the PA's new U.S.-trained security forces, which frequently worked in collaboration with Israel. Humanitarian organizations accused these forces of using torture. By 2010 there were accusations of corruption in the government. Leading members of Fatah resigned from their positions in the PA, protesting the Fayyad government. Abbas and Fayyad were increasingly viewed as being controlled by the United States and Israel.

As Fayyad's two-year deadline for building a Palestinian county approached in July 2011, the PA in the West Bank was once again facing a financial crisis, caused mainly by donor nations lagging behind in their financial aid.

Reconciliation

Even during the split between the West Bank and the Gaza Strip, Abbas had continued to press for the creation of a Palestinian state. He hoped to obtain a UN resolution recognizing the Palestinian state. He knew this would be impossible with the Gaza Strip and the West Bank divided. Abbas had other problems, as well. While Hamas and Fatah carried on their bitter feud, the Palestinian people grew increasingly disheartened with both parties. They had witnessed the power of ordinary people to drastically change their governments in the Arab Spring of 2011, a series of prodemocracy uprisings in the Middle East and North Africa. (For more information, see **The Arab Spring: 2011.**) By mid–March, small protests aimed at the PA had begun to break out in the West Bank. Although there was little agreement on anything between Fatah and Hamas, a reconciliation between these two organizations seemed necessary for their survival and for the advancement of the Palestinians' goal of a country of their own.

Abbas met with representatives of Hamas in March 2011. He proposed that they form a temporary government that would then quickly hold legislative and presidential elections. He argued that with democratic elections underway, the PA would have more success with its application to the UN for membership. This would make Israel's refusal to deal with Hamas less of an obstacle in the Palestinians' attempt to build their own country.

Hamas unexpectedly agreed to Abbas's proposal. In April Egypt sponsored a series of secret meetings between Abbas and Mashaal in Cairo, Egypt. The agreements between these two longtime opponents were few: an end to hostilities, the formation of a new interim government, and to proceed with presidential and legislative elections within the year. Many huge problems were not addressed. But the will of the Palestinian people to get back on the track of democratic elections was honored.

In September 2011, Abbas appeared before the United Nations Security Council and presented his application for UN recognition of a

Mahmoud Abbas holds up a copy of the letter requesting Palestinian statehood as he speaks before the United Nations General Assembly at UN headquarters in New York City, September 23, 2011.
STAN HONDA/AFP/GETTY IMAGES.

Palestinian state. Minor success was achieved in October, when the United Nations Educational, Scientific and Cultural Organization (UNESCO) granted Palestine full membership in that organization. But by November, the Security Council committee that was considering the application for UN recognition had failed to come to a agreement, and it was clear to authorities worldwide that the bid for statehood was doomed to fail. Because the proposed Palestinian state sits on land that is technically controlled by Israel, any agreement that does not include Israel would be nearly impossible to enforce.

For More Information

BOOKS

Brown, Nathan J. *Palestinian Politics after the Oslo Accords: Resuming Arab Palestine.* Berkeley: University of California Press, 2003.

Khalidi, Rashid. *The Iron Cage: The Story of the Palestinian Struggle for Statehood.* Boston, MA: Beacon, 2006.

Milton-Edwards, Beverly, and Stephen Farrell. *Hamas: The Islamic Resistance Movement.* Cambridge, England: Polity Press, 2010, p. 5.

Myre, Greg, and Jennifer Griffin. *This Burning Land: Lessons from the Front Lines of the Transformed Israeli-Palestinian Conflict.* Hoboken, NJ: Wiley, 2010.

Wright, Robin. *Dreams and Shadows: The Future of the Middle East.* New York: Penguin, 2008, pp. 26, 44.

PERIODICALS

"Gaza Strip," *New York Times* (August 11, 2011). Available online at http://topics.nytimes.com/top/news/international/countriesandterritories/gaza_strip/index.html (accessed November 30, 2011).

Mashaal, Khaled. "We Will Not Sell Our People or Principles for Foreign Aid," *The Guardian* (January 31, 2006). Available online at http://www.guardian.co.uk/world/2006/jan/31/comment.israelandthepalestinians (accessed November 30, 2011).

WEB SITES

"Hamas Covenant 1988." *The Avalon Project, Yale Law School.* http://avalon.law.yale.edu/20th_century/hamas.asp (accessed on November 30, 2011).

"Operation Cast Lead." *GlobalSecurity.org.* http://www.globalsecurity.org/military/world/war/operation-cast-lead.htm (accessed on November 30, 2011).

Saleh, Mohsen Mohammad. "Evaluating Salam Fayyad's Government in Ramallah." *Middle East Monitor* (December 30, 2010). http://www.middleeastmonitor.org.uk/articles/middle-east/1898-evaluating-salam-fayyads-government-in-ramallah (accessed on November 30, 2011).

"Who Are Palestine Refugees?" *UNRWA.* http://www.unrwa.org/etemplate.php?id=86 (accessed on November 30, 2011).

9

Syria and Lebanon: 1936 to 1990

Until the twentieth century, Syria and Lebanon were both part of a region in the Middle East called Greater Syria, which included the present-day countries of Syria, Lebanon, Israel, and Jordan, as well as the present-day territories of the West Bank and the Gaza Strip. The region was home to some of the oldest cities of the world. In ancient times, the area had land that was good for farming, and it had popular trade and military routes crossing through it. Many conquering forces invaded and ruled over Greater Syria over the years, including Egyptians, Mesopotamians, Romans, the Islamic Empire, and Christian Crusaders, all bringing with them different religious beliefs and traditions. (Crusaders were soldiers who participated in the Crusades, a series of military campaigns ordered by the Roman Catholic Church between 1095 and 1291 with the main goal of taking the Holy Land from the Muslims.) Under the rule of the Ottoman Empire (the vast empire of the Ottoman Turks which included southwest Asia, northeast Africa, and southeast Europe, and lasted from the thirteenth century to the early twentieth century), the people of Syria and Lebanon were, for the most part, allowed to rule themselves. The different ethnic and religious groups were encouraged to form their own locally governed communities, called *millets*. This led the many different sects (groups) of Islam and Christianity to maintain their own traditions, practices, and local rule.

In the early twentieth century the Ottoman Empire came to an end, and its former territories became Western mandates, or territories entrusted to foreign administration. Greater Syria was divided up, and Lebanon and Syria were established as French mandates. France divided Syria and Lebanon in a way that heightened tensions between the existing sects in those countries. In Lebanon the French created a sectarian government, which is a government that distributes political and institutional power among its various religious sects and ethnic communities on

WORDS TO KNOW

Alawis: Also spelled Alawites; followers of a sect of Shia Islam that live in Syria. Their belief system and practices vary from Shiites in several ways, particularly in the belief that Ali, the son-in-law of the prophet Muhammad, was the human form of Allah (the Arabic word for God).

Arab League: A regional political alliance of Arab nations formed in 1945 to promote political, military, and economic cooperation within the Arab world.

Arabs: People of the Middle East and North Africa who speak the Arabic language or who live in countries in which Arabic is the dominant language.

authoritarianism: A type of leadership in which power is consolidated under one strong leader, or a small group of elite leaders, who do not answer to the will of the people.

Ba'ath Party: A secular (nonreligious) political party founded in the 1940s with the goal of uniting the Arab world and creating one powerful Arab state.

Druze: Members of a small sect of Islam who believe that the ninth-century caliph Tariq al-Hakim was God.

mandate: A commission granting one country the authority to administer the affairs of another country. Also describes the territory entrusted to foreign administration.

Maronites: Members of an Arabic-speaking group of Christians, living mainly in Lebanon, who are in communion (share essential doctrines) with the Roman Catholic Church.

militia: Armed civilian military forces.

nationalism: The belief that a people with shared ethnic, cultural, and/or religious identities have the right to form their own nation. In established nations nationalism is devotion and loyalty to the nation and its culture.

Ottoman Empire: The vast empire of the Ottoman Turks which included southwest Asia, northeast Africa, and southeast Europe, and lasted from the thirteenth century to the early twentieth century.

Palestine: A historical region in the Middle East on the eastern shore of the Mediterranean Sea, comprising parts of present-day Israel and Jordan.

Palestine Liberation Organization (PLO): A political and military organization formed to unite various Palestinian Arab groups with the goal of establishing an independent Palestinian state.

Palestinians: An Arab people whose ancestors lived in the historical region of Palestine and who continue to lay claim to that land.

Pan-Arabism: A movement for the unification of Arab peoples and the political alliance of Arab states.

sectarian government: A government that distributes political and institutional power among its various religious sects and ethnic communities on a proportional basis.

sharif: A nobleman and political leader chosen from among descendants of the Muslim prophet Muhammad.

Shiites: Followers of the Shia branch of Islam. Shiites believe that only direct descendants of the prophet Muhammad are qualified to lead the Islamic faith.

socialism: A system in which the government owns the means of production and controls the distribution of goods and services.

Sunnis: Followers of the Sunni branch of Islam. Sunnis believe that elected officials, regardless of their heritage, are qualified to lead the Islamic faith.

a proportional basis. In Syria, France divided different ethnic, religious, and interest groups into separate provinces, with local governments that often engaged in competition for resources and in political rivalries. These divisions continued to grow long after Lebanon and Syria became independent nations. The divisions resulted in severe conflicts, including a fifteen-year civil war in Lebanon and an unstable government in Syria that was abruptly taken over by an authoritarian regime, in which power is consolidated under one strong leader, or a small group of elite leaders, who do not answer to the will of the people. Since independence, Syria has played a dominant role in regional conflict. It has been one of Israel's greatest enemies since it declared war on that country in 1948. It has been an instigator of civil unrest in Lebanon, using its power, including sending Syrian troops, to undermine stable governments in that country.

Background

Greater Syria became a part of the Ottoman Empire in 1516, and would remain so for four centuries. By the late eighteenth century, however, the empire had begun its decline. Many European nations were gaining world power at that time, as a result of major advances in their industry, trade, technology, global exploration and colonization, and also due to their innovations in weaponry and military skills. During the late nineteenth century, several European nations showed a growing interest in the affairs of Great Syria.

Great Britain began to negotiate with the Arab (people who speak the Arabic language) leaders of the region even before the Ottoman Empire collapsed at the end of World War I (1914–18; a global war between the Allies [Great Britain, France, and Russia, joined later by the United States] and the Central Powers [Germany, Austria-Hungary, and their allies]). Seeking help in the military struggle against the Ottomans, the British negotiated with Husayn ibn 'Ali (also spelled Hussein bin Ali; c. 1854–1931), the sharif of Mecca in present-day Saudi Arabia. (A sharif is nobleman and political leader chosen from among descendants of the Muslim prophet Muhammad [c. 570–632].) He promised the British that Arabs would revolt against the Ottoman Empire if the British agreed to support the creation of an independent Arab state that would fall within the boundaries of Greater Syria and Mesopotamia (present-day Iraq) after the war. The British agreed.

Husayn's two sons, Faisal (1885–1933) and Abdullah (1882–1951), led the Arab forces against the Ottoman Empire, greatly aiding the British in defeating the empire. In October 1918 Faisal captured Damascus, and the Arabs set about creating an independent Arab state.

As the victors of the war, the Allies, however, had developed other plans for the former Ottoman Empire. Through the treaties created after the war, they granted Great Britain a mandate (administrative authority) over Palestine and Iraq, while France was granted a mandate for the land on which present-day Syria and Lebanon are located. The administration of these mandates, which would be overseen by the League of Nations (an international organization of sovereign countries established after World War I to promote peace) was intended to guide them toward independence, and not to take them over as colonies. Not long after Damascus was captured by Faisal, the French moved their troops and administrators into the city.

Some countries around the world began to question the fairness of the British and French rule of these areas. In the summer of 1919, the United States appointed a group, called the King-Crane Commission, to investigate the wishes of the people of the Middle East. The commission concluded that a vast majority of the people of Syria and Palestine wanted independence for a united Greater Syria, including Palestine, and they wanted Faisal to be the king. The commission recommended that a mandate be formed under American supervision to establish the independent nation of Greater Syria. The British and French, however, never seriously considered the U.S. report and no plans were ever made for a U.S. mandate in Greater Syria. Instead, in April 1920, at a conference in San Remo, Italy, the international powers, heavily influenced by the powerful British and by France, granted Great Britain the mandate of Palestine (a historical region in the Middle East on the eastern shore of the Mediterranean Sea, comprising parts of present-day Israel and Jordan), as well as a mandate for Iraq. France was granted a mandate for a region called Syria, which included the present-day countries of Syria and Lebanon.

Ethnically and religiously divided

In 1920 a group of Arabs from Greater Syria convened a congress in which they proclaimed Faisal the king of Greater Syria. The kingdom's capital was in Damascus. The French refused to recognize Faisal as king, and soon forced him to leave Damascus. (The British, to make up for their broken promise, made Faisal king of Iraq, even though he had never lived in or visited that country.) Even without their king, the Syrians refused to accept French rule. They gathered a military force in an attempt to expel the French. In the Battle of Maysalun on July 23, 1920, the French defeated the Syrians and took their place as the rulers of Syria. But for the next few years, their efforts to rule were impeded by widespread uprisings of the Syrian people, who felt they had been robbed of the promised Arab state.

In the early twentieth century Syria had several large religious sects. An estimated 74 percent of its population was Sunni Muslims, followers of the Sunni branch of the Islam. Sunnis believe that the leader of Islam, called a caliph, can be selected from among any of the religious leaders, regardless of his heritage. Three other Muslim sects combined made up about 16 percent of the population. These were Shiite Muslims, Alawis, and Druze. Shiite Muslims are followers of the Shia branch of Islam, and they believe that only direct descendants of the Muslim prophet Muhammad are qualified to lead Islam. Alawis (also spelled Alawites) are members of a sect of Shiites who live mainly in Syria. Their beliefs and practices vary from Shiites, particularly in the belief that Ali, the son-in-law of the Muslim prophet Muhammad, was the human form of Allah (the Arabic word for God). The Druze are members of a small sect of Islam who believe that the ninth-century caliph Tariq al-Hakim was God. Various Christian groups made up another 10 percent of Syria's population. There was also a small Jewish community in Syria.

In order to maintain their power in Syria, the French tried to keep the religious groups separate. If the various sects competed against one another for political dominance and regional resources and trade, the French reasoned, then they would not be united in their fight against France. France, therefore, divided the region into states reflecting different sectors of the ethnically and religiously diverse region. These states were Damascus, Aleppo, Alawite, Jabal Druze, and Greater Lebanon. Damascus and Aleppo were the most powerful of the provinces. Both were large commercial centers with prosperous trade and businesses. Had they been united, they would have been better able to resist French rule. However, they competed with each other for trade, resources, and power, and their leaders often viewed each other as rivals rather than allies.

The state of Greater Lebanon was a special case among the Syrian states. Under the Ottoman Empire, the area known as Mount Lebanon, which is the central part of the present-day country of Lebanon, had long held a special status. The two major groups in Mount Lebanon were the

Druze and the Maronites, members of an Arabic-speaking group of Christians, living mainly in Lebanon, who follow the teachings of Saint Maron, a fifth-century monk, and share essential doctrines with the Roman Catholic Church. A conflict arose between the neighboring Druze and the Maronites in 1840 over power. As the conflict became especially bitter, France, a predominately Catholic nation, took an interest in the welfare of the Maronites. To protect the Maronites, in 1860 the French asked the Ottoman sultan to create two districts in Mount Lebanon, one for the Maronites and the other for the Druze. But the division created more hostility, and in 1861 the Druze attacked the Maronites, killing more than ten thousand people. After that, the Europeans pressured the Ottoman Empire to give a united Mount Lebanon more self-government, and over the years, France kept watch to make sure the Maronites were treated well.

By 1920, when France received the mandate for Syria, the Maronites of Mount Lebanon had long benefited from the attentions of their protector and called France "the Tender Mother." Favorable treatment extended to the creation of the borders of the new Lebanese state, Greater Lebanon. France added some key parts of Syria, namely the ports of Beirut, Tripoli, Sidon, and Tyre, and the rich Bekáa Valley, to the existing area of Mount Lebanon. France's expansion of Greater Lebanon's borders "more than doubled the territory and greatly altered the population ratios according to religious affiliation," according to Charles D. Smith in *Palestine and the Arab-Israeli Conflict.* These additions made Greater Lebanon economically stronger and weakened the rebellious Syrians who were still seeking their independence. The Maronites, who were a majority in Greater Lebanon at that time, supported France, while most other Syrians vehemently opposed its rule.

Independence and turmoil in Syria

France's attempts to divide the Syrians into competing states created many economic and political problems, but it did not prevent anti-France uprisings, as the French had hoped. In 1925 an uprising known as the Syrian Revolution erupted in the state of Jabal Druze. It quickly spread to Damascus and beyond. The French reacted with air strikes. In October 1925 they dropped bombs on Damascus, killing an estimated fourteen hundred civilians. Nevertheless, the massive revolt continued until 1927, at which time the Syrians were defeated but still defiant.

In 1925 the states of Aleppo and Damascus united in a Syrian federation. A year later, the state of Greater Lebanon, which had come to be known only as Lebanon, became a separate republic, although it remained under French administration. Syrians put together their own constitution and formed a government with which they intended to develop self-government and eliminate French oversight and interference in their country. Syria's local government, however, was unstable and lacked unity. Druze, Sunni, and Shiite factions fought bitterly over who would wield the most power. Despite the instability, Syrian discontent with France continued, and finally, in 1936, after much negotiation, the French agreed to Syrian independence.

Independence was delayed, however, first by unrest in Syria and then by World War II (1939–45; a war in which the Allies [Great Britain, France, the Soviet Union, the United States, and China] defeated the Axis Powers [Germany, Italy, and Japan]). Early in the war, in 1940 France was invaded by the Germans, and the French people came under the rule of the Vichy regime, a government that collaborated with the Germans. The Vichy regime installed governments in Syria and Lebanon, but in 1941, British and Free French forces (French troops loyal to their old government) regained the two countries. The Free French declared Syria an independent nation. Syria quickly applied to the United Nations for membership, which it received in 1945. (The United Nations is an international organization of countries founded in 1945 to promote international peace, security, and cooperation.) France tried to recover its rule over Syria after the war, but by then international recognition of Syria as an independent nation forced the French to withdraw in 1946. Syria was ruled solely by the republican government it had formed in the 1930s. It joined the Arab League (a regional political alliance of Arab nations formed in 1945 to promote political, military, and economic cooperation within the Arab world), and declared its independence on April 17, 1946.

After its struggle against France, Syria was suddenly faced with many internal divisions. Thomas Collelo describes the turmoil on the *Country Studies* Web site:

> Aleppines [people from the state of Aleppo] contested with Damascenes [people from the state of Damascus] for dominance in commercial and political life; the Druzes pledged allegiance to Druzes . . . and tribal peoples to tribal institutions. Alawis, the poorest yet largest of the minorities, tried to rebel from Sunni Muslim control. Rural leaders contended with urban leaders; the progressive, increasingly secularized [nonreligious], younger generation vied with the older, religious-minded leaders. Politicians differed over the kind of government Syria

should have—monarchy or republic, parliamentary or presidential democracy.... The cultural heritage of France and the American ideals of democracy induced many Syrians to look westward for friendship. Others looked north to the Soviet Union.

It was during this time of division and instability that Syria fought in the 1948 Arab-Israeli War, in which Israel established itself as an independent nation and defeated the major forces of the Arab nations, including Syria. After the war, Syrians were disgusted with their government because of its defeat to Israel and for other reasons as well. In 1949 in the first of a dizzying number of government takeovers, a group of military officers staged a coup (overthrow of the government) and installed an authoritarian regime in Damascus. (An authoritarian regime is a type of leadership in which power is consolidated under one strong leader, or a small group of elite leaders, who do not answer to the will of the people.) Within a year, this regime was overthrown, but as the new governing group worked to establish a constitution, yet another military coup installed another authoritarian government, which was then overthrown in 1954. A wide variety of political groups and parties emerged, each with its own ideas about how to run the unstable country.

The Ba'ath Party and Pan-Arabism

One of the groups that emerged in Syria was the Ba'ath Party, a secular (nonreligious) political party founded in the 1940s with the goal of uniting the Arab world and creating one powerful Arab state. *Ba'ath* is an Arabic word, meaning rebirth, and from the founding of the Ba'ath Party in 1947, Ba'athists sought a rebirth of Arab power. The founder of Ba'ath ideology was a Syrian Christian named Michel Aflaq (1940–1989). Ba'athism, with its motto of "Unity, Freedom, Socialism," promotes a secular (nonreligious) form of government in which private industries are nationalized, or brought under the ownership and control of the government, in order to provide work for all the people. This form of socialism was similar to that of the Soviet Union, but Ba'athists did not try to eliminate the influence of religion as did the Soviets. (Socialism is a system in which the government owns the means of production and controls the distribution of goods and services.) They recognized that Islam played an important role in unifying the Arab people. Early Ba'ath leaders wanted democratic rule as well as expanded personal freedoms, and the Ba'ath Party gained followers in many Arab nations, particularly in Syria and Iraq.

For a time, however, the party did not have enough votes or power to take over the Syrian government. Instead, Pan-Arabism, a movement for the unification of Arab peoples and the political alliance of Arab states, soon swept Syria.

Michel Aflaq, founder of the Syrian Ba'ath Party. © CLAUDE SALHANI/SYGMA/ CORBIS.

During the 1950s, Pan-Arabism was strongly promoted by Egyptian president Gamal Abdel Nasser (1918–1970). In 1958 Syria agreed to unite with Egypt and become the United Arab Republic (UAR). The two countries did not share a border, but they pursued a merger of their economies and political systems. Although Syrians were initially in favor of the union, once Egypt and Syria merged it began to appear to most Syrians that Nasser simply wanted to take over Syria. Popular resistance led to a military coup in Syria in 1961 that restored Syria's independence.

When it originated, the Ba'ath Party hoped to draw upon popular support to bring about a peaceful unification of Arab nations. Following the failure of the UAR in 1961, however, Syria's Ba'ath Party was taken over by military figures who sought to establish complete control over the Syrian government.

By 1970 the Ba'athists had placed Hafez Assad (also spelled al-Assad; 1930–2000) in power as Syria's leader. The move was controversial, because Assad was an Alawi. The Syrian constitution required Syria's leader to be a Muslim, and some Sunni Muslims in Syria did not consider Alawis to be Muslims at all because certain Alawi beliefs differed from Sunni beliefs. Most people thought the new administration would be as short-lived as the ones before it, but Assad fortified his position in several ways. For example, under Assad, Alawis, a minority in Syria, were given the most powerful positions in the government and in the military. They were extremely loyal to him because it was in their own best interest to be. Other sects, and anyone who voiced disagreement with Assad, did not fare as well. Assad was brutal to his opponents. In 1973 Syria enacted a new constitution, which required that the Ba'ath Party lead Syria, and a majority of seats in Syria's parliament were reserved for a group of politicians headed by the Ba'ath Party. In effect, Syrians voted in elections in which there was no choice but Assad's regime. His strict laws and the absence of any real democracy in Syria were a major departure from the Ba'ath Party's original ideals. Assad remained Syria's president until his death in 2000. Under Assad and the Ba'ath Party, Syria became a stable nation with an extremely strong military force, but Syrians paid for the stability with the loss of many freedoms.

A sectarian government in Lebanon

Like Syria, Lebanon was granted independence by the French during World War II. During the mandate period, France did a great deal to develop Lebanon, developing its roads, schools, and medical centers. But

Hafez Assad served as president of Syria from 1971 until his death in 2000. © WALLY MCNAMEE/CORBIS.

France also helped to prolong or cause conflicts between its peoples, particularly by favoring the Maronites over other religious groups. At the time of the mandate, Christians were in the majority, at about 50 percent of the population. Maronites dominated the Christian population, followed by members of the Greek Orthodox faith, Christians who had separated from the Catholic Church over a number of issues in the eleventh century. The Maronites allied themselves with France, a country ruled by Catholics, while the Greek Orthodox sect often looked to the Muslim population of Lebanon for support. Due to their large numbers, Maronites held many positions of power within the Lebanese government in the 1930s and 1940s.

When the French mandate ended in 1943, French officials used their influence to establish a system of government in Lebanon that favored French interests. The National Pact, an unwritten agreement reached among Lebanese leaders that year, created a division of power based on a 1932 census that showed the Maronites as a majority of the population. The National Pact called for a ratio of six Christians to every five Muslims in government. Every type of government job, from tax collector to public school teacher to policeman, was divided so that there were six Christians for every five Muslims. The government's highest positions were also divided under this agreement. Nominees for the Lebanese presidency were always chosen from among the Maronites, the prime minister was chosen from among the Sunnis, the speaker of the house from among the Shiites, and the chief of staff from the Druze. This form of government, which proportionally distributes political and institutional power among various religious and ethnic communities, is called sectarianism. In this system, everyone in Lebanon was grouped by religion for all political purposes.

Even though the government was divided by religious sects, Lebanon's constitution was strictly secular and allowed for freedom of religion. For a time the National Pact allowed Lebanon to be one of the most democratic of Middle Eastern nations. The pact allowed for power sharing between the major groups of the Christian and Muslim communities. The Maronites, who had long identified with the French, were guaranteed against losing power, despite the growth of Muslim communities in Lebanon in the late 1940s. The Muslims, on the other hand, found in the new government their own source of power, free from Western control. It was not a perfect system, but it worked for a time.

While the largest groups were guaranteed a place in government, the National Pact did not account for the political needs of all of the approximately seventeen different religious groups in Lebanon, each with its own distinct perspective on how to create a better life in the country. The differences in power among these ethnic and religious groups, and the actual representation of these groups in the Lebanese population, eventually became a source of internal strife in the country. Maronites guarded their political power by denying attempts to update the 1932 census information for decades, even as Muslim populations increased significantly in relation to the Maronite population. By 1970, Muslims were an estimated 60 percent of the total population.

A large group of Arab nationalists (people who want a country ruled by Arab Muslims) developed in the 1960s. In 1969 the nationalists formed the Lebanese National Movement. The movement's main goal was to end the National Pact of 1943, but it also focused on ongoing conflicts between Lebanon's social classes. Supporters of the movement sought social, political, and economic reform and a non-sectarian democracy with majority rule. They called for a new census knowing that this census would end Christian domination of the Lebanese government and place Muslims in high positions of power. But they soon realized that change would only come about through force. Soon both Christian and Muslim groups formed their own militias, or armed civilian military forces. These militias would soon lead Lebanon into a long period of violence between different its sects.

The Palestinian population in Lebanon

During the 1948 Arab-Israeli War, hundreds of thousands of Arab Palestinians fled from Israel to surrounding Arab countries. Southern Lebanon became a place of settlement for many Palestinians, who set up refugee camps even though the Lebanese government did not welcome them. Over the next decade thousands of Palestinians continued to arrive in southern Lebanon; some groups created refugee camps near Lebanon's capital city of Beirut. Caught up in their own political turmoil due to the power struggle between religious groups, Lebanese officials did little to regulate or even acknowledge the Palestinian refugees.

In the late 1960s Palestinians began launching attacks against Israel from inside Lebanon's borders. These attacks started as small raids on Israeli settlements near the border, but over time they grew more violent and larger in size. Some Palestinian groups based in Lebanon, including the Palestine Liberation Organization (PLO; a political and military organization formed to unite various Palestinian Arab groups with the goal of establishing an independent Palestinian state), began to use terrorism to draw the world's attention to the Israeli occupation of the lands the Palestinians considered their own. The PLO engaged in activities such as hijacking planes and kidnapping civilians. Lebanon ignored the Palestinian activities until December 1968, when Israel destroyed

---

Religious Groups of Lebanon

In 2011 Lebanon had seventeen different religious sects, with the main groups divided between Islam and Christianity. Muslims made up 59.7 percent of the population. They included Shiites, Sunnis, Druze, Alawis, and Isma'ilites (an Islamic sect that believes that Ismail, a direct descendant of Muhammad, and his descendants are the true leaders of the Islamic faith). Christians made up 39 percent of the population. They included Maronites, Greek Orthodox Christians, Melkite Catholics (Christians who sided with the Byzantine emperor Marcian in the 450s during a power struggle between Christian leaders), Orthodox Armenians, Syrian Catholics, Armenian Catholics, Roman Catholics, and Protestants. The remaining 1.3 percent of the population belonged to other religious groups.

A Palestinian refugee camp the outskirts of Beirut. Lebanon was one of many Arab countries to create refugee camps for Palestinians after Israel was formed. © BETTMANN/CORBIS.

thirteen Arab planes at the Beirut airport in retaliation for a Palestinian attack on an Israeli commercial flight earlier that year. It was the first time Israel had targeted a Lebanese-run establishment rather than punishing Palestinians directly. Lebanon needed to respond, but the Lebanese population was deeply divided over whether to support or oppose Palestinian political issues and the growing Palestinian population in Lebanon.

In 1969 the commander of the Lebanese armed forces granted the PLO the authority to control the Palestinian refugee camps in Lebanon. The PLO created its own laws and policies within these camps, many of which conflicted with the laws and policies of the Lebanese government. The PLO had long had its headquarters in Jordan, but over the years Jordan's leaders had grown tired of having the conflict between Israel and the Palestinians played out within its borders. In 1970 Jordan forced the PLO out of its country. Many PLO members quickly relocated to southern Lebanon and Beirut. Lebanon had become the group's main base.

The PLO became the largest militia in Lebanon in the 1970s, with members numbering in the thousands.

The Palestinian presence had a destabilizing effect on Lebanon's own bitter political divisions. PLO leaders sympathized with the pro–Arab National Movement. Looking for support, several Lebanese Muslim groups, including the Sunnis and Druze, allied themselves with the PLO in their fight against the Maronites in Lebanon. The Palestinian refugees, who were Sunnis, also made life difficult for Lebanese Shiites as the influx of Palestinians forced many Shiites off their land and into refugee camps near the Palestinians' Beirut camps. The Maronite-led government did not offer support to these Shiites or deter the further expansion of Palestinian immigration.

Problems with the Palestinian population in Lebanon grew. In April 1973 Israeli troops invaded Beirut and murdered three PLO leaders, also damaging parts of the city and wounding Lebanese civilians during the invasion. Palestinians began to suffer attacks by Lebanese militias, most notably the Maronite militias, who were unhappy with Palestinian support for the National Movement. Israel helped supply and train the powerful militia associated with the Christian Phalangists. The right-wing Phalangists had been founded as a militia in the 1930s by Lebanese political leader Pierre Gemayel (1905–1984) to protect Maronite Christian interests. The Phalangists had become the most formidable Maronite militia in Lebanon, and in 1958 developed into a political party called the Phalange Party (also known as the Kataeb Party), as well as a militia.

The Lebanese civil war

On April 13, 1975, in an unsuccessful attempt on Gemayel's life, unidentified gunmen murdered four Phalangists. Later that same day, the Maronites, assuming that these killings were carried out the PLO, attacked a bus in East Beirut and killed more than twenty Palestinians. The next day Phalangists and Palestinians fought each other throughout the streets of Beirut. Many residents hid in their homes, while militias from various groups joined the fighting.

As Lebanon's civil war began, neighborhoods where people of all religions and ethnicities had long lived comfortably together ceased to exist. Shiites moved to areas where Shiites predominated, such as southern Lebanon and the Bekáa Valley. Sunnis lived only in Sunni districts,

Maronites with Maronites, Druze with Druze, and so forth. Soon Lebanon was geographically divided among its sects.

The Lebanese army was destroyed by these divisions, when its soldiers allied themselves with the militias attached to their sect instead of with the army of the Maronite-controlled government. Similarly, the sectarian government could not effectively rule the country, since its representatives were drawn from Lebanon's different sects, which were at war with each other.

The war's destruction

At the outbreak of the civil war, militia members from all sects took up positions throughout the country. In Beirut large-scale battles occurred in the Palestinian refugee camp of Tel al-Zaatar and the neighboring Maronite community of Dekwaneh. Other fighting broke out in the Bekáa Valley between the predominantly Catholic population of the town of Zahleh and neighboring Shiites and Palestinians. Various Christian and Muslim militias secured positions on rooftops, bridges, and strategic streets throughout Beirut, making nearly every street in the city a potential battlefield. The fighting destroyed much of the once-thriving cities and countryside. Marketplaces were leveled by artillery shells. Bombs destroyed some buildings, and gunfire left others scarred with pockmarks from bullets. Communications systems were cut off, and roads were ruined. Farmlands were scarred by exploded landmines.

Before the civil war broke out in 1975, Beirut was a sprawling city with a coastline boardwalk called the Mediterranean Corniche and architecturally diverse buildings as well as modern skyscrapers. Lebanon had been a transfer point for trade between the West and the Arab countries, and that trade had brought a great deal of money into the country. Beirut was the center of the country's economy, which had grown by leaps and bounds since the early 1960s as an international banking and trading center.

When combat broke out, the newly constructed Hilton Hotel in Beirut had not even been open a year. The luxury hotel became the center of some of the most intense fighting in the war. Militias fought for control of the hotel, sometimes chasing each other from room to room. It was not long before the Lebanese government became desperate and turned to other countries to help them bring an unstable peace to the country, starting with the introduction of Syrian troops into the war in 1976.

Soldiers patrol a Beirut street during the Lebanese Civil War. Beirut was one of the main battlegrounds during the war and much of the city was destroyed. © REZA/WEBISTAN/CORBIS.

Syrian involvement in Lebanon

Syria's involvement in the Lebanese turmoil is complex. After France divided the two countries in 1920, Syria's leaders had not readily accepted Lebanon's status as a separate country and still viewed it as a part of Syria. Syria's president, Assad, wanted to establish Syria as a strong leader in the Middle East. In the aftermath of the 1967 Arab-Israeli War, in which Israel captured Syria's Golan Heights as well as parts of Egypt and Jordan, Syria had remained hostile toward Israel. Assad was therefore shocked in the early 1970s when Egypt's president, Anwar Sadat (also spelled al-Sadat; 1918–1981), made peace with Israel. Syrian leaders felt that Egypt's compromise undermined the goals of the Arab nations of the Middle East. Assad wished to pursue a more active leadership role among Arab nations. One of the ways to do that was to form an international alliance of Arab states, with Syria as leader and Lebanon as the first follower.

The Golan Heights

In the 1948 Arab-Israeli War Syria was among the Arab nations defeated by Israel. The defeat, however, did not stop the hostilities between Syria and Israel. A major source of ongoing conflict after the war was a 646-square-mile (1,673-square-kilometer) plateau called the Golan Heights, a mountainous region located on the border of Syria and Israel, northwest of the Sea of Galilee. The Golan Heights overlooks the plains of Galilee in Israel. From 1948 until 1967, Syrians used the Golan Heights as a vantage point from which to shoot artillery (mounted projectile-firing guns or missile launchers) at Israelis below, killing many civilians and interfering with daily life. Israel sought control over the Golan Heights for security purposes, but it also desperately wanted to divert the Golan Heights' fresh water supply to Israel to provide badly needed water to its citizens.

Most of the area of the Golan Heights was captured by Israel in the last two days of the 1967 Arab-Israeli War (a war fought between Israel and its Arab neighbors, Syria, Egypt, and Jordan). At that time, the estimated population of the Golan Heights was 130,000 Syrians of many ethnic and religious backgrounds. Historians believe that around 100,000 were forced to flee as the Israeli forces invaded, leaving dozens of villages and farms empty. Israel installed a military administration in the region, ignoring a United Nations resolution demanding that it withdraw from all the land it seized from Syria, Egypt, and Jordan during the war. Jewish settlers soon began building communities where the Syrians had once lived. Within a decade, there were about thirty Israeli settlements in the Golan Heights. Israel also began bringing water from the Golan Heights into Israel. It did not allow the Syrians who fled to return.

In the 1973 Arab-Israeli War, Syria, under the leadership of Hafez Assad (also spelled al-Assad; 1930–2000), tried to regain the Golan Heights. Although Syria's military performance in the war was stronger than in previous wars, Israel held on to the territory. In an agreement reached after the war, Israel returned a narrow tract of about 39 square miles (101 square kilometers) of Golan Heights land to Syria, and some of the territory's former residents returned to live there. Syria and Israel created a buffer zone (a neutral area separating two hostile countries) in the Golan Heights and agreed to have it monitored by a United Nations peacekeeping force. The force was still there in 2011.

In 1981 Israel annexed (made a permanent part of Israel) the Golan Heights, and was heavily criticized by the international community for doing so. Syria's leadership made it clear that it will never make peace with Israel until Israel returns the Golan Heights.

Within Lebanon, Syria first looked to the PLO and Lebanese Muslims for support. But when these groups seemed in position to win power in Lebanon, Syria became nervous. Assad feared that Israel would enter the Lebanese struggle on the side of the Maronites to keep the PLO out of power, thereby creating a Lebanese government friendlier to Israel than to

Syria. Syria therefore quickly switched its allegiance to the ruling Maronites when the civil war broke out in 1975, supplying troops to help maintain Christian power in the Lebanese government and to keep the Christian Maronites from siding with Israel.

Such wild swings of allegiance became increasingly common in Lebanon. In 1976, for example, both Syria (supported by the Soviet Union) and Israel (supported by the United States) offered Lebanon aid to fight the Palestinians. Israel also allowed Maronite militias to establish strategic strongholds along its border with Lebanon. Meanwhile, Syria worked to establish a strong Lebanese government that would limit the authority of Israeli-supported militias.

In 1976 the Arab League met in Riyadh, Saudi Arabia, to try to resolve the Lebanese crisis. The accords that emerged from this conference ordered a cease-fire in Lebanon and authorized the creation of a neutral military force called the Arab Deterrent Force (ADF) to supervise the cease-fire. The ADF was intended to be a made up of military units from a variety of Arab nations, all serving under the command of the Lebanese president. In the end, however, only about five thousand Arab troops were added to tens of thousands of Syrian forces already posted in Lebanon, and Syria refused to give up its command of the troops. Thus, the Riyadh accords made it more or less legitimate that forty thousand Syrian troops were stationed in Lebanon to maintain peace. The agreement did little to stop the tensions between various Maronite, Muslim, and Palestinian groups, however, and even the Syrian troops were unable to maintain the negotiated cease-fire. Within the year, Maronite militias were again battling with the PLO and the Lebanese National Movement. Israeli-supported Arab militias fought with the PLO, with Shiites in the south, and with Lebanese National Movement militias.

As a result of the fighting, Lebanon split in two. Christians controlled the north and Muslims and Palestinians controlled the south. The city of Beirut was divided along a border known as the Green Line, with a Christian sector in the east and a Muslim sector in the west. Moreover, Israel declared that it would not allow Syrian troops in Lebanon to cross what it called the Red Line, a territory south of the Litani River along the southern Lebanese border that Israel claimed as a security zone.

Over the coming years, Syria would struggle to gain influence over Lebanese politics and would switch alliances within Lebanon frequently to maintain its advantage in the country. The role of Lebanon as a battleground for Syria to fight Israel became clear in the 1980s. Syria tried to maintain a balance of power, supporting the PLO against Israeli attacks. However, it also condoned attacks on certain PLO authorities and supplied Shiite militias with weapons to attack the Palestinians in southern Lebanon. In 1982 Syria supported Maronite leader Suleiman Frangieh (1910–1992) in his election campaign against Israeli-supported Maronite Phalangist Bashir Gemayel (1947–1982) for the Lebanese presidency. Phalangists supportive of Gemayel fought with Syrian troops. To support the Phalangists, Israel air force bombers shot down two Syrian helicopters. Syria responded by setting up ground-to-air missiles in the region. Syria continued to fight for power in Lebanon in the 1980s and 1990s, and eventually emerged as the dominant force in the country.

Israel's relations with Lebanon

Three years into the Lebanese civil war, in 1978, Israeli troops invaded southern Lebanon in an attempt to secure its borders and remove the PLO from the region. They evicted both Palestinians and Lebanese Muslims from villages along the southern border in order to establish a buffer zone. Other countries generally disapproved of Israel's invasion of Lebanon. The United Nations Security Council called for the immediate withdrawal of Israeli troops. UN Resolution 425 established a peace-keeping force called the United Nations Interim Forces in Lebanon (UNIFIL) to oversee the withdrawal of Israeli troops and to secure a cease-fire in the area. The first UNIFIL troops arrived in Lebanon on March 23, 1978; over time the force grew to about six thousand soldiers. Most Israeli troops withdrew from Lebanon in 1978, but Israel did not waver from its goal of destroying the PLO.

Unable to maintain a cease-fire with the PLO, Israel invaded Lebanon again in 1982. Although the United Nations issued multiple resolutions calling for the withdrawal of Israeli troops and an end to hostilities, Israel pushed troops through southern Lebanon and into Beirut. Israel's military directive, known as Operation Peace for Galilee, had the objective of pushing the PLO far enough away from Israeli borders so that their rockets could not reach Israeli settlements. To this end Israel attacked Beirut, where thousands of PLO troops were assembled in fortified areas.

Israeli soldiers during the first invasion of Lebanon in 1978.
UZI KEREN/AFP/GETTY IMAGES.

The massacre at the Sabra and Shatila camps

By August 12, 1982, U.S. ambassador to Lebanon Philip Habib (1920–1992) successfully negotiated a plan to evacuate Israeli, PLO, and Syrian troops from Beirut, with the help of U.S. Marines, French troops, and Italian troops. These international forces arrived on August 20. But even in the presence of so many peacekeepers, peace could not be achieved in Lebanon.

In 1982, Bashir Gemayel was elected president of Lebanon. He was assassinated less than one month later, on September 14, killed by a bomb.

Lebanon's turmoil turned especially vicious after the bombing. The Phalangists, who immediately began to seek out the PLO fighters accused of the bombing, assumed that they were in the Palestinian refugee camps of Sabra and Shatila outside Beirut. As the Phalangists made their way to the camps, Israeli troops entered West Beirut, against rules set by international agreements. They surrounded the camps in time to watch as units of Phalangists swept into them. Over the next three days, the Phalangists massacred approximately one thousand Palestinians in the Sabra and Shatila camps. None of the people they killed were members of the PLO. Although the exact role of the Israeli troops is not known, observers throughout the world blamed them for their inaction during the shameful massacre. International pressure for Israel to leave Lebanon increased.

The United States negotiated another plan for withdrawal of Israeli and Syrian troops from Lebanon on May 17, 1983. Gemayel's brother, Amine (1942–), who had taken over as president, signed the agreement hoping to secure protection for Lebanon. The agreement aimed to remove all Syrian influence in Lebanon and maintain Israeli influence through military protection along the borders.

The plan backfired, igniting attacks against Americans. Although Israel withdrew from all but its security zone in the south by September 1983, Syria refused even to discuss withdrawal of its troops, claiming that the agreement signed by Lebanon and created by the United States (a country that claimed to be neutral in the situation) was focused on securing Maronite control in Lebanon instead of creating a stable peace. A growing number of opponents of the plan in Lebanon, including Druze leader Walid Jumblatt (1949–), came to view U.S. policies as hostile toward Arabs and Islam. Attacks on U.S. Marines in Lebanon escalated. A bombing of the American embassy in Beirut in June 1983 killed 63 people, and a suicide bomber killed more than 240 service personnel at a U.S. military barracks near Beirut in October 1983. Unable to secure peace in Lebanon, U.S. president Ronald Reagan (1911–2004) withdrew marines from Lebanon in February 1984.

The West leaves Lebanon to Syria

With the withdrawal of the United States, conflict between Lebanese Muslims and the Phalangists erupted. Western organizations within the country were bombed, and many Americans and other Europeans still working in Lebanon were killed or taken hostage. Without support from the United States, Gemayel withdrew his support from the agreement negotiated by the United States in 1983 and tried to get help from Syria.

Syria willingly stepped in. It proposed a power-sharing strategy that would retain Maronite control of the government and split the parliament between Muslims and Christians. By the end of 1985, Syria had succeeded in persuading the largest religious factions to support this new government structure. It sent several thousand troops with tanks and artillery to take control of West Beirut and central Lebanon. By 1988 the population Lebanon was split over whether or not Syria should remain in the country. A new group called the Lebanese Liberation Front had organized in 1987 with the intent to use violence to end Syria's control of the country. The group killed Syrian military and diplomatic personnel.

Struggles between supporters and opponents of Syrian intervention in Lebanon were so intense that the 1988 presidential elections could not be held, and Amine Gemayel's term as president came to an end that year. The division of power in Lebanon called for a Sunni Muslim prime minister and a Maronite president, but if Gemayel left office without an elected successor, the presidential authority would revert to the Sunni prime minister. To retain Maronite control of the government, Gemayel prepared for Lebanon to be ruled by a military-led government until proper elections could be held. He appointed the Maronite general Michel Aoun (1936–) as prime minister of that interim government just fifteen minutes before his term ended. Aoun was vehemently anti-Syrian. Once he was in power, he ordered aggressive military strikes against Syrian troops and against the various militias resisting his government's authority.

The Taif Accord and an end to battle

Finally, Lebanon's neighbors sought to negotiate an end to the seemingly endless conflicts in Lebanon. With support from both the Soviet Union and the United States, Saudi Arabia sponsored a meeting of the Lebanese parliament in 1989 in Taif, Saudi Arabia. There, Lebanese parliament members debated the future structure of the Lebanese government for three weeks. The result was the Taif Accord, which increased the size of the legislative chamber from 99 to 108 members and called for the seats to be divided equally between Christians and Muslims. Additionally, the agreement authorized Syria to provide military support in Lebanon for two years in order to securely establish the new government.

Michel Aoun, originally a Lebanese general, became prime minister of the interim government in 1988. © WAEL LADKI/REUTERS/CORBIS.

Aoun completely rejected the Taif Accord and did everything he could to block the formation of the new government, called the Second Lebanese Republic. As Aoun threatened and protested against the new government, his support waned and the new government grew stronger and gained new allies, including the United States. In October 1990 Syria bombed Aoun's stronghold and sent him into exile in France. Without Aoun stirring up resistance, Lebanon settled into a period of relative peace.

The civil war had torn the country apart. An estimated 150,000 people were killed and about 900,000 lost their homes. The different sects in the once-tolerant democracy had been, for the period of the war, hostile enemies. Lebanon proved to be resilient, however, and quickly began its rebuilding process. During the peaceful years after 1990, most independent militias were disbanded. One group, the militant Islamist organization known as Hezbollah, continued to grow more powerful, and its rise would eventually disrupt Lebanon's hard-won peace.

For More Information

BOOKS

Cobban, Helena. *The Making of Modern Lebanon*. London: Hutchinson, 1985.

Collelo, Thomas, ed. *Syria: A Country Study*. Washington: GPO for the Library of Congress, 1987. Available online at http://countrystudies.us/syria/ (accessed on November 30, 2011).

Cottrell, Robert C. *The Green Line: The Division of Palestine*. Philadelphia, PA: Chelsea House, 2005.

Diller, Daniel C., ed. *The Middle East*. 8th ed. Washington, DC: Congressional Quarterly, 1995.

Foster, Leila Merrell. *Lebanon*. Chicago, IL: Children's Press, 1992.

Hirst, David. *Beware of Small States: Lebanon, Battleground of the Middle East*. New York: Nation Books, 2010.

Pintak, Larry. *Seeds of Hate: How America's Flawed Middle East Policy Ignited the Jihad*. London: Pluto Press, 2003.

Sheehan, Sean. *Lebanon*. New York: Marshall Cavendish, 1997.

Smith, Charles D., ed. *Palestine and the Arab-Israeli Conflict: A History with Documents*. 7th ed. Boston: Bedford/St. Martin's Press, 2009.

PERIODICALS

"Analysis: New Lebanese Civil War Unlikely." *UPI Perspectives* (March 23, 2005).

Salhani, Claude. "Analysis: Syria to Redeploy Troops." *UPI Perspectives* (September 20, 2004).

WEB SITES

"Lebanon." *CIA World Factbook*. http://cia.gov/cia/publications/factbook/geos/le.html#People (accessed on November 30, 2011).

Moubayed, Sami. "Letter from Levant: Amin Gemayel Says His Family's History Runs Parallel to Lebanon's." *Washington Report on Middle East Affairs* (October 2001). http://www.wrmea.com/archives/october01/0110029.html (accessed on November 30, 2011).

"Q&A: Syria and Lebanon." *BBC News* (March 18, 2005). http://news.bbc.co.uk/1/hi/world/middle_east/4308823.stm (accessed on November 30, 2011).

"Syria Sets Deadline for Lebanon Pullout." *CNN* (April 3, 2005). http://www.cnn.com/2005/WORLD/meast/04/03/lebanon.syria/index.html (accessed on November 30, 2011).

The Rise of Hezbollah in Lebanon: 1990 to 2011

Hezbollah is a resistance group that emerged in Lebanon in the mid-1980s in the midst of the chaos of that country's civil war (1975–90). Within a few years it was best known for its large-scale acts of terrorism. Over the course of the next quarter century, Hezbollah also became one of Lebanon's major political forces. It had a solid political base among Lebanon's growing population of Shiites (followers of the Shia branch of the religion of Islam), who had long been underrepresented in Lebanon's government. In democratic elections in the early twenty-first century, Hezbollah members were elected into positions within the national government, winning a majority of votes. Around the world, observers anxiously watched this democratic process involving a group known for terrorism unfold.

Early Shiite resistance groups

In the 1970s Shiites grew to become the largest of the many religious groups in Lebanon. Despite their growing numbers, Shiites were poorly represented in Lebanon's democratic government. Lebanon had a diverse population, with seventeen different minority groups struggling for representation. Its government was sectarian, meaning that it distributed political and institutional power among its various religious sects (groups) and ethnic communities on a proportional basis. The proportions had been set many years ago and did not reflect the rapid rise in the Shiite population. (For more information, see **Syria and Lebanon: 1936 to 1990**.) Shiites, who lived primarily in the southern part of Lebanon, in the Bekáa Valley, and in some suburbs of the city of Beirut, were generally poorer than members of other religious sects and felt that they were the victims of discrimination.

WORDS TO KNOW

Arab League: A regional political alliance of Arab nations formed in 1945 to promote political, military, and economic cooperation within the Arab world.

Arab Spring: A series of prodemocracy uprisings in the Middle East and North Africa.

cleric: An ordained religious official.

Druze: Members of a small sect of Islam who believe that the ninth-century caliph Tariq al-Hakim was God.

guerrilla warfare: Combat tactics used by a smaller, less equipped fighting force against a more powerful foe.

Hezbollah: A Shiite militant group and political party based in Lebanon.

insurgency: An uprising, or rebellion, against a political authority.

Islamism: A fundamentalist movement characterized by the belief that Islam should provide the basis for the political, social, and cultural life in Muslim nations.

Maronites: Members of an Arabic-speaking group of Christians, living mainly in Lebanon, who are in communion (share essential doctrines) with the Roman Catholic Church.

militia: Armed civilian military forces.

occupation: The physical and political control of an area seized by a foreign military force.

Palestine: A historical region in the Middle East on the eastern shore of the Mediterranean Sea, comprising parts of present-day Israel and Jordan.

Palestine Liberation Organization (PLO): A political and military organization formed to unite various Palestinian Arab groups with the goal of establishing an independent Palestinian state.

Palestinians: An Arab people whose ancestors lived in the historical region of Palestine and who continue to lay claim to that land.

refugees: People who flee their country to escape violence or persecution.

sectarian government: A government that distributes political and institutional power among its various religious sects and ethnic communities on a proportional basis.

sharia: A system of Islamic law based on the Koran and other sacred writings. Sharia attempts to create the perfect social order, based on God's will and justice, and covers a wide range of human activities, including acts of religious worship, the law of contracts and obligations, personal status law, and public law.

Shiites: Followers of the Shia branch of Islam. Shiites believe that only direct descendants of the prophet Muhammad are qualified to lead the Islamic faith.

suicide bombing: An attack intended to kill others and cause widespread damage, carried about by someone who does not hope to survive the attack.

Sunnis: Followers of the Sunni branch of Islam. Sunnis believe that elected officials, regardless of their heritage, are qualified to lead the Islamic faith.

Shiites began to organize in the 1970s. One of the earliest Shiite groups was the Movement for the Disinherited (also called the Movement for the Deprived), founded in 1974 by Musa al-Sadr (1928–?), an Iranian-born Shiite cleric, an ordained religious official. The group provided aid and services, such as education and health care, to Lebanon's Shiite poor. It formed its own militia (an armed civilian military force), called Amal, in 1975. Al-Sadr mysteriously disappeared a few years later.

Musa al-Sadr, founder of the Movement for the Disinherited, an early Shiite group. © DIEGO GOLDBERG/ SYGMA/CORBIS.

During and after the 1948 Arab-Israeli War (a war fought between the newly declared state of Israel and its Arab neighbors) an estimated three hundred Palestinians (an Arab people whose ancestors lived in the historical region of Palestine, comprising parts of present-day Israel and Jordan, and who continue to lay claim to that land), became refugees, people who flee their country to escape violence or persecution. One of the countries that the Palestinian refugees fled to was Lebanon, where they lived in refugee camps and other dwellings mainly in the southern part of the country. In the 1970s, the Palestine Liberation Organization (PLO) established its headquarters in southern Lebanon. The PLO is a political and military organization formed to unite various Palestinian Arab groups with the goal of establishing an independent Palestinian state. Since the late 1960s, it had been increasingly employed guerilla warfare (combat tactics used by a smaller, less equipped fighting force against a more powerful foe) and terrorist acts, such as plane hijackings and kidnappings, to fight with Israel, hoping to draw the world's attention to Israel's occupation of lands the Palestinians considered their own. In Lebanon, the PLO became so powerful that it was virtually a state within a state, with its own government and militia. There was so much political turmoil in Lebanon at the time due to the power struggle between religious groups that Lebanese officials did not have enough resources to regulate the Palestinian refugees. The Lebanese Shiites were initially hostile to the Palestinians, because they had taken over Shiite territory and because the refugees were Sunnis, followers of the Sunni branch of Islam. By the 1980s Amal's main focus was to drive the Palestinian refugees out of the Shiite territory.

The PLO relentlessly attacked Israel from the border region of southern Lebanon. In 1982 Israel retaliated by invading Lebanon in an offensive called Operation Peace for Galilee. This offensive forced the PLO, as well as many other Palestinians and Muslim Lebanese, out of southern Lebanon. The Israeli troops remained in southern Lebanon, where they created a buffer zone (a neutral area separating two hostile countries) to protect Israelis from rockets launched across the border by the growing number of Shiite Lebanese militants.

Many Lebanese Shiites initially welcomed the Israeli invasion of 1982, hoping it would rid their country of the Palestinians. But soon the Israeli troops were making life difficult for the Shiites living in southern Lebanon. The troops raided villages to remove those suspected of committing attacks on Israeli positions, restricted local Lebanese access to markets in the north by putting up blockades, and brought Israeli merchandise into Lebanon and sold it at such low prices that local merchants suffered. Within a few years, many Shiites were ready to fight in an armed resistance against Israel, but they found that the leaders of Amal, who were still influenced by their anti-Palestinian focus, were not interested in taking on Israel. Many young warriors who wanted to fight Israel left Amal to start their own groups. A number of small militias emerged, ready to use any means available to fight the powerful Israeli forces.

Shiite support from Iran and Syria

The new militias had few resources, but it was not long before they found steady support from Iran. The 1979 Iranian Revolution (also known as the Islamic Revolution) transformed Iran from a secular (nonreligious) country into an Islamic country, in which the social, political, and economic institutions of the country are based on sharia, Islamic religious law. Iran, which is more than 90 percent Shiite, dispatched a group of about one thousand Iranian Revolutionary Guards (an elite Iranian security force) to Lebanon in the early 1980s. The guards set up recruiting and training programs in the mainly Shiite regions of southern Lebanon and the Bekáa Valley. These Iranian programs enabled the new militias to unite and organize themselves for their fight against Israel.

Iran was not the only foreign power supporting militants in Lebanon. Syrian president Hafez Assad (also spelled al-Assad; 1930–2000) had ambitions to rule a large Arab republic from Damascus, Syria's capital. He had long viewed Lebanon as a province of Syria and had sought to exercise his influence and power there. He did not want to see a liberal democratic party control Lebanon, because he did not believe he could manipulate it. About one year after the Lebanese Civil War broke out in 1975, the Arab League (regional political alliance of Arab nations formed in 1945 to promote political, military, and economic cooperation within the Arab world) had granted Syria permission to station forty thousand Syrian troops in Lebanon as part of a peace agreement. Assad quickly sent in his troops, beginning what would be a twenty-nine-year Syrian military occupation of Lebanon. It was Syria that encouraged its ally, Iran, to send the Revolutionary Guards to Lebanon to train the Shiite militias in 1982.

Hezbollah is born

From 1983 to 1985 the Shiite militias based in the Bekáa Valley and southern Lebanon began a new era of violence aimed at Israel. Since Israel had a powerful, well-armed, and well-funded military and intelligence network, the Shiites did not have the resources to fight them using conventional or even guerrilla warfare. The militias instead began to target unsuspecting civilians or unprepared troops. The practice of suicide bombing first came into use in the modern Middle East among these Shiite militias of the early 1980s. (A suicide bombing is an attack intended to kill others and cause widespread damage, carried about by someone who does not hope to survive the attack.) Kidnapping foreigners was another favored tactic of these militias.

In 1983, both the United States and France had troops in civil war-torn Lebanon in an effort to establish peace. That year, a suicide bomber drove a truck filled with explosives into a building at the Beirut airport that housed U.S. Marines on the peacekeeping mission, killing 241 people. At the same time another bomber blew up a structure housing French paratroopers, killing 58. Several days later, a suicide bomber drove a truck into an Israeli headquarters in southern Lebanon, killing 29 Israeli troops. These attacks and others like them succeeded in their purpose; in 1984 the United States and France withdrew from Lebanon and Israel pulled back its forces to a small region in southern Lebanon.

The impact of these attacks was immense. Small groups with little power or authority and few resources had found a means by which they could combat the worlds' most powerful militaries. Soon suicide bombings and kidnapping people, particularly those from the United States and Western Europe, became common events in the region. The Shiite militants, like the Iranians who trained them, resented Western interference in the Middle East and associated the United States, in particular, with Israel.

In 1985 the small militias that had arisen in response to the 1982 Israeli invasion merged into a new group called Hezbollah (*Hizb Allah* in Arabic, meaning "Party of God"). The group was Islamist, meaning it advocated a conservative interpretation of Islam, in which sharia provided the basis for political, social, and cultural life. But Hezbollah's immediate purpose was to drive Israeli forces, and all Western influences, out of Lebanon.

A group called Islamic Jihad claimed responsibility for the worst of the terrorist acts. Historians attribute most of the worst violence and terrorism that occurred from 1983 to 1985 to a man named Imad Mughniyah

(1962–2008), who was originally associated with Islamic Jihad but later with Hezbollah. It is not known for certain whether Islamic Jihad was just another name for Hezbollah, or if it was a separate group that merged into it. Although Mughniyah's role in Hezbollah has always been kept secret by the organization, many experts say he was a senior Hezbollah agent in charge of security and/or terrorist operations until his death.

From 1984, with the withdrawal of U.S. Marines from Lebanon, to the end of that decade, the Islamic Jihad was especially noted for its kidnappings. A few examples of its work are the 1984 murder of American University of Beirut president Malcolm Kerr (1931–1984) and the kidnapping of CIA Chief William Buckley (1928–1985). Buckley was tortured and died in captivity in Iran. In 1985 American journalist Terry Anderson (1947–) was kidnapped and held for nearly seven years before his release.

On February 16, 1992, Israeli forces assassinated Hezbollah's secretary-general, Abbas al-Musawi (c. 1952–1992) in a helicopter attack on his motorcade that also killed his wife and son. He was succeeded by Hassan Nasrallah (1960–).

Syria settles in

Lebanon's government had many problems during Hezbollah's early years due to the civil war. Its national security forces had broken down and many competing militias, including Hezbollah, had taken its place. In 1989, after a cease-fire had been established, members of the Lebanese parliament (legislature) met in Saudi Arabia for a conference that resulted in the Taif Accord. The agreement proposed a restructuring of Lebanon's government to more fairly represent the country's major religious and ethnic groups. The parties agreed on a restructuring of the Lebanese government that would better represent the country's different religious sects and the withdrawal of Syrian forces from the country, but in the end, the final agreement failed to call for the Syrian withdrawal. Instead, it proposed that Syria move its forces to the Bekáa Valley within two years; at that time another meeting between Syria and Lebanon would decide Syria's role in Lebanon. With this agreement, Lebanon's civil war ended.

Syria's immense involvement in Lebanon's affairs angered many Lebanese leaders. Lebanese prime minister Michel Aoun (1935–) was a former general of the Christian-dominated Lebanese army, which had been nonfunctioning during most of the civil war. Aoun was secular and charismatic, and he appealed to people of many different sects. Fearing that Syria would take over Lebanon, Aoun launched a major rebellion against the Syrians. In the end, however, the Syrian forces proved more powerful. Aoun was driven out of Lebanon, hundreds of his troops were killed, and Syria continued to occupy Lebanon.

In May 1991 the Lebanese government granted Syria control of Lebanon's internal affairs and soon handed over the management of its foreign policy and security issues as well. Most of the international community, including the United States, accepted Syria's role in Lebanon as a means of maintaining security and stability there. With the strength of the Syrian military behind them, Lebanon's first parliamentary elections since 1972 were held in 1992. The numerous militias were disbanded, and Lebanon began to rebuild its own national military. Of the many militias, only Hezbollah remained, with Syria's support. Hezbollah, beginning to change its image from a militia to a political party, placed candidates in the election and won several seats in Lebanon's parliament.

In the 1992 election, Rafiq Hariri (1944–2005) became Lebanon's prime minister. Born in Lebanon, Hariri spent the years of the civil war in Saudi Arabia as a highly successful building contractor. He was a billionaire by the time he returned to Lebanon in the early 1980s, and he contributed generously to political groups and foundations, earning himself the nickname "Mr. Lebanon". Hariri was one of the chief promoters of the Taif Accord. Although he was Sunni Muslim, Hariri led a secular government. He brought a businessman's sense to the job and set to work restructuring Lebanon's economy and reconstructing its buildings and roads. With the militias gone, Lebanese citizens could move throughout the country freely for the first time in years. Trade and communication networks resumed, and Beirut, where so much of the civil war violence had occurred, was transformed into an attractive, modern city and a major tourist destination, as it had been before the civil war.

Hezbollah's victory

While Lebanon was rebuilding, Hezbollah's struggle against Israel continued. Hezbollah had developed a strong military force, and its attacks on Israeli troops in southern Lebanon employed suicide bombers and rocket launchers called Katyushas, supplied by Iran. The group took credit for killing an estimated sixteen hundred Israelis in Lebanon between 1982 and 2000.

Rafiq Hariri, seen as his home in Beirut in 2000. Hariri became Lebanon's prime minister in 1992. © MAHER ATTAR/SYGMA/CORBIS.

The link between Hezbollah and Iran had remained strong. Iran's population is almost entirely Shiite, like the members of Hezbollah. Both promote the idea of an Islamic Middle East, run by clerics under a rigid interpretation of sharia. After its Islamic Revolution, Iran pledged to

An Israeli soldier, carrying the Israeli flag that had flown at an Israeli outpost in Lebanon, on his way out of Lebanon. Hezbollah's goal of expelling Israelis from Lebanon succeeded in 2000 with the withdrawal of Israeli soldiers. MENAHEM KAHANA/AFP/ GETTY IMAGES.

spread Islamism, and it also strove to destroy Israel. In funding Hezbollah, it hoped to accomplish both objectives.

Hezbollah's persistent attacks on Israel succeeded. In May 2000 the Israeli occupation of Lebanon, which had lasted more than eighteen years, ended with the withdrawal of Israeli soldiers. It was a huge victory. Hezbollah was celebrated by both Lebanese Christians and Muslims and by Muslims worldwide for this victory against Israel.

Along with its show of military might, Hezbollah had become a potent political force. With funding from Iran, Hezbollah's secretary-general Hassan Nasrallah led major efforts to provide aid to poor Shiite communities. Hezbollah built schools and health clinics, distributed fresh water, established garbage collection services, and instituted many other necessary programs that the Lebanese government lacked the resources to provide.

By 1990, Lebanon's Shiite community had grown to make up about 45 to 50 percent of the Lebanese population. Although some of Hezbollah's more militant leaders opposed working within the government, it was clear to Nasrallah that Shiite support would bring Hezbollah votes at election time. A highly charismatic leader, Nasrallah broadcast rousing

Supporters listen to the speech of Hezbollah leader Hassan Nasrallah through a video link in October 2010. Nasrallah broadcast rousing political speeches on Hezbollah's communications network on a regular basis. © NABIL MOUNZER/EPA/CORBIS.

political speeches on Hezbollah's communications network on a regular basis. Even as it tried to change its public image, however, Hezbollah refused to give up its independent military force. With a significant force of trained fighters and a large arsenal of missiles, Hezbollah's militia was stronger than the forces of the Lebanese government.

The assassination of Hariri

After the civil war, the Syrian government's influence in Lebanon became increasingly oppressive. Syria provided power and resources to the Lebanese politicians who supported it, thus ensuring that the Lebanese parliament was filled with pro-Syrian ministers. It used its sophisticated intelligence network, arbitrary arrests, and whatever other means were necessary to suppress opposition and maintain its enormous influence in Lebanon. In 1998 Hariri resigned as prime minister due primarily to clashes with the Lebanese president, Emile Lahoud (1936–), who was a strong ally of Assad.

Assad died in 2000, and his son, Bashar Assad (1965–), took his place as Syria's president. Many in Lebanon, including Hariri, hoped Syria's new leader would adopt more gentle policies for Lebanon. Hariri ran for prime minister and was once again elected. But in 2004, Syria used its influence within Lebanon's government to force a vote to amend the constitution in order to extend Lahoud's presidency by three years. Many Lebanese leaders objected, saying the constitutional amendment would destroy Lebanon's democracy. Hariri hoped to negotiate with Bashar Assad, but in August, the Syrian leader called Hariri to Damascus, where he told him to push through the constitutional amendment. After the amendment passed, Hariri resigned. He turned his attention to establishing the Future Movement, a political organization dedicated to Lebanon's unity and independence.

On February 14, 2005, Hariri was assassinated in Beirut by a powerful bomb that blew up his armored car. Twenty-two others, mostly Hariri's bodyguards, were killed in the incident. Hariri's son, Saad Hariri (1971–), quickly took over as the head of the Future Movement, determined to continue his father's work. The assassination provoked strong feelings among the Lebanese people. Even many who had not been supporters of Hariri were deeply affected by his murder. Most people in Lebanon blamed Syria, even though Syria denied involvement.

March 8 Alliance versus March 14 Coalition

On the day of Rafiq Hariri's funeral, people of all faiths and ethnicities showed up by the tens of thousands to pay their respects. Emotions ran so strong that the funeral turned into a long-term protest demonstration. The protesters called for Lebanon's government (the prime minister and the parliament, but not the president) and security chiefs to resign, for Syria to withdraw from Lebanon, for free elections to be held, and finally, for an international investigation into Hariri's murder. The government did resign after two weeks, and the United Nations began what would be a five-year investigation into the murder. (The United Nations is an international organization of countries founded in 1945 to promote international peace, security, and cooperation.) But President Lahoud and the occupying Syrian forces remained, although they could not stop the protests.

Hezbollah was strongly linked to Syria. Nasrallah, who had been positioning his group to take over a large number of parliamentary seats in the upcoming elections, realized that the anti-Syrian fever would hurt Hezbollah's chances in the election. He used his influence to call together a mass demonstration on March 8, 2005, in an attempt to counter the ongoing anti-Syrian protest. The March 8 counterdemonstration took place in downtown Beirut and brought together several pro-Syrian groups, headed by Hezbollah, who expressed gratitude to Syria for helping to end the civil war. The groups involved in this demonstration became known as the March 8 Alliance. It was not strong enough at that time, however, to effectively counter Lebanese rage at Syria.

One month after the assassination of Hariri, on March 14, 2005, an estimated one million Lebanese citizens took to the streets in a demonstration called the March 14 Movement (later called the Cedar Revolution) to protest Syrian presence in Lebanon. In addition, calls for Syria's withdrawal mounted around the world, with Russia, Germany, and especially Saudi Arabia, which had maintained close ties with Hariri, putting pressure on Syria. The pressure was too much, even for Syria. In April Syrian troops withdrew from Lebanon, ending Syria's twenty-nine-year military presence there.

Shortly after Syria's withdrawal, Lebanon held its first elections free of Syrian control in decades. The election pitted Hezbollah's Shiite supporters against the March 14 Coalition, a group led by Saad Hariri and the Future Movement and comprised of Lebanon's Maronites, Sunni Muslims, and Druze (a small sect of Islam that believes that the ninth-century caliph Tariq al-Hakim was God). The March 14 Coalition won seventy-two seats, the majority of the votes. It promised an era of political and economic reform. Hezbollah and the March 8 Alliance won thirty-five parliamentary seats.

Israel's thirty-three-day war on Hezbollah

On July 12, 2006, Hezbollah attacked a small force of Israeli troops who were patrolling Israel's border with Lebanon, killing eight, wounding several, and taking two hostage. Israel unexpectedly responded to Hezbollah's raid with extreme force. Israel's attack began as an attempt to recover its kidnapped soldiers. But as the battle escalated, Israeli leaders saw it as an opportunity to destroy Hezbollah once and for all. Israel launched air, naval, and ground attacks at Hezbollah targets in Lebanon. Hezbollah, in

On March 14, 2005, Lebanese demonstrators gathered in Martyrs Square in Beirut, near the grave of former prime minister Rafiq Hariri, to protest Syrian presence in Lebanon. RAMZI HAIDAR/AFP/GETTY IMAGES.

turn, fired about four thousand rockets into northern Israel, some reaching as far as the city of Haifa. Forced into hiding, Nasrallah still broadcast speeches day and night throughout the war.

The war between Israel and Hezbollah lasted for thirty-three days, ending in what appeared to be a stalemate (having no clear winner). The destruction in many Shiite communities in Lebanon was devastating. In one month of fighting, about 1,200 Lebanese and 159 Israeli civilians and soldiers were killed. Nearly one million Lebanese were displaced from their homes, and some parts of Lebanon had been utterly destroyed by bombs. Hezbollah had lost a large portion of its missiles and trained soldiers. Nevertheless, Nasrallah hailed the war as a victory for Hezbollah. It had inflicted harm on Israel and forced its civilians to experience warfare firsthand. The main victory was that Hezbollah had survived Israel's all-out attack. People throughout the Middle East celebrated Hezbollah's triumph over Israel. In Lebanon Hezbollah's popularity soared.

Nasrallah explained through his broadcast speeches that he had not foreseen Israel's explosive retaliation for the Hezbollah attack and apologized to the Lebanese people for his error. Then he put Hezbollah to work rebuilding the damaged neighborhoods and roads.

Disruption in the government

In November 2006 Lebanon's coalition government (a government in which political parties cooperate with each other, because no party holds the majority) fell apart when Hezbollah's ministers in parliament resigned to protest what they viewed as unequal Shiite representation. The majority of the parliament refused to agree to Hezbollah's demands for equal representation for fear of giving the group the power of veto (the power to block any legislations or actions) in the coalition government.

Over the next two years, political chaos ensued. The Hezbollah resignations prevented a presidential election to replace Lahoud when his term was over in 2007, and Lebanon suddenly found itself without a president. Hostilities between the March 14 Coalition government and the March 8 Alliance grew. In 2008 the government fired at least one top official with known associations to Hezbollah and closed down Hezbollah's communication network. Hezbollah struck back with force. On May 8, 2008, Hezbollah members swarmed several areas of Beirut, taking over the party headquarters and communications networks of their rivals and even burning the offices of the newspaper run by the Hariri family. They quietly withdrew two days later, but the clashes had killed eighty-one people and spread new fears of civil war.

On May 21, 2008, all factions of the Lebanese government met in Doha, Qatar, and worked out a resolution in which Hezbollah received the power of veto in the government. The Doha agreement paved the way for new presidential elections in 2009, in which Saad Hariri and the March 14 Coalition won 71 of the 128 parliament seats and Hezbollah and the March 8 Alliance won 58 seats. With only a small majority, Hariri, the new prime minister, offered to build a coalition government with his opponents. In an attempt at balance, the proportions were set at fifteen ministers of parliament for the March 14 Coalition, ten for the March 8 Alliance, and five for the president, who was considered neutral. Lebanon's new government functioned for more than a year. During that time, Hezbollah shored up its power by allying with the ever-popular and powerful Aoun, who had returned from exile and threw his support behind Hezbollah. With this political alliance, which added about half of Lebanon's Christians to the March 8 Alliance, Hezbollah had achieved a majority in government.

In the meantime, the United Nations continued to investigate Rafiq Hariri's assassination. In March 2009 the Special Tribunal for Lebanon, a court based in the Netherlands specifically to prosecute Hariri's killers under Lebanese law, was established under an agreement by the United Nations and Lebanon. By the beginning of 2011 the tribunal had decided to indict (formally charge) four Hezbollah members for Hariri's murder. Nasrallah claimed that the tribunal was controlled by Israel and the United States. He denied Hezbollah's part in the murder and requested that the prime minister reject the tribunal's findings. Saad Hariri, who had sought the investigation into his father's death in the first place, refused to deny its findings. In January 2011 March 8 Alliance ministers of parliament resigned their posts in protest of the tribunal. Hariri's coalition government collapsed.

As the majority party, Hezbollah was responsible for forming a new government. In June 2011 Hezbollah nominated Najib Mikati (1955–) as prime minister and asked him to form a new government. Mikati is a wealthy Sunni businessman who describes himself as politically moderate. He is a family friend of Syrian president Bashar Assad, and Hariri refused to recognize him as a legitimate prime minister. Mikati formed a thirty-seat government in which Hezbollah and its allies control eighteen seats.

In 2011 Hezbollah nominated Najib Mikati (pictured) as prime minister. ANWAR AMRO/AFP/GETTY IMAGES.

Hezbollah on the defensive

The new government of Lebanon was formed during the Arab Spring, a series of pro-democracy uprisings that swept the Middle East and North Africa in 2011. Nasrallah and other leaders had long portrayed Hezbollah as a friend of the people, and they had spoken in support of the uprisings in Egypt, Tunisia, Yemen, Bahrain, and Libya. But when the protests in the region inspired the people of Syria to rise up against President Assad, Hezbollah was caught off guard. As protests in Syria continued and Syrian forces grew increasingly brutal in their crackdowns on civilians, Hezbollah found itself in a highly unpopular position. When Nasrallah took a public stand in support of Assad, calling the Syrian protesters thugs and gangs, he immediately faced criticism from his usual supporters at home and around the world. But he could not join in the popular criticism of Assad, since Hezbollah was dependent on Syria's funding and its supplies of weapons.

On June 30, 2011, the Special Tribunal for Lebanon officially indicted the four Hezbollah members in the assassination of Rafiq Hariri. One of the accused was the brother of long-time Hezbollah operative Imad Mughniyeh, one of the world's most wanted terrorists who had himself been assassinated in 2008. Nasrallah announced that he would never allow the arrest of any members of his group for this crime and vowed that no one would ever find the accused.

For Westerners and many moderates in the Middle East the rise of Hezbollah in the Lebanese government made a long-held fear a reality. Although most had wanted to see democratic reforms in Lebanon as elsewhere in the Middle East, they also feared that in democratic elections people would vote for increasingly popular militant groups, like Hezbollah. Some feared that these groups might impose rigid religious laws. There were also concerns that while these groups were clearly prepared for combat, they were not really ready to govern a nation. The greatest fear was that a group that practiced terrorism and committed itself to the destruction of Israel could be in control of a modern nation and its resources. Political analysts are watching Lebanon as a possible key to the future of democracy other in Middle East countries. They are looking to see whether Hezbollah, in its role as the elected governing majority, will escalate violence and hostilities, transform itself into a more mainstream political party, or lose its popular appeal and gradually fade from the government.

For More Information

BOOKS

Hirst, David. *Beware of Small States: Lebanon, Battleground of the Middle East.* New York: Nation, 2010.

Wright, Robin. *Dreams and Shadows: The Future of the Middle East.* New York: Penguin, 2008, p. 146.

Young, Michael. *The Ghosts of Martyrs Square: An Eyewitness Account of Lebanon's Life Struggle.* New York: Simon and Schuster, 2010.

WEB SITES

"Background Note: Lebanon." *U.S. Department of State* (May 23, 2011). http://www.state.gov/r/pa/ei/bgn/35833.htm#history (accessed on November 30, 2011).

"Bullets to Ballet Box: A History of Hezbollah." *Frontline World.* www.pbs.org/frontlineworld/stories/lebanon/history.html (accessed on November 30, 2011).

Prados, Alfred B. "CRS Report for Congress: Lebanon." *U.S. Department of State* (November 29, 2006). http://fpc.state.gov/documents/organization/77712.pdf (accessed on November 30, 2011).

Slim, Randa. "Hezbollah's Most Serious Challenge." *Foreign Policy* (August 5, 2011). http://mideast.foreignpolicy.com/posts/2011/05/03/hezbollah_s_most_serious_challenge (accessed on November 30, 2011).

11

The Iran-Iraq War: 1980 to 1988

The Iran-Iraq War (1980–88) was a brutal eight-year war between the nations of Iran and Iraq. It created terrible upheaval in both countries and revealed divisions among peoples of the Middle East that would be at the root of major conflicts in the region in the following years. The war pitted Persians, the people of Iran who generally speak Farsi or other Persian languages and have a unique ethnicity, identity, and culture, against Arabs, the people of the Middle East and North Africa who speak Arabic or live in countries in which Arabic is the dominant language. Sunni Muslims (followers of the Sunni branch of the religion of Islam) struggled against Shiites (followers of the Shia branch of Islam). Pan-Arabists (advocates of the unification of Arab peoples and the political alliance of Arab states) opposed Pan-Islamists (advocates of the unification of Muslims under a single Islamic state where Islam provides the basis for political, social, and cultural life). The war also pitted two ambitious authoritarian leaders against one another: Iran's Supreme Leader Ruhollah Khomeini (c. 1900–1989) and Iraq's president Saddam Hussein (1937–2006).

The Iran-Iraq War forced people in both countries to question which form of identity was most important or unifying: their ethnic group, their religious sect (group), or their nationality. On a global level, the war demonstrated the power of other countries to influence the outcome of war in the Middle East. At the national level in Iran and Iraq, however, the war accomplished little or nothing and at great cost. Although the bloody conflict seemed to solidify the idea of nationalism (devotion and loyalty to the nation and its culture), neither Iran or Iraq gained territory from or political authority over the other, and both suffered hundreds of thousands of casualties and severely damaged economies.

A history of of conflict

One of the conflicts that led to the Iran-Iraq War was a dispute over the shared border between the two countries. At the heart of this conflict was

233

WORDS TO KNOW

Arabs: People of the Middle East and North Africa who speak the Arabic language or who live in countries in which Arabic is the dominant language.

ayatollah: A high-ranking Shiite religious leader.

Ba'ath Party: A secular (nonreligious) political party founded in the 1940s with the goal of uniting the Arab world and creating one powerful Arab state.

chemical weapons: Toxic chemical substances used during armed conflict to kill, injure, or incapacitate an enemy.

dynasty: A series of rulers from the same family.

genocide: The deliberate and systematic destruction of a group of people based on religion, ethnicity, or nationality.

Islamism: A fundamentalist movement characterized by the belief that Islam should provide the basis for the political, social, and cultural life in Muslim nations.

Kurds: A non-Arab ethnic group who live mainly in present-day Turkey, Iraq, and Iran.

mandate: A commission granting one country the authority to administer the affairs of another country. Also describes the territory entrusted to foreign administration.

nationalism: The belief that a people with shared ethnic, cultural, and/or religious identities have the right to form their own nation. In established nations nationalism is devotion and loyalty to the nation and its culture.

Ottoman Empire: The vast empire of the Ottoman Turks which included southwest Asia, northeast Africa, and southeast Europe, and lasted from the thirteenth century to the early twentieth century.

Pan-Arabism: A movement for the unification of Arab peoples and the political alliance of Arab states.

Pan-Islamism: A movement for the unification of Muslims under a single Islamic state where Islam provides the basis for political, social, and cultural life.

refugees: People who flee their country to escape violence or persecution.

sharia: A system of Islamic law based on the Koran and other sacred writings. Sharia attempts to create the perfect social order, based on God's will and justice, and covers a wide range of human activities, including acts of religious worship, the law of contracts and obligations, personal status law, and public law.

Shiites: Followers of the Shia branch of Islam. Shiites believe that only direct descendants of the prophet Muhammad are qualified to lead the Islamic faith.

Sunnis: Followers of the Sunni branch of Islam. Sunnis believe that elected officials, regardless of their heritage, are qualified to lead the Islamic faith.

---

a 120-mile (193-kilometer) river called the Shatt al Arab, which is formed by the joining of the Euphrates and Tigris rivers. The Shatt al Arab flows past Iraq's port of Basra and the Iranian city of Abadan before entering the Persian Gulf at the Iraqi port of Al Faw. The southern half of the river forms the long-disputed boundary between Iraq and Iran. The Shatt al Arab is important to both nations; it is Iraq's only access to the Persian Gulf and it provides a strategic waterway for both Iran and Iraq for shipping their oil and other products. Since the seventeenth century, the people of both the region known as Mesopotamia (present-day Iraq) and the region known by Westerners as Persia (which officially became known as Iran in 1935) a have at times claimed the river, or at least one of its banks, as part of their lands.

The border conflict began anew at the end of World War I (1914–18; a global war between the Allies [Great Britain, France, and Russia, joined later by the United States] and the Central Powers [Germany, Austria-Hungary, and their allies]), when the victorious Allies divided up the lands of the defeated Ottoman Empire, the vast empire of the Ottoman Turks which included southwest Asia, northeast Africa, and southeast Europe and lasted from the thirteenth century to the early twentieth century. Great Britain was granted a mandate (administrative authority) to govern Iraq, and in creating the mandate of Iraq, Britain included some border areas that Iran claimed as its own. When Iraq tried to declare its independence in 1932, Iran refused to recognize it as a nation until these border claims were resolved. Iran and Iraq agreed to a treaty in 1937 that defined their boundaries along the east bank of Shatt al Arab, which favored Iraq. For a time, the treaty brought resolution, but the monarchies that ruled these countries ended in the 1950s. The new rulers were not as willing to submit to the terms of the treaty as the earlier rulers had been.

Problems arose near the end of the 1960s, when the Ba'ath Party, a political party that had originated in Syria, took control of Iraq. The party was secular (nonreligious), and its original objective was to bring about a peaceful unification of Arab nations. The Ba'ath Party leaders of Iraq took the idea to a new level, envisioning Iraq as the central force in the united Arab world of the future. This was disturbing to Iran, since Iran's population is Persian and not Arab. Mohammad Reza Pahlavi (1919–1980), the shah of Iran, did not want a powerful union of Arab countries so close to Iran.

With this hostility already festering, the shah demanded that the boundaries along the Shatt al Arab be changed in Iran's favor. In order to pressure the Iraqis to agree to his terms, the shah began to interfere in Iraq's internal problems with the Kurds, a non-Arab ethnic group who lived along Iraq's northern border. The Kurds had been fighting for self-rule within Iraq since the 1920s. In the mid–1970s the Kurds began attacking Iraqi targets in an attempt to gain self-rule. In retaliation the

Iraqi government began an organized effort to drive the Kurds living along the Iran-Iraq border out of the country. Much to the dismay of Iraq, Iran began to support the Kurds, providing them with weapons, safe refuge, and other types of aid and support, within its borders. (It is important to note, however, that Iran had its own population of Kurds who also wanted self-rule, and Iran did not support their efforts or grant them self-rule.)

Under these pressures, the two governments decided to negotiate. In 1975 Iran and Iraq signed the Algiers Agreement, in which Iran agreed to end its aid to the Iraqi Kurds and Iraq gave up full control of the Shatt al Arab. According to the agreement, the boundary between Iran and Iraq would be in the center of the Shatt al Arab. Each country would have

A young Kurdish fighter in Iraq, near the Iraq-Iran border. In the mid–1970s the Kurds began attacking Iraqi targets in an attempt to gain self-rule. AFP/GETTY IMAGES.

rights to one bank and its half of the river. But this agreement would soon prove to be unstable.

Borders and Kurds were not the only sources of friction between Iran and Iraq. A new political movement arising in Iran would significantly add to the hostility. Starting in the 1960s, Iranian Muslim religious leader Ayatollah Ruhollah Khomeini began to encourage Iran to isolate itself from the rest of the world. He protested against modern, and, specifically, Western values. Many Iranians disliked the control that foreign powers had over the shah. During the years following World War II, Iran's oil industry had been controlled by British and American companies and the Soviet Union had begun to support Iranian Communist groups that were trying to overthrow the shah. (Communists are advocates of Communism, a system of government in which the state plans and controls the economy and a single political party holds power.) In 1953, in an effort to regain control of Iranian resources and government, Iran's prime minister led an uprising in which he seized control of Iran's oil industry and forced the shah into exile. The United States, however, had been unwilling to lose control in Iran, particularly given the Soviet Union's interest in the country and the U.S. interest in its oil. The United States helped a small group of Iranians stage a coup (overthrow of the government) that returned the shah to power in 1954. After that, the shah was one of the United States' strongest allies in the Middle East. Throughout his rule, the United States supplied Iran with billions of dollars' worth of military equipment, in the hope of deterring the Soviet Union's power in the region, and had bought billions of dollars of Iranian oil.

Khomeini declared that in modernizing Iran, the shah had created policies that went against the teachings of Islam and ancient Persian tradition. Khomeini felt that the power and influence of foreigners in Iran were damaging to the dignity of the Iranian people. He was especially disgusted by the preferential treatment given to American soldiers in Iran. In 1964, a new law was enacted that gave U.S. military personnel and their families immunity from Iranian criminal laws. According to Robin Wright in *Dreams and Shadows: The Future of the Middle East*, Khomeini thought that Americans were given these freedoms in Iran because the United States had just loaned the shah's government $200 million. As quoted by Wright, Khomeini remarked: "If the shah himself were to run over a dog belonging to an American, he would be prosecuted. But if an American cook runs over the shah, the head of state, no one will have the right to interfere with him. . . . Are we to be trampled underfoot by the boots of

America simply because we are a weak nation and have no dollars?" For his outspoken criticism of the shah, Khomeini was arrested and in 1964 he was forced into exile. First exiled to Turkey, he soon moved to Iraq, where for the next thirteen years he continued to preach his opposition to the shah and his government.

During the years when Khomeini was exiled in Iraq, Shiites formed the majority, at about 60 percent of that country's population, but Iraq's ruling Ba'ath Party was made up of Sunni Muslims. Khomeini, who was a charismatic figure and a Shiite, began to develop a strong following among the Iraqi Shiites. He was also open in his criticism of the high-ranking Ba'ath Party member Saddam Hussein, who was then in charge of Iraq's internal security. Khomeini called him an infidel (unbeliever). Saddam was so concerned about Khomeini's perceived power that he had him driven out of Iraq in 1978.

The Ayatollah Khomeini waves to supporters after his return to Iran in 1979. Khomeini became the leader of the Islamic Revolution and eventually the leader of Iran. © ALAIN DEJEAN/SYGMA/CORBIS.

Saddam comes to power

Saddam had joined the Ba'ath Party in his youth. Even in his early years as a Ba'athist, Saddam envisioned himself as the leader of a pan-Arab country. When Saddam was only twenty-two, the Ba'ath Party assigned him to help in the assassination of Iraq's military leader, which failed. After other secret and often violent missions, Saddam emerged in the 1960s in a high position within the party. By the late 1960s, as the head of Iraq's internal security, he began to use the system to purge the country of all enemies of the Ba'ath Party by having them driven out of the country, imprisoned, or killed. By the late 1970s Saddam had also begun to ruthlessly eliminate members of his own party who he perceived as rivals to his political ambitions.

Saddam became president of Iraq in July 1979. Once he had taken office, he ordered the executions by firing squad of hundreds of high-ranking Ba'ath Party members and officers of the Iraqi military—anyone he thought might threaten his power in Iraq. He ruled as the absolute dictator of Iraq, brutally eliminating those who threatened to oppose him. Once in power, he set his sights on expanding his realm. The Soviet Union had been an ally of Iraq's for decades, and had supplied it with enough weapons to enable a powerful assault on its neighbors when the time seemed right.

Khomeini comes to power

The same year that Saddam became president, 1979, Khomeini returned to Iran. It was a time of great upheaval. The monarchy of Mohammad Reza Pahlavi, heir to the Pahlavi dynasty (series of rulers from the same family) that had transformed Persia into the modern state of Iran starting in 1925, was collapsing. The shah had modernized and secularized Iran, creating a wealthy class. He led a secular government and was his rule was heavily influenced, in terms of culture, politics, and economy, by the West. But many Iranians, especially the devotedly religious and the poor who had not benefited from the new economy, feared that their traditions, values, and Persian identity were being wiped away by modernization and the shah's allegiance to the Western world.

These disgruntled Iranians banded together, and in 1979 popular protest escalated into an Islamic revolution, an Islamist movement intended to bring the laws and regulations of the country under the control of Islam. The revolution sent the shah into exile. Led by Khomeini, Iran formed an

Islamic republic, which granted the ayatollah ultimate command of the country as its Supreme Leader. A Council of Guardians, made up of six Islamic clergy members appointed by the ayatollah, oversaw legislative acts created by an Islamic Consultative Assembly of 290 elected legislators. The new government adopted a constitution that used sharia as its guiding principles for Iran's laws and regulations.

The Islamic republic placed strict rules on society. It took control of the country's industries and businesses and enforced adherence to sharia in all aspects of life. Women were forced to wear traditional Muslim dress, usually including a chador, a veil that covers their body and hair. Textbooks were rewritten to better represent Islamic values. Government employees were subjected to loyalty tests. Opponents to the new government were arrested or executed. Khomeini hoped to inspire other Shiites around the globe to rise up and create Islamic countries according to his pan-Islamic ideology. Like Saddam, Khomeini aspired to rule a larger territory than his own country and was willing to take extreme measures to make this happen.

Hostilities rise

Saddam knew that Khomeini was a rival to his own ambitions in the Middle East, and he was also concerned about the effects the Islamic Revolution in Iran might have on his own country. There was good reason to doubt the loyalty of Iraqi Shiites, for Iraq had a long history of oppressing its Shiite population. In 1972 the Iraqi government had forced nearly seventy thousand Shiites out of the country and in March 1980, Saddam had seized the property and homes of nearly thirty thousand Iraqi Shiite men and exiled them to Iran.

With Iran controlled by Islamists after 1979, Iraqi leaders also worried about Iraq's access to the Persian Gulf along the Shatt al Arab waterway. Iraq relied on secure access to the gulf to transport oil, its main export. After 1979, hostilities between Iran and Iraq grew over control of the disputed islands of Abu Musa and the Greater and Lesser Tunbs in the Persian Gulf and over the oil-rich Khuzistan, an Iranian province located at the head of the Persian Gulf that borders Iraq. In the spring of 1980, an Iranian group tried to kill Iraqi foreign minister Tariq Aziz (1936–), who was Saddam's close adviser. Saddam retaliated by deporting thousands of Iranians and by ordering the extremely brutal execution of the leader of the Iranian group suspected of attempting to kill Aziz.

By April 1980 both Khomeini and Saddam began to incite the public against each other, using speeches that were broadcast to both Iran and Iraq. Khomeini appealed to Iraqis to "wake up and topple this corrupt regime in your Islamic country before it is too late." Saddam responded, "Anyone who tries to put his hand on Iraq will have his hand cut off," as quoted in *The Middle East*, edited by Daniel C. Diller.

Iraqi invasion

Saddam decided to strike before Khomeini's new government became established, hoping Iran would be unprepared for war so soon after the Islamic Revolution. On September 17, 1980, Saddam broadcast his rejection of the 1975 Algiers Agreement by destroying a copy of it on television. He claimed the Shatt al Arab for Iraq alone. Khomeini responded by announcing that Iran would no longer abide by the agreement either and started to fund Iraqi insurgents (people rebelling against the Iraqi government), especially the Kurds, once again.

Iraq mounted the first offensive. Iraqi troops crossed the Iranian border near Baghdad on September 22, 1980, and then, farther south, they crossed the Shatt al Arab. By October Iraq controlled much of the Khuzistan province. Oil, being the main source of income for both countries, was the main target of these early attacks. Iran and Iraq bombed each other's oil wells and refineries, and each tried to destroy the other's trading routes. As Iraq had hoped, the new Islamic republic had had little time to organize a military, and it was overwhelmed by Iraq's superior weaponry and established military. Iraq quickly captured Shatt al Arab and a long strip of Iranian territory along the border. Observers around the world thought the war would be over within a few weeks. But they were wrong.

International attention

Rather than destroying the new Iranian regime, the Iraqi attacks actually inspired a sense of nationality among the Iranians. Thousands volunteered to join the military and fight their new enemy. According to many historians, the new soldiers were extremely committed to the fight, because they connected it to the recent Islamic Revolution and felt they were fighting for their religion as well as their country. As Iran strengthened its forces and Iraqi war casualties mounted, Saddam's hopes for a quick victory were dashed. Though the Soviet Union had been an ally in the past, it had declared it neutrality when the war broke out and

Iranian soldiers during the Iran-Iraq War. Iraqi attacks actually inspired a sense of nationality among the Iranians and thousands volunteered to join the military and fight Iraq. © MAHMOUDREZA KALARI/SYGMA/CORBIS.

temporarily stopped supplying Iraq with weapons, although it would resume in 1982. Saddam soon appealed to Khomeini and the international community to negotiate a peace settlement.

The pleas and bargaining efforts of neighboring Arab states and the United Nations (an international organization of countries founded in 1945 to promote international peace, security, and cooperation) failed to bring peace. Khomeini announced that he would not stop fighting until he had established "an Islamic government in Iraq" and destroyed "the Iraqi regime in the same way as we destroyed the shah," as quoted by Diller. Khomeini's plan frightened many in the Arab and Western worlds who feared the growth of the Islamist country and the power of its authoritarian leader.

International fears increased when Iranian counterattacks started pushing Iraqi troops back across the border. Iran had begun using human wave attacks, in which a large line of volunteer soldiers rushes toward enemy lines in a formation that is many men deep. The enemy can kill the men in front with machine guns and cannons, but because of their sheer numbers, the soldiers just keep coming in waves and their attack continues. This form of warfare is rarely used, because it results in a large loss of life. The Iraqis were overwhelmed by the Iranians, and by 1982 Iraqi troops had retreated to their home soil, where the battles would be fought for the remainder of the war.

Both Iran and Iraq had few allies when the war began in 1980. Neither had asked other countries to send troops to help them or for money or weapons until the peace negotiations failed in 1982. But after the attempts for peace failed and Iraqi troops had been driven across the border, Saddam turned to the West for help.

Although the West was reluctant to support either Saddam or Khomeini, Saddam seemed the one most likely to assist in protecting Western interests in Middle East oil, which both Iran and Iraq had in abundance. Neighboring Arab countries with huge oil reserves but small militaries feared being targeted by Iran as part of its Islamic Revolution; they also supported Iraq in the war. France sold weapons to Iraq, while Kuwait, Saudi Arabia, and other countries along the Persian Gulf loaned it billions of dollars in the hope that an Iraqi victory would protect them from the spread of Khomeini's style of Islamism.

The United States, which had not had relations with Iraq since 1967, sided with Iraq as well. Like other countries coming to Iraq's aid, the United States "was willing to ignore the brutality of [Saddam's] regime in order to prevent the spread of the kind of Islamic radicalism and anti-U.S. sentiment represented by Khomeini," writes William L. Cleveland in *A History of the Modern Middle East*. But the main U.S. interest in the Middle East was oil. Before being deposed (removed from office). After the revolution, the relationship between the United States and Iran changed drastically. The ayatollah announced his intentions to rid the entire Middle East of American influence. Immediately after the Islamic revolution in Iran, the U.S. embassy in the capital city, Tehran, was overtaken by a group of Iranian students, who took the entire U.S. staff, as well as several bystanders, hostage. They demanded that the shah, who was receiving medical treatment in the United States, be returned to Iran to face trial. Some of the hostages were initially released, but fifty-two Americans were held hostage for

444 days. The United States, not surprisingly, came to view the ayatollah, who openly supported the hostage-taking, as its enemy. The United States supported Iraq with troops and naval vessels to keep the Persian Gulf open for oil tankers to pass.

Iran gained support from Libya and Syria during the war. Both Libya and Syria were Arab countries that hoped that Iran would help them in battles against the West and other foes in the Middle East. The alliance between Iran and Syria would prove to be important and long-term for both countries, but during the Iran-Iraq War, Iran relied mainly on its vast population and huge oil wealth for its needs.

A map showing the cities where major battles occurred during the Iran-Iraq War. MAP BY XNR PRODUCTIONS, INC./CENGAGE LEARNING.

A brutal war

Empowered by international aid and support, both Iran and Iraq continued to launch offensives in the mid–1980s, aimed at destroying each other's resolve to continue the fight. Hundreds of thousands of casualties on both sides resulted from these attacks. Territory was continually gained and lost. Iranian and Iraqi oil tankers were sunk, depriving both sides of much-needed income. In 1985 densely populated civilian centers became military targets. Iraq directed its superior supply of missiles at Tehran, the capital of Iran. Even though Iran had far fewer missiles and those that they had were less powerful, it retaliated by launching them at Baghdad, the capital of Iraq. Although Iraq's attacks were decidedly more devastating, the population in both countries was rapidly growing weary of the war.

In the late 1980s Iran announced new attacks against Iraq, making it seem as if Iran was making progress toward winning the war. But these attacks were held off by Iraqi resistance. One of Iran's attacks in 1986 sent waves of soldiers into the Iraqi port of Basra, located 75 miles (121 kilometers) up the Shatt al Arab from the Persian Gulf. After two months, Iran had gained little in territory or strategic position and thousands of Iranian soldiers had been killed.

Saddam Hussein inspecting the Basra front. In 1986 Iran sent waves of soldiers into the Iraqi port of Basra. © THE PRINT COLLECTOR/ALAMY.

Halabja and the Iraqi War on Kurds

Since Iraq gained its independence in 1932, the Kurds living in Iraq's northern region, who comprise nearly 20 percent of the country's population, have struggled to obtain self-rule within Iraq. The Kurds' distinctiveness of being non-Arabs living in an Arab country sets them apart, especially as the Ba'ath Party came to power in Iraq in the 1960s. The Ba'ath Party supported a Pan-Arabism (a movement for the unification of Arab peoples and the political alliance of Arab states) and suppressed religious or ethnic groups that opposed its control of Iraq. Although many of the Kurds were Sunni Muslims, like members of the Ba'ath Party, they did not support the Ba'ath Party's attempts to unify the country and challenged the government by fighting for self-rule in the northern Iraqi province of Kurdistan, where most Kurds lived. The Iraqi government refused to allow the Kurds self-rule in Kurdistan, mainly because of the rich oil reserves located there.

In 1970 the Kurds signed a peace agreement with the Iraqi government, ending fifteen years of war. But the Kurds and the ruling Ba'ath Party did not make amends. In 1974 the Iraqi government tried to intimidate Kurds by destroying two Kurdish towns and bombing and burning others. It also forced Kurds from their homes and moved Arabs into the emptied Kurdish towns. An estimated 1.5 million Kurds became refugees in Iraq and another 100,000 fled to Iran. (Refugees are people who flee their country to escape violence or persecution.) By 1975 the Iraqi government tried to evict the Kurds from the country, forcing residents out of eight hundred Kurdish villages near the Iran border.

Although the Iran-Iraq War turned the Iraqi government's attention from the Kurds for a short while, toward the end of the war Iraq recommitted itself to ridding the country of Kurds. Kurds of Iraq had united in 1987 in the hope of gaining autonomy, or self-government, within Iraq. The Iraqi government fought hard to stop their efforts, and in 1988 began an operation called Anfal that was designed to destroy the Kurdish population in Iraq. From February through September 1988 the Iraqi government sent airplanes to bomb Kurdish villages, destroying Kurdish homes and farmlands and forcing tens of thousands of Kurds to flee. Many fled to Iran, Turkey, and Syria, where there were large populations of Kurds.

In March 1988 the Iraqi government attacked the Kurdish town of Halabja. They used poison gases, such as sarin, which kills by destroying the central nervous system, and mustard gas, which burns the lungs and causes blisters on the skin. The attack on Halabja killed an estimated five thousand Kurds and wounded an estimated ten

Iranian resolve to fight faltered not only due to the high rate of death in battle but also because Iraq had begun to use chemical weapons, or toxic chemical substances used during armed conflict to kill, injure, or incapacitate an enemy. Early in the war Iraq used mustard blister gas, which causes blistering of the skin and eyes and lung irritation, but has a fairly low death rate. Later it used sarin gas, which can enter the body through contact with the skin or by being inhaled and can quickly kill the victim. Use of chemical thousand. Iraqi leader Saddam Hussein's use of these gases against his country's own citizens horrified the world, but no country came to the assistance of the Kurds, despite Kurdish pleas for help.

Conflicts between Iraqi troops and Kurds resulted in many more deaths. Many Kurds were even shot as they tried to surrender to Iraqi soldiers. The extermination campaign waged by Saddam against the Kurds in 1988 claimed an estimated one hundred thousand Kurdish lives and forced nearly sixty thousand Kurds to become refugees. Many years later, in 2006, Saddam was found guilty of war crimes, crimes against humanity, and genocide (the deliberate and systematic destruction of a group of people based on religion, ethnicity, or nationality). The Anfal campaign and the chemical attack on Halabja were among the crimes that led to his execution in 2006.

A man walks through the Halabja Memorial Cemetery, where victims of the 1988 chemical weapons attacks against the Kurds are buried. © PHILIP CHEUNG/CORBIS.

weapons violates the 1925 Geneva Protocol, an international law. Iraq had been accused of using chemical weapons since the mid–1980s. It had used large quantities of poison gas to regain the Al Faw Peninsula at the mouth of Shatt al Arab after it was captured by Iran in early 1986. The poison gas caused hundreds of casualties. The international community publicly condemned Iraq for its use of these weapons but did not stop its aid to the nation, and Iraq continued to use chemical weapons.

Despite Iran's occupation of large tracts of Iraqi land by the late 1980s, none of its offensives seemed dramatic enough to end the war in its favor. Even with public knowledge of its use of chemical weapons, Iraq continued to enjoy international support, and by 1987 countries from the West, especially the United States, were working hard to end the war in Iraq's favor. On July 20, 1987, the United Nations passed Resolution 598, calling for a cease-fire and a withdrawal of troops to the borders between Iran and Iraq that had existed before the war. Although the resolution favored Iraq, Iran did not flatly reject it. Instead, Iran asked to modify it.

Before any alterations to the resolution were made, Iraq increased its bombings of Iranian targets. In February 1988 Iraq launched approximately one hundred missiles at Tehran. By April 1988 Iraq had forced the majority of Iranian troops from its borders and advanced on Iranian territory. The Iraqi government went so far as to launch a devastating campaign of chemical warfare against its own citizens, the Kurdish inhabitants of the border village of Halabja, whom it suspected of aiding Iran.

Iraq used more chemical weapons against Iranians in subsequent offensives in May and June 1988. By July 1988 Iran's morale was broken. Khomeini agreed to the original Resolution 598 cease-fire proposal. On July 21, 1988, Khomeini announced to his country that although he believed the cease-fire to be "in the best interests of the revolution and the [Islamic republic]," he considered the agreement to be "more lethal to me than poison," as quoted by Shaul Bakhash in *The Reign of the Ayatollahs: Iran and the Islamic Revolution.* A final cease-fire took effect on August 20, 1988.

The legacy of war

At the end of the Iran-Iraq War, both countries were in shambles. Nearly one million people had died in the battles, with approximately twice as many Iranians as Iraqis killed. More than one million people, mostly from near the border, were forced to flee from their homes in cities that had been destroyed by the eight-year war. Both countries' ports, oil refineries, roads, and farm irrigation systems were in desperate need of repair.

One of the more remarkable elements of the war was what did not happen. Contrary to some expectations, Shiite Muslims in Iraq did not rise up and join their fellow Shiites from Iran; similarly, ethnic Arabs living in Iran's Khuzistan province remained loyal to Khomeini and did not follow Saddam in a pan-Arab revolution. Religion and ethnicity, thought to be such powerful forces in the region, proved to be less powerful than

An Iranian soldier watches as smoke rises from burning oil refineries in Iran. While neither Iraq nor Iran gained territory in the Iran-Iraq war, both countries lost resources such as oil. © HENRI BUREAU/SYGMA/CORBIS.

nationalism. This was considered confirmation that the relatively young countries of the Middle East (most had achieved independence between 1920 and 1950) had attained a stable national identity. The Iran-Iraq War was the greatest show of nationalist sentiment seen yet in the Middle East.

Iran, which had used its own finances and huge population to fund and execute the war, immediately turned its attention to reconstruction. Khomeini ruled strictly and often harshly in order to control Iran's internal disagreements about the best way to start reconstructing cities and industry and provide for the welfare of the country's huge internal refugee population of people who had lost their homes in the war. Nearly two thousand opponents to Khomeini's rule were executed in the months following the end of the war. Actual reconstruction of homes and business began after Khomeini died in 1989.

Rather than plunge into the challenges of reconstruction, Iraq took a completely different path after the war. Saddam continued his quest to dominate the Arab countries of the Middle East and poured money into rebuilding Iraq's military. Iraq had borrowed billions of dollars to finance its war efforts. Rather than repay its debts, Iraq set its sights on controlling its former allies. Two years after the Iran-Iraq War, in 1990, Iraq invaded and annexed (took over) Kuwait. Its aggression soon started the Persian Gulf War (1990–91). This time the international community fought against Iraq, and Iraq suffered a major defeat that further damaged the country. While Saddam did eventually begin to rebuild Iraq after the Persian Gulf War, it was clear that Iraq, much like Iran, would never be as strong as it had been before the start of the Iran-Iraq War.

For More Information

BOOKS

Bakhash, Shaul. *The Reign of the Ayatollahs: Iran and the Islamic Revolution.* New York: Basic Books, 1984.

Cleveland, William L. *A History of the Modern Middle East.* 3rd ed. Cambridge, MA: Westview, 2004.

Diller, Daniel C., ed. *The Middle East.* 8th ed. Washington, DC: Congressional Quarterly, 1995.

Dudley, William, ed. *The Middle East.* Opposing Viewpoints Series. San Diego, CA: Greenhaven Press, 2004.

Karsh, Efraim. *The Iran-Iraq War, 1980–1988.* Oxford: Osprey, 2002.

Kort, Michael G. *The Handbook of the Middle East.* Brookfield, CT: Twenty-First Century Books, 2002.

Ojeda, Auriana. *The Middle East.* Current Controversies Series. San Diego, CA: Greenhaven Press, 2003.

Smith, Charles D., ed. *Palestine and the Arab-Israeli Conflict: A History with Documents.* 4th ed. New York: St. Martin's, 2001.

Wright, Robin. *Dreams and Shadows: The Future of the Middle East.* New York: Penguin, 2008, pp. 26, 266.

PERIODICALS

MacFarquhar, Neil. "Saddam Hussein, Defiant Dictator Who Ruled Iraq With Violence and Fear, Dies," *New York Times* (December 30, 2006). Available online at http://www.nytimes.com/2006/12/30/world/middleeast/30saddam.html?pagewanted=3 (accessed on November 30, 2011).

WEB SITES

"1981: Tehran Frees US Hostages After 444 Days." *BBC.* http://news.bbc.co.uk/onthisday/hi/dates/stories/january/21/newsid_2506000/2506807.stm (accessed on November 30, 2011).

12

The Gulf Wars: 1991 to 2011

In the early twenty-first century, the "gulf wars" referred to two wars primarily involving the United States and Iraq. The first one, the Persian Gulf War (1990–91), is also commonly called the Gulf War, the First Gulf War, and Operation Desert Storm. The second one, the Iraq War (2003–11), is often referred to as the Second Gulf War, the War in Iraq, and Operation Iraqi Freedom. In both of these wars U.S.-led forces clashed with the forces of Iraq's ambitious and ruthless president, Saddam Hussein (1937–2006) and his Ba'athist government. In the Persian Gulf War, the United States and its allies engaged in military action in order to restore the nation of Kuwait, which Iraq had invaded in a dispute over land and oil reserves. In the Iraq War, the United States and its allies attacked Iraq, claiming that it had weapons of mass destruction. The U.S. role in each of these wars was extremely different.

Saddam and the Ba'ath Party in Iraq

The Ba'ath Party of Iraq was an offshoot of the Ba'ath Party founded in Syria in 1947. Initially the party sought unity among Arabs (people who speak the Arabic language) and promoted a secular (nonreligious) and democratic form of government that protected individual freedoms. In both Syria and Iraq, however, the Ba'ath Party developed into authoritarian systems, in which power is consolidated under one strong leader, or a small group of elite leaders, who do not answer to the will of the people.

In Iraq the Ba'ath Party first came into power in 1963, but the party was divided between moderates and extremists and was soon overthrown. Saddam Hussein had been born into a clan (family) of Sunni Arabs from the town of Tikrit. Sunnis are followers of the Sunni branch of Islam.) This clan gained control of the Ba'ath Party during the 1960s. Then, in 1968, the Ba'athists staged a coup (overthrow of the government) and

WORDS TO KNOW

Arabs: People of the Middle East and North Africa who speak the Arabic language or who live in countries in which Arabic is the dominant language.

Arab League: A regional political alliance of Arab nations formed in 1945 to promote political, military, and economic cooperation within the Arab world.

authoritarianism: A type of leadership in which power is consolidated under one strong leader, or a small group of elite leaders, who do not answer to the will of the people.

Ba'ath Party: A secular (nonreligious) political party founded in the 1940s with the goal of uniting the Arab world and creating one powerful Arab state.

ethnicity: Groupings of people in a society according to their common racial, national, tribal, religious, language, or cultural backgrounds.

insurgency: An uprising, or rebellion, against a political authority.

Islamism: A fundamentalist movement characterized by the belief that Islam should provide the basis for the political, social, and cultural life in Muslim nations.

Kurds: A non-Arab ethnic group who live mainly in present-day Turkey, Iraq, and Iran.

militia: Armed civilian military forces.

occupation: The physical and political control of an area seized by a foreign military force.

Organization of Petroleum Exporting Countries (OPEC): An organization formed in 1960 by the world's major oil-producing nations to coordinate policies and ensure stable oil prices in world markets.

Ottoman Empire: The vast empire of the Ottoman Turks which included southwest Asia, northeast Africa, and southeast Europe, and lasted from the thirteenth century to the early twentieth century.

refugees: People who flee their country to escape violence or persecution.

sanctions: Punitive measures adopted by the international community against a nation that has violated international law, usually in the form of diplomatic, economic, or social restrictions.

sect: A social unit within a society that is defined by its distinct beliefs or customs.

Shiites: Followers of the Shia branch of Islam. Shiites believe that only direct descendants of the prophet Muhammad are qualified to lead the Islamic faith.

suicide bombing: An attack intended to kill others and cause widespread damage, carried about by someone who does not hope to survive the attack.

Sunnis: Followers of the Sunni branch of Islam. Sunnis believe that elected officials, regardless of their heritage, are qualified to lead the Islamic faith.

Taliban: An Islamic militant and political group that controlled Afghanistan from 1996 to 2001.

weapons of mass destruction: Any nuclear, chemical, or biological weapons capable of killing or injuring large numbers of people.

secured complete control over the Iraqi government, placing Saddam's cousin, Ahmed Hassan al-Bakr (1914–1982), in the position of president. Al-Bakr conferred great power upon Saddam, as the head of Iraqi security and later as the vice president of the country. By 1979 Saddam had edged his cousin out of power.

Saddam used the Ba'ath Party as a tool to enforce his personal control over all political activity in Iraq. He eliminated his enemies and opponents through exile, imprisonment, torture, rape, and murder. He controlled the press and allowed no freedom of speech, and he initiated devastating wars resulting in hundreds of thousands of deaths. He even used weapons of mass destruction (nuclear, chemical, or biological weapons capable of killing or injuring large numbers of people) to kill thousands of Iraqi citizens. At the same time Saddam's administration was developing Iraq's abundant oil fields, bringing some economic stability in harsh times. Iraq experienced a growing middle class and greatly improved education and health programs, so living conditions for some portions of the population stabilized. Saddam was rigorously secular in his rule, and for a time there was relative peace among Iraq's three major groups, the Shiites (followers of the Shia branch of Islam), the Sunnis, and the Kurds (a non-Arab ethnic group).

Like many parts of the Middle East, Iraq is divided by its sects (social units within a society that are defined by their distinct beliefs or customs) and by ethnicity (groupings of people in a society according to common racial, national, tribal, religious, linguistic, or cultural backgrounds). Shiites are Iraq's majority religious sect, at about 60 to 65 percent of the population. Sunnis, who make up from 32 to 37 percent of the Iraqi population, are in the majority in every Arab nation except Iraq. (They are also a minority in Iran, where the dominant language is Persian, not Arabic.) The Kurds makes up about 17 percent of Iraq's population. Kurds may belong to any religious sect, although the majority of Kurds in Iraq are Sunni. Most Kurds speak the Kurdish language and live in a region called Kurdistan, a borderless territory that spans the countries of Turkey, Iran, Iraq, and Syria. Kurds constitute the fourth largest ethnic group in the Middle East.

Saddam had not been president of Iraq long when he launched a bloody, expensive, and long war on Iran over territory, oil reserves, and dominance in the region. (For more information, see **The Iran-Iraq War: 1980 to 1988**.) Saddam had managed to get most of the Western powers on his side in the Iran-Iraq War (1980–88), but beginning in

1990 his actions gained him the condemnation of the international community, and the United States led in efforts to stop him.

Controlling the flow of oil

By the end of the Iran-Iraq War in 1988, Iraq's economy was severely damaged. Saddam's regime turned to vigorous oil production for revenue. High oil prices would secure much-needed profits for Iraq, but oil prices at the time were dropping due to the overproduction of oil. The oil market was shared by about a dozen oil-producing countries, many in the Middle East. Since the price of oil is largely determined by the amount of oil each country produces, the Organization of Petroleum Exporting Countries (OPEC; an organization formed in 1960 by the world's major oil-producing nations to coordinate policies and ensure stable oil prices in world markets) establishes limits on production. Saudi Arabia had long served as OPEC's overseer, limiting its own production to keep oil prices steady regardless of overproduction of oil by other nations. By the late 1980s and early 1990s, however, Saudi Arabia had grown tired of other OPEC members' overproduction and announced that it would no longer abide by production limits. Without Saudi limits on production, the market was flooded with oil, and prices dropped.

Even though Iraq had been overproducing oil throughout the early 1980s to support its war efforts, in 1990 Saddam called for a stop to the overproduction of oil by all OPEC nations. Several countries, including Saudi Arabia, finally agreed to Saddam's proposed limits. Neighboring Kuwait tried to establish an agreement with Iraq in 1990, but the negotiations broke down because Kuwait would not agree to the conditions Iraq demanded. First, Kuwait refused to agree to an oil price increase among OPEC nations. In addition, Kuwait wanted full repayment of loans it had made to Iraq during the Iran-Iraq War, despite Iraq's request for a reduction in the amount it owed. Kuwait also continued pumping oil from the Rumaila oil field, a large oil field that Kuwait shared with Iraq, and Iraq accused Kuwait of using slant-drilling techniques that allowed Kuwait to drain oil from Iraq's portion of the field.

Saddam grew increasingly hostile toward Kuwait, and his actions began to threaten Saudi Arabia, as well. Disagreements with Kuwait over oil were not Saddam's only reasons for his antagonism. He had long harbored hopes to be the leader of a united Arab world, yet countries such as Kuwait and Saudi Arabia were in his way. Both were led by monarchs who lived luxurious lifestyles, made possible by their nation's large oil revenues. These monarchs often refused to take part in programs proposed by the Arab League or by Iraq. (The Arab League is a regional political alliance of Arab nations formed in 1945 to promote political, military, and economic cooperation within the Arab world.) These oil-rich nations also often had cooperative relationships with the West, especially the United States. Saddam began to publicly criticize the Kuwaiti and Saudi regimes. According to Daniel C. Diller in *The Middle East*, "No one symbolized those rich elites better than the ruling families of Kuwait and Saudi Arabia." Saddam hoped to take advantage of popular opposition to the wealthy members of the population in these countries in order to gain power for himself in the region. Saddam was allied with the West during the Iran-Iraq War, but with his continued harassment of Kuwait he strove to redefine himself as an anti-Western leader among Arabs. By criticizing the decadent rulers of Arab countries in the Middle East, Saddam hoped to gain support for himself among the masses of poorer Arabs.

The Persian Gulf War

In the summer of 1990, Saddam increased his public accusations against Kuwait in an attempt to get Kuwaiti leaders to agree to limited oil production and higher oil prices. In his speeches Saddam highlighted Kuwait's alliances with the West, the United States and Israel in particular, maintaining that overproduction of oil among Arab nations was "inspired by America to undermine Arab interests and security," according to Diller. On July 17, 1990, Saddam threatened Kuwait with an attack. Days later Saddam began to gather thousands of troops along Iraq's border with Kuwait.

The OPEC nations finally agreed to lower oil prices on July 26, 1990, but Saddam remained convinced that gaining control of Kuwait would enhance his position in the Arab world. By controlling Kuwait, Saddam reasoned that he could ease his country's debt, have a stronger voice in OPEC decisions, and increase Iraqi access to important trading ports along an expanded Persian Gulf coastline.

Iraqi claims to the land of Kuwait were not new. Both before and during the rule of the Ottoman Empire (the vast empire of the Ottoman Turks which included southwest Asia, northeast Africa, and southeast Europe, and lasted from the thirteenth century to the early twentieth century),

Major Events of the 1990–91 Gulf War

On February 22, 1991, the CIA initiates a plan to kill Saddam Hussein. F-117 stealth bombers are sent to bomb an air base northwest of Baghdad, where Saddam is reportedly hiding. Saddam is not there and the operation fails. As a result, Saddam Hussein remains in power.

On August 2, 1990, Iraq invades Kuwait. The Iraqi army drives into Kuwait City and easily gains control. The Iraqis would loot the city, set 500 oil fields on fire, and dump millions of barrels of oil into the Persian Gulf, causing extensive environmental damage.

On August 7, 1990, U.S. troops arrive in Saudi Arabia to help protect Saudi Arabia's oil fields from invasion by Iraq. When Saddam Hussein refuses to withdraw troops from Kuwait by January 15, 1991, Operation Desert Storm is launched. After a 100-hour ground battle, President Bush declares a cease-fire on February 17, 1991.

A map showing the location of some of the major events of the Persian Gulf War. MAP BY XNR PRODUCTIONS, INC./ CENGAGE LEARNING.

Kuwait and Iraq had been part of a united region. But Kuwaiti tribes broke their allegiance with the Ottoman rulers at the beginning of World War I (1914–18), and had been protected by Great Britain until gaining their independence in 1961. Iraq had periodically claimed that Kuwait was rightfully a part of Iraq, but Great Britain and other Western nations had always intervened to put a stop to any Iraqi aggression. In his move on Kuwait, Saddam played upon long-held Iraqi suspicions that the West had taken a portion of Iraqi land by supporting Kuwait as a separate nation.

The Iraqi strike Deploying 140,000 ground troops and dispatching long columns of tanks supported by fighter jets and bombers, Iraq invaded Kuwait on August 2, 1990. Within four hours Iraqi troops had captured Kuwait City, the capital of Kuwait. Later that same day the United Nations (UN; an international organization of countries founded in 1945 to promote international peace, security, and cooperation) called for Iraq to withdraw from Kuwait. Iraq refused, declaring instead that it was annexing, or taking possession of, Kuwait. On August 6, 1990, the UN passed Resolution 661, which imposed a trade and financial sanctions on Iraq. (Sanctions are punitive measures adopted by the international community against a nation that has violated international law, usually in the form of diplomatic, economic, or social restrictions.) The resolution froze Iraq's financial assets held in foreign banks, and essentially cut Iraq off from the world markets by prohibiting the sale of its oil or the import of goods. Many in the international community hoped that without access to trade, Iraq would soon give up its fight and leave Kuwait.

Iraq's attack on Kuwait immediately drew the attention of the United States. Although it had been an ally of Iraq during its war with Iran and still considered Iran a major threat, the United States feared that Saddam's aggression might threaten U.S. oil supplies and other strategic interests in the region. U.S. president George H.W. Bush (1924–) quickly organized a coalition of more than thirty countries to challenge Iraq's advances. The coalition included support from several Middle Eastern nations. Bush explained the intentions of U.S. involvement as "preserving oil supplies, containing Iraq's program to develop nuclear weapons, supporting the security of Israel, and maintaining the credibility of America as the sole remaining world military power," as summarized by Peter Huchthausen in *America's Splendid Little Wars*. Saudi Arabia, which feared that Iraq's quick seizure of Kuwait meant that Iraq would next target Saudi Arabia, requested a U.S.-led coalition to protect it from Iraq.

The United States worked closely with the UN and relied on the other thirty or so UN member nations to support the military mission, plus an additional eighteen countries that supplied economic, humanitarian, and other assistance. Supporters of this effort included Arab, Asian, and European nations. The objective of the mission, called Operation Desert Shield, was to guard against an Iraqi invasion of Saudi Arabia and to force Iraq to withdraw from Kuwait. One of the largest military missions in decades, Operation Desert Shield soon had five hundred thousand troops participating.

The coalition attacks Even though the UN sanctions had cut Iraq off from nearly 90 percent of its imports by November, Iraq gave no signs of withdrawing from Kuwait. The UN issued an ultimatum, or a final statement of warning, declaring that if Iraq did not withdraw from Kuwait by January 15, 1991, coalition forces would end the Iraqi occupation by force.

Saudi Arabian troops gather in the desert to protect the country's oil reserves from Iraq. Saudi Arabia joined the coalition against Iraq during the Persian Gulf War. ©J.A. GIORDANO/CORBIS SYGMA.

(Occupation is the physical and political control of an area seized by a foreign military force.) Iraq did not withdraw, and on January 16, 1991, an offensive campaign called Operation Desert Storm began. Coalition bombers, armed helicopters, and gunships in the Persian Gulf hit targets in Iraq and Kuwait with bombs and cruise missiles for forty-three days. In addition to strategic strikes against such targets as the Iraqi nuclear weapons plant and Iraqi government buildings in Baghdad, Iraq's capital, Huchthausen reports that "during the [Persian] Gulf War, 2,780 coalition aircraft, 75 percent of which came from the United States, flew more than twenty-three thousand sorties [armed attacks] against Iraqi ground forces, who proved to be a predictable enemy on open terrain. The results were devastating to Iraq."

In hopes of breaking Arab support away from the UN coalition, Saddam directed the Iraqi army to launch missiles into Israel, a longtime foe of many Arab nations in the region. If Israel returned fire, Saddam reasoned, it would be difficult for Arab nations to remain loyal to the Western-led coalition. In the past, Arab nations had often banded together against Israel, and Saddam believed that many would not continue to fight Iraq, an Arab country, if it was being attacked by Israel. Mindful of this possibility, the UN persuaded Israel to let the coalition forces protect it. Israel did not return fire, and the coalition remained dominant until the war's end.

On February 24, 1991, the coalition began a ground campaign, and coalition troops forced the retreat of Iraqi forces from Kuwait. Within one hundred hours, Iraq was defeated. On February 27, President Bush announced the coalition's victory, the liberation of Kuwait, and a cease-fire. The war had claimed the lives of 240 coalition soldiers and an estimated 100,000 Iraqi soldiers (although Iraq officially claimed a loss of 20,000). In defeat, Saddam's regime ordered Iraqi soldiers to destroy Kuwait's oil wells. The soldiers opened the pipelines so the oil would pour into the sea, and they also set fire to more than seven hundred oil wells, causing massive losses and environmental damage. Another result of the war was that many thousands of Iraqi and Kuwaiti citizens became refugees, people who flee their country to escape violence or persecution. The war triggered "what is now regarded as one of history's largest, fastest, and most widespread migrations," writes Peter Cipkowski in *Understanding the Crisis in the Persian Gulf.* During the Iraqi invasion of Kuwait, nearly 1.5 million people fled Iraq and Kuwait to seek refuge in other Arab nations in the region; another 65,000 left during the coalition attacks.

At the end of the Persian Gulf War, Kurds in northern Iraq and Shiites in the south revolted against Saddam and the Sunni Ba'athist regime. They expected help from the U.S.-led coalition but did not receive any. Saddam's troops crushed them and drove them from their lands. The failed revolt resulted in another two million people leaving Iraq after the war's end.

A decade of tension

The end of the Persian Gulf War restored the contested territory between Iraq and Kuwait to its prewar state. Kuwait maintained its original borders, restored its monarchy, and began the lengthy process of repairing the devastation of its cities and oil production capabilities. Saddam

Oil wells burning outside Kuwait City. At the end of the Persian Gulf War, Iraqi soldiers were ordered to destroy Kuwait's oil wells.
© CORBIS.

remained in charge of Iraq, with command over a formidable military. Iraq, however, remained cut off from trade due to the UN sanctions, and its industry and infrastructure were severely damaged. Saddam's rule became more strict, destroying opposition and doing everything possible to suppress internal conflict.

One controversy at the end of the war was that the coalition had declined to remove Saddam from power. Many in the international community disapproved of foreign interference in Iraq's government, and most assumed that Iraq would eventually have a revolution in which the Shiite majority would take over. President Bush decided that the price of removing Saddam was too steep for both the United States and for the Iraqis. In a 2003 article called "Reasons Not to Invade Iraq," Bush explained that although his administration wished to see Saddam removed from power, "Trying to eliminate Saddam, extending the ground war into an occupation of Iraq, . . . would have incurred incalculable human and political costs. . . . Going in and occupying Iraq, thus unilaterally exceeding the U.N.'s mandate, would have destroyed the precedent of international response to aggression we hoped to establish. Had we gone the invasion route, the U.S. could conceivably still be an occupying power in a bitterly hostile land." Saddam remained in power, and the tensions between Iraq and the United States continued to grow.

The post-war decade

In the years following the Persian Gulf War, Saddam made it difficult for UN officials to verify that Iraq had fulfilled the terms of the 1991 cease-fire agreement. The main issue was whether or not Iraq continued to possess weapons of mass destruction. Saddam had notoriously used chemical weapons on Iranian troops and on Iraqi Kurds during the Iran-Iraq War. Although coalition air strikes during the Persian Gulf War had destroyed several weapons laboratories, and UN commissions destroyed the rest of the known remaining weapons plants after the war, many observers throughout the world speculated that Iraq was still building weapons of mass destruction in secret weapons factories. Suspicions grew during the mid–1990s when the Iraqi government frequently refused to allow UN weapons inspectors access to all requested areas within the country to search for these weapons. Despite his unwillingness to cooperate, Saddam insisted that all weapons of mass destruction and the means to produce them had been destroyed.

The international community tried many tactics during the mid–1990s to force Iraq to comply with UN weapons inspectors' demands, including bombing raids against Iraq by the United States, Great Britain, and France, but this did little to sway the Iraqi government or Saddam. The bombing destroyed the country's infrastructure (basic physical and organizational structures and facilities, such as roads, bridges, water pipes, and power lines), making conditions for Iraqi citizens worse. The UN also left its sanctions against Iraq in place after the war, not only to press for compliance with the cease-fire agreement, but also to weaken Saddam's rule.

The embargo on Iraqi trade with foreign countries made life increasingly difficult for the Iraqi people. Industrial and agricultural production stalled due to a lack of necessary machinery, spare parts, and supplies. The war's destruction of power plants made it difficult for Iraq to offer reliable electricity or safe drinking water to its citizens. Food and medicine came into Iraq from international humanitarian agencies, but the Iraqi government often distributed it to groups supportive of the government, leaving specific ethnic and religious groups, such as the Kurds and the Shiites, who had revolted against Saddam's rule, with less. Malnutrition (a condition where the body does not get essential vitamins and minerals) and disease increased throughout the country. The Iraqi government initiated an effective food rationing system that prevented Iraq from suffering a famine, a widespread shortage of food leading to massive starvation.

After years of sanctions, observers around the world began to question their effectiveness. Many humanitarian organizations contended that the sanctions ultimately punished Iraq's innocent citizens and probably had little effect on Saddam's powerful regime. To rectify the harm the sanctions were causing the Iraqi people, the UN launched a food-for-oil program in 1995 that enabled Iraq to sell some of its oil to buy food and medical supplies for its people. The suffering continued despite the new program, with severe poverty leading to starvation and increased deaths among parts of the population. In the end, the sanctions may have actually united the Iraqi people and their leader; Saddam was perceived by many Iraqis and others in the region as standing up to the United States and the UN.

The election of George W. Bush (1946–), the son of former U.S. president George H. W. Bush, to the U.S. presidency in 2000 brought several changes in the way that the international community, especially the United States, responded to Iraq. Bush appointed several of his father's former advisers to positions within his administration. Most significantly, Dick Cheney (1941–), secretary of defense during the Persian Gulf War, became Bush's vice president. Many of these advisers, including Cheney, felt that not enough had been done to remove Saddam from power during the Persian Gulf War. They believed that Iraq was still a threat to the United States and to other Western countries, despite the UN being unable to discover any weapons of mass destruction in Iraq or the means to produce such weapons. The UN stated that even though Iraq had not fully complied with the cease-fire agreement, there was no proof that it possessed these weapons, and it would not support attacks against Iraq without evidence that Iraq was a threat to other countries.

The war on terror

American views on foreign policy changed greatly after the September 11, 2001, terrorist attacks on the United States in which nearly three thousand people were killed. The United States declared a "war on terror" and vowed to fight terrorism around the world. The men who attacked the United States on September 11th were either members of or affiliated with al-Qaeda, a terrorist group led by Saudi militant Osama bin Laden (1957–2011). Al-Qaeda operated terrorist training camps in Afghanistan, where the Taliban (an Islamic militant and political group that had controlled Afghanistan since 1996) had granted bin Laden refuge. After the September 11th attacks, the United States quickly put together an international coalition to support military action against al-Qaeda and the Taliban government, which refused to hand bin Laden over to the United States. In October 2001 the United States launched an invasion of Afghanistan and removed the Taliban from power. Although it captured many al-Qaeda members, U.S. forces were unable to locate bin Laden.

Having succeeded in its first strike in the war on terror, the United States was determined to fight the terrorists before they could attack again. Many nations around the world were supportive of this effort but were uncertain about what criteria should be used to determine a terrorist threat. For instance, some groups were called terrorists by some nations while other nations considered them freedom fighters. In addition, terrorists are present in many societies around the world and do not represent their nations or the general populace in the nations where they live. Many countries had concerns about the United States using pre-emptive (preventive or anticipatory) military force to invade other nations.

In November 2002 the U.S. government voiced mounting concerns about Iraq. Many of President Bush's advisers were disturbed by Iraq's continued failure to comply with the demands of UN weapons inspectors. After September 11th, the United States was more concerned than ever about the threat of weapons of mass destruction, and Saddam was known to have used such weapons against Iraqi Kurds during the 1980s. The Bush administration argued that Iraq posed a threat to the security and safety of the Middle East and to the West, including the United States.

In his January 2003 State of the Union address, President Bush labeled Iraq, along with North Korea and Iran, as part of an "axis of evil." Bush criticized Iraq, saying "The Iraqi regime has plotted to develop anthrax, and nerve gas, and nuclear weapons for over a decade." Bush requested that the UN take action against Iraq for resisting the UN weapons inspectors' attempts to search for weapons of mass destruction. The UN, however, had already imposed stricter guidelines for Iraq to prove its compliance with weapons inspectors, and it felt that Saddam and the Iraqi government were being more open to inspectors than they had in the 1990s. Because no evidence of weapons of mass destruction had been found in Iraq up to that point, the UN refused to take further action against Iraq.

The United States, using information that later proved to be inaccurate, contended that there was enough evidence that Saddam was continuing to develop weapons of mass destruction to present a threat to Western countries. Many people who worked with the Bush administration at the time noted that Saddam's noncompliance with weapons inspections was only one motivation for the build-up to war. In 2003 Deputy Defense Secretary Paul Wolfowitz (1943–), who was an adviser to Cheney during the Persian Gulf War, suggested that a major motivation was to spread democracy in the Middle East. He said, as quoted by Robin Wright in *Dreams and Shadows: The Future of the Middle East*, "I don't think it's unreasonable to think that Iraq, properly managed... really could turn out to be, I hesitate to say it, the first Arab democracy." He goes on to predict that an Iraqi democracy could then influence Iran and Syria and the rest of the Middle East.

In early 2003 the United States declared that Iraq was a terrorist threat to the United States and the international community, and attempted to organize a coalition to invade Iraq and overthrow Saddam's government. The UN refused to be part of the coalition. Some nations pledged support for the U.S. effort, including Great Britain, while many others, even some that had supported earlier U.S. actions in the war on terror, refused to take part.

The Iraq War

The United States and Great Britain put together a coalition of forces, consisting mainly of American and British units but with support from Australia, Denmark, Poland and other countries. By March 125,000 U.S. troops and 45,000 Brisith troops had mobilized in Kuwait with Kuwait's permission. On March 19, the coalition launched what was called a "shock and awe" attack, beginning with an intense air strike on Baghdad, followed by a ground attack on April 5. Four days later, on April 9, a small group of Iraqis supported by the U.S. Marines pulled down a statue of Saddam in Baghdad's Firdaws Square, marking the end of Saddam's long dictatorship. Saddam went into hiding, and both of his sons, who had been high-ranking Iraqi government officials, were killed.

The coalition disbanded the Iraqi army, dismissing about one hundred thousand Iraqi soldiers, and ousted about thirty thousand government officials who had been associated with Saddam's Ba'athist regime, a process that became known as de-Ba'athification. Unlike its quick exit from the region after the Persian Gulf War, the United States did not leave Iraq immediately, because Iraq now lacked a functioning government and a leader. The United States set up an occupation government, called the Coalition Provisional Authority (CPA), to run the country until the Iraqis could establish a new government. President Bush declared a

U.S. troops entering Iraq in 2003, as part of the ground offensive in the Iraq War. © PETER TURNLEY/CORBIS.

victory in the war on May 1, 2003, but even as he was making the victory speech, new hostilities were erupting.

From celebration to upheaval Across Iraq, many people celebrated Saddam's removal from power. Especially among Shiite and Kurdish communities, long the victims of Saddam's violence, the relief was profound. However, for many, emotions were mixed. Iraqis had to face the elimination of their entire government and all of its security structures. Some feared the occupation by the United States. With the police force disbanded as part of the de-Ba'athification effort, celebrations turned into looting and then to upheaval. Some Iraqi rebels quickly organized to fight against the occupation of Iraq by the United States military, sent suicide bombers into Iraqi cities to kill U.S. and coalition troops and the Iraqis who had helped them. (A suicide bombing is an attack intended to kill others and cause widespread damage, carried about by someone who does not hope to survive the attack.) On August 19, 2003, a suicide bomber drove a truck into the UN headquarters in Iraq, killing the UN's special representative to Iraq.

After the de-Ba'athification purges, many Ba'athist military members found themselves suddenly unemployed. Many joined in the insurgency (an uprising, or rebellion, against a political authority) against coalition forces. Saddam and the Ba'ath Party had been members of the Sunni minority in Iraq. As the Americans ejected Ba'ath Party members from government, it appeared that they were isolating not just the Ba'ath Party, but all Sunnis. Sunnis feared that with the help of the Americans, the Kurds and Shiites would seize power in Iraq and treat Sunnis as inferiors or exact revenge on them for the past wrongs of Saddam and his associates. Former Ba'ath Party leaders and military officers, who had experience and had managed to take some of the former government's resources and funds, frequently led the bands of Sunni insurgents in their fights against the coalition troops.

On December 13, 2003, U.S. forces captured Saddam, who was found hiding in a hole in the ground, and took him into custody. Despite the American success in toppling Saddam, Iraqis grew increasingly hostile to the American occupation. By 2004 it became clear that the information that the U.S. government had used to justify the attack on Iraq had been faulty; investigations showed that Iraq had not possessed weapons of mass destruction since the late 1990s. In March 2004 Iraqis became outraged when photos were released to the public that showed Iraqi prisoners being beaten and sexually humiliated by U.S. soldiers at Abu Ghraib, a prison in Baghdad where the United States was holding its detainees. More gruesome details emerged as the U.S. military charged several soldiers with prisoner abuse and found them guilty. The CPA, under increasing attack, was forced to erect barriers around the section of Baghdad where most embassies and government offices are located and the heavily fortified section became known as the Green Zone.

By 2004 international terrorist groups had begun to filter into Iraq from neighboring Arab countries. A new group called al-Qaeda in Iraq, led by the Jordanian-born Abu Musab al-Zarqawi (1966–2006), began kidnapping and sometimes brutally murdering Westerners. The group drew the world's attention with grisly videos of beheadings and other murders that were posted on the Internet. The foreign militant groups led Iraqis in antigovernment and anti-U.S. campaigns and trained Iraqi warriors in violent methods of insurgency. They also stirred up trouble between Iraq's sects, hoping to add to the chaos. Al-Qaeda in Iraq established bases in the Iraqi city of Fallujah, and from there it launched attacks on coalition troops.

To fight the insurgency, the United States joined the newly formed Iraqi military troops. In the first Battle of Fallujah the coalition forces turned the fighting over to the Iraqi Fallujah Brigade. The Iraqi unit collapsed, leaving the city in the hands of the insurgents. In the late fall of 2004, the coalition forces evacuated the majority of civilians from Fallujah and then, in a carefully planned campaign, attacked the city. After heavy fighting, the coalition cleared the city, although they were unable to capture al-Zarqawi.

Foreign militants were only part of the reason for the escalating violence in Iraq, however. Sectarian violence (fighting between the different sects) began to occur, slowly at first. Despite widespread resentment of the Ba'athists, Shiites and Sunnis had generally lived peacefully together in Iraq before the Iraq War, particularly in Iraq's cities, where they shared neighborhoods and frequently intermarried. In the first years of the war, Shiites often fought alongside the Sunni insurgents. One very popular Iraqi Shiite leader, Muqtada al-Sadr (1973–), who came from a prominent family of religious and political leaders, used his influence to put together a militia called the Mahdi Army that was originally an anti-American force. Al-Sadr had a large following among Shiites nationwide, but particularly in the poor suburbs of Baghdad. In 2004, under al-Sadr's leadership, the rapidly growing Mahdi Army joined the Sunni insurgents to fight against the Americans. But conflicts between Sunnis and Shiites mounted. Within a year the Mahdi Army would be fighting in bloody battles against Sunnis.

A supporter holds up a portrait of Shiite leader Muqtada al-Sadr. Al-Sadr's militia, called the Mahdi Army, joined insurgents to fight Americans in Iraq. AHMAD AL-RUBAYE/ AFP/GETTY IMAGES.

A new Iraqi government In January 2005 the United States organized democratic elections in which Iraqis could vote for a transitional government. This was applauded as a huge step for democracy. Although the voter turnout was a relatively high 58 percent, Sunnis boycotted the elections, fearing their loss of power and scorning the American imposition of an Iraqi government. Shiite candidates, led by the Ayatollah Ali al-Sistani (1930–) won 48 percent of the vote, and Kurdish candidates won 25.6 percent. The transitional government's job was to draft a new constitution, which it did. The Iraqi public voted on it in October and passed it (although just barely, because the Sunnis objected to it). In December 2005 elections for a permanent government were held. The turnout was 80 percent, and the Sunnis were well represented among the more than two hundred parties running for parliament. The Shiite United Iraqi Alliance party won the majority and by April 2006 had formed a government headed by the new prime minister, Nouri al-Maliki (1950–), a Shiite leader who had led a resistance movement against Saddam before the war.

Even though Iraq now had a new government, the United States continued its military occupation, fearing that if it withdrew its troops out of Iraq, the country would fall into a civil war and that other nations, such as Syria or Iran, would exert their influence in Iraq and further destabilize the country. The concerns about civil upheaval were soon justified. Despite the new constitution and democratic elections, Iraq's sectarian hostilities were increasing, and the years 2006 and 2007 were the bloodiest of the Iraq War.

Nightmarish violence began on February 22, 2006, after a group of bombers blasted the Askariya Mosque in Samarra, one of the Shiites' holiest shrines. Experts tied the bombing to al-Qaeda in Iraq and Sunni extremists. Outraged Shiites blamed the Sunnis and prepared for revenge. Shiite men formed militias (armed civilian military forces) that swept into Sunni mosques and neighborhoods, beating and killing Sunnis. Sunnis in turn armed themselves and bombed and attacked Shiites in revenge. An estimated one thousand deaths ensued, and hundreds of thousands of Iraqis were forced to flee their homes. After these massacres, Iraq's mixed neighborhoods no longer existed. Sunnis lived only in Sunni neighborhoods, and Shiites lived only in Shiite neighborhoods. The militias continued to terrorize the streets, and according to many reports, it was not uncommon to see dead bodies lining the city streets after a night of sectarian gang violence.

Another long-standing conflict among Iraq's peoples centered around the Kurds. After the Persian Gulf War ended in 1991, the Kurds who remained were finally able to enjoy limited self-government in their region in northern Iraq under the protection of Western forces. By 2002 the Iraqi Kurds had formed a functioning regional parliament called Kurdistan Regional Government. They developed a large militia called the Pesh Merga. Saddam's removal from office had been a welcome event for them, and thousands of Kurdish troops had volunteered to help the U.S. effort in Iraq. In April 2005 Jalal Talabani (1933–) became the first Kurdish president of Iraq. Many Arab Iraqis resented the Kurds' support for the United States and their growing strength. Fears that the Kurds were in the process of declaring their independence led to violent incidents. An independent Kurdish state was unacceptable, largely because the Kurds' traditional lands in Iraq are situated on rich oil fields. Disputes with Arab Iraqis arose over control of the northern oil city of Kirkuk, which has a multiethnic population but has long been considered Kurdish. Tensions built up along the line dividing the Arab lands and the Kurdish lands of Iraq.

By the end of 2006, Iraq appeared to be on the verge of civil war. In an article for *Foreign Affairs*, Emma Sky, the chief political adviser to the commanding general of coalition forces, describes the situation: "Tens of thousands of Iraqis had fled their homes, and Baghdad had degenerated into armed sectarian enclaves [enclosed territories that are distinct from the surrounding territory]. Insurgent groups, criminal gangs, and militias of political parties used violence to achieve their particular objectives. Neighboring countries backed them with funding, paramilitary training, and weapons, further fomenting instability."

Violence declines On December 30, 2006, Saddam was hanged after being convicted by an Iraqi tribunal for crimes against humanity, but his death did not stop the violence in Iraq. In January 2007 the Bush administration announced that it would add twenty thousand more U.S. troops to the combat scene, an effort called "the surge." Although many Americans were calling for their troops to be brought home, the Bush administration deemed the surge necessary in order to stem Iraq's sectarian violence and to train Iraqi security forces to take over. U.S. troops began to work with Sunni insurgents, many of them former Ba'athists. These new Iraqi forces soon turned against al-Qaeda in Iraq and other foreign militant groups. Iraqis had come to hate the terrorist

Former Iraqi president Saddam Hussein appears before the Iraqi Special Tribunal in Baghdad, in 2005. Saddam was convicted on charges of crimes against humanity. © IRAQ SPECIAL TRIBUNAL/HANDOUT/REUTERS/CORBIS.

groups because of their attacks on Iraqi civilians. Al-Zarqawi had been killed in 2006. The level of violence in Iraq dropped, but the fighting continued.

The United States attributed much of the sectarian violence to al-Sadr and his Mahdi Army. The British had handed over control of the Iraqi city of Basra to Iraqi forces in December 2007. In 2008, with al-Qaeda in Iraq suppressed, the Mahdi Army's strongholds in Basra and Sadr City (a poor suburb of Baghdad) remained the greatest threats to Iraq's new government and security forces. Prime Minister al-Maliki and al-Sadr were both Shiites, and al-Sadr had helped the prime minister to gain his position, but they disagreed over the American military presence in Iraq. Al-Maliki needed to prove his actions were intended for the national good, rather than to support sectarian interests. He sent his increasingly strong Iraqi forces to combat the Mahdi Army. After a drawn-out battle in Basra, the Iraqi forces gained some, though not full, control in Basra and Sadr City.

U.S. troops prepare to leave In 2008 the United States handed over control of the province of Anbar to Iraqi forces. Although it was calm in 2008, Anbar had been a base for extremist groups, and one of the most violent areas earlier in the war. The insurgents had been successfully suppressed, and this, among other factors, led the United States to prepare to withdraw troops from Iraq and declare an end to the war. In November 2008, after intense negotiations, the Iraqi government approved an agreement that called for the withdrawal of U.S. troops from Iraqi cities by the end of 2009 and the withdrawal of all troops from the country by December 2011.

With a schedule for the departure of U.S. troops in place, long-delayed national elections were held in March 2010. The democratic process did not go smoothly or easily. Out of the sixty-two hundred candidates for Iraqis to choose from, the two top candidates were the incumbent prime minister, al-Maliki, and Iyad Allawi (also spelled Ayad Allawi; 1945–), who had served as the prime minister in the transitional government of 2005. Both leaders sought to win the votes of a broad spectrum of Iraqis, appealing to national interests rather than sectarian ones. The election was held despite multiple bombings in several cities and violence along the Kurdish-Arab borders. Allawi's party won ninety-one seats in parliament, while al-Maliki's won eighty-nine. Nine months of bitter debate and deal-making efforts in the attempt to form Iraq's new government followed. During that time, the bitter dispute between the two leaders nearly halted the government.

Al-Sadr had gone into exile in Iran during or after the 2008 battle at Basra. From there, he led a political party created from his militia forces and his Shiite supporters. Al-Sadr's party won forty seats in parliament. Eventually, in November 2010, al-Sadr announced his support of al-Maliki, and with his influence, a new government was formed. From Iran, al-Sadr had urged his followers to cease fighting and to vote in Iraq's elections. In January 2011 al-Sadr returned to Iraq amid much publicity. Commentators worldwide noted that he was becoming a potent political force in Iraq.

In the meantime, on August 19, 2010, U.S. president Barack Obama (1961–) declared the U.S. combat mission in Iraq over. While ninety thousand U.S. troops had been withdrawn, fifty thousand remained in an advise-and-assist role in the new U.S. mission called Operation New Dawn, with the objective of training Iraqi security forces. Operation New Dawn was scheduled to end in December 2011. On December 15, in a quiet ceremony at Baghdad International Airport, military officials lowered the U.S. flag, marking the official end of the Iraq War.

Effects of the Iraq War

Although most Iraqis were glad that Saddam was gone, many blamed the United States for what they suffered after he was driven from power. By most estimates, about 100,000 Iraqis lost their lives during the Iraq War. From 2003 to 2011 more than 3 million Iraqis fled from their homes. During the war, more than 4,000 American soldiers died, and 32,000 were wounded.

Aside from the terrible loss of life and community in Iraq and the U.S. casualties, the Iraq War took a large toll on international relations. As the war came to an end, few experts, even those who had supported the war, denied that it had hurt relations between the United States and Middle Eastern countries, causing distrust and anger. There have been concerns that Iran would gain power in Iraq; and in 2011 China and Russia were also exerting increasing influence in the Iraqi economy and politics. The war provided terrorist groups with opportunities to grow and to cause death and destruction for a time. Nevertheless, Iraq had a democratically elected government in 2011; future perceptions of the war will depend on how well that government fares.

For More Information

BOOKS

Arnove, Anthony, ed. *Iraq Under Siege: The Deadly Impact of Sanctions and War.* Cambridge, MA: South End Press, 2000.

Bratman, Fred. *War in the Persian Gulf.* Brookfield, CT: Millbrook Press, 1991.

Cipkowski, Peter. *Understanding the Crisis in the Persian Gulf.* New York: Wiley, 1992.

Diller, Daniel C., ed. *The Middle East.* 8th ed. Washington, DC: Congressional Quarterly, 1995.

Huchthausen, Peter. *America's Splendid Little Wars: A Short History of U.S. Military Engagements: 1975–2000.* New York: Viking, 2003.

Nardo, Don. *The Persian Gulf War.* San Diego, CA: Lucent Books, 1991.

Wright, Robin. *Dreams and Shadows: The Future of the Middle East.* New York: Penguin, 2008, p. 396.

WEB SITES

Bush, George H.W. "Reasons Not to Invade Iraq." *Global Policy Forum* (April 19, 2003). http://www.globalpolicy.org/component/content/article/169/36409.html (accessed on November 30, 2011).

Bush, George W. "Address Before a Joint Session of the Congress on the State of the Union." January 2003. *GPO Access.* http://frwebgate.access.gpo.gov/cgi-bin/getdoc.cgi?dbname=2003_presidential_documents&docid=pd03fe03_txt-6 (accessed on November 30, 2011).

"The Gulf War." *Harper's Magazine.* http://www.harpers.org/GulfWar.html (accessed on November 30, 2011).

"The Gulf War: an In-Depth Examination of the 1990–1991 Persian Gulf Crisis." *PBS Frontline.* http://www.pbs.org/wgbh/pages/frontline/gulf/ (accessed on November 30, 2011).

Kennedy, Edward M. "The Axis of War: Cheney, Rumsfeld, and Wolfowitz." Speech to the Center for American Progress." *All Salon* (January 14, 2004). http://www.salon.com/news/opinion/feature/2004/01/14/kennedy_speech (accessed on November 30, 2011).

"Refugees and Health." *Costs of War.* http://costsofwar.org/article/refugees-and-health (accessed on November 30, 2011).

Sky, Emma. "Iraq, from Surge to Sovereignty: Winding down the War in Iraq." *Foreign Affairs* (March–April 2011). http://www.foreignaffairs.com/articles/67481/emma-sky/iraq-from-surge-to-sovereignty (accessed on November 30, 2011).

"Timeline: The Life and Times of Donald Rumsfeld." *PBS Frontline.* http://www.pbs.org/wgbh/pages/frontline/shows/pentagon/etc/cronfeld.html (accessed on November 30, 2011.

13

Terrorism Based in the Middle East

On September 11, 2001, nineteen men affiliated with the terrorist organization al-Qaeda hijacked four American airliners filled with passengers and directed them at targets in the United States. Two of the planes slammed into the World Trade Center towers in New York City. Both towers collapsed within two hours of being struck. The third plane flew into the Pentagon, the headquarters of the U.S. military located in Virginia, just outside the nation's capital of Washington, D.C., creating a large hole in the side of the building and killing more than one hundred of its occupants. The fourth plane crashed into a field in Pennsylvania, after the passengers and crew tried to retake control of the plane. All the passengers and crew aboard the four planes were killed. These were the worst terrorist attacks that have ever occurred on American soil, killing nearly three thousand people. For many Americans, the attacks created a new awareness of terrorism. But in the quarter century prior to September 11th there had been many terrorist attacks of a similar nature on Western or American targets. A significant portion of them originated in the Middle East, and there were many more such attacks on targets in the Middle East.

Terrorism has existed in many forms since ancient times. Every region of the world has been troubled by it at one time or another. Terrorism became a major problem in the Middle East in the early twentieth century and continued to be a problem into the twenty-first century. Two Middle East conflicts in particular have generated small groups of extremists who have resorted to violence against civilians to get their point across. One is the conflict between Arabs (people who speak the Arabic language) and Israelis, and the other is the conflict between Islamists (those who seek a government based on the religion of Islam) and advocates of a secular (nonreligious) government.

Many contemporary terrorist groups of the Middle East have roots the Muslim Brotherhood, an Islamic fundamentalist group organized in

275

WORDS TO KNOW

Fatah: A Palestinian militant group and political party dedicated to the establishment of an independent Palestinian state.

fatwa: A statement of religious law issued by Islamic clerics.

fundamentalism: A movement stressing adherence to a strict or literal interpretation of religious principles.

Haganah: The underground defense force of Zionists in Palestine from 1920 to 1948. It became the basis for the Israeli army.

Hamas: A Palestinian Islamic fundamentalist group and political party operating primarily in the West Bank and the Gaza Strip with the goal of establishing a Palestinian state and opposing the existence of Israel. It has been labeled a terrorist organization by several countries.

Hezbollah: A Shiite militant group and political party based in Lebanon.

Irgun Zvai Leumi: A militant underground group founded in 1931 that worked to secure Israeli independence by staging violent attacks on British and Arab targets. Also known simply as Irgun.

Islamism: A fundamentalist movement characterized by the belief that Islam should provide the basis for the political, social, and cultural life in Muslim nations.

jihad: An armed struggle against unbelievers, in defense of Islam; often interpreted to mean holy war. The term also refers to the spiritual struggle of Muslims against sin.

martyr: A person who dies for his or her religion.

Muslim Brotherhood: An Islamic fundamentalist group organized in opposition to Western influence and in support of Islamic principles.

occupied territories: The lands under the political and military control of Israel, especially the West Bank and the Gaza Strip.

Palestine: A historical region in the Middle East on the eastern shore of the Mediterranean Sea, comprising parts of present-day Israel and Jordan.

Palestine Liberation Organization (PLO): A political and military organization formed to unite various Palestinian Arab groups with the goal of establishing an independent Palestinian state.

Palestinian Authority (PA): The recognized governing institution for Palestinians in the West Bank and the Gaza Strip, established in 1993. Also known as the Palestinian National Authority.

Palestinians: An Arab people whose ancestors lived in the historical region of Palestine and who continue to lay claim to that land.

sharia: A system of Islamic law based on the Koran. Sharia attempts to create the perfect social order, based on God's will and justice, and covers a wide range of human activities, including acts of religious worship, the law of contracts and obligations, personal status law, and public law.

Shiites: Followers of the Shia branch of Islam. Shiites believe that only direct descendants of the prophet Muhammad are qualified to lead the Islamic faith.

suicide bombing: An attack intended to kill others and cause widespread damage, carried about by someone who does not hope to survive the attack.

Sunnis: Followers of the Sunni branch of Islam. Sunnis believe that elected officials, regardless of their heritage, are qualified to lead the Islamic faith.

weapons of mass destruction: Any nuclear, chemical, or biological weapons capable of killing or injuring great numbers of people.

The World Trade Center in New York City, after it was hit during al-Qaeda terrorist attacks on the United States, September 11, 2001. AP PHOTO/JIM COLLINS.

opposition to Western influence and in support of Islamic principles that was established in Egypt in 1928. The Muslim Brotherhood was not initially a terrorist organization, but by the 1940s some of its members began using acts of violence as a method of promoting their political cause. The movement spread rapidly throughout the Middle East, starting in the 1950s. At that time another conflict was brewing that would eventually lead to terrorist activities. Jews established the state of Israel in Palestine (a historical region in the Middle East on the eastern shore of the Mediterranean Sea, comprising parts of present-day Israel and Jordan), and the 1948 Arab-Israeli War erupted in response. During that war, hundreds of thousands of the Arab Palestinians, people who had lived for centuries on the land that Israel claimed, were forced to flee their homes and livelihoods. Many of the Palestinian refugees relocated to refugee camps in the West Bank, area on the west bank of the Jordan River that was part of Jordan; in the Gaza Strip, a narrow strip of land along the eastern shore of the Mediterranean Sea that was part of Egypt; and in other neighboring Arab countries. Palestinians continued to press their claim to territory within the former region of Palestine, but for a time, they were too poor and poorly organized to fight the powerful Israeli Army. By the 1970s however, Palestinians had begun to organize. Some Palestinians joined local Muslim Brotherhood branches, and in places like the Gaza Strip and Lebanon, the objectives of the two groups were combined. By the late 1980s, there were several powerful groups that used terrorism in their attempts to eliminate Western influences from the Middle East, establish governments based on Islamic law, and fight against Israel. Among these groups were Hamas, Islamic Jihad, Hezbollah, and later, al-Qaeda.

Throughout history, terrorist groups have frequently changed their tactics and become a part of the mainstream political process. In the twenty-first century some of the groups, such as Hamas and Hezbollah, have deliberately turned themselves into political parties, running candidates in national elections and participating in the government of their countries. To some observers, members of terrorist organizations who are elected into positions in government are simply terrorists in office, but others view them as the people's chosen representatives in a democracy. There are other terrorist groups, however, such as the various branches and offshoots of al-Qaeda, that scorn participation in political processes.

Defining terrorism

The horrific attacks on the United States on September 11, 2001, by al-Qaeda are easily identified as terrorism. Many acts, though, are not as easy to label. What is called terrorism by some people may well be considered a necessary step in a fight for freedom by others. The United Nations (UN; an international organization of countries founded in 1945 to promote international peace, security, and cooperation) has struggled for many years to arrive at a definition of terrorism, without success. The lack of a clear definition is an obstacle to the ongoing international efforts to fight terrorism and to prosecute terrorists under international laws.

The U.S. Department of State considers terrorism to be deliberate, politically motivated violence committed against noncombatant targets (civilians, off-duty soldiers, unarmed soldiers, or places, such as buildings) by groups that do not directly represent the government of a nation, although they may be supported by a government. Other definitions note that acts of terrorism intend to create great fear in the public at large because the violence is random and could happen to anyone and at any time. Some definitions note that acts of terrorism are usually designed to pressure a government or other political institution into doing what the terrorists want.

Acts of war are not considered terrorism. When countries declare war on one another and there is open warfare, the actions of soldiers are acts of war and generally are not classified as terrorism. Even if soldiers harass or murder the civilian inhabitants of a country during war, the action is called a war crime, not terrorism. Also in war, if civilians use bombs and rocket launchers to attack soldiers, the act is often called guerrilla warfare or insurgency, indicating that loosely organized and less equipped rebel groups are fighting against an organized army or government. In conflicts in which war has not been declared by governments, however, it can be difficult to distinguish between terrorist acts and other uses of violence.

Use of the word *terrorism* became so common by the early twenty-first century that it was often meaningless. In the fight between Palestinians and Israelis, each side has frequently accused the other of terrorism even when the acts do not fit any generally accepted definition. While there is no doubt that terrorism has played a large role in Arab-Israeli conflict, sometimes the word is used more to stress that an action was cruel or unjust than to actually identify an act of terrorism.

Terrorist beginnings in Palestine

Most historians point out that terrorism has ancient roots in the Middle East. Two ancient terrorist groups of the Middle East stand out, perhaps because of some similarities to modern conflicts. The Zealots of Judea (the southern kingdom of ancient Israel) was a first-century Jewish religious and political group that rebelled against Roman rule in Judea. Too few in numbers to stage an all-out revolt, the Zealots of Judea began to secretly murder Roman officials and the Jews who helped them. The second group, the Assassins, arose one thousand years later in northern Iran. The group was a faction of eleventh-century Muslims who felt that the top rulers of Islam were corrupting the religion with their worldly ways and needed to be eliminated. Generally the Assassins sent a lone killer to publicly stab the designated ruler or religious leader. These were suicide missions. The killer did not try to escape after the murder, considering it an honor to die as a martyr, a person who dies for his or her religion.

Contemporary forms of terrorism in the Middle East began early in the twentieth century in Palestine. Beginning in the late nineteenth century, Zionists (supporters of an international political movement that called for the creation of an independent Jewish state in Palestine) began to immigrate to Palestine, the site of the ancient Jewish kingdom. There they hoped to escape the sometimes violent anti-Semitism (prejudice against Jews) they faced in Europe and elsewhere. (For more information, see **Palestine and Zionist Settlement: Nineteenth Century to 1948**.) As increasing numbers of Jews immigrated to Palestine, Jews and Arabs began to clash over access to land, as well as access to religious holy sites in the city of Jerusalem. By the 1920s the clashes between the Jews and the Arabs had become violent.

Irgun Zvai Leumi

In the early twentieth century, Palestine was being administered as a mandate (a territory entrusted to foreign administration) under British rule. Zionist organizers in Palestine were determined to reach their political goal: the creation of a Jewish state in Palestine. Some Zionists used legitimate means to pursue their goal. They lobbied the mandate's British officials, organized political parties, and prepared to defend themselves by getting military training, collecting arms, and developing defense plans. But other Zionists felt that extreme strategies were necessary. These Zionists formed what many consider to be one of the first contemporary terrorist groups in the region: the Irgun Zvai Leumi, better known as Irgun. The group was founded in 1931 by those who felt that the underground Zionist defense force, Haganah, was not as effective as it should be, because it did not strike directly against Arab targets.

From 1931 through 1948, Irgun conducted many attacks against Arab civilians and against British officials who wanted to limit Jewish immigration to Palestine in a belated attempt to ease the conflict between the huge influx of Jewish immigrants and the Arabs who lived there. One of Irgun's well-known attacks was the July 22, 1946, bombing of the King David Hotel in Jerusalem, which targeted British criminal investigators headquartered at the hotel who were investigating Irgun. The bombing killed 91 people, including hotel guests, and injured 45 more. The leader of Irgun at that time was Menachem Begin (1913–1992), who went on to serve as prime minister of Israel in the late 1970s and early 1980s. Irgun's most notorious act came during Israel's fight for independence in the 1948 Arab-Israeli War, when Irgun forces attacked the Palestinian village of Deir Yassin. The number of Palestinians killed in this attack is uncertain. Some sources say that around two hundred fifty men, women, and children were killed; other sources place the number closer to one hundred.

Irgun Zvai Leumi troops. The Jewish militia Irgun conducted missions that some countries considered to be terrorism.
© BETTMANN/CORBIS.

Once Israel became a nation in 1948, the Irgun forces were absorbed into the Israeli military, called the Israel Defense Forces (IDF). The views of the former Irgun fighters influenced many military actions in Israel. The new nation of Israel was surrounded by hostile Arab nations that were unhappy that Jews had taken land from Arab Palestinians to create their new nation. Many of these neighboring Arab nations vowed to destroy Israel. Israeli policy makers, including Israel's first prime minister, David Ben-Gurion (1886–1973), thought that if they over-looked even minor attacks on Israeli borders, then it would give the impression that the country was weak and unstable. They established a policy, called "Ben-Gurionism," that any attack on Israel would be met with an overwhelming display of force. Many Israelis believed the IDF was justified in its use of extreme force to respond to minor conflicts, but in the years after Israel became an internationally recognized and accepted nation, observers throughout the world began to question this use of excessive force.

Israeli military occupation

On June 5, 1967, Israel, believing an attack from neighboring Arab countries was imminent, attacked Egypt, Jordan, and Syria. In just six days, Israel seized the Gaza Strip and the entire Sinai Peninsula from Egypt, the West Bank from Jordan, and the Golan Heights (a mountainous region located on the border of Syria and Israel, northwest of the Sea of Galilee) from Syria. From almost the moment the 1967 Arab-Israeli War (known in Israel as the Six-Day War) ended, what to do with the captured lands became a divisive issue both inside and outside Israel. Of particular issue was the West Bank and the Gaza Strip, which were populated largely by Palestinians who had fled to these regions during the 1948 Arab-Israeli War. Israeli military forces were sent in to occupy these lands, and some of the tactics they used to keep the peace were cruel and at times extreme. The Israeli Army issued curfews, forcing all Palestinians into their homes at defined hours regardless of work or school schedules. They also used roadblocks and travel bans to limit travel; even travel to work or to visit family members was often denied. At times, Palestinians who worked in areas outside of the occupied territories (lands under the political and military control of Israel) were not allowed back to their homes once they had left. Any resistance or failure to comply with restrictions was punished by military force. The Israeli military detained and imprisoned thousands of Palestinians in the 1970s and 1980s, and often beat and harassed those Palestinians who did not obey their orders.

In late 1987 the Palestinian people rose up against the Israeli military occupation in an uprising called the First Intifada (1987–91). Palestinians in the West Bank and the Gaza Strip rioted and threw rocks at Israeli soldiers. The IDF responded with tanks and rifle fire. Soon, television images that showed stick-and-stone throwing Palestinian youths facing a powerful military force were broadcast to countries around the world. The Palestine Liberation Organization (PLO; a political and military organization formed to unite various Palestinian Arab groups with the goal of establishing an independent Palestinian state) stated that the IDF forces had been terrorizing Palestinians in the occupied territories since 1967. Israel replied that it was ensuring its own security, and that the measures taken by the military were not of a terrorist nature since the government of Israel had determined that such force was necessary to protect the nation.

Palestinian terrorism

The 1967 Arab-Israeli War marked a turning point in the history of the Middle East. In the years after the war, the Palestinians organized to fight back. They could not, however, hope to match the strength of their powerful, well-armed foe. In the late 1960s small groups of Palestinians attacked Israeli settlements and military targets using basic weaponry. By the early 1970s better-organized militant groups had formed, including Fatah and the Popular Front for the Liberation of Palestine (PFLP), all operating under the central leadership of the Palestine Liberation Organization (PLO). These groups used their operational bases in neighboring Jordan, Lebanon, and Syria to attack Israel from across the border, using stronger weapons, such as handheld rockets. This kind of attack, using a variety of rocket types with varying ranges, occurred on a regular basis throughout the end of the twentieth century and into the early years of the twenty-first century. Israel viewed these attacks as acts of terrorism, but to the Palestinians and their Arab supporters, they were acts of warfare designed to reclaim territory Israel had taken from the Palestinians in the Arab-Israeli wars of 1948 and 1967.

PFLP hijackings

Some Palestinian militant groups felt that even more dramatic tactics were necessary to fight Israel. In 1968 three members of the PFLP hijacked an

Israeli jetliner and diverted it to Algeria, a North African nation sympathetic to the Palestinians. By their actions the PFLP hoped to draw attention to the plight of the Palestinians in the occupied territories and in refugee camps in Arab countries, where many Palestinians had fled after being forced from their homes during the 1948 and 1967 Arab-Israeli Wars. For forty days the hijackers negotiated with Israeli officials and made their demands known to the international media. Eventually the hijackers and the hostages went free. No deaths resulted from this hijacking. The international attention that resulted from this attention-grabbing act encouraged the PFLP and similar groups to continue to stage terrorist acts.

After the 1968 hijacking, the PFLP became infamous for terrorist activities. Its members blew up a supermarket in Jerusalem, set off bombs at Israeli embassies in several European cities, and in 1970 blew up a Swissair flight bound for Israel, killing forty-seven people. In September 1970 the PFLP hijacked four jets flying from Germany, Switzerland, and the Netherlands and diverted one to Egypt and three to Jordan. The hijackers did not kill anyone, but they did blow up three of the jets. The terrorist attacks caught the world's attention, but they did not, as the PFLP had hoped, result in greater support for the Palestinians' plight. Many nations reacted by increasing airport security and arresting and detaining potential terrorists who attempted to enter or leave the country.

The PFLP destroyed three jets that its members hijacked in 1970 to draw attention to the treatment of Palestinians by Israelis.
© BETTMANN/CORBIS.

For a few years after the 1967 Arab-Israeli War, Jordan had allowed the PLO to operate from within its borders. The PLO served as the coordinator of groups such as the PFLP and thus was considered by most observers to be involved in the terrorist activities. Jordan wanted to avoid war with Israel over the PLO's activities, and it also wished to avoid the condemnation of other nations for supporting terrorism. For that and other reasons, Jordan evicted the PLO in a violent purge called Black September.

The Munich massacre

In 1972 some PLO members split from the organization and created an independent group that operated under the name Black September (a reference to Jordan's 1970 purge of the PLO). The group conducted one of the most publicized terrorist acts in the history of the Arab-Israeli conflict. On September 5, 1972, in Munich, Germany, members of Black September used stolen keys to let themselves into apartments occupied by members of the Israeli Olympic team, who were in Munich to participate in the Olympic Games. The terrorists immediately killed two Israelis and took nine more hostage; they demanded the release of 234 Palestinians who had been jailed in Israel for reasons they considered unjust. Israeli officials refused to negotiate with Black September, fearing that giving in to the group's demands would encourage more violent acts. During a rescue attempt by German police, Black September murdered the hostages, and the police killed five of the Black September members.

The Munich Massacre, as it came to be known, horrified the international community. Governments around the world increased security measures against groups that used terrorist tactics. Within Israel, high-ranking politicians authorized Mossad, Israel's intelligence service, to use any means necessary to eliminate terrorist actions against Israel. Mossad conducted a number of operations against Palestinian groups, including Black September, the PFLP, the PLO, and Fatah. Using a variety of techniques, including letter bombs, car bombs, and sniper attacks, Mossad killed high-ranking members of these groups over the next several years. The militant Palestinian groups responded to the killings with more violence.

Abu Nidal

One of the most hunted and feared terrorists of the 1970s and 1980s was an independent Palestinian known as Abu Nidal (also known as Sabri al-Banna;

1937–2002). Abu Nidal initially worked with Fatah and the PLO in their struggle to retake land from Israel through violent means. When those groups began to take more moderate positions in the late 1970s, Abu Nidal left and began to fight Israelis on his own.

To further his cause, Abu Nidal formed a small and secretive group called the Abu Nidal Organization. The Abu Nidal Organization attacked anyone who opposed the goal of reclaiming Palestinian land and did not limit its targets to military and government sites. It attacked Jewish targets, such as a group of Jewish schoolchildren in the early 1980s, as well as Palestinians whom Abu Nidal accused of betraying the Palestinian cause. Abu Nidal himself tried to assassinate PLO chairman Yasser Arafat (1929–2004). All told, the Abu Nidal Organization is credited with more than one hundred terrorist attacks in twenty countries over twenty-five years, killing three hundred and wounding another six hundred. Abu Nidal's terrorist activities stopped around 1990.

Abu Nidal Organization militants, during training exercises at their camp in Lebanon, in 1980. The Abu Nidal Organization attacked anyone who opposed the goal of reclaiming Palestinian land. © ALAIN NOGUES/SYGMA/CORBIS.

The rise of Islamist terrorism

The Palestinian terrorism of the late 1960s and the 1970s is considered the first wave of modern Middle East terrorism. Another brand of terrorism, known as Islamist terrorism, emerged in the 1980s and became the dominant form of terrorism in the Middle East in the 1990s and the early twenty-first century.

Islamist terrorism should not be confused with Islamism. Islamism is a movement that advocates organizing governments and societies according to Islamic law and teachings. Islamists believe that Islam is a complete philosophy of life that should be the basis of religious, social, and political institutions. Using the Koran (also spelled Qur'an or Quran; the holy book of Islam) as their guide, Islamists seek to build ideal Muslim societies. Many Muslims accept that their religion should be the primary shaping force in all areas of social life, including politics. They reject the common Western notion that religion should be set apart from social institutions, such as government, justice systems, and the economy. Many advocates of Islamism are also strong supporters of democracy and human rights.

Islamic terrorists usually have rigid interpretations of the Koran and Islamic law. According to Robin Wright in *Dreams and Shadows: The Future of the Middle East*, the most extreme Islamists are purists who "believe Islam was perfect and absolute in its original form. They see the early generations of Muslims, particularly the first three in the seventh century, as the model for all Islamic life in any age." These extremists seek a return to the days of the Islamic empires, when the caliphs (the spiritual, political, and military leaders of the world's Muslims) ruled a huge empire with their great military forces and spread Islam throughout vast regions of the world. (For more information, see **The Ancient Middle East: From the First Civilizations to the Crusades**.) Many support a movement for world dominance by Islam. Islamists who use terrorist methods are willing to hurt or kill people to achieve their goals. Besides creating a society based on their interpretation of Islam, one of the top objectives of Islamist terrorists in the Middle East is the removal of all Western influences from their region, including Israel, which they see as a symbol of Western strength within a mainly Arab (and Muslim) region.

The Muslim Brotherhood

The largest force in Islamist organizations during the twentieth century was an Egyptian-based group called the Muslim Brotherhood. The group was founded in Egypt in 1928 by Hassan al-Banna (1906–1949). At that time, Egypt had gained its independence but it remained under the heavy influence of Great Britain, with a large force of British troops stationed there for the long term. Al-Banna felt that the presence of foreign customs and philosophies was corrupting Egyptian Muslims. Rather than the British-inspired, secular, Western-style government, al-Banna taught that Islam should be the center of all aspects of Egyptian life. Sharia (Islamic religious law) should provide the legal structure and the Koran should be the basis of social interaction, including the economy.

Beginning as a protest movement against the British presence in Egypt, the Muslim Brotherhood quickly grew in size and strength by forming social institutions, such as labor unions, schools, and social aid programs that would improve Egyptian society. People from every walk of life joined the movement; by the 1940s, the Muslim Brotherhood had an estimated one million members. When Egypt led the fight against the

Hasan al-Banna, founder of the Muslim Brotherhood. AP PHOTO/NADER DAOUD.

newly independent Israel in the 1948 Arab-Israeli War, the membership in the Muslim Brotherhood soared. It was around that time that the organization began to actively arm and train its members for the fight against the British, the Israelis, and the Egyptian government, which they felt had been corrupted.

In December 1948 the Egyptian chief of police and the prime minister were assassinated, and the Egyptian government blamed both deaths on the Muslim Brotherhood. The organization was outlawed and hundreds of its members were arrested. Two months later, Hassan al-Banna was assassinated, and many accused the Egyptian government of his murder. Starting in the early 1950s, some leaders of the organization moved to neighboring Arab countries to establish new branches.

The 1950s were a difficult time for the Muslim Brotherhood in Egypt. Egyptian president Gamal Abdel Nasser (1918–1970) disbanded all political parties. He saw the Muslim Brotherhood, with its large membership, as a threat to his power, and he blamed the group for an attempt on his life in 1954. Throughout Nasser's reign, the Muslim Brotherhood was outlawed. It continued to exist in secret, but many of its members were imprisoned and others fled the country.

Sayyid Qutb and the Muslim Brotherhood In 1951 a young Egyptian scholar named Sayyid Qutb (1906–1966) returned to Egypt from a lengthy stay in the United States and joined the Muslim Brotherhood. He had been appalled at what he considered to be a lack of morals and an overall indecency in American society. Qutb allied himself with the segment of Egyptian society that was preparing for armed resistance. He was arrested in 1954 for plotting to overthrow the government and spent almost all of the next twelve years in prison, facing frequent torture, before he was hanged in 1966. While he was in jail, he wrote influential works on Islamic fundamentalism, a movement stressing adherence to a strict or literal interpretation of religious principles.

Qutb contrasted the modern Middle East civilization with the pre-Islam era—the Middle East prior to the coming of its prophet Muhammad. He considered all contemporary Arab leaders corrupt infidels (unbelievers), because they had replaced the authority of God with other, worldly authorities. Qutb's writings call for following the Koran exactly and purging oneself of the influences of modern life. He believed that the true Muslim path is to isolate oneself for a period of time to intensely study the Koran and then to use the knowledge of Allah (the

Arabic word for God) gained in isolation to organize others and carry out jihad against infidels. Jihad is the spiritual struggle of Muslims against sin. It also refers to armed struggle against unbelievers, in defense of Islam. This concept is often interpreted to mean holy war. Qutb believed it was through this struggle that true Islam could be established once again on Earth as it had been by Muhammad when he formed the Islamic empire in the seventh century. Many scholars cite Qutb as one of the most influential thinkers of the Middle East of the twentieth century. Interpretations of his works vary, however, and some have formed the basis of extremism, such as that of the Taliban (an Islamic militant and political group that controlled Afghanistan from 1996 to 2001), as well as terrorist groups, such as al-Qaeda.

Radical branches form The majority of the large membership of the Muslim Brotherhood was not violent or involved in terrorism. When Anwar Sadat (also spelled al-Sadat; 1918–1981) became president of Egypt in 1970, he allowed the Muslim Brotherhood to reorganize and to freely gather and publish a newspaper. During the 1970s, the Muslim Brotherhood officially rejected violence and reorganized as a political party. Those members with more militant goals broke away to form new groups, some of which were violent and extremist. In 1981 Sadat was assassinated; Egyptian Islamic Jihad, one of the new militant groups that had broken off from the Muslim Brotherhood, was responsible.

Over the years, branches of the Muslim Brotherhood formed in about seventy countries. These branches frequently formed new identities. For example, a fourteen-year-old Egyptian named Ayman al-Zawahiri (1951–) was a member of the Muslim Brotherhood in Egypt. He broke away from that group to cofound the Egyptian Islamic Jihad and from there he went on to help Osama bin Laden (1957–2011) form al-Qaeda, which he led after bin Laden's death in 2011. Many of the Islamist groups that were terrorist groups in the twenty-first century, such as Hamas, Hezbollah, Islamic Jihad, and al-Qaeda, have roots in the Muslim Brotherhood, although the connections to the older organization have generally long been severed.

The Muslim Brotherhood offshoot that formed in Syria had a large headquarters in the city of Hama and bases in many other cities. In the 1980s Syrian president Hafez Assad (also spelled al-Assad; 1930–2000) felt that his power was threatened by the popularity of the movement and went after the organization with full military force. In 1982 he launched a brutal attack on the city of Hama. His forces leveled parts of the city and killed more than ten thousand of the city's inhabitants. Assad's forces also attacked Muslim Brotherhood bases in the Syrian cities of Latakia, Aleppo, and Homs.

Although the original Egyptian Muslim Brotherhood had reorganized itself as a political party, it could not function as one because the Egyptian constitution prohibited religious groups from running candidates in elections. Still, the Muslim Brotherhood was very popular in Egypt. When the United States launched the Iraq War (2003–11) in 2003, many Egyptians joined the Muslim Brotherhood as a means of protesting the foreign presence in the Middle East. (For more information on the Iraq War, see **The Gulf Wars: 1991 to 2011**.) A significant segment of Muslim Egyptians in 2011 believed their government should be led, to greater or lesser degrees, by the principles of their religion. Many moderate Islamists responded enthusiastically to the Muslim Brotherhood's current motto, "Islam is the solution." The Muslim Brotherhood successfully ran some of its members in elections as independent candidates. Since the Arab Spring of 2011, a series of prodemocracy uprisings in the Middle East and North Africa, the organization has taken a leading role in Egyptian politics. The U.S. State Department does not include the Muslim Brotherhood on its list of terrorist organizations.

The Egyptian Islamic Jihad

One of the major Egyptian offshoots of the Muslim Brotherhood was the Egyptian Islamic Jihad, a group that openly advocated the use of terrorist methods in its mission to establish an Islamic state in Egypt and to eventually achieve world domination by Islam. The group's terrorist activities were based on the belief that it was the duty of Muslims to mount jihad against any government or institution that corrupts Islam. The group broke off from the Muslim Brotherhood in the mid–1970s, because it was working too closely with the Egyptian government, which the group considered corrupt. Another small Islamic terrorist group, al Gamaa al-Islamiyya, formed when its leaders broke off from the Egyptian Islamic Jihad.

The Egyptian Islamic Jihad was structured in individual cells, or small groups of members who worked together. The members of the cells knew only their own assignments and did not know anything about other cells. Thus, if they were caught, they were unable to inform police about the group's overall activities. In 1981 members of the Egyptian

U.S. State Department List of Terrorist Organizations: Middle East and North Africa, 2011

The list that follows is comprised of the names of Middle East and North African organizations selected from the U.S. Department of State's list of Foreign Terrorist Organizations (FTOs). The list is monitored and maintained by a division of the State Department called the Office of the Coordinator for Counterterrorism (S/CT). The S/CT investigates the activities of possible terrorist organizations to identify those that might be designated as FTOs. For inclusion on this list, the S/CT selects either groups that have carried out actual terrorist activities or those that have engaged in planning possible future acts of terrorism or that have the capability and intent to carry out acts of terrorism.

When the S/CT decides to designate an organization as an FTO, it notifies the U.S. Congress, which has a week to review the decision and approve or reject it. The designated organization may seek a review of the designation from the U.S. Court of Appeals within thirty days. The FTOs may petition once every two years to have their names removed from the list, and if the organization does not petition, the S/CT will review the designation every five years.

Abu Nidal Organization (ANO; West Bank and Gaza Strip, Iraq, Sudan)

Al-Aqsa Martyrs Brigade (AAMS; West Bank and Gaza Strip)

Ansar al-Islam (AAI; Iraq)

Asbat al-Ansar (Lebanon)

Gama'a al-Islamiyya (Islamic Group; Egypt)

HAMAS (Islamic Resistance Movement; Gaza Strip and West Bank)

Hizballah (also spelled Hezbollah; Party of God; Lebanon)

Kahane Chai (Kach; Israel)

Kata'ib Hizballah (KH; Iraq)

Kongra-Gel (KGK, formerly Kurdistan Workers' Party, PKK, KADEK; Turkey)

Libyan Islamic Fighting Group (LIFG)

Moroccan Islamic Combatant Group (GICM)

Mujahedin-e Khalq Organization (MEK; Iran)

Palestine Liberation Front (PLF)

Palestinian Islamic Jihad (PIJ)

Popular Front for the Liberation of Palestine (PFLP)

PFLP-General Command (PFLP-GC)

al-Qaeda in Iraq (AQI)

al-Qaeda (AQ; Afghanistan, Sudan, Pakistan)

al-Qaeda in the Arabian Peninsula (AQAP; Yemen, Saudi Arabia)

al-Qaeda in the Islamic Maghreb (formerly GSPC; Algeria)

Army of Islam (AOI; the Gaza Strip)

"FOREIGN TERRORIST ORGANIZATIONS." *U.S. DEPARTMENT OF STATE.* (MAY 19, 2011). HTTP:// WWW.STATE. GOV/S/CT/RLS/OTHER/ DES/123085.HTM (ACCESSED ON NOVEMBER 30, 2011).

Islamic Jihad were executed for participating in Sadat's assassination. At that time, the police uncovered the entire Islamic Jihad membership list; nearly eight hundred members of Islamic Jihad were arrested, including a large portion of its leaders and central members, but by no means all of them. Al-Zawahiri, wanted by the law, fled Egypt. He soon began working with bin Laden in Pakistan, bringing with him his thorough knowledge of the workings of both the Muslim Brotherhood and Egyptian Islamic Jihad.

Throughout the 1990s, the Egyptian Islamic Jihad carried out a series of terrorist activities, including the 1995 bombing of the Egyptian embassy in Islamabad, Pakistan. By the end of the 1990s, the Egyptian Islamic Jihad worked mainly as an arm of al-Qaeda. In this capacity the group carried out the orders of al-Zawahiri and bin Laden and bombed U.S. embassies in Kenya and Tanzania, killing 258 people and injuring thousands. In 2011, Egyptian Islamic Jihad is generally considered to be part of al-Qaeda.

The Palestine Islamic Jihad

The Palestine Islamic Jihad (PIJ) was an offshoot of the Palestinian Muslim Brotherhood, which was a fairly moderate group. PIJ became radical in the late 1980s, when the PLO began to negotiate with Israel and renounced violence. This step angered many Palestinians who wanted to continue to fight the Israelis. Radicals began to organize for armed resistance against the Israeli occupation of the West Bank and the Gaza Strip. The Islamic Jihad, one of the militant groups in Palestine, arose in the Gaza Strip in the 1980s, but later in the decade the group moved to Lebanon. Its goal was the creation of an Islamic state throughout the lands of historic Palestine and the destruction of Israel. Its history of suicide bombings, shootings, and car bombs from the 1980s to present times have been directed at Israeli targets.

Despite conflicts between different branches of Islam, radical groups cooperated at times in their fight against Israel. The Palestine Islamic Jihad is Sunni Muslim in its origins (Sunnis are followers of the Sunni branch of Islam) but it was sponsored by the Islamic Republic of Iran (which has a Shiite majority) and by the militant Lebanese Shiite group, Hezbollah. (Shiites are followers of the Shia branch of Islam) At times the Palestine Islamic Jihad worked with the militant Palestinian group Hamas, which is also Sunni.

In the early years of the twenty-first century the Palestine Islamic Jihad again came to the world's attention for its frequent use of suicide bombers against Israeli targets. The Islamic Jihad is especially noted for its use of teenage boys and women as suicide bombers. Statements from the group indicate that it is unwilling to give up its terrorist activities until Israel is destroyed.

Hamas

The most powerful Palestinian Islamist group is Hamas (also known as the Islamic Resistance Movement), which was founded in 1987, emerging out of the Muslim Brotherhood. Over the years Hamas has built itself into an important political group with widespread public support, especially in the Gaza Strip. For much of its existence, its goal was to destroy Israel and create an Islamic state in a Palestinian nation that would emerge after Israel's destruction. Hamas became active during the First Intifada and continued its terrorist attacks during the Second Intifada (2000–2005). Hamas is most notorious for its attacks on Israeli settlements using rocket launchers, and, after the Second Intifada, for sending suicide bombers into public places in Israeli towns and cities, killing bystanders and creating great fear and confusion throughout the country.

Thousands of Hamas supporters attend a rally in Gaza City, Palestine, in 2006. Over the years Hamas has built itself into an important political group with widespread public support. MAHMUD HAMS/AFP/GETTY IMAGES.

Hamas's violent attacks on Israeli targets were only a small part of its operation. It also ran a huge nonmilitary wing that provided education, medical services, orphanages, and many other social services to thousands of poverty stricken Palestinian refugees, mainly in the Gaza Strip. The organization is viewed by most Palestinians as less corrupt than the Palestinian Authority (PA), the recognized governing institution for Palestinians in the West Bank and the Gaza Strip, established in 1993. Hamas became very popular among people in the West Bank and the Gaza Strip.

After Arafat's death in 2004, Hamas's role in the Palestinian government was greatly altered. In 2005, Palestinians elected Mahmoud Abbas (1935–), a moderate leader who had been closely connected to Arafat and took his place as the head of Fatah, to be president of the PA. Many observers hoped the turn to democracy, with free elections for the president and parliament of the Palestinian Authority in 2005 and 2006, would encourage Hamas to modify its methods and its anti-Israel position. In 2005 Israel withdrew its troops from the Gaza Strip and forced Jewish settlers to leave, giving the PA greater power there. In 2006 Hamas unexpectedly won the majority vote in elections for the PA legislative council. For a time, the organization participated in a coalition government with representatives of Fatah and President Abbas.

In 2007, however, persistent clashes between Hamas and Fatah erupted into a short, but violent civil war. Hamas took control of the Gaza Strip and Fatah, under Abbas, put together a new government in the West Bank. Hamas refused to recognize Israel as a legitimate nation or to denounce violence. Israel, in turn, refused to recognize the Gaza Strip's new government, led by Hamas. In September 2007 Israel declared Hamas a terrorist organization and the Gaza Strip hostile territory. Israel had long exercised control over the Gaza Strip's borders, but after 2007, it imposed a tight blockade, stopping the movement of people through its borders and preventing many supplies from entering or leaving the territory. The blockade greatly harmed the Gaza Strip's economy and caused great suffering among the people. The United States and many European countries supported the blockade, isolating Hamas while at the same time supporting Abbas's government. Hamas, which viewed Israel's blockade as a type of military occupation, continued launching rockets from the Gaza Strip into Israel. In December 2008 Israel launched a fierce twenty-two-day military campaign called

Operation Cast Lead against Hamas that killed more than thirteen hundred Gazans and caused billions of dollars worth of destruction. With few resources and little money, the Hamas government in the Gaza Strip struggled on, relying on the help of sympathetic countries, organizations, and individuals worldwide. (For more information on the Gaza War, see **The Palestinian Authority: 2004 to 2011**.)

In April 2011 Abbas met with Hamas leaders in Cairo, where Hamas reconciled with Fatah, at least temporarily ending the division in the PA government in order to stage new elections. Some Western governments were now uncertain about how to deal with Hamas. The organization they had designated as a terrorist group was, at least for the time being, also an elected political party representing the Palestinian people.

Hezbollah

In 1982, the PLO was headquartered in Lebanon, and PLO fighters were attacking Israel from the border regions in the southern part of the country. Israel retaliated by invading Lebanon in an offensive called Operation Peace for Galilee. This offensive forced the PLO, as well as many other Palestinians and Muslim Lebanese, out of southern Lebanon. The Israeli troops remained in southern Lebanon, where they made life difficult for the Shiites who lived there. The troops raided villages to remove those suspected of committing attacks on Israeli positions, restricted local Lebanese access to markets in the north by putting up blockades, and brought Israeli merchandise into Lebanon and sold it at such low prices that local merchants suffered. Soon many Shiites were ready to fight in an armed resistance against Israel. Between 1983 and 1985, several small, unorganized, militant Shiite groups formed in resistance to the occupying Israeli forces in Lebanon. These groups employed terrorist tactics in their fight.

The small, militant, Shiite groups of Lebanon were the first to adopt the practice of suicide bombing in the modern Middle East. One of the first incidents was the 1983 suicide bombing in which a truck containing several hundred pounds of explosives was driven into the U.S. embassy in Beirut, Lebanon, killing sixty-three people inside. The act was in protest of U.S. support for Israel's invasion of Lebanon the previous year. Also in 1983, in Beirut, a suicide bomber in a truck struck a building at the airport that housed U.S. Marines on a peacekeeping mission, killing 241 people. Simultaneously, a bomber blew up a building that housed French troops;

58 people died in the attack. Several days later, another suicide bomber drove his truck into an Israeli headquarters in southern Lebanon, killing 29 Israeli troops. The attacks succeeded in their purpose; the United States and France withdrew from Lebanon, and Israel pulled back its forces to a small region in southern Lebanon. The impact of these successful attacks was immense. Small groups with few resources had found a means by which they could combat the world's most powerful militaries. By 1985 the members of all the small, radical groups had united to form Hezbollah. Over the years, Hezbollah built up a large and powerful militia. It engaged in warfare with Israel in 2006.

Hezbollah, like Hamas, is modeled on the original Muslim Brotherhood organization. It provides much-needed aid to poor Shiite communities. It has built schools and health clinics, distributed fresh water, established garbage collection services, and instituted many other necessary programs that the Lebanese government lacks resources to provide. By 2000, its secretary-general, Hassan Nasrallah (1960–) had changed Hezbollah's overall objective from violent activism to political participation, and it became very popular among Lebanon's Shiites.

Hezbollah differed from other political parties, though, in that it had a well-trained militia that was stronger than the Lebanese national military and a huge arsenal of weapons. To the frustration of opponents in Lebanese politics, the organization was unwilling to give up the militia and reserved the right to fight Israel and defend itself. Gradually, Hezbollah members gained seats in Lebanon's parliament. In January 2011 Hezbollah had sufficient representatives in parliament to choose Lebanon's prime minister. Interactions within the parliament, however, were turbulent. (For more information on Hezbollah, see **The Rise of Hezbollah in Lebanon: 1990 to 2011**.)

Al-Qaeda

The terrorist group al-Qaeda, which is well-known for its attacks outside of the Middle East, did not originate from the same conflicts that produced the PLO, Hamas, and the Islamic Jihad. Bin Laden, the founder of al-Qaeda, came from a wealthy family in Saudi Arabia, where the royal family's adherence to Wahhabism (a conservative branch of Islam) makes Saudi Arabia one of the most conservative religious countries in the Middle East. Bin Laden, however, was deeply critical of his nation's close ties to some nations in the West, including the United States. He thought that

Muslim nations should obey the strictest forms of Islamic religious law, and he wanted to rid the Muslim nations of all traces of Western influence, which he considered to be corrupt.

Bin Laden became a mujahideen (a warrior, or a person who carries out jihad) during the Soviet invasion of Afghanistan (1979–89). In response to the Soviet invasion, many young Muslims around the world journeyed to Afghanistan to fight the non-Muslim invaders. The twenty-three-year-old bin Laden had money to help fund the jihad against the Soviets, and he created funding networks with other countries to aid in the fight. When the Soviets left Afghanistan in 1989, bin Laden decided to maintain the group of mujahideen. He initially moved to Sudan, where he established al-Qaeda headquarters. Al-Qaeda began to recruit mujahideen from countries with large Muslim populations, and it built secret bases on which to train these fighters.

In 1990 Iraq invaded Kuwait. (For more information see, **The Gulf Wars: 1991 to 2011**.) Saudi Arabia, which had requested help from the United States to stop the Iraqis, allowed American troops to be stationed on Saudi soil. Having Americans on Muslim land near the holy cities of Mecca and Medina outraged bin Laden and many others. In bin Laden's eyes, the United States had become the greatest enemy of Islam. In 1998 bin Laden publicly declared in a statement called "Jihad Against Jews and Crusaders" that it was the duty of every Muslim "to kill the Americans and their allies—civilians and military...in any country in which it is possible to do it." Israel, which had taken land away from Arab Muslims, was also a target.

Al-Qaeda became one of the deadliest terrorist organizations in history. It was run as a network of small cells, or groups of people, that existed in many countries. At least some of the cells did not communicate with one another. Cells were thought to exist for years at a time without acting and were therefore almost impossible for security forces to detect. Al-Qaeda was well funded, and its recruits were trained in special fields of terrorism.

From the beginning, al-Qaeda mainly attacked Americans. In the early 1990s, it bombed hotels housing American soldiers in Yemen. On June 25, 1996, al-Qaeda engineered a huge truck bomb that blasted the Khobar military complex in Dhahran, Saudi Arabia, killing nineteen U.S. soldiers and injuring hundreds. In 1998 bin Laden and al-Zawahiri put together a plan for bombing the U.S. embassies in Kenya and

Al-Qaeda leader Osama bin Laden. AP PHOTO.

Tanzania. They assigned the actual bombing to the Egyptian Islamic Jihad to carry out. On October 12, 2000, al-Qaeda operatives pulled a small boat alongside the USS *Cole*, a navy destroyer anchored in the port of Aden in Yemen, and detonated a bomb that ripped a large hole in the ship, killing seventeen and injuring thirty-nine. The group's most dramatic and deadly attack was the September 11, 2001, attacks on the United States.

The U.S. war on terror

September 11th prompted a U.S. "war on terror" that began almost immediately. On October 7, 2001, the United States sent troops to rid Afghanistan of bin Laden and the al-Qaeda training camps, as well as the Taliban government, which was providing shelter for them. Al-Qaeda was forced to flee Afghanistan, moving to the border regions of Pakistan.

In early 2003 the United States presented information (which later proved inaccurate) to the United Nations that Iraqi leader Saddam Hussein (1937–2006), in defiance of a ban that had existed since the 1990s, was producing weapons of mass destruction (any nuclear, chemical, or biological weapons capable of killing or injuring large numbers of people). Expanding its war on terror, on March 19, 2003, the United States and a small coalition of countries invaded Iraq, removed Hussein's government from power, and established a large number of U.S. and coalition troops in the region. (For more information on the Iraq War (2003–11), see **The Gulf Wars: 1991 to 2011.**)

The military operations were only one part of the U.S. war on terror. The United States also conducted many covert (secret) operations worldwide. It invested heavily in its intelligence organizations (government agencies responsible for gathering and interpreting information about enemies to the United States). These organizations began to work together and to coordinate with international intelligence organizations. They quickly began to identify and capture suspects of terrorism and to track, and often stop, terrorist financing networks worldwide. There were also anti-terrorism measures at home, such as the creation of the Office of Homeland Security; heightened security measures in airports and other threatened public places; and the 2001 enactment of the USA PATRIOT Act (or Uniting and Strengthening America by Providing Appropriate Tools Required to Intercept and Obstruct Terrorism), which granted a wide range of new powers to domestic law enforcement and intelligence agencies. These enhanced efforts to stop terrorism achieved some of their goals. There were no terrorist attacks on American soil in the decade after September 11th, and the terrorist groups lost many of their top leaders. However, the war on terrorism was not a total success. The wars in Afghanistan and Iraq caused bad relations between the United States and many Middle Easterners, and it took ten years and the combined efforts of the most powerful nations in the world to locate and kill Osama bin Laden in 2011.

Branches of al-Qaeda

Another negative aspect of the war on terrorism was that it caused al-Qaeda to scatter its forces to avoid capture. Within a few years, there were several branches of the organization, and all were deadly. When coalition forces attacked Iraq in the Iraq War, a new branch of al-Qaeda formed in Iraq to create a resistance movement. Its goals were to force the U.S.-led troops to withdraw from Iraq, eliminate the temporary Iraqi government, heighten conflicts between the Iraqi Shiites and Sunnis, and establish an Islamic nation in Iraq. Fighters came from around the Arab world to fight against the U.S.-led military occupation of Iraq. Al-Qaeda, which was a Sunni organization, also recruited and trained Iraqi Sunnis in the methods of insurgency against the Western occupation. The group caused tremendous chaos and catastrophic violence in the war torn country, hoping that from the utterly devastated nation would arise the new Islamic state they had envisioned. Many of the terrorist acts of this group targeted Iraqi Shiites, rather than Westerners, and eventually al-Qaeda in Iraq violence became too harsh even for Iraqis that had initially joined in the effort. Al-Qaeda in Iraq was greatly weakened by strong U.S. and Iraqi campaigns against it in 2008, and was nearly inactive for a few years, but by 2011 the group had become active once again.

Al-Qaeda in Iraq was only one of several al-Qaeda branches in the twenty-first century. Al-Qaeda in the Islamic Maghreb is a North African branch based in Algeria. The other major al-Qaeda group, al-Qaeda in the Arabian Peninsula, based in Yemen, was formed from two separate branches: al-Qaeda in Yemen and al-Qaeda in Saudi Arabia. In 2011 experts believed al-Qaeda in the Arabian Peninsula to be the most powerful of the branches. Yemen was undergoing social upheaval due to uprisings. Experts on security issues fear that without a strong government in Yemen to hold it in check, al-Qaeda in the Arabian Peninsula has grown more powerful and will present a threat to Westerners in the future.

The end of an era

In the early hours of May 2, 2011, nearly a decade after September 11th, bin Laden was killed by a U.S. Navy SEAL (Sea, Air, and Land) team in a large compound in Abbottabad, Pakistan. His death weakened al-Qaeda's image of being invulnerable to the powerful forces of the United States, but most observers did not believe it would hurt al-Qaeda's operations. Bin Laden's longtime deputy, al-Zawahri, who had been in the forefront of al-Qaeda for years, quickly took over as its leader, and al-Qaeda was still an established network with many powerful branches. Experts believed that its branches, al-Qaeda in Iraq, al-Qaeda in the Maghreb, and al-Qaeda in the Arabian Peninsula, were well placed to take over the bulk of the operations targeting Westerners and secular governments in the Middle East. This was made clear in August 2011, when a series of attacks throughout Iraq was carried out by suicide bombers, gunmen, and car bombers, killing eighty-nine people and injuring hundreds more. After the attacks, al-Qaeda in Iraq issued a warning that it would carry out one hundred attacks in revenge for the death of bin Laden.

In the last quarter of the twentieth century, Islamic extremism had grown into one of the most potent forces in the Middle East. During that era, there were few political movements for the general public in the Middle East to join. The governments of the Middle East were mainly authoritarian, meaning that power was consolidated under one strong leader, or a small group of elite leaders, and the people who lived there had little voice in their governments and could not freely oppose them. Militant groups like al-Qaeda arose during a time of frustration with the Western powers and Israel, and the frustration was also a product of the lack of political freedom in most Middle Eastern countries. By 2011, though, many analysts questioned whether al-Qaeda's network was still as much of a threat as it had been in the past. When the Middle East became swept up in the Arab Spring in 2011, the people of the Middle East called for democracy. Modernization, particularly the rise of communication through the Internet, allowed political expression in a way that was impossible only a decade earlier. There seemed to be little public interest in trying to recapture the glories of the seventh-century Islamic empire. Although few believed that terrorist groups like al-Qaeda would stop terrorizing, many political experts expressed a cautious hope that there would be fewer fires to ignite militant movements with the opening up of political expression in the Middle East.

For More Information

BOOKS

Anderson, Sean, and Stephen Sloan. *Historical Dictionary of Terrorism*. Lanham, MD: Scarecrow Press, 2002.

Burke, Jason. *Al-Qaeda: Casting a Shadow of Terror*. London: Tauris, 2003.

Cleveland, William L. *A History of the Modern Middle East.* 3rd ed. Boulder, CO: Westview Press, 2004.

Currie, Stephen. *Terrorists and Terrorist Groups.* San Diego, CA: Lucent Books, 2002.

Katz, Samuel M. *Jerusalem or Death: Palestinian Terrorism.* Minneapolis, MN: Lerner, 2004.

Randal, Jonathan. *Osama: The Making of a Terrorist.* New York: Knopf, 2004.

Rapoport, David C. "Terrorism." In *Encyclopedia of Violence, Peace, & Conflict.* Vol. 3. 2nd ed. Edited by Lester Kurtz. San Diego, CA: Academic Press, 2008, pp. 2087–2104.

Wright, Robin. *Dreams and Shadows: The Future of the Middle East.* New York: Penguin, 2008, pp. 3, 170.

PERIODICALS

Beinin, Joel. "Is Terrorism a Useful Term in Understanding the Middle East and the Palestinian-Israeli Conflict?" *Radical History Review* no. 85 (Winter 2003): 12–23). Available online at http://www.why-war.com/files/85.1beinin.pdf (accessed on November 30, 2011).

Ripley, Amanda. "Assisted Suicide? In Baghdad, Notorious Extremist Abu Nidal Meets a Violent, Mysterious End—One Worthy of His Life." *Time* (September 2, 2002): 35.

Whitaker, Brian. "The Definition of Terrorism." *Guardian* (May 7, 2001). http://www.guardian.co.uk/world/2001/may/07/terrorism (accessed on November 30, 2011).

WEB SITES

"Abu Nidal Organization." *Council of Foreign Relations.* http://www.cfrterrorism.org/groups/abunidal.html (accessed on November 30, 2011).

"Al-Qaeda (a.k.a. al-Qaida, al-Qa'ida)." *Council on Foreign Relations* (June 17, 2011). http://www.cfr.org/terrorist-organizations/al-qaeda-k-al-qaida-al-qaida/p9126 (accessed on November 30, 2011).

Burke, Jason. "The Making of Osama bin Laden." *Salon.* http://dir.salon.com/news/feature/2001/11/01/osama_profile/index.html (accessed on November 30, 2011).

"Foreign Terrorist Organizations." *U.S. Department of State.* (May 19, 2011). http://www.state.gov/s/ct/rls/other/des/123085.htm (accessed on November 30, 2011).

"Hunting Bin Laden." *PBS Frontline..* http://www.pbs.org/wgbh/pages/frontline/shows/binladen/ (accessed on November 30, 2011).

"The 9/11 Commission Report." *National Commission on Terrorist Attacks Upon the United States.* http://www.9-11commission.gov/report/911Report_Exec.htm (accessed on November 30, 2011).

Bin Ladin, Osama. "Jihad Against Jews and Crusaders." (February 23, 1998). *Federation of American Scientists (FAS)* . http://www.fas.org/irp/world/para/docs/980223-fatwa.htm (accessed on November 30, 2011).

14

Conflicts Within: Repressive Governments of the Middle East in the Early Twenty-First Century

Beginning in the 1970s, the countries of the world shifted heavily toward democracy, a form of government in which the citizens have the power to govern themselves, usually through elected representatives and majority votes. Prior to 1974, only 40 of the world's 196 nations were democracies, but by the early years of the twenty-first century, more than 115 countries had some type of democratic government. In the Middle East and North Africa, however, all nations except Israel, Turkey, and Lebanon were ruled by some form of authoritarian government (a government in which power is concentrated in the hands of one strong ruler or a small group of elite leaders, who do not answer to the will of the people). Even in the three Middle Eastern countries that had some democratic institutions, to most Westerners their governments frequently seemed undemocratic.

Many of the authoritarian rulers of the Middle East in the early twenty-first century were well-known, partly because they had been in power for so long. Hosni Mubarak (1928–) was president of Egypt for thirty years, from 1981 to 2011. Saddam Hussein (1937–2006) was president of Iraq from 1979 to 2003. Hafez Assad (also spelled al-Assad; 1930–2000) ruled Syria from 1971 until his death in 2000, and then his son Bashar Assad (also spelled al-Assad; 1965–) took power. Zine el-Abdine Ben Ali (1936–) was the president of Tunisia from 1987 to 2011. Several monarchies of the Middle East maintained power over their countries within a single family for generations. The Hashemite family, for example, has ruled Jordan since King Abdullah I (Abdullah I bin al-Hussein; 1882–1951) established the monarchy in 1921. Although King Abdullah Bin-Abd-al-Aziz Al Saud (1924–) has only been the monarch of Saudi Arabia since 2005, the Saud family has ruled there

WORDS TO KNOW

Alawis: Also spelled Alawites; followers of a sect of Shia Islam that live in Syria. Their belief system and practices vary from Shiites in several ways, particularly in the belief that Ali, the son-in-law of the prophet Muhammad, was the human form of Allah (the Arabic word for God).

Arab League: A regional political alliance of Arab nations formed in 1945 to promote political, military, and economic cooperation within the Arab world.

Arab Spring: A series of prodemocracy uprisings in the Middle East and North Africa.

authoritarianism: A type of leadership in which power is consolidated under one strong leader, or a small group of elite leaders, who do not answer to the will of the people.

ayatollah: A high-ranking Shiite religious leader.

Ba'ath Party: A secular (nonreligious) political party founded in the 1940s with the goal of uniting the Arab world and creating one powerful Arab state.

cleric: An ordained religious official.

Islamism: A fundamentalist movement characterized by the belief that Islam should provide the basis for the political, social, and cultural life in Muslim nations.

Muslim Brotherhood: An Islamic fundamentalist group organized in opposition to Western influence and in support of Islamic principles.

Pan-Arabism: A movement for the unification of Arab peoples and the political alliance of Arab states.

sharia: A system of Islamic law based on the Koran and other sacred writings. Sharia attempts to create the perfect social order, based on God's will and justice, and covers a wide range of human activities, including acts of religious worship, the law of contracts and obligations, personal status law, and public law.

Shiites: Followers of the Shia branch of Islam. Shiites believe that only direct descendants of the prophet Muhammad are qualified to lead the Islamic faith.

socialism: A system in which the government owns the means of production and controls the distribution of goods and services.

Sunnis: Followers of the Sunni branch of Islam. Sunnis believe that elected officials, regardless of their heritage, are qualified to lead the Islamic faith.

---

since 1932. Morocco and the Arab states of the Persian Gulf also have long-term ruling families. The longest rule by an individual leader, however, was that of Mu'ammar al-Qaddafi (also spelled Moammar al-Gaddafi; 1942–2011), who ruled Libya for more than four decades, from 1969 until 2011.

In the early twenty-first century, authoritarian rulers throughout the region were holding onto power by stifling opposition, reform, and innovation. The persistent view of the Middle East by observers worldwide was that the region was failing to advance. Gideon Rose, a contributor to *The New Arab Revolt*, notes in the book's introduction, "As most of the world transformed...one area remained frozen in time: the Arab Middle East." Historians and Middle East scholars theorized that the cultures of the Middle East were not receptive to democracy. But in the first years of the twenty-first century, studies and polls repeatedly showed that the vast majority of people of the Middle East and North Africa, whether Muslim, Christian, Jewish, Arab, or non-Arab, wanted some form of democratic government for their country. Thus, tensions between citizens and their authoritarian rulers smoldered. Protests erupted frequently, and even though governments tried to suppress them, they continued to occur. When the Arab Spring, a series of prodemocracy uprisings, swept the Middle East and North Africa in 2011, the people of the Middle East expressed their desire for democracy and political freedom in hundreds of protest movements, many of which involved great personal risk to the protestors. Several of these uprisings succeeded in removing authoritarian leaders from power. (For more information, see **The Arab Spring: 2011**.)

Authoritarian government in the Middle East

An authoritarian government usually consists of a strong central power, either a sole ruler or a small group of elite leaders, within a nation. This central power may consult with elected councils or judges, but it holds the ultimate authority and is not obligated to follow the findings of its councils or court systems. In the Middle East in the last quarter of the twentieth century, there were varying forms of authoritarian government and varying degrees of authoritarianism. There were dictatorships (led by rulers with unrestricted powers), monarchies (ruled by a king or queen) that either lacked written constitutions (the set of basic principles by which a nation is governed) or had constitutions that failed to ensure citizens a voice in the government. Some countries looked like democracies. They had presidents with elected parliaments and a written constitution, but still failed to give their people a voice in the government. The revolutionary government of the Islamic Republic of Iran was unique, with a blend of elected and unelected, and religious and secular (nonreligious), leaders. Even so, the Iranian government adopted authoritarian methods after its formation in 1979.

Although authoritarian rulers may at times bring prosperity or stability to a nation, they can also cause great harm. Because authoritarian leaders are not in power by the choice of the country's citizens, they often have to exert a great deal of effort to keep themselves in power. They usually do not allow open opposition to their government and use special security forces to suppress people who oppose them. Thus, individual freedoms, such as freedom of speech, the freedom to assemble, and freedom of the press, are limited. Often authoritarian governments successfully hide their operations from the public. Many have been found to be corrupt, with people in the top levels of government taking money that rightfully belongs to the citizens. Most authoritarian rulers place a small number of loyal individuals, such as family members, friends, and military officials, in the country's top government positions, creating a privileged power elite that they trust to help them maintain their power.

Most modern governments strive for "rule of law," a concept that dates back to ancient times. In its simplest form, rule of law calls for a written form of law to which everyone in a nation, including the kings and presidents, must adhere. This prevents those who are in power from ruling on an arbitrary basis, according to their own individual judgment or whim. Often these written laws include checks and balances, systems in which separate branches of the government have the power to amend or veto acts of other branches in order to prevent any one branch from exerting too much power. In the United States, for example, there are three branches of government: the executive (the presidency), the judicial (the courts), and the legislative (Congress). Although many Middle Eastern nations of the late twentieth century did have written constitutions, most did not achieve rule of law or a successful system of checks and balances. In some cases the constitutions did not provide sufficient checks on the central power's authority, and in other cases the constitutions were not followed by leaders at all.

In the very early twenty-first century, Egypt, Syria, and Tunisia were examples of secular single-party authoritarian regimes with some outward appearance of democracy. These nations, though different, had some noteworthy similarities. They all mounted a fight against Islamism (a fundamentalist movement characterized by the belief that Islam should provide the basis for the political, social, and cultural life in Muslim nations); they declared extremely prolonged states of emergency, under which citizens' constitutional rights were suspended; and they had powerful security forces that suppressed opponents.

Egypt From 1954 until 2011, Egypt had only three presidents: Gamal Abdul Nasser (1918–1970) from 1956 to 1970, Anwar Sadat (also spelled al-Sadat; 1918–1981) from 1970 to 1981, and Mubarak from 1981 to 2011. Nasser was part of a military group called the Free Officers Movement that overthrew Egypt's constitutional monarchy (a form of government in which a monarch rules under the authority of a constitution) in 1952 and established a government ruled mainly by the military. This revolutionary government created a socialist nation (one in which the major means of production and distribution are owned, managed, and controlled by the government) that was ruled by a one-party system, meaning that no opposition or other political parties were legal. By 1954 Nasser had taken power, with the military completely in his charge to support him. He set the tone of authoritarianism for many years to come, maintaining tight control over the parliament (legislature), the court system, the economy, and Egypt's media systems.

Shortly after succeeding Nasser in 1970, Sadat put together a team of legal, political, and religious experts to create a new constitution. Sadat strove to move away from Nasser's brand of socialism and authoritarianism, but he did little to limit the power of the presidency. The constitution of 1971 called for democratic reforms, but it also kept the president firmly at the center of power, able to undo any of the reforms at will.

Egypt's 1971 constitution called for the formation of the People's Assembly, the lower house of parliament. All but ten of the deputies of the People's Assembly were elected by the Egyptian people, and the constitution gave the People's Assembly the authority to nominate the country's president and to enact laws. Although this seemed to be a step in the direction of democracy, the People's Assembly never acted independently of the president's regime. This was partly because the president had the power to veto any legislation passed by parliament and to dismiss the entire parliament at will. It was also because with only one political party, the majority of parliament was loyal to the president. The people who ran for office were his handpicked associates. Those who got into office were generally well rewarded with access to power and resources. Elections rarely offered any real choices and, not surprisingly, voter turnout in Egypt was usually very low.

Under the 1971 constitution, the president was authorized to declare states of emergency, during which the president could suspend normal governmental operations and rule by decree (an order that has the force of law). Egypt was already in a state of emergency when the constitution was written, and it remained so almost continuously from 1967 to 2011. During the thirty-year rule of Mubarak, there was never a break in the state of emergency. In a state of emergency the people's constitutional rights are suspended; the central government can prohibit demonstrations and censor speech, communications, and the press; and it can arrest people for political reasons and hold them in prison for long periods of time without charging them with a crime.

Mubarak repeatedly justified Egypt's decades-old state of emergency rule as a necessary measure due to the government's constant fight against extremists and terrorists. He referred mainly to Egypt's large Islamist movement, which has generated some extreme factions that practice terrorist methods. In the 1990s and into the twenty-first century, the Egyptian security force, the powerful State Security Intelligence (SSI), went after the extremist groups in full force. In its zeal to stomp out terrorism, the SSI was accused of arresting thousands of political opponents who were not terrorists. Many were imprisoned for years without charges or a trial. The SSI was also accused of torturing prisoners and of "disappearing" people (taking them into custody, after which they were never seen again). Perhaps the best-organized opposition group was the Muslim Brotherhood, an Islamic fundamentalist group founded in 1928 in opposition to Western influence and in support of Islamic principles that was very popular and active in the last decades of the twentieth century. The group, which had renounced violence decades earlier, had begun to serve as a political opposition group to the central government and may have been deemed a threat by the Mubarak regime. The Muslim Brotherhood acted with great caution, and it had so many supporters that it endured despite the government's repression of the group.

The Egyptian court system was another area of contention. Since Nasser's rule, the judges of Egypt's courts have struggled to gain independence from the executive (presidential) branch of government and to assert their role in overseeing elections. In 1969 the General Assembly of the Egyptian Judges Club called for an independent judiciary. Nasser retaliated against them with a series of harsh measures, and more than one hundred judges were fired. Thereafter, the leaders in the judiciary tended to be those who went along with the central government's policies. Judges who could be persuaded to do the president's bidding were granted better salaries and other benefits. Under the constitution, judges were responsible for overseeing elections, although it was not clear in what way they should supervise. The role that was allotted to them by the Egyptian

Hosni Mubarak repeatedly justified Egypt's decades-old state of emergency rule as a necessary measure to combat extremists and terrorists.
© VARIO IMAGES GMBH & CO.KG/ALAMY.

government was too limited to make a true difference in electoral processes. Thus, through 2005, the courts were unable to act as a check against excessive executive power.

Mubarak was elected president five times, to six-year terms. All presidential elections until 2005 were uncontested, meaning that there was only one candidate. In 2005 Egypt changed its constitution to allow multiparty elections but then restricted the political parties that could run to those that were already in existence, which meant that no real rivals to Mubarak were eligible to run. Mubarak was, by then, in his late seventies, and he had never named a successor, although many thought his son, Gamal (1963–), was being groomed to take over. With no true reforms or changes in view, the Egyptian people were beginning—quietly at first—to revolt. These revolts would soon evolve into revolution in the Arab Spring uprisings of 2011, which led to the ousting of Mubarak. (For more information, see **The Arab Spring: 2011**.)

Syria Although Syria calls itself a parliamentary republic, it is considered by political authorities worldwide to be an authoritarian government. It has long been ruled by a president, a small elite circle of his associates, and the Arab Socialist Ba'ath Party, which took control of Syria in 1963 in a military coup (overthrow of the government). The Ba'ath Party is a secular (nonreligious) political party founded in the 1940s with the goal of uniting the Arab world and creating one powerful Arab state. After the 1963 coup, the party's top positions were assumed by officers in the military, most of whom were Alawis (also spelled Alawites), followers of a sect of Shia Islam who live mainly along the Turkish border of Syria and whose belief system and practices vary from Shiites in several ways. Alawis are a minority in Syria, at about 12 percent of its population; the majority of the population is Sunni (followers of the Sunni branch of Islam). The Syrian constitution, adopted in 1973, mandates that the Ba'ath Party is to lead society and the nation. A majority of seats in Syria's 250-member parliament are reserved for a group of politicians headed by the Ba'ath Party.

One of the Alawi military officers of the Ba'ath Party was Hafez Assad. He staged a coup in 1970 and assumed the presidency in early 1971. Assad immediately bolstered his own authority, greatly limiting the ability of any opposition parties to form in Syria. He was respected by some for bringing stability to Syria, which had a history of coups and revolts. But he was also greatly feared for his harsh, and at times brutal, repression of all opposition. In 1982 he ordered a crackdown on a Syrian branch of the Muslim Brotherhood in the city of Hama. An estimated ten thousand or more people, many of whom were innocent civilians, were killed in the raid, and this was only one of several against the Muslim Brotherhood. Other opponents were imprisoned for long periods of time without trials. Assad was repeatedly reelected president by a yes-or-no vote until he died in 2000.

The Ba'ath party then nominated Assad's son, Bashar Assad, to the presidency. At first, it seemed that the new president was liberalizing the government when, upon taking office, he released hundreds of political prisoners. But expected reforms never took place, and according to international observers, Syrians had little political freedom in the early twenty-first century. The media in Syria was tightly controlled and communications were restricted, including use of the Internet.

Along with Bashar Assad, many other members of the Assad family held powerful positions in the Syrian government. His brother Maher Assad (1967–), who is next in power, is the head of Syria's elite security force and has a reputation for ruthlessness. In a U.S. State Department report titled *2010 Human Rights Report: Syria* Syria's security forces are described in harsh terms:

> The government systematically repressed citizens' ability to change their government. The security forces committed arbitrary or unlawful killings, caused politically motivated disappearances, and tortured and

Syrian president Bashar Assad in his office high above Damascus. © ED KASHI/CORBIS.

physically abused prisoners and detainees with impunity. Security forces arrested and detained individuals under poor conditions without due process. Lengthy pretrial and incommunicado [without means of communication] detention remained a serious problem. The judiciary [court system] was not independent. There were political prisoners and detainees, and during the year the government sentenced to prison several high-profile members of the human rights and civil society communities.

During the first decade of Bashar Assad's presidency, many political observers worldwide commented on Syria's stability, its rising middle class, its freedom from conflict among religious sects, and its modernization. Although it was well known that the government violated international standards regarding human rights, many authorities believed that Assad's regime was well-supported by Syrians. A pro-democracy movement began in 2005 in Syria, but it was repressed by the government and many of its members were imprisoned. Syria was initially quiet when the Arab Spring revolts of 2011 began in Tunisia and Egypt, but gradually a determined opposition movement rose up to nonviolently protest Assad's authoritarian government. When Assad's forces launched into a brutal crackdown, the opposition grew stronger and more determined than ever to oust their leader. (For more information, see **The Arab Spring: 2011**.)

Tunisia The North African nation of Tunisia gained independence from France in 1956 and adopted its constitution in 1959. Habib Bourguiba (1903–2000) served as president from 1956 to 1987. Under different names, the Democratic Constitutional Rally (RCD) was the sole legal political party for decades. Bourguiba was a charismatic leader who worked to modernize Tunisia, updating its tourism, industry, and oil production, and bringing prosperity to the country. He also solidified his own powers, operating as a dictator (absolute ruler) despite a constitution that should have prevented it. Bourguiba ran unopposed for election and in 1974 was named "president for life." He appointed his cabinet and prime minister. He did not allow any dissent and was particularly intolerant of Islamism.

During economic crises in the 1980s, Tunisia's prime minister, Zine el-Abdine Ben Ali, forced Bourguiba out of office on grounds of medical disability. Ben Ali seemed to be moving toward reform, and in terms of economics and living conditions, Tunisia rated fairly high. People had more money, women had more rights, and education advanced greatly. Still, people had no say in their government. Elections were uncontested and the Tunisian government allowed no opposition. Tunisia's security forces were ruthless against opposition and virtually eradicated the Islamist groups in the country. Like Syria, Tunisia was viewed worldwide as one of the more successful and modern governments in the Middle East, even though its human rights issues were apparent. The people of Tunisia, particularly the hard hit Islamists, grew increasingly resentful of Tunisia's harsh oppression of opposition and its lack of democracy. They became the first to revolt in the Arab Spring uprisings of 2011. (For more information, see **The Arab Spring: 2011**.)

Authoritarianism and oil

Many of the countries of the Middle East lie upon vast oil fields that bring in equally vast sums of money. Some of these countries get from 70 to 90 percent of their export income from oil and gas. These countries are called "rentier" states, because their governments receive economic rents, or oil revenue, from other countries. Some rentier countries are Saudi Arabia, Iran, Qatar, Kuwait, Bahrain, the United Arab Emirates, Algeria, and Libya. The governments of rentier countries take in oil income and use it to fund the country's government, infrastructure, and public institutions, and sometimes distribute portions of the oil money in direct payments to the people. When oil production is good and prices are high, this can make the entire population of a small nation quite wealthy. In countries with high oil revenue, the people do not have to pay any taxes. All of this would seem very positive, but for a number of reasons, most rentier countries lack democracy.

There are many theories about why rentier countries lack political freedom. One is that, since they do not collect taxes, the governments do not feel accountable to the people. If a country does not need the people's money to fund itself, the theory goes, then it does not need their consent for any actions it wants to take. Another theory is that in rentier states most of the country's people are involved in the oil business, which means a large percentage of the population works for the government and it is not in their interest to rebel. Some rentier states are so focused on oil that they do not have other types of business and investment, and therefore lack the kind of modernization and innovations made by business developers and investors. Also, a wealthy country can support a powerful security force and is therefore able to suppress opposition. Rulers who are reluctant to lose their position because of the enormous available wealth are likely to fight democratic transfers of power. In a January 2010 article for the *Journal of Democracy*, Larry Diamond observes that, for many of these countries, oil "distorts the state, the market, the class structure, and the entire incentive [motivation] structure," and notes that "not a single one of the 23 countries that derive most of their export earnings from oil and gas is a democracy today."

Saudi Arabia Saudi Arabia is a prime example of a rentier country. Although it is the world's largest oil exporter, Saudi Arabia is rated in *Economist* magazine's 2010 Democracy Index as the seventh most authoritarian regime from among the 167 countries rated.

Saudi Arabia is an Islamic absolute monarchy. All of its kings to date have been sons of Abd al-Aziz ibn Abd al-Rahman (1876–1953), more commonly known as Ibn Saud, who founded the modern nation of Saudi Arabia in 1932. Polygamy (marrying more than one spouse) is legal in

Saudi Arabia. With his many wives, Ibn Saud fathered forty sons and thus had many heirs. The powerful Saudi king works in association with the ulema, a body of religious leaders and legal experts from Wahhabism, the traditional form of Islam practiced by most Saudis. The Saudi king does not answer to any other government bodies, but it is necessary for him to consult and maintain the peace within the royal family, and there were thousands of members of the royal family in the early twenty-first century.

Saudi Arabia does not have a constitution, but in 1992 King Fahd (1921–2005) compiled a code called the Basic Law. The Basic Law confirms that Saudi Arabia's constitution is the Koran (also spelled Qur'an or Quran; the holy book of Islam) and other texts that teach about the life of the prophet Muhammad (c. 570–632). The Basic Law also proclaims that sharia (Islamic religious law) is the law of the land. The Basic Law also sets forth some governing procedures, and it prohibits

An oil refinery in Saudi Arabia. As the world's largest oil exporter, Saudi Arabia is a prime example of a rentier state, or a nation that receives economic rents, in the form of oil revenue, from other countries. © ART DIRECTORS & TRIP/ALAMY.

the government from certain abuses of the public. It does not, however, protect the freedoms of belief, expression, assembly, or political participation.

Libya under Al-Qaddafi

Oil brought great wealth to the small, and once very poor, North African nation of Libya, and it also brought great power to Mu'ammar al-Qaddafi, who ruled Libya for more than four decades. In 1969 he was part of a small military group that overthrew Libya's king. Although he promised that Libya would never be under the power of any individual leader, and he went only by titles such as "brother leader of the revolution," al-Qaddafi quickly became the de facto head of state (the ruler in fact, but not necessarily by right or law).

Al-Qaddafi's early efforts in governing Libya were generally well received by the Libyan people. He focused on the popular Pan-Arabism movement (a movement for the unification of Arab peoples and the political alliance of Arab states), for example, which raised cultural pride among his people. At the same time, al-Qaddafi renegotiated Libya's oil contracts with foreign countries, gaining for Libya a majority share of the revenues from its own oil production—an unusual accomplishment in the Middle East at that time. Western corporations had been instrumental in developing the oil fields and had taken the majority of the oil profits in most Middle Eastern countries up to that time. With oil prices high throughout the 1970s, the nation flourished. Al-Qaddafi used funds coming in from oil revenue to provide free health care, education, and low-cost housing to the people of Libya. He also supported women's rights.

In the mid–1970s al-Qaddafi turned his attention to writing his political philosophy, which he called the Third Universal Theory, in *The Green Book* (1976–78). The book, which addresses many different topics, calls for a form of socialism in which people rule themselves and control their economy through people's committees, all under the guiding principles of sharia. Al-Qaddafi applied *The Green Book* principles in restructuring his country and in 1977 Libya officially became the Socialist People's Libyan Arab Jamahiriya (*jamahiriya* means "rule of the masses" in Arabic). He relentlessly promoted his book to the people of Libya. According to Middle East scholar Dirk Vandewalle in an interview on National Public Radio (NPR), "Usually, when television came on in the afternoon in Libya, it would open up with a citation from *The Green*

Libyan leader Mu'ammar al-Qaddafi reading The Green Book *in 2007. Al-Qaddafi describes his political philosophy in the book, written in the mid–1970s.* © LOUAFI LARBI/REUTERS/CORBIS.

Book. So in a sense, it was everywhere. It was on public television. It was on the radio. It was in the schools. Children had to read it. You simply could not avoid it." Following the principles of the book, people were expected to join one of the hundreds of Basic People's Congresses, which were local deliberative bodies that met every few months.

It was not long before Libyans realized that their local congresses had no power, and that al-Qadaffi's regime was all-powerful. Other frustrations followed. In the 1980s oil prices fell. Libya did not have other industries to fall back on, and its economy deteriorated. Meanwhile, al-Qaddafi had become involved in international terrorism. Using Libyan oil money, he supported a number of anti-Western militant groups. In 1986 he was accused of being behind the bombing of a nightclub in Berlin, Germany, that was a regular hangout for U.S. troops. The United States retaliated by bombing Libya in an attempt to kill al-Qaddafi, who U.S. president Ronald Reagan (1911–2004) called the "mad dog of the Middle East." Two years later, Pan Am Flight 103 from London to New

York exploded in the sky over Lockerbie, Scotland, due to a terrorist's bomb, killing 243 passengers as well as the 16 crew members. Libya, and al-Qaddafi in particular, were suspected of being involved in the bombing.

After the Lockerbie incident, the international community condemned al-Qaddafi and stopped trading with Libya. The country suffered, and there was at least one attempt to overthrow al-Qaddafi. He responded with harsh measures against any opposition. Al-Qaddafi's powerful security forces were accused of using torture, long imprisonments, disappearances, and executions to silence opponents. His forces were especially hard on Islamist groups, which sought to change the government. When the Libyan military seemed to be turning against him in 1993, al-Qaddafi eliminated many of its top officers and installed his allies in their positions.

Around 1998, al-Qaddafi began to focus on uniting African nations. He used billions of dollars of Libyan oil money to invest heavily in sub-Saharan Africa, where he acquired a large following of devoted fans. After the September 11, 2001, terrorist attacks on the United States in which nearly three thousand people were killed, the eccentric al-Qaddafi turned abruptly away from his long hatred of Westerners to join the United States in its fight against terrorism. His reasons for making such odd changes in policy were not always apparent.

Over the four decades of his rule, al-Qaddafi kept a tight grip on the Libyan people. Despite his political theorizing, his regime gravely violated the human rights of his opponents and restricted freedom of speech, assembly, and the press. In an article for the *BBC News* Web site, correspondent Martin Asser writes, "The result of [al-Qaddafi's] theory, underlined with absolute intolerance of dissent or alternative voices, was the hollowing out of Libyan society, with all vestiges [traces] of constitutionality, civil society and authentic political participation eradicated."

Many Libyans lived in fear of their leader for years. In 2011, however, inspired by the Arab Spring uprising in other nation, they rose up in force, calling for al-Qaddafi to step down. Al-Qaddafi responded with a deadly crackdown on the protesters, and a violent, civil war ensued that ended with al-Qaddafi's capture and death at the hands of rebel forces. (For more information, see **The Arab Spring: 2011.**)

Iran's Islamist republic

Iran was distinct among Middle East nations in the last quarter of the twentieth century for having undergone a revolution in 1979 in which it eliminated its authoritarian government and replaced it with a new form of constitutional government. The new government, however, developed into an authoritarian regime, as well.

Iran had been ruled since 1925 by the Pahlavi family, a monarchy ruled first by Reza Shah Pahlavi (1878–1944), a military officer who crowned himself shah after taking power. After 1941, his son, Mohammad Reza Pahlavi (1919–1980), ruled Iran. With growing oil income, Iran experienced prosperity and developed a new middle class throughout the 1950s and 1960s. Pahlavi modernized the country's industry and cultural institutions. Over the years Pahlavi became increasingly pro-Western and was closely allied with the United States. He won a great deal of support from the West, but at home he restricted political freedom and allowed no opposition. By the 1970s he had angered large segments of Iran's population. The country's conservative Islamic clerics (ordained religious officials) and their many followers disliked the Western-influenced lifestyle of Pahlavi and his elite circle of followers. The country's poor, who were barely able to eke out a living, resented the lavish wealth of the elite. Advocates of democracy condemned Pahlavi's harsh repression of those who disagreed with him. By 1978 people of many different political groups and social backgrounds furiously demanded Pahlavi's removal from office.

In 1979 Pahlavi's regime collapsed, and he fled the country. The foremost leader of Pahlavi's opposition was Ayatollah Ruhollah Khomeini (1902–1989), a respected Shiite religious scholar, who immediately returned to Iran. (An ayatollah is a high-ranking Shiite religious leader.) Pahlavi had expelled Khomeini from Iran for his outspoken criticism of the regime, and for fifteen years Khomeini continued to speak out against Pahlavi from Iraq and later from Paris, France. Upon his return Khomeini took the lead in the revolutionary movement, although at the time the revolutionaries were made up of a wide variety of interests, both secular and Islamist, liberal and conservative. Because there was little agreement on what kind of government should replace Pahlavi's regime, the task of writing a constitution greatly divided the revolutionary movement. According to prominent Iranian political philosopher Abdolkarim Soroush (1945–), as quoted by Robin Wright in *Dreams and Shadows:*

The Future of the Middle East, "Our revolution was a haphazard, chaotic, and theory-less revolution, in the sense that it wasn't well thought out—not by the leader, not by the people." After many disagreements and rejected drafts of constitutions, Khomeini urged a group of clerics, called the Assembly of Experts, to do the writing. Not surprisingly, the clerics based the new constitution on Islamic principles, but they mixed these principles with a unique form of democracy.

The constitution called for a complex government for the new republic that was to be both democratic and Islamist. The government is made up of two sides, an unelected side and an elected side. At the top of the hierarchy on the unelected side is the Supreme Leader, who oversees all branches of the government and appoints the head of the judiciary, six of the twelve members of the Guardian Council, the commanders of all the armed forces, and the country's broadcasting systems. The Supreme Leader's position is permanent, unless revoked for a failure to do his duties.

Under the Supreme Leader on the unelected side is the Guardian Council, a powerful branch of the government that consists of six clerics appointed by the Supreme Leader and six lawyers who are nominated by the courts and approved by parliament. The Guardian Council's function is to approve or veto all bills passed by parliament, and it has the power to bar candidates from running in parliamentary, presidential, and Assembly of Experts elections. Because it has always been a conservative Islamist branch, the Guardian Council usually bars people from running in elections when it feels they do not hold the same Islamist principles as the council.

On the elected side of the government is the president. The supreme leader, however, has the authority to veto the president's acts. Although the president is elected by the people, the Guardian Council screens all potential candidates and eliminates those who do not seem to uphold the principles of the Islamic revolution.

The constitution also called for an Assembly of Experts, which is comprised of 86 Islamic scholars who are elected by the people and responsible for appointing the Supreme Leader and overseeing his performance. The assembly can remove the Supreme Leader if he is failing to carry out his duties. The assembly is open only to clerics, and any cleric who wishes to run for this office must first pass the screening of the Guardian Council.

Iranian President Mahmoud Ahmadinejad holds up his identification papers as he registers as a candidate for the 2009 presidential elections. Iran's Guardian Council screens all potential candidates and eliminates those who do not seem to uphold the principles of the Islamic revolution. AP PHOTO/VAHID SALEMI.

The framers of the Iranian constitution initially aimed for a system of checks and balances that would prevent the new government from becoming authoritarian, while at the same time giving greater weight to the religious leader than to the political leader. Although the Supreme Leader had almost unlimited authority, his actions were to be kept in check by the Assembly of Experts. At first, the position of president was to be filled only by nonclerics. But in the first years after the revolution, there was a major, violent clash between the clerics and elected government officials, and Khomeini decided that clerics could run for the presidency. In 1981 Ali Khamenei (also spelled Khāmen'i; 1939–), a conservative religious scholar and associate of Ayatollah Khomeini, was elected president. With both sides of the government overseen by conservative clerics, the checks and balances established by the constitution stopped functioning.

In 1997 Iranian voters surprised everyone by overwhelmingly electing a reform-minded cleric, Mohammad Khatami (1943–), as president. But Khatami's efforts to open Iran to political freedom were stifled by the other branches of the government. Publications were shut down, journalists were arrested, student demonstrations were stopped, and many students were arrested. Some of Khatami's reformist associates in the government were arrested and imprisoned as well.

In the years since, elections in Iran have not presented the voters with much choice. The Guardian Council has prevented thousands of candidates from running in elections, allowing only a few handpicked loyalists to run. By the 1990s many Iranians felt that with the 1979 revolution they had exchanged one authoritarian government for another. Some also criticize the government's conservative view of Islam. Many of the conservative clerics in the government do not see democratic principles as being in accordance with Islamist principles, but there are many religious and political scholars in Iran and throughout the world who argue that an Islamist government can also be a democracy. According to political analysts, most Iranians hope that reform to the existing constitution of Iran can still accomplish what many had hoped for, a democratic Islamist republic.

Lack of foreign intervention

There are many reasons why other nations did not intervene when they perceived human rights abuses under authoritarian governments in the Middle East. The Arab-Israeli conflict (the ongoing fighting between Arabs and Israel over the land that is the present-day nation of Israel and the territories of the West Bank and the Gaza Strip) has often served to distract people in the Middle East from the abuses of their own governments. Authoritarian rulers, facing upheaval, can often redirect the public wrath toward Israel. (Israel is a Jewish nation and most of the Arab nations in the Middle East side with the Arab Palestinians in the ongoing conflict.) Sometimes authoritarian rulers even use the Arab-Israeli conflict to get aid and allies from the West. The United States, which has a long history of strong relations with Israel, in particular has often supported governments that are willing to have peaceful relations with Israel.

The Arab League, a regional political alliance of Arab nations formed in 1945 to promote political, military, and economic cooperation within

Democracy Index 2010

In 2006 *Economist* magazine's Intelligence Unit compiled its first Democracy Index, which measures the level of democracy in 167 of the world's nations. The index is based on a concept of degrees of democracy, from a full democracy, to a flawed democracy, to a hybrid democratic/authoritarian government, to a full authoritarian government. The ranking is from 1 to 167, with the most democratic nation as number 1 and the least democratic nation at 167. The overall score, with 10 being best and 1 being worst, is determined by several factors the *Economist* considers vital to democracy, such as: 1) the fairness of the electoral process and whether or not minority groups are respected and allowed to maintain their cultural traditions; 2) the protection of civil liberties and fundamental rights, such as freedom of speech and religion; 3) the ability of the government to function; 4) the level of public participation in politics 5) whether or not the political culture promotes democracy.

The *Economist* updates the Democracy Index every two years. In the 2010 index Norway ranked first, and North Korea ranked last. The United States ranked 17 and had an overall score of 8.18. Below are the 2010 index results for fifteen countries of the Middle East.

Democracy Index 2010

Country	Rank (out of 167)	Overall Score (10 is highest)
Israel	37	7.48
Lebanon	86	5.3
Turkey	89	5.73
Palestine	93	5.44
Iraq	111	4.0
Kuwait	114	3.88
Jordan	117	3.74
Egypt	138	3.01
Tunisia	144	2.79
Yemen	146	2.64
United Arab Emirates	148	2.52
Syria	152	2.31
Libya (tied with Iran)	158	1.94
Iran (tied with Libya)	158	1.94
Saudi Arabia	160	1.84

ECONOMIST INTELLIGENCE UNIT. *DEMOCRACY INDEX 2010.* AVAILABLE ONLINE AT HTTP://GRAPHICS.EIU.COM/ PDF/DEMOCRACY_INDEX_2010_WEB.PDF (ACCESSED ON NOVEMBER 30, 2011).

the Arab world, was intended to be a forum in which leaders of the various Arab nations can intervene in a country whose leader has taken excessive or abusive power. But in fact, the organization is made up of many autocratic leaders and its founding charter does not even mention democracy or political freedom. Throughout much of its history it has failed to intervene when abuses were clear. A notable exception to the Arab League's lack of intervention occurred in November 2011, when it suspended Syria's membership, because of its violent crackdown on protesters.

Despite their harsh laws and powerful security forces stifling opposition, many of the authoritarian governments of the Middle East have been supported with financial aid and military support by Western nations at one time or another. The policies of Western nations toward the authoritarian regimes in the Middle East have been erratic at best. The United States, for example, has at different times supported the president of Egypt, the shah of Iran, the kings of Saudi Arabia, Saddam Hussein in Iraq, and Mu'ammar al-Qaddafi in Libya. Many Western foreign policies regarding the Middle East are heavily influenced by self-interest and dependence on oil. Others are geared toward forming strong allies in the region.

At times, human rights violations have disturbed Westerners enough that they put pressure on Middle East governments to reform. But for the most part foreign intervention to rectify the abuses of Middle Eastern leaders has been slight. For example, the United States contributed billions of dollars to Egypt in military and economic aid during Mubarak's thirty-year presidency. At times it pressured Mubarak to adopt democratic reforms. He took some measures, but most of them were empty gestures that changed little. In his article in the *Journal of Democracy* Diamond calls this "managed reform," in which authoritarian governments "adopt the language of political reform in order to avoid the reality [of reform], or embrace limited economic and social reforms to pursue modernization without democratization." Managed reform clearly did not appease the citizens who lived under authoritarian rule. In 2011 the Arab Spring uprisings spread across the Middle East and North Africa as citizens rose up against the oppressive authoritarian governments, bringing an end to the rule of several authoritarian leaders.

For More Information

BOOKS

Carothers, Thomas, ed. *Uncharted Journey: Promoting Democracy in the Middle East.* Washington, D.C.: Carnegie Endowment for International Peace, 2005.

Council on Foreign Relations/Foreign Affairs. *New Arab Revolt.* New York: Council on Foreign Relations, 2011.

Wright, Robin. *Dreams and Shadows: The Future of the Middle East.* New York: Penguin, 2008, p. 277.

PERIODICALS

Diamond, Larry. "Why Are There No Arab Democracies?" *Journal of Democracy* 21, no. 1 (January 2010).

Economist Intelligence Unit. *Democracy Index 2010.* Available online at http://graphics.eiu.com/PDF/Democracy_Index_2010_web.pdf (accessed on November 30, 2011).

Jamal, Amaney, and Mark Tessler. "The Democracy Barometers: Attitudes in the Arab World." *Journal of Democracy,* Vol. 19, No. 1. Available online at http://www.princeton.edu/~ajamal/Jamal_Tessler.97-110.pdf (accessed November 30, 2011.

Masoud, Tarek. "The Upheavals in Egypt and Tunisia: The Road to (and from) Liberation Square," *Journal of Democracy,* July 2011, Vol. 22, No. 3. Available at http://www.journalofdemocracy.org/articles/gratis/Masoud-22-3.pdf (accessed November 30, 2011.

WEB SITES

Asser, Martin. "The Muammar Gaddafi Story." *BBC News* (October 21, 2011). http://www.bbc.co.uk/news/world-africa-12688033 (accessed on November 30, 2011).

Brown, Nathan J., and Hesham Nasr. "Egypt's Judges Step Forward." *Carnegie Endowment for International Peace* (May 2005). http://www.carnegieendowment.org/files/PO17.borwn.FINAL.pdf (accessed on November 30, 2011).

United Nations Development Programme. *Arab Human Development Report, 2002: Creating Opportunities for Future Generations.* http://www.arab-hdr.org/publications/other/ahdr/ahdr2002e.pdf (accessed on September 5, 2011).

U.S. Department of State. *2010 Human Rights Report: Syria* (April 8, 2011). http://www.state.gov/g/drl/rls/hrrpt/2010/nea/154473.htm (accessed on November 30, 2011).

Vandewalle, Dirk, interview by Melissa Block. *NPR* (March 3, 2011). http://www.npr.org/2011/03/03/134239733/Whats-In-Gadhafis-Manifesto (accessed on November 30, 2011).

The Arab Spring: 2011

I n Sidi Bouzid, Tunisia, one man's act of frustration on December 17, 2010, sparked a protest movement that rapidly expanded throughout the Middle East and North Africa, launching the series of pro-democracy uprisings that came to be known as the Arab Spring. (Arabs are people who speak the Arabic language or who live in countries in which Arabic is the dominant language). After this incident, Tunisians rose up against their authoritarian leader Zine el-Abdine Ben Ali (1936–), forcing him to flee the country. Inspired by the success of the Tunisian protests, the citizens of other Middle East and North African nations launched similar demonstrations.

Bouazizi inspires Tunisian uprising

Twenty-six-year-old Mohamed Bouazizi (1984–2011) was a poor man living in Sidi Bouzid. His father had died young, and Bouazizi was forced to quit school in his teens to support his mother, uncle, and siblings by selling fruits and vegetables from a cart. Bouazizi was known as an honest man who, despite his own poverty, often gave fruit and vegetables to the needy. At times local officials stopped him on his way to market. According to the people of the town, the officials bullied him and fined him, probably for lacking a permit to sell his produce. Bouazizi hoped for better work, but there were few employment opportunities in Sidi Bouzid.

On the morning of December 17, Bouazizi was once again stopped by police. A policewoman attempted to take away the electronic scales he used for weighing produce and, when Bouazizi resisted, the officer slapped him. Then two other officers forced him to the ground and took away his scales, as well as his fruits and vegetables. Bouazizi, badly humiliated by the experience, made his way to the city government building to try to get back his property and report the abuse. He was turned away. The young man left, but he quickly returned with a can of paint thinner. In front of many witnesses, he doused himself with the

WORDS TO KNOW

Alawis: Also spelled Alawites; followers of a sect of Shia Islam that live in Syria. Their belief system and practices vary from Shiites in several ways, particularly in the belief that Ali, the son-in-law of the prophet Muhammad, was the human form of Allah (the Arabic word for God).

Arab League: A regional political alliance of Arab nations formed in 1945 to promote political, military, and economic cooperation within the Arab world.

Arabs: People of the Middle East and North Africa who speak the Arabic language or who live in countries in which Arabic is the dominant language.

authoritarianism: A type of leadership in which power is consolidated under one strong leader, or a small group of elite leaders, who do not answer to the will of the people.

Ba'ath Party: A secular (nonreligious) political movement founded in Syria in the 1940s with the goal of uniting the Arab world and creating one powerful Arab state.

Hamas: A Palestinian Islamic fundamentalist group and political party operating primarily in the West Bank and the Gaza Strip with the goal of establishing a Palestinian state and opposing the existence of Israel. It has been labeled a terrorist organization by several countries.

Islamism: A fundamentalist movement characterized by the belief that Islam should provide the basis for the political, social, and cultural life in Muslim nations.

Kurds: A non-Arab ethnic group who live mainly in present-day Turkey, Iraq, and Iran.

Muslim Brotherhood: An Islamic fundamentalist group organized in opposition to Western influence and in support of Islamic principles.

Palestinian Authority (PA): The recognized governing institution for Palestinians in the West Bank and the Gaza Strip, established in 1993. Also known as the Palestinian National Authority.

Palestine Liberation Organization (PLO): A political and military organization formed to unite various Palestinian Arab groups with the goal of establishing an independent Palestinian state.

Palestinians: An Arab people whose ancestors lived in the historical region of Palestine and who continue to lay claim to that land.

sharia: A system of Islamic law based on the Koran and other sacred writings. Sharia attempts to create the perfect social order, based on God's will and justice, and covers a wide range of human activities, including acts of religious worship, the law of contracts and obligations, personal status law, and public law.

Shiites: Followers of the Shia branch of Islam. Shiites believe that only direct descendants of the prophet Muhammad are qualified to lead the Islamic faith.

socialism: A system in which the government owns the means of production and controls the distribution of goods and services.

Sunnis: Followers of the Sunni branch of Islam. Sunnis believe that elected officials, regardless of their heritage, are qualified to lead the Islamic faith.

flammable liquid and set himself on fire. Suffering from severe burns covering 90 percent of his body, Bouazizi was taken to a hospital, where he later died. Bouazizi's humiliation and his self-immolation (burning of himself) hit a nerve among the people of the city. His friends and family quickly gathered at the police station to protest his abusive treatment.

By the next day, the protest had grown, and it soon spread to other parts of the country. Throughout Tunisia, people drew courage from seeing others protesting injustices similar to ones they had suffered in silence for many years. Many empathized with Bouazizi's loss of dignity at the hands of the authorities. Tunisians were angry with their president of twenty-three years, Zine el-Abdine Ben Ali, and his authoritarian regime, which stifled expression and allowed no opposition. They were disgusted with the propaganda campaign that plastered pictures of Ben Ali on city walls everywhere and broadcast his virtues and heroism on the national media. Although Tunisia had a relatively stable economy, there was a high rate of unemployment among young people, and outside the capital city of Tunis there was widespread poverty. The lavish lifestyle of the president and his circle of friends and family contrasted sharply with many Tunisians' difficult circumstances. Both Tunisian and international observers accused Ben Ali and his circle of gaining their immense wealth through corruption (the misuse of public office and resources for personal gain). The worst part of life in Tunisia, however, was living in fear of Ben Ali's harsh security forces, which frequently took political prisoners and held them for long periods of time, subjecting them to torture and isolation. Young Tunisians had never known any ruler but Ben Ali, but they were well aware that citizens of other countries had more freedoms they did.

The local protest against Bouazizi's treatment quickly transformed into a national protest against Ben Ali's regime. When Tunisian police responded harshly to the early protesters, beating them and shooting tear gas into the crowds, long-suppressed anger exploded. By the thousands, Tunisians took to the streets, shouting and chanting for Ben Ali's removal. The government tried to suppress news of the protest, but activists posted the news and videos of the protest on the Internet. The story was then picked up by some of the Middle East's satellite television news stations, such as Al Jazeera, an independent news channel based in Qatar. Students, lawyers, labor unions, and teachers went on strike (stopped working) and joined in the protests. In most places the protesters were peaceful, but angry rioting, including the burning of several police stations, broke out in some places. The police in turn attacked protesters, arresting, wounding, and even killing them. A video that recorded the gruesome death of one young protester was viewed by tens of thousands of Tunisians on *YouTube*, a video-sharing Web site, and *Facebook*, a social networking Web site, compelling more protesters to join the revolt.

The demonstrations continued into the new year. They were so fierce that the Tunisian army withdrew its support for Ben Ali. Unprotected, he was forced to flee the country on January 14. Normally, an act such as Bouazizi's would not have received much attention outside his hometown. But to people throughout the vast regions of the Middle East and North Africa, the act became a symbol of the frustration of life under authoritarian rulers. These were governments in which those in power did not have to answer to the people; communications were censored; basic rights were suspended under decades-long states of emergency (a government's declaration of special circumstances, in which it gives itself special powers to try to control a difficult or dangerous situation, often limiting people's freedom); and brutal security forces used beatings, torture, imprisonment, and murder to stop opposition. Bouazizi's expression of anger and frustration had unleashed the rage of millions.

A Tunisian man places flowers on the newly renamed Mohamed Bouazizi Martyr Street in Tunis, in February 2011. The death of Bouazizi, who set himself on fire in protest, sparked the Tunisian revolution and the Arab Spring uprisings. FETHI BELAIP/AFT/GETTY IMAGES

The fall of Tunisia's president prompted pro-democracy demonstrations in Egypt and Libya that would unseat two more long-term rulers, Egyptian president Hosni Mubarak (1928–) and Libyan leader Mu'ammar al-Qaddafi (also spelled Moammar al-Gaddafi; 1942–2011). In the following months, major revolts would erupt in Yemen, Bahrain, and Syria, and significant demonstrations for democratic reforms would affect other Middle East and North African countries, including Morocco, Jordan, and Algeria. The uprisings came to be called the Arab Spring, even though the turmoil in the Middle East and North Africa continued well past the spring of 2011, becoming more violent and complicated as time passed.

Roots of the Arab Spring

Syria By the turn of the twenty-first century, the nations of the Middle East and North Africa, with the exception of Israel, Turkey, and Lebanon, had been ruled by some form of authoritarian government for decades. (For more information, see **Conflicts Within: Repressive Governments of the Middle East in the Early Twenty-First Century**.) Fear of secret police and repressive measures had kept most people from rising up against their governments. But in the first few years of the twenty-first century there was a notable public movement toward democracy in the Middle East.

One of the first countries to experience a "spring," or time of renewal after a long period of repression, was Syria. Hafez Assad (also spelled al-Assad; 1930–2000), Syria's authoritarian president for twenty-nine years, died in 2000. Syria's ruling Ba'ath Party named Assad's son, Bashar Assad (also spelled al-Assad; 1965–), as the new president. At first Assad appeared to be a much milder leader than his father. He promised democratic reform but warned that it would take time to develop. Syria's economy, as well as its government, had long ago been shaped on the model of the former Soviet Union, with many of its industries

The Term "Arab Spring"

The name "Arab Spring" was created by Western media and is not used in the Middle East. According to Rami G. Khouri in the *Daily Star*, a newspaper based in Lebanon, most people of the Middle East speak of the prodemocracy uprisings that spread across the Middle East and North Africa in 2011 as "the revolutions." Other common terms are *intifada* (uprising), *sahwa* (awakening), and *nahda* (rebirth). Among Westerners the phrase "Arab Spring" comes from several earlier historical revolutionary events in Europe that were also called "springs" to denote that they were a time of awakening or rebirth after repressive governments were overthrown. Perhaps the most famous example of an earlier "spring" was the Prague Spring of 1968, in which Czechoslovakian leaders made reforms to their government in an attempt to end the Soviet domination of their country.

KHOURI, RAMI G. "DROP THE ORIENTALIST TERM 'ARAB SPRING.'" *DAILY STAR* (AUGUST 17, 2011).

nationalized (owned and controlled by the government). Assad initiated economic reforms to build independent businesses and led Syria into the modern era of technology. He also released hundreds of political prisoners. By 2001 a period known as the Damascus Spring had begun. (Damascus is Syria's capital city.) For the first time in decades, Syrians openly talked about change in government and individual freedom. Syria's media was run by the government, but after 2001 independent newspapers that printed opposing points of view competed with the government media.

As suddenly as the Damascus Spring arose, it was crushed. Some Middle East experts speculate that the leaders of the Ba'ath Party overrode Assad's reforms and organized a crackdown on those who expressed any kind of opposition to, or criticism of, the government. By 2002 hundreds of writers, activists, and educators had been arrested by security forces. Many were imprisoned for years, sometimes in solitary confinement. In 2005, from among these victims of the crackdown, the writers of the Damascus Declaration for Democratic National Change emerged. The declaration was a statement signed by two hundred fifty members of opposition parties from many of Syria's diverse religious, ethnic, and political groups. The Damascus Declaration condemned Syria's authoritarian government. The declaration called for the formation of a democratic government but urged that it be established through slow and peaceful reforms "founded on accord, and based on dialogue and recognition of the other." The efforts of the activists who created the declaration, however, were stifled by the government. In 2008 twelve members of the Damascus Declaration National Council were found guilty of spreading false information and weakening national morale and sentenced to several years in prison.

Iraq By 2005 the roots of the Arab Spring also began developing elsewhere in the Middle East. In January war-torn Iraq held its first multiparty elections in more than fifty years, just two years after a U.S.-led coalition toppled Saddam Hussein (1937–2006), Iraq's president for more than two decades in the Iraq War (2003–11). (For more information, see **The Gulf Wars: 1991 to 2011**.) With a growing insurgency (a revolt against a political authority that falls short of revolution) creating violence throughout the country, large numbers of Iraqis risked their lives to exercise their right to vote. The process, it was hoped, would begin the difficult path of constructing a democratic government in the middle of war.

Lebanon Lebanon experienced a reform movement in February 2005, after former Lebanese prime minister Rafiq Hariri (1944–2005) was assassinated. Many Lebanese blamed Syria, which had a twenty-nine-year military presence in Lebanon and a heavy influence over the Lebanese government. Outraged at Hariri's murder, thousands of Lebanese took to the streets in protest. Lebanon's elected government soon resigned, but Syria maintained its troops in Lebanon. On March 14, 2005, an estimated one million Lebanese citizens took to the streets in a demonstration called the March 14 Movement (later called the Cedar Revolution) to protest Syrian presence in Lebanon. The pressure forced the Syrian troops to withdraw. Lebanon then held its first elections free of Syrian control in decades.

Palestine January 2006 marked a democratic milestone for the Palestinian Authority (PA), the recognized governing institution for Palestinians in the West Bank and the Gaza Strip. (Palestinians are an Arab people whose ancestors lived in the historical region of Palestine, comprising parts of present-day Israel and Jordan, and who continue to lay claim to that land). The PA was established in 1993 under terms of the Oslo Accords, a peace agreement between Israel and the Palestinians. The newly formed PA was to govern as the democratically elected representative of the Palestinian people living in the West Bank and the Gaza Strip, areas that had been occupied by Israel since the 1967 Arab-Israeli War. Democracy had not followed, largely because, prior to the creation of the PA, Yasser Arafat (1929–2004), head of the Palestine Liberation Organization (PLO), had served as the representative of Palestinians for decades. (The PLO is a political and military organization formed to unite various Palestinian Arab groups with the goal of establishing an independent Palestinian state.) Arafat became president of the PA, and, according to most observers, Arafat's regime had become corrupt and authoritarian.

Arafat died in 2004. Mahmoud Abbas (1935–), a close associate of Arafat's and his successor as head of the PLO was elected president in 2005. After many delays, in January 2006 the PA held its first national legislative elections to elect members of the Palestinian National Council, the PA's legislature. Hamas, a militant Islamist group (Islamists believe that Islam should provide the basis for the political, social, and cultural life in Muslim nations), won the majority of the seats in the council.

Although many feared the results of the election might create foreign policy turmoil (many Western nations considered Hamas to be a terrorist organization), start war with Israel, or restrict the rights of women and people with differing religious views, others hailed the fact that the Palestinians had carried out fair and free elections.

Kuwait In June 2006 Kuwait held its first elections in which women were allowed to vote and to run for office. Although Kuwait had been one of the first Arab countries to adopt a parliamentary system, it was relatively late in allowing women to vote and participate in politics. Advancing the rights and roles of women in the Middle East is viewed by many as vital to democracy. U.S. Secretary of State Hillary Rodham Clinton (1947–) voiced this view in a 2011 speech in which she asserted that, as quoted by Merle David Kellerhals Jr. in an article for the *allAfrica.com* Web site, "women have to be part of the future. And it's imperative that as constitutions are created, as political parties are organized, as elections are waged and won, nobody can claim a democratic future if half the population is marginalized or even prevented from participating."

Iran In June 2009 a non-Arab nation in the Middle East, the Islamic Republic of Iran, experienced what seemed to be a brief preview of events to come throughout the Middle East. That year, the increasingly authoritarian government held presidential elections in which conservative incumbent Mahmoud Ahmadinejad (1956–) ran against a reform-minded candidate. When officials announced that Ahmadinejad had won, many Iranians claimed the elections had been rigged by the government in Ahmadinejad's favor. Hundreds of thousands of Iranians poured into the streets demanding Ahmadinejad's resignation and major reforms to their government in an event that became known as the Green Movement. The government quickly banned foreign journalists, shut down Internet connections, and sent security forces to crush the protests. Thousands of protesters were arrested, and by some estimates, as many as one hundred people were killed. For several weeks, the protesters used cell phones and cameras to document beatings and other acts of police violence, posting photos and videos on the Internet. Eventually government militias regained control of the streets, and the protesters went home, but demonstrations continued intermittently in the years that followed.

After Iran's 2009 presidential elections, which many claimed to be fraudulent, hundreds of thousands of Iranians poured into the streets demanding Ahmadinejad's resignation and major reforms to their government. SIPA VIA AP IMAGES.

Egypt Egypt had its own brief political spring in 2005. At that time, the United States, Egypt's ally and greatest financial contributor, pressured Mubarak to institute democratic reforms in Egypt. More pressure on the government arrived in May 2005, when a group of Egyptian judges announced that the judges of Egypt would boycott their role as supervisors of Egypt's elections unless the government passed new laws reforming judicial (court) powers. Mubarak's regime gave in to the pressure by holding more open voting in the parliamentary elections of November and December 2005. While in the past only one party, Mubarak's National Democratic Party, had been allowed to run, the 2005 elections allowed other parties to participate. A significant number of candidates from other parties (although not a majority) won seats in parliament. For a brief time, Egypt's powerful security forces relaxed their rigid restrictions of public speech and assembly. With the easing of security measures, a small but energetic youth movement soon emerged.

In the early years of the twenty-first century, the entire Middle East had a young population. Approximately 60 percent of the population in the region was under the age of thirty, and the median age was only twenty-six years old (by comparison, the median age in the United States was thirty-seven years old). However, as education opportunities grew in Egypt, job opportunities decreased, particularly among the young. The better-educated youth were the least employed of Egyptian groups, and their frustrations were increasingly directed at their government. They wanted more political freedom. Their problem was how to fight the government without falling prey to its powerful security forces.

In 2004 a group of young Egyptians of many different political beliefs established a movement with the goal of ending Mubarak's rule and establishing a system of free elections in Egypt. The group's name was Kifaya (also spelled Kefaya; which means "enough"). For a short time Kifaya organized a series of well-attended anti-Mubarak street demonstrations that drew international attention. Within a year, however, Mubarak's security forces renewed their efforts against opposition. They brutally suppressed the group, arresting and beating many of its leaders. Kifaya had nearly vanished by 2006, but many of its members went on to lead Egypt's 2011 revolt.

By 2007 Mubarak put a decisive end to the reform era with a set of constitutional amendments that eliminated the full judicial supervision of elections, limited who could run in elections, and strengthened the president's state-of-emergency powers, which enabled Mubarak to continue to run what most people considered a police state. Mubarak's huge police forces, the Central Security Forces, the State Security forces, and a large unofficial group of hired strongmen called the *baltagiya* (hired thugs or gangsters), were comprised of an estimated 1.5 million agents, and they were notoriously corrupt and abusive.

Egyptian activists organize through Facebook In 2008 youth activists, many of whom had their start in Kifaya, helped to organize a textile (cloth) workers' strike planned for April 6. They used *Facebook* to aid in organizing the strike, and it worked better than anyone had anticipated. The new movement, called the April 6th Movement, soon had a *Facebook* membership of seventy thousand, making it Egypt's largest activist group. *Facebook* provided a way for protesters to communicate without the danger involved in a physical gathering. Many young people who had never before participated in political efforts were drawn to the April 6th *Facebook* page. And while the authorities prohibited group meetings, blocked news reporting, and intercepted e-mail and telephone conversations, they had not, as yet, blocked social media. The April 6th Movement, under the leadership of some dedicated prodemocracy reformers, drew together people of many backgrounds and beliefs and narrowed their objective to one goal: to remove Mubarak from office. The members of the movement began to study methods of nonviolent protest and strategies for mass protests.

The April 6th Movement was not alone in finding *Facebook* a handy tool for organizing against the government. By 2010 another popular *Facebook* page for activists was that of Mohamed ElBaradei (1942–), the Egyptian Nobel Peace Prize winner and former director of the International Atomic Energy Agency, an organization that seeks the peaceful use of nuclear energy worldwide. ElBaradei had become a leader in the anti Mubarak efforts, and many hoped to see him run for president of Egypt.

Activism on *Facebook* soared after an incident in June 2010 in which Khaled Said, a young Egyptian businessman, was arrested while sitting in an Internet café in Alexandria. Said had recently posted a video on the Internet that showed Egyptian policemen stealing marijuana during a drug raid. According to witnesses, two detectives burst into the café and arrested him. They dragged him outside, handcuffed him, and then viciously beat him to death despite outcries from bystanders. Afterward, the police department claimed that Said died from choking on illegal drugs he had attempted to swallow upon his arrest. A grisly photo of Said's battered face, posted on the Internet shortly after the fatal beating, showed that the police claim was unlikely. Said's skull had been fractured, his jaw dislocated, his teeth knocked out, and his nose broken. A photo of Said's corpse was anonymously placed on a *Facebook* page called "We Are All Khaled Said." The page drew thousands of outraged viewers.

The Egyptian youth, and older generations as well, became even more disgusted with Mubarak's regime after the November 2010 parliamentary elections, in which 97 percent of the seats were reportedly won by the ruling party. Many people in and out of Egypt claimed that massive vote rigging had occurred.

The Arab Spring spreads to Egypt

In the first weeks of 2011, activists from the April 6th Movement and other Egyptian groups were organizing a large demonstration against police brutality for January 25, which is a national holiday in Egypt known as Police Day, when they learned that a massive revolt in Tunisia had forced Ben Ali to flee. Greatly inspired, Egyptians took to the streets in massive numbers on January 25. Tens of thousands of protesters positioned themselves in Tahrir Square in the capital city of Cairo. They went beyond denouncing police brutality, demanding an end to Mubarak's rule.

The protest's leaders were mainly young, both male and female, and mainly secular (nonreligious). The crowds were made up of Egyptians of all generations, social backgrounds, and religious beliefs. For days, the protesters refused to go home, despite a curfew (a regulation requiring people to be off the streets for a certain period of the day) and many arrests. In the eighteen days of the revolt, from January 25 to February 11, as many as two million people gathered in Tahrir Square. In Alexandria an estimated three-quarters of a million protesters took to the streets and in Mansour another one million people demonstrated.

Egyptian protesters gather at Tahrir Square in Cairo on February 11, 2011. PEDRO UGARTE/AFP/GETTY IMAGES.

In the early days of the uprising, Mubarak's regime launched its police forces against protesters, but the protesters bravely faced them and through their sheer numbers eventually overwhelmed the police. Violence soon erupted between anti-Mubarak protesters and pro-Mubarak protesters (reportedly the paid thugs hired by Mubarak's regime). Mubarak first tried threatening the protesters and cutting off Internet and cell phone service. As it became apparent that the protesters could not be frightened into going home, he gave in to some of their demands, but it was too late.

Unlike the police, the Egyptian military took a neutral role. After the protests started, the military leaders reviewed the situation and decided the best course was to separate the military from the unpopular president. Many of the protest leaders, in turn, advocated a partnership between the protesters and the military. On February 1 Field Marshall Hussein Tantawi (1935–) announced that the army would not fire on the demonstrators. Finally the army withdrew its support from Mubarak altogether. Without protection, he was forced to resign. The Supreme Council of the Armed Forces (SCAF), headed by Tantawi, then assumed power in Egypt. On February 13, Tantawi announced that the 1971 Egyptian constitution would be suspended, the parliament would be dissolved, and the military would run the country for a transition period of about six months, until democratic elections could be held.

Uprisings spread and motivate reform

Meanwhile, massive demonstrations broke out all over the Middle East in rapid succession. On January 21, for example, thousands of demonstrators encouraged by the revolt in Tunisia took to the streets in several cities in Jordan, protesting economic policies and demanding the resignation of the prime minister, who had been appointed by King Abdullah II (1962–). The king quickly took limited reform measures, such as dismissing the prime minister and taking steps to lower fuel and food prices and to stimulate jobs. In late September 2011 he approved several constitutional amendments that provided, among other things, for a constitutional court and the supervision of general elections by an independent body.

In late February 2011 demonstrations for democratic reform rocked Morocco's capital city of Rabat, as well as the cities of Casablanca, Marrakech, and Tangier. Although Morocco's King Mohammed VI (1963–) was respected in his country for the reforms he had initiated, such as

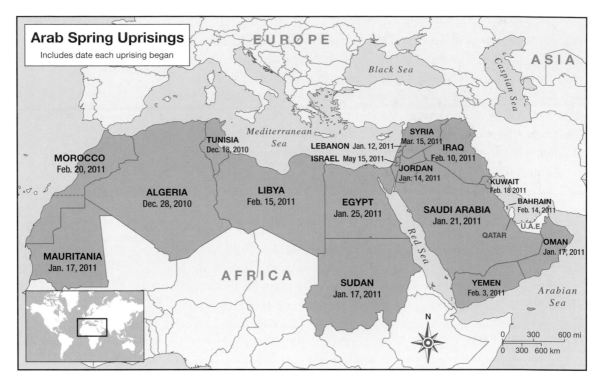

A map showing the locations of the Arab Spring uprisings, with the date each uprising began. MAP BY XNR PRODUCTIONS, INC./CENGAGE LEARNING.

extending women's rights and allowing limited forms of political protest, many felt it was not enough. When the demonstrations started, however, Moroccan security forces avoided violence, and the protesters, in turn, agreed to work with the government for a slow, peaceful process toward reform.

Fear of an Arab Spring movement within its borders forced the Algerian government, led by President Abdelaziz Bouteflika (1937–), to take measures to keep its people content, including helping to reduce the high price of food, ending Algeria's nineteen-year-old state-of-emergency law, and releasing thousands of political prisoners.

Peaceful protests in Yemen turn violent

Antigovernment protests began in Yemen in January 2011. Yemen is the poorest country in the Middle East, and long before 2011, its people had risen up against the government only to be overpowered by its forces.

Until 1990, Yemen was two countries: the Yemen Arab Republic (or North Yemen) and the People's Democratic Republic of Yemen (or South Yemen). Ali Abdullah Saleh (1942–) became president of the Yemen Arab Republic in 1978, and when the north and south were united in 1990, he took over as president of the whole country. Deep hostility continued between the north and south despite the 1990 union. The former People's Democratic Republic of Yemen unsuccessfully revolted against Saleh's rule in the 1994, resulting in civil war. The north won the battle and took over the south, but the south continued to accuse the Saleh administration of corruption and discrimination against southerners and threatened to secede (withdraw) from Yemen.

Saleh stayed in power by stifling opposition. He shored up his power over the military by placing friends and family in the top positions. Many Yemenis also accused him of making deals with the increasing numbers of terrorist groups, including al-Qaeda, that were moving into several areas of southern Yemen. Although Saleh committed his country to aiding the United States in its war on terror in the early twenty-first century, many experts believe that he had been making deals with the al-Qaeda leaders stationed in southern Yemen for many years.

There were other divisions within the country, as well. Yemen has a long history of tribal conflict. (Tribes are social groups, usually made up of many families or clans that identify strongly with their membership to the tribe and its leaders.) Disputes between Yemeni tribes have often resulted in violence, which provokes revenge killings, creating long-term cycles of violence. Saleh had a reputation for manipulating tribal conflicts to his own advantage, and he frequently paid tribal leaders for their loyalty. Another division in Yemen, as in several other Arab countries, is one between Shiite Muslims and Sunni Muslims. Shiites are followers of the Shia branch of Islam, who believe that only direct descendants of the prophet Muhammad (c. 570–632) are qualified to lead the Islamic faith. Sunnis, followers of the Sunni branch of Islam, believe that elected officials, regardless of their heritage, are qualified to lead the Islamic faith. In the northern reaches of Yemen, a group of Shiite Muslims called the Houthis had long battled with the central government.

Many political analysts contend that Saleh purposely inflamed the hostilities among his people, knowing that a divided country would be too weak to rebel. By most accounts, Saleh's rule was corrupt; his family made billions of dollars from Yemen's rapidly shrinking oil fields while most of the country was impoverished.

Tawakkul Karman

Tawakkul Karman (1979–) is a Yemeni activist and journalist who played a major role as a leader in the 2011 revolution against Yemen's president, Ali Abdullah Saleh (1942–), and his regime. Karman has devoted most of her life to trying to improve political conditions in her country. In 2005 Karman cofounded an organization called Women Reporters Without Chains, an organization that worked to promote freedom of the press in Yemen. She began organizing local demonstrations about specific injustices, such as unfair imprisonments and corrupt local officials.

Karman is a member of the Islah, an Islamist opposition political party linked to the Muslim Brotherhood. She is a moderate Islamist seeking democracy and human rights. Karman has taken a strong stand for women's rights: She has battled for minimum wages for women, worked against child marriages, and taken to wearing a head scarf rather than the *niqab*, a face veil worn by many traditional Muslim women in Yemen that covers the lower part of the face up to the eyes. In her protests and her strong stands

for women's rights, Karman angered some traditional Yemenis. She received death threats that targeted herself and her three children, but she did not stop fighting.

In 2011, when Karman learned about the successful uprising in Tunisia, she quickly organized Yemeni students to protest against their government. Protesters set up a tent city in the center of Sana'a, demanding that Saleh resign, and Karman stationed herself in a tent, leaving her children in the care of family members. She remained in the tent city for months, braving the brutal retaliation of Saleh's security forces, watching in horror as her fellow demonstrators were killed by government snipers, and getting arrested and released. Through it all she maintained her solid belief in nonviolent demonstration. She allowed her face to become a symbol of the revolt, particularly among the foreign media. She soon became known as the woman behind the revolution.

In 2011 the Nobel Peace Prize was awarded to three women who had used nonviolent means to

In January 2011 a group of nonviolent youth activists began to demonstrate against the Saleh regime. The peaceful movement began in the southern Yemeni city of Taiz, but by February tens of thousands of young Yemeni men and women had flocked to the capital city of Sana'a and several other cities to participate. The demonstrators camped out on the city streets, refusing to leave until Saleh resigned, remaining there for months. In a main street of Sana'a, the protesters erected what became known as Change Square, a 1-mile-long (1.6-kilometer) encampment of shelters made of tarp and concrete blocks. Saleh's forces responded to the protests with vicious attacks. In one attack on March 18, 2011, an estimated fifty demonstrators were killed by snipers (skilled marksmen who shoot people from hidden places). The violence outraged some of fight for women's rights and peace, and Karman was one of them. She accepted the prize on behalf of all the revolutionary fighters in Yemen, but particularly the women fighters. She pointed out that before the revolution, women in Yemen were not allowed out of their houses after a 7 PM curfew. This changed during the revolt. Karman explains, as quoted in the *Sydney Morning Herald*, "If you go to the protests now, you will see something you never saw before: hundreds of women. They shout and sing, they even sleep there in tents. This is not just a political revolution, it's a social revolution."

Thorbjoern Jagland, chairman of the Nobel Committee, noted how difficult it was to choose just one recipient from all the activists of the Arab Spring. The committee chose Karman because of her courage and because it wanted to honor the women who have been at the core of the revolutions. Jagland said, as quoted in *CNS News.com*, "If one fails to include the women in the revolution and the new democracies, there will be no democracy."

Tawakkul Karman. © EUROPA NEWSWIRE/ALAMY.

AMLAND, BJOERN H., AND KARL RITTER "NOBEL PEACE PRIZE GOES TO WOMEN'S RIGHTS ACTIVISTS." *CNS NEWS.COM* (OCTOBER 7, 2011).

"WOMEN OF STRENGTH SHARE NOBEL PEACE PRIZE." *SYDNEY MORNING HERALD* (OCTOBER 10, 2011).

the army officers; despite government orders to attack, they ordered their troops to protect the demonstrators. The courageous demonstrators faced the attacks without weapons, contending that Yemen's long history of violence could not be overcome with more violence.

The peaceful anti-Saleh movement was soon taken over by other forces. Along with the defecting army officers, some of the tribal leaders that had once been loyal to Saleh saw a chance to overthrow him by joining the movement. They brought arms and violence to the conflict, despite the wishes of the original protesters.

In May Saleh's armed foes attacked the president's compound, killing some of Saleh's staff. Saleh was badly wounded and quickly left for

Smoke rises from Peal Square in Bahrain after police assaulted the protest camp there in March 2011. JOSEPH EID/AFP/GETTY IMAGES.

Saudi Arabia for medical treatment. He did not return to Yemen until September 23, but his forces, under the command of his son and two nephews, remained in control of the military. In southern Yemen a lack of government presence allowed al-Qaeda and other extremist forces to gain control, at least for a time, of cities near the seaport city of Aden. Many feared that the once-peaceful revolt was turning into a bloody civil war or, worse, into utter lawlessness and chaos. By late fall Yemen's economy was near collapse. The United States called for the resignation of Saleh. Several times he implied that he would resign, but then did not. On November 23, 2011, Saleh transferred his power to his vice president, Abed Rabbo Mansour al-Hadi (1945–). After his resignation, however, Saleh continued to issue orders as if he were still in control of the country, and people loyal to him allegedly killed more protesters. Presidential elections were set for February 21, 2012, in which Hadi was expected to be the only candidate.

Bahrain crushes demonstrators

Bahrain has been ruled by the Al Khalifa family as a monarchy since the eighteenth century. The Al Khalifas are Sunni, while about two-thirds of Bahrain's population is Shiite. The Shiite majority claims to have faced discrimination by the Sunni rulers. Hamad ibn Isa Al Khalifa (1950–), who became emir (ruler) of Bahrain in 1999, declared himself king in 2002. He also introduced a new constitution with democratic elections for the lower house of the National Assembly. Shiites won a majority of the seats, but some forms of discrimination against them continued. On February 14, 2011, after uprisings forced Ben Ali in Tunisia and Mubarak in Egypt out of office, masses of young people, the majority of whom were Shiites, took over Pearl Square in Bahrain's capital city of Manama. Most were seeking democratic reforms in their country and not necessarily the overthrow of their government.

Soon after the protesters took over Pearl Square, the government's security forces attacked them, but the protesters refused to go home. When its own forces failed, Bahrain asked Saudi Arabia for help. The Saudi royal family led an authoritarian monarchy itself and had no desire to see a democratic revolution next door. Furthermore, the Saudis are Sunni Muslims. They have an ongoing rivalry with the Iranians, who are Shiite, and feared that an uprising of Shiites in Bahrain could provide Iran access to the country. The Saudis therefore sent twelve hundred troops and police forces to Bahrain. The Saudi and Bahrain forces brutally crushed the Pearl Square demonstrators. Afterward, Bahrain used its own forces to terrify its people into silence, resulting in at least a temporary halt to the revolt. Many Shiite dissidents were arrested and tortured, others lost their jobs. Shiite mosques (places of worship) and other buildings were destroyed. The U.S. Fifth Fleet, a huge unit of U.S. Navy warships, is based in Bahrain, and, to the frustration of many Bahrainis, the United States was slow to criticize Bahrain's abuses of its people.

Bahrain's extreme police measures and its arrest and holding of thousands of Bahrainis as political prisoners months after the uprising caused deep bitterness in the country. Many experts viewed Bahrain as a likely spot for further conflict. A September 24, 2011, article in *Economist* magazine quotes Matar Matar, a Bahraini opposition politician who was imprisoned and beaten for three months by the government, as saying "People are not afraid anymore." He explains, "They have seen the worst that the government can do and they have kept coming back.

They want something tangible now. They want freedom. It is the only way out of this."

Libya's leader falls

On February 15, 2011, a group of lawyers gathered outside a police station in the Libyan city of Benghazi. They were there because a fellow attorney, a human rights activist who was representing victims of brutality in a Libyan prison, had been arrested that day. The lawyers chanted for his release. Crowds gathered around them. Young activists joined in, calling for an end to the rule of Mu'ammar al-Qaddafi, Libya's president of more than forty years. By the next day the Benghazi demonstration had swelled in numbers and another large demonstration was underway in Libya's capital city of Tripoli.

Al-Qaddafi's response was swift and brutal. On February 17, al-Qaddafi's security forces and the Libyan army fired machine guns directly at the unarmed demonstrators. When photos and videos of the killed and maimed protesters appeared on the Internet, thousands of enraged Libyans joined the movement. Several top military leaders turned against al-Qaddafi and joined the demonstrators. Libya rapidly descended into civil war.

Al-Qaddafi had never allowed any sort of opposition to form in Libya, so the rebel forces were a haphazard mixture of mainly untrained volunteers. Writer Jon Lee Anderson describes them in a *New Yorker* article:

> The hard core of the fighters has been the *shabab*—the young people whose protests in mid-February sparked the uprising. They range from street toughs to university students (many in computer science, engineering, or medicine), and have been joined by unemployed hipsters and middle-aged mechanics, merchants, and storekeepers. There is a contingent of workers for foreign companies: oil and maritime engineers, construction supervisors, translators. There are former soldiers. . . . And there are a few bearded religious men, more disciplined than the others.

In the city of Benghazi, a group of protesters formed the National Transitional Council, a political body, and by early March proclaimed it the legitimate representative, or government, of the Libyan people during the time of transition.

Al-Qaddafi was widely hated by many Libyans after decades of an eccentric and brutal rule. During the last two weeks of February, rebels in the towns and cities of eastern Libya, inspired by their hatred, overpowered al-Qaddafi's security forces and destroyed their headquarters. These acts uncovered proof of some of the horrors Libyans had long suffered. "All across eastern Libya, the collapse of Qaddafi's regime exposed an unknown world of walled military compounds and torture rooms belonging to the Leader [al-Qaddafi] and his gang," writes Robert Worth in an April 3, 2011, *New York Times* article. "Protesters burned and destroyed almost all of them, police stations, jails, security branches—and there were so many: external security, internal security, national security, intelligence."

In the early weeks of March, al-Qaddafi's forces struck back with vengeance. Al-Qaddafi had intentionally weakened the Libyan military in order to prevent it from rebelling against him. In its place he had trained elite security units that were usually formed from Libya's most powerful tribal groups and included large numbers of foreign fighters from sub-Saharan African nations (those south of the Sahara desert). His sons took command of these powerful units with superior weapons and trained soldiers. Al-Qaddafi used everything in his power, including air strikes, to crush the rebels. His forces quickly regained control of many of the towns the rebels had taken a few weeks earlier.

In mid–March al-Qaddafi's forces were approaching the rebels' stronghold, the city of Benghazi. It appeared to observers worldwide that the well-armed forces would crush the untrained and disorganized rebels and retake Benghazi. At the last minute, help came from outside Libya. The United Nations Security Council had been reviewing the threat of a major massacre of civilians if al-Qaddafi's forces retook Benghazi. As the forces approached the city, the United Nations (UN; international organization of countries founded in 1945 to promote international peace, security, and cooperation) passed a resolution to establish and enforce a no-fly zone (a territory over which military aircraft are prohibited from flying) over Libya and endorsed military action to protect Libyan civilians. On March 19, the United States led a coalition of forces from several nations in a mission called Operation Dawn Odyssey. The coalition employed strategic strikes from the air and from ships and submarines to support the rebels in their fight. On March 31 the North Atlantic Treaty Organization (NATO; an international organization created in 1949 for purposes of collective security), took over the mission. With NATO support, the rebels at Benghazi resisted al-Qaddafi's forces.

With NATO supporting them with air strikes, the Libyan rebels slowly pressed forward toward Tripoli. Al-Qaddafi's forces were strong, despite the desertions of many military leaders. The battles created nightmarish situations for civilians. According to Amnesty International, a nonprofit organization that works to protect human rights worldwide, the al-Qaddafi forces committed gross violations of international humanitarian law during the fighting, including killing, torturing, kidnapping, and arresting civilians and intentionally destroying their residences. They also laid siege to territories held by their opponents, leaving the residents with no food, water, medicine, or other vital necessities and no means of escape. Telephone and Internet services were disconnected, and journalists were killed and arrested in an attempt to prevent news of the brutality from spreading.

Amnesty International also accuses the rebels of committing war crimes, although on a smaller scale. They were said to have abused captured al-Qaddafi forces, including killing and torturing them. Because al-Qaddafi's forces were staffed by foreigners from sub-Saharan Africa, there were reports that the rebels had violently attacked sub-Saharan Africans regardless of whether they were involved in the war or not.

In August the rebel forces overtook Tripoli. By that time, al-Qaddafi had moved most of the government operations from the capital to Sirte, the city where he was born. Although al-Qaddafi's forces held out in Sirte and several other bases, by September the rebels' political group, the National Transitional Council, had received the recognition of the international community as the legitimate government of the Libyan people.

Libya faced huge hurdles in forming a democratic nation out of the broken pieces left by al-Qaddafi's eccentric rule. Al-Qaddafi had instituted a quirky form of socialism under which, in principle, people ruled themselves and controlled their economy through revolutionary people's committees called Basic People's Congresses. (Socialism is a system in which the government owns the means of production and controls the distribution of goods and services.) In practice, however, these Basic People's Congresses; were headed by al-Qaddafi's associates. Libyans found they had no power in these committees and came to fear and detest the committee leaders. The buildings where these revolutionary committees convened were some of the first to be burned as the rebels took the cities. In Libya there was no previous government or constitution to work from as there had been in Tunisia and Egypt. The military was also in dire straits.

In September, speaking from Tripoli, National Transitional Council leader Mustafa Abdel-Jalil (1952–) called for a new Libya with a democratic government based on Islam, cautioning that no extremism would be acceptable in Libya's new social order. After Tripoli fell, Abdel-Jalil promised to bring the National Transitional Council to the capital to form a transitional government there. Elections were to be held eight months after the fall of Sirte. Despite Abdel-Jalil's calls for unity, however, by the autumn of 2011 different groups of Libyans were vying against one another for power, particularly those who sought a Western-style secular government versus those who sought a government based on Islam.

On October 20, 2011, al-Qaddafi was captured while fleeing from Sirte as the rebels overtook the city. He was killed shortly after his capture. Though the exact circumstances of his death remain unknown, many observers theorized that his captors had killed him, although the rebels claimed he was caught in crossfire. The next day, his body was laid out for public view, as Libyans rejoiced over the end of his long regime. On October 23, the eight-month civil war was declared over. The National Transitional Council estimated that about twenty-five thousand people had been killed and about twice as many had been wounded.

Syria receives international condemnation

Syria's prodemocracy protests came relatively late in the Arab Spring, causing some, including Syria's president Bashar Assad, to speculate that the country might avoid them altogether. Syria's secret police, the *mukhabarat*, were tremendously effective in instilling fear in the Syrian people. Syria also has a long history of internal differences, with strong rivalries between cities and religious and ethnic sects. Syria's population is religiously divided, with about 74 percent Sunni Muslim, 10 percent Alawi (followers of a sect of Shia Islam that live in Syria), 6 percent other Muslim sects, and 10 percent Christian. Another faction in Syria is the Kurds, the largest ethnic group in the world that does not have its own country. Kurds are a non-Arab people who have traditionally lived in a region called Kurdistan, a vast area that spreads across parts of Iraq, Iran, Turkey, and Syria. The Kurds make up about 10 percent of Syria's population (they may be of any religion), and they have long complained of government discrimination against them.

Assad and members of the ruling Ba'ath Party are Alawis, and over the years of rule by Assad and his father before him, Syria's Alawis became a privileged elite; many of them held top positions in the government. In 2011 with the large majority of Sunnis in Syria, the powerful Alawi leaders feared they would be targeted for reprisal (revenge) for their past privileges if the Assad regime should fall. Many Syrian Christians, too, worried that they would lose their protection if the Sunni majority took control. The Syrian people had only to look to their close neighbors for terrible examples of what might happen. Lebanon had experienced a fifteen-year civil war, from 1975 to 1990, due to sectarian conflicts, and Iraq had descended into sectarian violence after a U.S.-led military coalition removed Saddam Hussein and his authoritarian regime from power in the Iraq War. Some Syrians feared that without the rigid control of Assad's regime, Syria, too, could fall into chaos.

There was, therefore, little outward reaction in Syria about the events in Tunisia and Egypt in the first months of 2011, but in mid–March, a grim incident pitted many Syrians against their government. In the southern Syrian town of Dara'a, fifteen teenagers, all under the age of seventeen, had painted anti-Assad graffiti on a school wall. They were arrested, beaten, and tortured. Hundreds of townspeople rose up in protest. On March 18, local security forces fired on them, killing three protesters. On March 20, the Dara'a protesters burned the local Ba'ath Party office and the governor's office and began openly calling for revolution. The protest soon began to spread to other cities.

Assad reassured the Syrian people that he would investigate the teenagers' arrests and make necessary reforms in his government. At the same time, his regime claimed that the protests were the work of extremists and terrorists. The government banned all foreign journalists from entering Syria and shut down Internet and telephone service. Soon brutal and deadly crackdowns on protesters began. In April, right after Assad fulfilled his promise to end Syria's forty-eight-year-old state of emergency, he ordered a military assault on the town of Dara'a, using tanks, bombs, and automatic weapons. Many townspeople were killed in this violent crackdown, hundreds were arrested, and the rest were forced to remain for weeks in their homes without food or water or face death or arrest. As people in other parts of Syria heard about the siege of Dara'a, they took to the streets in larger numbers than ever before. In reprisal, the government launched severe military assaults on the cities of Homs, Baniyas, and Moadamiya, a suburb of Damascus, killing many protesters and arresting thousands. Protests then erupted in Latakia, Hama, and Deir al-Zour, and vicious military sieges took place in these cities as well.

A Syrian woman protests outside the Syrian embassy in Jordan, in April 2011.
© JAMAL NASRALLAH/EPA/
CORBIS.

By summer the United States, the European Union (EU; an economic and political association of European countries), and even Arab nations, such as Saudi Arabia, had condemned Syria for shedding the blood of its own people. U.S. president Barack Obama (1961–) stopped just short of demanding action. Assad's "calls for dialogue and reform have rung hollow while he is imprisoning, torturing, and slaughtering his own people. The time has come for President Assad to step aside," Obama said, as quoted by *PBS Newshour* on August 18.

In early September Mohammed Adnan al-Bakkour, the attorney general of Hama, resigned his job in protest. He described hundreds of killings, arrests, and torture of nonviolent demonstrators at the hands of the government's security forces. By October large segments of the Syrian military were defecting to join the protesters, and armed battles were taking place between the military and these defectors. Although the demonstrators had started the uprising as a nonviolent campaign seeking a peaceful transition to democracy, by fall many observers predicted civil war. When the UN failed to pass a resolution against Assad's regime to help the protesters, rebels in Homs and Hama began actively seeking shipments of weapons from other countries.

The protesters were from a wide variety of religious sects, political beliefs, and geographic areas, and they had long lacked a united group to lead them. On October 2 the opposition forces announced that they had formed the Syrian National Council, a political body similar to Libya's Transitional National Council. According to an October 2011 article in the *New York Times*, the Syrian National Council "included representatives from the Damascus Declaration group, a pro-democracy network; the Syrian Muslim Brotherhood, a banned Islamic political party; various Kurdish factions; the Local Coordination Committees, a group that helps organize and document protests; and other independent and tribal figures."

In the first months of the uprising, Syria's Kurds did not actively participate in the protests. This changed on October 7, when four masked gunmen stormed the house of one of the most popular and respected Kurd leaders, Mashaal Tammo (1958–2011), and killed him. Tammo was one of the founding members of the Syrian National Council and a longtime advocate of a democratic Syria. Although the government blamed the attack on terrorists, most of the Kurdish community blamed the government's security forces. An estimated fifty thousand enraged Kurds gathered to attend Tammo's funeral and to protest the killing on October 8. At the funeral, shooting broke out and five mourners were killed. Kurdish leaders accused government forces of these killings.

By December 2011 the UN estimated that there had been more than five thousand deaths in the Syrian uprising, and fourteen thousand people had been arrested by government forces. On November 17, the Arab League (a regional political alliance of Arab nations formed in 1945 to promote political, military, and economic cooperation within the Arab world) officially suspended Syria, and on November 27, the Arab League imposed economic sanctions on Syria, under which many top Syrian officials were prohibited from traveling outside the country; the government's assets held in other Arab countries were frozen, meaning that Syria would not be able to access those funds; and Arab countries stopped transacting business with Syria's central bank. The United Nations reported grave human rights violations by Syria's security forces, including torture, sexual assaults, disappearances, and the killing of children of dissidents.

An uncertain future

As the end of 2011 approached, the wave of triumph among protesters at having unseated longtime authoritarian rulers was subdued by some grim realities. Libya was struggling to create a new government from scratch. Yemen faced a collapsing economy, and Syria was headed for civil war. The economies of most of the Arab Spring countries were in shambles. Protests and crackdowns had shut down or reduced many businesses, such as tourism and most trade. For the young men and women who had bravely led the uprisings, jobs were even more scarce than they had been at the start.

Among Arab Spring states, Tunisia was considered by political commentators to have the easiest path to democracy. On October 24, 2011, Tunisia held elections to choose members for a Constitutional Assembly, a group that would take over the transitional government and at the same time rewrite Tunisia's constitution. Sixty or more political parties soon began to organize, a complicated process, because the former regime had never allowed this. A moderate Islamist party, Ennahda (also called Nahda, meaning "Renaissance"), won the majority of the votes, and began immediately to form a coalition government, in which political parties cooperate with each other, because no party holds the majority. Ennahda would also name the prime minister and wield the greatest influence over the new constitution. Once the rewritten constitution was approved, elections for the new Tunisian government could take place.

In Egypt, although plans were in place for democratic elections, the situation was more complicated. During the revolt, the military and the protesters had worked together. After the revolt, the Supreme Council of the Armed Forces (SCAF) headed by Field Marshall Tantawi took charge of the transitional government. The SCAF appointed a committee to amend Egypt's existing constitution and scheduled parliamentary elections for a new government for November 28, 2011. In the meantime, protests continued in Tahrir Square, sometimes drawing large and angry crowds who felt that the military leaders were not pressing ahead with democratic reforms. Many experts on Egypt's government were concerned that military leaders had only outwardly gone along with some democratic reform while holding onto the base power they had always exercised. Just one week before the scheduled elections, tens of thousands of protesters rallied in Tahrir Square, calling for an end of the military government and the resignation of Tantawi. The military used tear gas and rubber bullets to try to clear the square; some protesters said they used live fire from guns, as well. In these demonstrations, more than forty protesters were killed. On November 21, the government resigned. Tantawi and his administration immediately appointed a new prime minister, who would form another cabinet, but the protesters refused to leave Tahrir Square until the military government had been handed over to a civilian government. When the first round of parliamentary elections took place in

Egypt on November 28, however, Egyptian voters showed up to vote in large numbers. Many of the protesters left Tahrir Square only long enough to vote and then returned to their protest. The military government has refused to cede its power until the new constitution has been written and a president has been elected. Presidential elections were scheduled for the summer of 2012.

In the late fall of 2011 most commentators agreed that, although no one could foresee what would happen at the end of the Arab Spring, the unexpected series of tumultuous events revealed a great deal about the spirit of the people of the Middle East and North Africa. Libyan writer Hisham Matar summarizes the Arab Spring in the *New Yorker*. He writes, "The final outcome—if there ever is such a thing as a final outcome in history—of our revolutions remains unclear. We might not succeed in building a better future. But no one can question the authenticity of our desire, or how much we are prepared to sacrifice for the opportunity to gain self-determination, dignity, and justice."

For More Information

BOOKS

Al Aswany, Alaa. *On the State of Egypt: What Made the Revolution Inevitable.* New York: Vintage Books, 2011.

Council on Foreign Relations/Foreign Affairs. *The New Arab Revolt: What Happened, What It Means, and What Comes Next.* New York: Council on Foreign Relations, 2011.

Wright, Robin. *Dreams and Shadows: The Future of the Middle East.* New York: Penguin, 2008.

PERIODICALS

Anderson, Jon Lee. "Who Are the Rebels?" *New Yorker* (April 4, 2011). Available online at http://www.newyorker.com/talk/comment/2011/04/04/110404taco_talk_anderson (accessed on November 30, 2011).

Associated Press. "Anti-Assad Dissidents Form Syrian National Council." *New York Times* (October 3, 2011). Available online at http://www.nytimes.com/2011/10/03/world/middleeast/anti-assad-dissidents-form-syrian-national-council.html (accessed on November 30, 2011).

"A Bitter Stalemate." *Economist* (September 24, 2011): 58.

Khouri, Rami G. "Drop the Orientalist Term 'Arab Spring.'" *Daily Star* (August 17, 2011). Available online at http://www.dailystar.com.lb/Opinion/Columnist/2011/Aug-17/Drop-the-Orientalist-term-Arab-Spring.ashx#axzz1ZMX0FZfe (accessed November 30, 2011).

Matar, Hisham. "The Light." *New Yorker* (September 12, 2011): 36.

Shapiro, Samantha. "Revolution, Facebook Style." *New York Times* (January 22, 2009). Available online at http://www.nytimes.com/2009/01/25/magazine/25bloggers-t.html (accessed November 30, 2011).

Steavenson, Wendell. "Roads to Freedom: The View from within the Syrian Crackdown." *New Yorker* (August 29, 2011): 26–32.

"Women of Strength Share Nobel Peace Prize." *Sydney Morning Herald* (October 10, 2011). Available online at http://www.smh.com.au/world/women-of-strength-share-nobel-peace-prize-20111009-1lfqe.html#ixzz1aIkfpLGs (accessed on November 30, 2011).

Worth, Robert F. "The Eruption of Benghazi." *New York Times Magazine* (April 3, 2011): 32–39.

Worth, Robert F. "Yemen on the Brink of Hell." *New York Times Magazine* (July 24, 2011): 24–31, 46.

WEB SITES

Amland, Bjoern H., and Karl Ritter "Nobel Peace Prize Goes to Women's Rights Activists." *CNS News.com* (October 7, 2011). http://cnsnews.com/news/article/nobel-peace-prize-goes-womens-rights-activists-5 (accessed on November 30, 2011).

"The Battle for Libya: Killings, Disappearances, and Torture." *Amnesty International* (September 2011). http://www.amnesty.org/en/library/asset/MDE19/025/2011/en/8f2e1c49-8f43-46d3-917d-383c17d36377/mde190252011en.pdf (accessed on November 30, 2011).

"Egypt Warns of 'Iron Fist' Response after Clashes." *BBC News* (May 8, 2011). http://www.bbc.co.uk/news/world-middle-east-13325845 (accessed on November 30, 2011).

Kellerhals, Merle David, Jr. "Clinton: Women's Political Participation Vital to Democracy." *allAfrica.com* (September 20, 2011). http://allafrica.com/stories/201109210884.html (accessed on November 30, 2011).

"Shirin Ebadi's Nobel Peace Prize Speech." *Muslim Women's League.* http://www.mwlusa.org/news/shirin_ebadi_acceptance_speech.htm (accessed on November 30, 2011).

"Bahrain News: The Protests (2011)." *New York Times* (September 26, 2011). http://topics.nytimes.com/top/news/international/countriesandterritories/bahrain/index.html (accessed November 30, 2011).

"World Leaders Echo Obama's Call for Syria's Assad to Step Down." *PBS Newshour* (August 18, 2011). http://www.pbs.org/newshour/bb/world/july-dec11/syria1_08-18.html (accessed on November 30, 2011).

16

Western Views of the Middle East

Relations between the "West" (a term generally used to refer the nations of North America and Europe) and the "Middle East" (the region that spans from northern Africa to southwestern Asia) are tremendously complex, and deeply influenced by a long history of interaction between the two regions, as well as the views that each maintains about the other. Some of these views are based on stereotypes, rather than fact. Many North Americans and Europeans still know very little about the people of the Middle East. Westerners often misunderstand and distrust the Middle East. For the most part, these feelings are mutual. Many people of the Middle East regard people of the West with misunderstanding and distrust, too. In her introduction to a synopsis of a seminar titled "The Middle East and the West: Misunderstandings and Stereotypes," Katerina Dalacoura of the London School of Economics and Political Science describes these mutually negative views: "The Middle East is all too often depicted [by Westerners] as a violent, threatening society from which emanate terrorism, hijackings, bombings and reactionary revolutions. Equally, the West is seen as the perpetrator of all kinds of imperialism, an instigator of plots, and an oil-hungry and self-interested actor." Dalacoura notes that it is a common mistake to view the Middle East or the West as a single entity in which all people are the same. While the many countries of the Middle East are similar, each has its own history and culture. Within each country there are people of different religious and political beliefs, some traditional and some modern, males and females, young and old, radical and moderate. Likewise, within the West, there are some large differences between the viewpoints of Americans, Canadians, and Europeans, as well as many cultural and political differences within each country.

The terrorist attacks on the United States on September 11, 2001, in which nineteen men from the Middle East, all affiliated with al-Qaeda,

WORDS TO KNOW

authoritarianism: A type of leadership in which power is consolidated under one strong leader, or a small group of elite leaders, who do not answer to the will of the people.

capitalism: An economic system in which the means of production and distribution are privately owned.

Cold War: A period of intense political and economic rivalry between the United States and the Soviet Union that lasted from 1945 to 1991.

Communism: A system of government in which the state plans and controls the economy and a single political party holds power.

Crusades: A series of military campaigns ordered by the Roman Catholic Church between 1095 and 1291 with the main goal of taking the Holy Land from the Muslims.

fundamentalism: A movement stressing adherence to a strict or literal interpretation of religious principles.

Hamas: A Palestinian Islamic fundamentalist group and political party operating primarily in the West Bank and the Gaza Strip with the goal of establishing a Palestinian state and opposing the existence of Israel. It has been labeled a terrorist organization by several countries.

Holocaust: The mass murder of European Jews and other groups by the Nazis during World War II.

Islamism: A fundamentalist movement characterized by the belief that Islam should provide the basis for the political, social, and cultural life in Muslim nations.

jihad: An armed struggle against unbelievers, in defense of Islam; often interpreted to mean holy war. The term also refers to the spiritual struggle of Muslims against sin.

Koran: Also spelled Qur'an or Quran; the holy book of Islam.

mandate: A commission granting one country the authority to administer the affairs of another country. Also describes the territory entrusted to foreign administration.

Muslim Brotherhood: An Islamic fundamentalist group organized in opposition to Western influence and in support of Islamic principles.

occupation: The physical and political control of an area seized by a foreign military force.

Ottoman Empire: The vast empire of the Ottoman Turks which included southwest Asia, northeast Africa, and southeast Europe, and lasted from the thirteenth century to the early twentieth century.

Palestine: A historical region in the Middle East on the eastern shore of the Mediterranean Sea, comprising parts of present-day Israel and Jordan.

Palestine Liberation Organization (PLO): A political and military organization formed to unite various Palestinian Arab groups with the goal of establishing an independent Palestinian state.

Palestinians: An Arab people whose ancestors lived in the historical region of Palestine and who continue to lay claim to that land.

settlements: Communities established and inhabited in order to claim land.

sharia: A system of Islamic law based on the Koran and other sacred writings. Sharia attempts to create the perfect social order, based on God's will and justice, and covers a wide range of human activities, including acts of religious worship, the law of contracts and obligations, personal status law, and public law.

used airliners for a devastating attack on U.S. soil that killed nearly three thousand people, greatly magnified the distrust of the West toward the Middle East. Although these were not the first acts of terrorism to target Americans on their own soil, they were the worst. September 11th was one of many defining moments in the troubled relations between the West and the Middle East, but it was not the beginning of the mistrust and misunderstandings. There have been many events and policies that have led to bitter feelings between the West and the Middle East throughout the history of their relations.

Early relations between the West and the Middle East

Western views of the Middle East have been shaped by some of the world's major historical events. In early times the most basic Western attitudes toward the Middle East were awe and reverence. This is because the three major monotheistic (worshipping one god) religions of Judaism, Christianity, and Islam arose in the Middle East. The city of Jerusalem has long been held sacred by Jews, Christians, and Muslims all over the world. Throughout history, reverence for Jerusalem has been mixed with intense rivalry over who controls it. Israel claims the city as its capital, although many other nations (including the United States) do not recognize it as such and maintain their embassies in Tel Aviv. Palestinians, in turn, claim East Jerusalem as the capital of a proposed Palestinian state. (Palestinians are an Arab people whose ancestors lived in the historical region of Palestine, comprising parts of present-day Israel and Jordan, and who continue to lay claim to that land.)

The golden age of Islam Not long after the rise of Islam in the seventh century, Muslim armies began their rapid conquest of vast areas of the Middle East, and over the next centuries expanded into areas of Asia and Europe, building a series of Muslim empires that came to be collectively known as the Islamic empires (632–1299). As the Middle East grew strong, however, the West was losing strength. In the fifth century the western part of the Roman Empire (a vast territory surrounding the Mediterranean Sea that was ruled by the Romans from about 43 BCE to 467 CE) collapsed. After the fall of Rome, most European countries lost their central governments. People were ruled mainly by local lords and the Roman Catholic Church. Life for Europeans became increasingly isolated and rural. The Islamic empire was flourishing at this time, with lucrative trading within its vast regions. The Islamic golden age, extending from about 750 to 1200, came after the fall of the Roman Empire. During the golden age, people of the Middle East made tremendous advances in the arts, education, science and math, medicine, architecture, and philosophy. Europeans regarded the Middle East of these times as an exotic and mysterious place. The people of the Middle East were proud of their prosperous empire and sophisticated civilization. They looked down on Europeans as barbarians (uncivilized people) and as their inferiors.

The Crusades In 1095 the Roman Catholic Church launched the Crusades, a series of military campaigns to take control of the Holy Land (roughly present-day territory of Israel, the Palestine territories, and parts of Jordan and Lebanon), which was under the control of the Islamic Empire. Of special concern to the pope (the leader of the Roman Catholic Church) was the city of Jerusalem. In a speech in Clermont, France, in 1095 the pope called on Catholic men to fight the people of the Middle East, whom he called, as quoted in *Lend Me Your Ears: Great Speeches in History* edited by William Safire, "an accursed race, wholly alienated from God." The pope went on to implore Catholic men to "wrest that land from a wicked race, and subject it to yourselves. Jerusalem is a land fruitful above all others, a paradise of delights." He ended with the rousing call: "God wills it!" In the view of the world expressed by the pope, a deep and extremely hostile division existed between the people of the Middle East and the West.

The Christian crusaders outmatched the Muslim and Jewish defenders of Jerusalem in 1099, and a massacre ensued in which tens of thousands of Muslim men, women, and children were brutally killed. In 1187 Muslim forces led by a skilled leader named Saladin (1138–1193) regained Jerusalem. After the bloody era of the Crusades was over in 1291, Europeans tended to romanticize the brutal wars in heroic poems, songs, paintings, and tales about the European knights who valiantly fought the Muslims, whom they considered infidels (nonbelievers). In the Middle East the Crusades left bitter feelings toward the Western invaders.

Power shift

After the Crusades ended in the thirteenth century, much of the Middle East came under the rule of the Ottoman Empire, the vast empire of the Ottoman Turks which included southwest Asia, northeast Africa, and southeast Europe, and lasted from the thirteenth century to the early twentieth century. For centuries, the Ottomans were in many ways stronger

Pope Urban II delivering his famous speech at Clermont calling on Catholic men to fight against Muslims in the Middle East. The Crusades would have a lasting impact on relations between the West and the Middle East. © THE ART GALLERY COLLECTION/ALAMY.

than Europeans, winning battles and taking European lands. But by the end of the sixteenth century the Ottoman armies were slowly weakening, while Western armies grew stronger. The age of European colonialism had begun. (Colonialism is the practice of acquiring new lands, establishing colonies there, and making a profit from the natural resources of the land.) Western shipbuilding and weapons-making technology made it possible for Europeans to explore the globe, enriching themselves by conquering foreign lands.

In the eighteenth century, the Industrial Revolution began in England, and it soon spread throughout Europe and North America. During this period, the invention of machines dramatically improved manufacturing, transportation, and agriculture. Due to the new technology Europe was able to produce goods on a large scale, and it needed new markets for all of the additional goods, as well as new trading routes to get the goods to distant new markets. The Middle East soon fell behind Europe in economic strength, technology, and military skills. Europeans began to view the region not as the proud empire of history, but as a market for their products, a source of needed resources, and a route to faraway colonies.

By the late nineteenth century European powers had begun to reconquer many of the European lands that had long been part of the Ottoman Empire. Europeans increasingly viewed the Middle East as a weak and failing empire that would soon be within their grasp. Newspapers in European capitals referred to the Ottoman Empire as the "Sick Man of Europe," and diplomats spoke of the "Eastern Question," arguing over which of the powerful European nations would rule the regions of the vast empire after the Ottoman rulers were gone. Many present-day historians, however, contend that the Europeans underestimated the power of the Ottoman Empire and that their views of the "Sick Man" were based largely on self-interest.

Great Britain and France were particularly intrigued with the idea of building of an artificial waterway through Egypt that would connect the Red Sea in the south to the Mediterranean Sea in the north. This would allow European shippers easy access to Africa, India, and the Far East. With the consent of the Ottoman khedive (governor) of Egypt, a French company built that waterway, Egypt's Suez Canal, which opened in 1869. The khedive owned a significant part of the Suez Canal Company, but in 1875, he needed to raise money. He sold his share of the company and Great Britain, which had major interests in Egypt already, purchased them. The British government then became a partner with the French investors in the canal company. In 1882, the British took control of Egypt.

Imperialism and Orientalism

Many historians date the beginning of the European Age of Imperialism at around 1870. Imperialism is the policy of extending the power of a nation over foreign regions, either directly, by acquiring the territory as a colony, or indirectly, by gaining control over the political or economic life of the region. Around 1870, the modern and industrialized nations of western Europe, mainly Great Britain, France, the Netherlands, and Italy, were expanding their power and territory both by colonizing and by investing heavily in economic opportunities in territories that were less developed than Europe.

Imperialism shaped Western attitudes toward non-Western regions. European imperialists tended to justify their colonial rule with the assumption that the people in the lands they controlled were inferior to, and less civilized than, Europeans. They argued that they were actually aiding the backward people in their colonies by advancing their civilization and modernizing their cultures with technology, weapons, and Western religion. Many imperialists believed in social Darwinism, the theory that the strongest or fittest survive and flourish, while the weak do not and that the people who are the elite of a society (those with power and wealth) are biologically superior in the struggle for survival.

During the Age of Imperialism, European readers were drawn to eighteenth- and nineteenth-century translations of *The Thousand and One Nights*. This popular book is a compilation of ancient folk stories that had originally been related orally among people in the Middle East and other parts of Asia. It first appeared in written form in eleventh-century Iraq but did not reach Europe until it was translated—and highly edited

An illustration of Sinbad the Sailor from The Thousand and One Nights. *This collection of Middle East folk tales became extremely popular in the West during the eighteenth and nineteenth centuries.*
© POODLESROCK/CORBIS.

and rewritten—by French translator Antoine Galland (1646–1714). In his twelve-volume edition, Galland added many stories to the collection, including some of the most famous in the West, such as the tales of Ali Baba, Sinbad, and Aladdin.

The Thousand and One Nights has a main story that serves as a base for additional tales: A bitter king who distrusts all women carries out his plan to marry, and then kill, one woman every day. Then he marries a woman named Scheherazade. Each night Scheherazade tells the king an intriguing story but stops before the end, promising to finish the story the next day. Desiring to hear the end of each tale, the king refrains from killing her. *The Thousand and One Nights* was translated into many languages and was a hit in late-nineteenth-century Europe. With its tales of genies, magic, enchantresses, and heroes, it is credited with establishing the fairy-tale genre in the West, and it has shaped Western literature from nineteenth-century poets to twenty-first-century horror novelists.

Some of the original appeal of *The Thousand and One Nights* was its depiction of an exotic culture that was unlike anything previously known to Europeans. In nineteenth-century Great Britain and France, a demand arose for other Middle Eastern arts, such as paintings and tapestries. In elite society, a new social trend arose, based in part on the logic that a colonial power should be acquainted with the cultures of the people it ruled. The new fashion, called Orientalism, consisted of scholarly attempts to define or describe the East (generally referring to Asia, including the Middle East) and artistic attempts by Western writers and painters to imitate Eastern cultures.

In his influential book *Orientalism*, (1978) renowned literary scholar Edward Said (1935–2003) contends that Westerners' romantic image of the East, which was called "the Orient" at the time, was simply one more aspect of the imperialistic view. The Orientalists and their followers depicted the people of the Middle East and Asia as exotic, but also weak, backward, and uncivilized, a population that would therefore benefit from Western imperialism. The images of the Middle East were generally not based on actual knowledge of the culture or people but were primarily a product of the imaginations of the Western Orientalists. According to Said, Orientalism basically divided the world into two opposing groups: the people of the West, who were "us," and the people of the East, who were the "other."

The end of the Ottoman Empire

The Ottoman Empire collapsed during World War I (1914–18; a global war between the Allies [Great Britain, France, and Russia, joined later by the United States] and the Central Powers [Germany, Austria-Hungary, and their allies]). After the war, the victorious Allies divided up the former empire. By that time, political opinion in the West was turning away from the outright forms of imperialism like colonization. The prevailing view, upheld most strongly by the United States, was that nations should govern themselves (although this view never stopped Western nations from attempting to dominate in the politics and economics of the Middle East). Most European leaders did not believe that the various populations of the Middle East were ready to govern themselves after being ruled for so long by the Ottomans. The newly founded League of Nations (an international organization of sovereign countries established after World War I to promote peace) therefore created a mandate system, under which Great Britain and France were to govern the former lands of the Ottoman Empire with the goal of leading the people to eventual independence. Because the United States had not, up to that point, been involved in imperialism in the Middle East, some Middle Eastern societies looked to the United States for help against European interference in their lands, but the United States did not want to confront its Western allies.

Great Britain became the strongest power in the Middle East, with control of Egypt and economic interests in the region that would become Iraq. A British corporation, the Anglo-Iranian Oil Company, which would later change its name to British Petroleum (BP), had already begun to exploit the vast oil fields in the area that later became Iran. Great Britain had promised its support to a variety of groups that were competing for local control in the region, including an Arab independence movement centered in Mecca (in present-day Saudi Arabia) and the supporters of Zionism, an international political movement originating in the late nineteenth century that called for the creation of an independent Jewish state in Palestine. France had its own interests in the region that later became Lebanon and Syria. In a series of post–World War I treaty conferences in the 1920s, mainly following the directives of Great Britain and France, the the victorious Western powers divided the Middle East into the nations that exist in the early twenty-first century.

In its decisions, the League of Nations did not consider the ethnic, religious, or political customs of the inhabitants. According to Alan R.

Taylor, author of *The Superpowers and the Middle East*, the Western powers behaved as if "the Middle East represented a declining civilization, one whose peoples and governments were inept and incapable of dealing with reality and whose cultures and institutions were not to be taken seriously." Not surprisingly, the Western powers created national boundaries and established local governments based on what would best serve their own interests. Some of the results of this division were disastrous. France manipulated the various religious and cultural sects (groups) in the region in which is created the present-day nations of Lebanon and Syria in a way that deepened the existing divisions among the people. The two nations have experienced nearly continuous conflict into the twenty-first century. Great Britain's inability to negotiate an effective compromise between the Jewish and Arab inhabitants within its mandate of Palestine contributed to the persistent violence throughout the Middle East that continued well into the twenty-first century. As Great Britain and France, as well as several other European powers that did not operate under mandates, slowly withdrew their involvement from the region, they left behind a troubling legacy of conflict.

The impact of the Cold War

At the end of World War II (1939–45; a war in which the Allies [Great Britain, France, the Soviet Union, the United States, and China] defeated the Axis Powers [Germany, Italy, and Japan]), the European powers withdrew from the Middle East, and a very different, but powerful, Western influence emerged in the region. The world's two new superpowers (powerful and dominating nations), the Soviet Union and the United States had become locked in an intense political and economic rivalry known as the Cold War (1945–91). The Soviet Union strove to spread Communism (a system of government in which the state plans and controls the economy and a single political party holds power) to other nations; the United States tried to spread democracy and capitalism (an economic system in which the means of production and distribution are privately owned).

Rather than impose their systems on other nations through war, the Soviet Union and the United States used a variety of strategies, such as providing countries with large loans or supplies of weapons, to make allies. The United States, struggling to prevent the Soviets from gaining access to oil in the Middle East, began to intervene in several countries that Great Britain and France were just leaving. It supported Middle Eastern leaders who pledged to prevent Communism from taking root in their countries, often overlooking the fact that these leaders were authoritarian (ruling with absolute power, often prohibiting democratic processes and free expression and denying rights to court trials or political opposition).

Egypt was a prime example of a U.S. Cold War ally. In the 1950s and 1960s, much to the distress of the United States, Egyptian president Gamal Abdel Nasser (1918–1970) adopted socialist policies and turned to the Soviet Union for regional support. But when Anwar Sadat (also spelled al-Sadat; 1918–1981) took over the Egyptian presidency after Nasser's death in 1970, he eliminated many socialist policies and sent the Soviet advisers home. Then the United States and Egypt achieved friendly relations, and by the mid–1970s, Sadat became the first Arab leader to enter into peace negotiations with Israel. Sadat's successor, Hosni Mubarak (1928–), who took office in 1981, continued a policy of maintaining ties with Israel and the United States. The United States valued having a strong ally in the Middle East. For the more than thirty years Mubarak was in office, the United States provided Egypt with approximately two billion dollars in aid per year, despite its knowledge that the seemingly democratic systems put in place by Mubarak were, for the most part, only for show and did not give the people a voice in the government, and that he stifled criticism of his regime, using violence and imprisonment to silence any opposition among Egyptians.

The Arab-Israeli conflict

In the mandate era after World War I, control of the British mandate of Palestine was hotly disputed between native Arabs of the region and Jewish immigrants, particularly with the massive Jewish immigration into Palestine after the war. Throughout the 1920s and 1930s, the Jewish community in Palestine, organized and funded by European Zionists, grew strong. By the mid–1930s, major clashes between Arab Palestinians and the Jews led Great Britain to formulate a plan in 1939 to limit Jewish migration into Palestine.

U.S. support of a Jewish homeland With the British limiting the number of Jews who could enter Palestine, the Zionists came to believe they could not rely on Great Britain to protect their interests. The center of support for the Zionist effort gradually shifted from England to the United States. In

1942 some six hundred American Zionists met in New York City to announce their support for the creation of a Jewish state and to call on all democratic nations to offer their support. The United States embraced this role.

After World War II ended in 1945, support for a Jewish homeland increased. People around the world felt profound sympathy and compassion for the Jewish people after it was discovered what they had suffered during the war. At the end of the war Allied forces found the concentration camps that had been operated by the Germans during the war, and they were full of horribly malnourished people and piles of dead bodies. (Concentration camps are complexes built by the Germans for the confinement and extermination of political opponents and ethnic minorities, especially Jews.) The Nazis had slaughtered millions of European civilians, including an estimated six million Jews, in these camps. The Holocaust, as the mass murder of European Jews and other groups came to be known, horrified the world. Most world leaders sought to provide the Jewish people of the world with a secure national home and a refuge from persecution. The United State continued to be one of the main supporters of a Jewish home in Palestine. In 1946 it requested that Great Britain accept one hundred thousand Jewish survivors of the Holocaust in Palestine (after refusing to accept the refugees into the United States).

In 1948 the Jews created Israel, declaring it an independent nation. In the 1948 Arab-Israeli War that followed, the neighboring Arab nations invaded Israel, attempting to crush the new nation and return the land to Palestinians. But Jewish forces prevailed, gradually gaining control of large areas of Palestine. Their victories forced approximately 750,000 Palestinians to flee their homes and take refuge in neighboring Arab countries.

The United States was the first nation to recognize the newly created country of Israel, and it took on the mission of providing for Israel's security and survival. Most Arab nations supported the Palestinians in their quest to return to their homes in Palestine. Arab nations would fight a series of wars with Israel in the following years, and they consistently denied Israel's right to exist. U.S. support for Israel angered Arab leaders and contributed greatly to the negative image of the United States in the Middle East. Israel thus became a symbol for the great cultural clash between the West and the Arab countries of the Middle East.

The problems intensified in 1967, when Arab nations began to mass their forces along their borders with Israel. Believing that an Arab invasion

Jewish Holocaust survivors arrive in Palestine in 1946. The end of World War II was a time of profound sympathy and compassion for the Jewish people. ZOLTAN KLUGER/GPO VIA GETTY IMAGES.

was imminent, Israel launched an attack in which it gained substantial territory from surrounding Arab nations, including the Sinai Peninsula and the Gaza Strip from Egypt, the West Bank from Jordan, and the Golan Heights from Syria. After the 1967 Arab-Israeli War (known in Israel as the Six-Day War), Israel established military occupations (the physical and political control of an area seized by a foreign military force) in the Gaza Strip, the West Bank, and the Golan Heights, defying requests from the international community to return them to its Arab neighbors.

The Palestinians After the 1967 war, Palestinians began organizing themselves to fight Israel to get their land back. With few resources and no standing army, they faced a powerful opponent. The militant Palestinian groups began by engaging in guerilla warfare (combat tactics used by a smaller, less equipped fighting force against a more powerful foe) against Israel. Later, some Palestinian groups engaged in kidnappings, plane hijackings, and other violent crimes to draw attention to their cause and to retaliate against Israel. As the Palestinians carried out these violent and illegal acts from the late 1960s through the late 1980s, many Western nations considered them to be terrorists. Even after 1988, when Palestinian leader Yasser Arafat (1929–2004), publicly denounced violence against Israel and agreed to recognize Israel as a nation, Palestinian militants continued to resort to violence and even terrorist acts, launching rockets on Israeli targets and, after 2000, sending suicide bombers into public places within Israel, where they caused great devastation. Slow progress was made over the next twelve years toward creating a Palestinian state, and in 1993, the Palestinian Authority (PA), a new governing body for the Palestinians, was established. A true Palestinian self-governing state with its own sovereign land was not established, however, and the Arab-Israeali conflict continued into the twenty-first century.

In 2006 the PA held elections for its legislative council (parliament). The militant group Hamas, long considered a terrorist group by the West, won a majority of the seats. Fatah, the party of the moderate PA president, Mahmoud Abbas (1935–) and Hamas had a long history of conflict, and it was difficult for the members of the two parties to work together. Clashes between the two groups led to a short, violent civil war in 2007. Afterwards, Hamas took over the rule of the Gaza Strip while Fatah ruled in the West Bank.

After the split in the PA, the conflict between Hamas and Israel remained a violent one. Militants in the Gaza Strip launched rocket attacks on Israel, and in 2007 Israel invaded the Gaza Strip, causing major death and destruction. In 2007 Israel blockaded the Gaza Strip, preventing vital necessities from being imported into the region. According to many nongovernmental organizations, the blockade caused a humanitarian crisis (an event that harms the health, safety, and security of people) for the Gazans.

Meantime, Israel continued to build Jewish settlements (communities established and inhabited in order to claim land) in the West Bank and in East Jerusalem. The settlements are located in lands where the Palestinians want to establish their own self-governed nation. With their rapidly growing populations, the Jewish communities threaten Palestinians' hopes for eventual self-rule and take away their resources. By 2010 most Western leaders and humanitarian organizations were growing increasingly concerned about Israel's blockade on the Gaza Strip and its settlements in the West Bank and Jerusalem.

Western views of the Arab-Israeli conflict Although there are no formal treaties or alliances between the United States and Israel, the United States has long been one of Israel's greatest supporters in its struggles in the Middle East and remained so in the early twenty-first century. This support has taken many forms, including large monetary donations. In the first decade of the twenty-first century the United States contributed about three billion dollars per year to Israel for economic and military support. The United States supports Israel for a number of reasons, including a desire to support democratic countries in the Middle East; a sense of shared traditions between Christians and Jews; a need for allies in the region; cooperation in intelligence gathering in the war against terror; and the knowledge that Israel, though powerful, is isolated in a hostile environment. Some also ascribe the United States' commitment to Israel in part to strong U.S.-Israel lobby organizations that seek to influence politicians, such as the American Israel Public Affairs Committee (AIPAC), a pro-Israel political lobby with a twenty-first-century membership of more than sixty thousand that has significant influence over elected officials and the ability to push many pro-Israel measures through the U.S. Congress.

U.S. support of Israel has meant that the United States often finds itself in opposition to the other Middle Eastern countries that are in conflict with Israel. This position has frequently caused the United States to form alliances with those regimes in the Middle East that support Israel, even when the regimes are antidemocratic.

Europeans and Americans did not view the Arab-Israeli conflict in the same way. In a 2008 *WorldPublicOpinion.org* poll Europeans and Americans were asked if their governments should take Israel's side, the Palestinians' side, or neither side in the conflict. In Great Britain 2 percent chose Israel's side, 8 percent chose the Palestinians' side, and 79 percent chose neither side. In France 4 percent chose Israel, 6 percent chose the Palestinians, and 79 percent chose neither. In the United States 21 percent chose Israel, 3 percent chose the Palestinians, and 71 percent chose neither.

In a random sample of Europeans in a 2011 Middle East Monitor poll, 49 percent of the respondents said that they viewed Israel as the occupying force in Palestine, and 47 percent viewed the Palestinians as the conflict's primary victims. When asked what obstacles lay in the path of compromise in the conflict, 40 percent of Europeans named the Israeli settlements and 41 percent named Israeli oppression of Palestinians, while 39 percent named Palestinian terror attacks on Israelis.

Since the 1970s, the American public has maintained a positive attitude toward Israel and a fairly negative one toward Palestinians. Little has changed in these general views over the years. In a May 2011 Pew Research poll of Americans, 48 percent said they sympathized more with Israel in the Arab-Israeli dispute, while 11 percent sympathized more with the Palestinians and 15 percent did not sympathize with either. Americans are not of one mind in this matter. The Pew poll revealed that 75 percent of conservative Republicans sympathize more with Israel than the Palestinians, and only 32 percent of liberal Democrats sympathize more with Israel.

Oil and alliances in the Middle East

In addition to Israel the United States also has a strong, long-term relationship with Saudi Arabia. In the years following the collapse of the Ottoman Empire, Saudi Arabia was a poor country. In 1933 the Saudi king, Abd al-Aziz ibn Abd al-Rahman (1876–1953), more commonly known as Ibn Saud, granted Standard Oil of California permission to drill for oil in Saudi Arabia. The company paid the king a small fee for each ton of oil the Saudi wells produced. In the early 1940s the American Oil Company (later renamed the Arabian American Oil Company, or ARAMCO) took the place of Standard Oil, and by mid-decade, it had developed the world's largest petroleum reservoir in Saudi Arabia. ARAMCO and Ibn Saud agreed to split the oil income equally. At the same time, the United States entered into an agreement to provide Saudi Arabia with strong security and defense measures. As oil revenue made Saudi Arabia very wealthy, ARAMCO went to work developing and modernizing the country, building roads, railroads, water wells, and schools, to better support their large workforce, made up of both Americans and Saudis. Over the years, Saudi Arabia obtained a larger share of ownership of ARAMCO, and in 1980 it took over the company completely.

The Saudi kings come from a conservative branch of Islam and have one of the most authoritarian governments in the Middle East. During the Cold War, however, the United States was glad to have Saudi Arabia as an ally in the Middle East, because Saudis strongly oppose Communism. The United States also wanted to ensure a steady oil supply at reasonable prices. Saudi Arabia, in turn, valued the products it received from the United States, including advanced technology, weapons, and fighter jets.

In 1991 Iraq invaded Saudi Arabia's neighbor, Kuwait. (For more information, see **The Gulf Wars: 1991 to 2011**.) The Saudi government felt threatened by Iraq's aggression and asked the United States for help. As a result, five thousand American troops came to be based in Saudi Arabia. Many people throughout the region, including many Saudis, were offended at the presence of Westerners in their lands. Al-Qaeda leader Osama bin Laden (1957–2011), who was originally from Saudi Arabia, was so outraged by American soldiers in Saudi Arabia that he began targeting Americans with acts of terrorism. Although the United States and Saudi Arabia disagree about many things, including the Arab-Israeli conflict, the alliance remained strong well into the twenty-first century.

Iran's Islamic revolution

In the 1950s the Soviet Union began to support Communist groups that were trying to overthrow Mohammad Reza Pahlavi (1919–1980), the shah of Iran. The Communists were among many Iranian groups that disliked the control foreign powers had over the shah, particularly in regard to oil. Iran had the world's third- or fourth-largest oil reserves, and from the beginning of the twentieth century, they had been developed by the Anglo-Iranian Oil Company. By the 1940s Iranians resented the fact that, under the contracts established between the oil company and the Iranian government which allowed the Anglo-Iranian Oil Company to develop the oil fields, the company was making more money from Iranian oil than Iran was.

Iran's government at that time was a constitutional monarchy, meaning it had both a shah and an elected parliament. In 1951 Iran's elected prime minister, Mohammad Mosaddeq (1882–1967), led a movement to nationalize (bring under government ownership and control) Iran's oil industry. He also tried to institute democratic reform. By 1953 Mosaddeq had enough popular support to force Pahlavi into exile. The United States became concerned that a new leader might reject Western influence, particularly at a time when the Soviets were showing interest in the country. It was also concerned about maintaining access to Iran's oil. Thus, the U.S. Central Intelligence Agency (CIA) supported a group of Iranians in overthrowing Mosaddeq from his position as prime minister and returning Pahlavi to power. Pahlavi, greatly indebted to the United States, maintained strong relations with it. He led Iran into a period of relative prosperity and introduced many Western customs into Iran, including modernization and protection of women's rights. But many of the Western influences Pahlavi brought to Iran, such as the lavish Western lifestyle led by his family and immediate circle of associates, deeply offended many Iranians. His secret police force suppressed opposition to his rule but anger mounted.

Iranians began to revolt in 1978, forcing Pahlavi to leave the country in early 1979. Suffering from cancer that would soon take his life, Pahlavi was allowed into the United States to seek medical treatment. In the meantime, the Iranian revolutionaries created a new constitution, establishing an Islamic government based on sharia. The government was to be ruled both by clerics (ordained religious officials) and by democratically elected representatives. The most powerful figure in the new Islamic Republic of Iran was the Supreme Leader, the Ayatollah Ruhollah Khomeini (1902–1989). Khomeini was intensely anti-Western and particularly anti-American. On November 4, 1979, a large mob of Iranian students overran the U.S. Embassy in Tehran, Iran's capital, taking the entire U.S. staff and some bystanders hostage. They demanded that the shah, who was receiving medical treatment in the United States, be returned to Iran to face trial. Khomeini supported the militants' actions, although his prime minister resigned in disapproval. Some of the hostages were initially released, but 52 Americans were held hostage for 444 days before being released.

The hostage crisis in Iran was deeply disturbing to Americans, as were the events that followed. Khomeini openly called the United States the "Great Satan," and Iranians rallied in the streets in support of the hostage taking, shouting "Death to America." Even after the hostages were released, other acts of terrorism were linked to Iran, among them the bombings of the U.S. Embassy and the Marine barracks in Lebanon. The new Islamic Republic of Iran vowed that it would actively spread its form of Islamism. In the years after the revolution, it gave support to militant groups designated as terrorists by the United States and other Western nations, such as Hezbollah in Lebanon and Hamas in Palestine, and provided weapons to insurgents in the Iraq War (2003–11). In the twenty-first century, Western nations greatly feared that Iran was developing nuclear weapons, and Iran became one of the Middle East nations most feared by the United States and other Western countries. The anti-Western aspect of the Iranian Islamic revolution also caused many Westerners to fear Islamism, which had not previously been a large concern.

Iranian students storm the U.S. Embassy in Tehran during the Iranian Revolution. They seized fifty-two American hostages, who were held for more than a year. AFP/GETTY IMAGES.

The "clash of civilizations" theory

In 1991 the Soviet Union collapsed, and the United States became the sole superpower. At the time no other country could compete with the tremendous military and economic strength of the United States. In 1993 political scientist Samuel P. Huntington wrote an article titled "The Clash of Civilizations?" in the journal *Foreign Affairs*. In the article Huntington theorizes that in the post–Cold War world, the nature of world conflict would change. In Huntington's view, future conflicts would erupt between civilizations rather than between nations, and they would be based on differences in culture rather than differences in ideology (the body of ideas held by a group or culture) or economic systems.

Huntington argues that Western culture had become pervasive in non-Western civilizations by the 1990s, and that non-Western people, especially Muslims, did not necessarily accept the West's most basic values. "Western ideas of individualism, liberalism, constitutionalism, human rights, equality, liberty, the rule of law, democracy, free markets, the separation of church and state, often have little resonance [appeal] in Islamic" and other cultures, Huntington notes. Yet the Western powers continued to spread their own cultural values and systems, as if they represented the "universal civilization" of the world. This caused bitter resentment in places like the Middle East, which sought to renew its own culture with a resurgence of Islamism. Huntington predicts that this will give rise to violent, global conflict between the West and the Islamic civilization.

Renowned Middle East historian Bernard Lewis strongly supports Huntington's views. In his 1990 article, "The Roots of Muslim Rage," Lewis writes of the bitter anger Muslims worldwide feel toward Westerners. Lewis describes the history of relations between the West and the Middle East, or more generally, between Christendom and Islam, as a "long series of attacks and counterattacks, jihads [armed struggles against unbeleivers] and crusades, conquests and reconquests." He describes a general trend among Muslims toward a holy war waged against the West.

Many historians strongly disagreed with Lewis, but a tremendous onset of terrorist activity targeting Americans took place during the 1990s which seemed to confirm Lewis's theories. In 1993 a bomb exploded in the parking garage of the World Trade Center in New York, killing 6 people and injuring more than 1,000 others. In 1995 a car bomb killed 5 U.S. military servicemen at a U.S. military headquarters in Riyadh, Saudi Arabia. In 1996 a truck bomb in Dhahran, Saudi Arabia, killed 19 U.S. servicemen and injured hundreds more. In 1998 the U.S. embassies in Nairobi, Kenya and Dar es Salaam, Tanzania were blown up by truck bombs, killing 224 people and injuring thousands more. In 2000 a suicide bomber in a small boat sailed alongside the U.S. Navy destroyer USS *Cole* while it was in port in Aden, Yemen and detonated his explosives, blowing a hole in the side of the ship and killing 17 sailors. Less than a year after the attack on the *Cole*, the attacks of September 11, 2001, occurred in the United States. Many of these terrorist attacks were linked to al-Qaeda, and all of them were connected to militant Islamic groups with anti-Western, anti-Israel messages. In 1998 bin Laden had issued a chilling fatwa (a statement of religious law issued by Islamic clerics), that signaled al-Qaeda's war against the United States. The fatwa, available on the *PBS Newshour* Web site, stated: "The ruling to kill the Americans and their allies—civilians and military—is an individual duty for every Muslim who can do it in any country in which it is possible to do it."

After September 11th, the U.S. government, persuaded to some extent by the Huntington's theory, declared a war on terror. To many, it appeared that the "clash of civilizations" had begun.

By the time the United States entered into the bloody and lengthy War in Afghanistan (2001–) and the Iraq War, Huntington's "clash of civilizations" theory was accepted by many historians and U.S. foreign policy makers. The American news media bolstered this view of a raging Muslim world. In an article on the *Teach Mideast* Web site Mohamed El Mansour writes,

> Instead of treating terrorist attacks as an aberration [unusual occurance] and acts by a radical minority, most of the analysts and commentators would exaggerate their importance and portray them as part of a systematic war against Western civilization. In this sense terrorism has poisoned even more US-Arab and US-Muslim relations.

Many scholars of the Middle East, however, continued to object to the theory. They argued that the world's Muslim population is a highly diverse group of people with wide ranging belief systems; one entity known as the Islamic civilization is a gross and inaccurate generalization. They also argued that the theory employs a misreading of the Koran (also spelled Qur'an or Quran; the holy book of Islam) and many Islamic terms.

The Council on American-Islamic Relations (CAIR) held Huntington, Lewis, and other followers of the clash of civilizations theory responsible for pervasive Islamophobia (an unfounded fear of or hostility toward Islam) in the United States. According to CAIR, in an article titled "Islamophobia" on its Web site,

> Islamophobia has resulted in the general and unquestioned acceptance of the following: Islam is monolithic [characterized as one rigid and fixed uniform whole rather than a combination of diverse parts] and cannot adapt to new realities; Islam does not share common values with other major faiths; Islam as a religion is inferior to the West. It is archaic, barbaric and irrational; Islam is a religion of violence and supports terrorism; Islam is a violent political ideology.

Islam and democracy

Another issue that arose from the clash of civilizations theory is the concept that Muslims, in general, do not value political freedom and human rights in the same way that Westerners do and that Islam might be incompatible with democracy. This issue was, for the most part, put to rest in 2011, when major prodemocracy revolts broke out in Tunisia,

Egypt, Libya, Bahrain, Yemen, and Syria, a series of uprisings that came to be known as the Arab Spring. Long-term authoritarian rulers were forced out of office in Tunisia, Egypt, and Libya. The protesters, who had organized their protests via the Internet and social media, came out in the millions. They were mostly young and mostly secular. Their overwhelming message was that they wanted political freedom and democracy, and many risked their lives in the fight to gain it.

When Tunisia, Egypt, and Libya scheduled democratic elections to replace their authoritarian governments in 2011, concerns arose about the popularity of Islamism in those countries, particularly the possibility of Islamist groups being elected to government positions. Although the Islamic groups of Tunisia and Egypt had not actively organized the protests, they were strong, ready to run candidates, and well positioned to win seats in the new governments of both countries. For example the Muslim Brotherhood (an Islamic fundamentalist group organized in opposition to Western influence and in support of Islamic principles) was suppressed by Egypt's government for decades. It has a long tradition of assisting the needy and working to improve society through the principles of Islam. For decades, the Muslim Brotherhood has called for democracy in Egypt. Some of its members participated in the pro-democracy uprising.

Many Americans, along with many liberal and secular people in the Middle East, fear that popular Islamist groups, such as the Muslim Brotherhood, will rise to power through democratic elections and that once in office they will impose unwanted religious restrictions upon non-Islamists, withhold political freedoms, and limit women's rights. Academics and Middle East specialists debate about the prospects of elected Islamist governments in the Middle East. Some fear them. In a February 2011 interview with David Horovitz in the *Jerusalem Post*, Bernard Lewis called the Muslim Brotherhood "a very dangerous, radical Islamic movement" and warned that "if they obtain power, the consequences would be disastrous for Egypt." Lewis explained his overall view:

> We, in the Western world particularly, tend to think of democracy in our own terms . . . to mean periodic elections in our style. But I think it's a great mistake to try and think of the Middle East in those terms and that can only lead to disastrous results, as you've already seen in various places. They are simply not ready for free and fair elections.

In testimony before a U.S. House of Representatives subcommittee in 2011, political scientist Nathan J. Brown expressed a very different view of the Muslim Brotherhood. Brown testified that, as quoted in the article "U.S. Policy and the Muslim Brotherhood" on the *Carnegie Endowment for International Peace* Web site, "Despite its radical roots, the Muslim Brotherhood has clearly and consistently renounced violence for decades and is deeply committed to peaceful political change." Noting that the organization has many different branches throughout the Middle East and that it is dedicated to many social functions beyond politics, Brown contends that the Muslim Brotherhood is not as politically powerful as some other experts seem to fear. He concluded, "There is every reason to be interested in the Brotherhood's myriad (and surprisingly diverse) country-based movements, but there is no reason to fear it as a menacing global web." Brown believes that moderate Islamism is fully compatible with a democratic society that upholds human rights and political freedom. His view was shared by many Middle East scholars in 2011, but most agreed that how an Islamist democracy might come into being and how it would operate cannot be foreseen.

Stereotypes

Most American perceptions about people of the Middle East come from popular entertainment, such as the movies and television, or from the news media. According to the American Arab Anti-Discrimination Committee (ADC), children receive many negative images of people from the Middle East from American television and film. One notable example is the Disney animated film *Aladdin* (1992). According to Marvin Wingfield and Bushman Karaman, in their 1995 article for the ADC titled "Arab Stereotypes and American Educators," the film offended many Arab Americans with "characters who are dark-skinned, swarthy and villainous—cruel palace guards or greedy merchants with Arabic accents and grotesque facial features." The ADC particularly objected to the lyrics of the opening song, as quoted by Wingfield and Karaman:

> Oh, I come from a land, from a faraway place
> Where the caravan camels roam
> Where they cut off your ear
> If they don't like your face
> It's Barbaric, but hey, it's home.

With this song, the ADC stated, "The film immediately characterizes the Arab world as alien, exotic, and 'other.' Arab Americans see this film as perpetuating the tired stereotype of the Arab world as a place of deserts and camels, of arbitrary cruelty and barbarism."

Jack Shaheen, author of the book *Reel Bad Arabs: How Hollywood Vilifies a People*, surveyed nine hundred Hollywood films with Arab characters made over the entire history of film and found that the vast majority of them contained offensive stereotypes. Films such as *True Lies* (1994), *Back to the Future* (1985), and *Raiders of the Lost Ark* (1981) depict Arabs as evil villains, murderous fanatics, lecherous rapists, or lazy, rich sheikhs. Arab women, Shaheen writes, are portrayed either as half-clad belly dancers or as veiled nonentities. "Taken together, her mute on-screen non-behavior and black-cloaked costume serve to alienate the Arab woman from her international sisters, and vice versa. Not only do the reel [movie] Arab women never speak, but they are never in the workplace, functioning as doctors, computer specialists, school teachers" as are the women of most Arab countries.

Stereotypes of the women of the Middle East are widespread. According to the article "Arab Woman between East and West" on the UNESCO Web site:

> In both the East and the West, Arab women are often portrayed through stereotypical representations and discourses in which they have no voice. The Western popular imagination, nurtured by a media which commonly lacks sensitivity to complex realities, is quick to associate Arab women with oppression and subordination. Meanwhile, the Eastern media tends to value and project a comforting image of women as housewives, wives and mothers and devote little attention to independent and politically active women.

The article concludes that this stereotyping is harmful because women are the "essential actors in the development of the Arab region, and it is indispensable that their position at the heart of all contemporary social, political, economic and cultural matters be recognized in both the East and West."

Middle Eastern immigrants in the West

Western fears and mistrust of people of the Middle East leads to hostility toward Middle Eastern immigrants. Since the terrorist attacks in the United States on September 11, 2001, Middle Eastern immigrants in Europe and the United States have faced increasing incidents of hate crimes (crimes that are carried out against people because of their race,

An Arab woman. Stereotypes of women from the Middle East are widespread, in both the Middle East itself and the West.
© GRAPHEAST/ALAMY.

religion, gender, or sexual orientation), racial profiling (the consideration of race, ethnicity, or national origin by law enforcement in identifying a criminal suspect), workplace discrimination, and other abuses.

Europe has experienced its own terrorist attacks and has had a large influx of Middle Eastern immigrants in the past few decades. Some European countries have passed laws that seem prejudicial against Muslims. Many laws are aimed at preventing Muslims from upholding their cultural distinctions in their new homes. For example, in 2009, Switzerland passed an amendment to its constitution that banned the building of minarets (the tall slender towers of mosques with one or more balconies from which the summons to prayer are called). In 2011 France banned women from wearing full-face veils. For many Muslim women it is a custom to dress according to *hijab*, a principle of dressing modestly. Although many Muslim women do not wear any type of head covering, and some wear simple head scarves that do not cover the face, more traditional Muslim women wear burkas and *niqabs*, veils that cover the entire face except the eyes. Of the approximately six million Muslims living in France, fewer than two thousand women wear the full-face veil. The French president claimed the law forbidding full-face veils is meant to support women's dignity, but most commentators believe it is an attempt to discourage Muslim fundamentalism.

Of the many forms of discrimination that Muslims face in the United States in the twenty-first century, one of the most pronounced was the impassioned objections to the building of mosques, Muslim places of worship. In 2010 a proposal to build a Muslim center and mosque two blocks from Ground Zero, the site of the September 11th terrorist attacks in New York (where the World Trade Center towers once stood), met with a furious protest that was taken up by Internet bloggers. (Bloggers are authors of online journals called blogs.) Overlooking the constitutional right to freedom of religion in the United States, the bloggers proclaimed that Islam is a threat to the United States. Also in 2010 the Islamic Center of Temecula Valley proposed building a mosque in the conservative Southern California city of Temecula. The announcement drew local protesters.

Anti-Muslim rhetoric (use of language through writing or speaking) on the Internet and in protests has become disturbingly hateful and irrational. In 2010 a pastor of a fundamentalist Christian church in Florida drew media attention when he organized a Burn a Koran day on September 11, using the social networking Web site *Facebook* to recruit people to help him burn thousands of copies of the holy book of Islam. He was stopped from carrying out the burning, but in March 2011, he publicly burned a Koran in front of a small crowd of onlookers.

Messages from the U.S. government

In the first decade of the twenty-first century, there were many examples of officials of all levels of the U.S. government making offensive, inaccurate statements about Muslims, but those in the nation's highest office sent a more reasoned message. In 2001, not long after the September 11th terrorist attacks, President George W. Bush (1946–) made an appearance at an Islamic center. There he carefully distinguished between the millions of peace-loving followers of Islam and the few violent followers of extreme Islamist groups, like al-Qaeda. He entreated the American people not to retaliate against Muslims.

In June 2009 President Barack Obama (1961–) addressed the Muslim people of the world in a speech called "A New Beginning," from Cairo, Egypt. In his speech, Obama acknowledged that conflicts between the United States and the Middle East were complex. He called on the younger generations in all countries to view the world without the blinders imposed by the worn-out traditions of hostility and division and to dismiss the divisive theories, like the clash of civilizations, in order to move forward. He said, in part, as quoted by the *New York Times*,

> I know there are many—Muslim and non-Muslim—who question whether we can forge this new beginning. Some are eager to stoke the flames of division, and to stand in the way of progress. Some suggest that it isn't worth the effort—that we are fated to disagree, and civilizations are doomed to clash. Many more are simply skeptical that real change can occur. There is so much fear, so much mistrust. But if we choose to be bound by the past, we will never move forward. And I want to particularly say this to young people of every faith, in every country— you, more than anyone, have the ability to remake this world.

For More Information

BOOKS

Kalin, Ibrahim. "Roots of Misconception: Euro American Perceptions of Islam before and after September 11." In *Islam, Fundamentalism, and the Betrayal of Tradition: Essays by Western Muslim Scholars.* Edited by Joseph E.B. Lumbard. Bloomington, IN: World Wisdom, 2004, pp. 144–187. Available online at http://www.worldwisdom.com/uploads/pdfs/58.pdf (accessed on November 30, 2011).

Safire, William, ed. *Lend Me Your Ears: Great Speeches in History.* New York: Norton, 2004, p. 93.

Taylor, Alan R. *The Superpowers and the Middle East.* New York: Syracuse University Press, 1991, p. 9.

PERIODICALS

Ghosh, Bobby. "Islamophobia: Does America Have a Muslim Problem?" *Time* (August 19, 2010). Available online at http://www.time.com/time/printout/ 0,8816,2011936,00.html (accessed on November 30, 2011).

Horovitz, David. "A Mass Expression of Outrage against Injustice." *Jerusalem Post* (February 25, 2011). Available online at http://www.jpost.com/Opinion/Columnists/Article.aspx?id=209770 (accessed on November 30, 2011).

Huntington, Samuel P. "The Clash of Civilizations?" *Foreign Affairs* 72, no. 3 (Summer 1993). Available online at http://www.polsci.wvu.edu/faculty/hauser/PS103/Readings/HuntingtonClashOfCivilizationsForAffSummer93.pdf (accessed on November 30, 2011).

ICM Research. *Public Perceptions of the Israel-Palestine Conflict.* (January 2011). Available online at http://aljazeera.net/mritems/streams/2011/3/15/1_1048049_1_51.pdf (accessed on November 30, 2011).

WEB SITES

"Al Qaeda's Fatwa." *PBS Newshour* (February 23, 1998). http://www.pbs.org/newshour/terrorism/international/fatwa_1998.html (accessed on November 30, 2011).

"Arab Woman Between East and West." *UNESCO.org.* http://portal.unesco.org/culture/en/ev.php-URL_ID=36006&URL_DO=DO_TOPIC&URL_SECTION=201.html (accessed on November 30, 2011).

"The Balfour Declaration.' *Israel Ministry of Foreign Affairs.* http://www.mfa.gov.il/MFA/Peace%20Process/Guide%20to%20the%20Peace%20Process/The%20Balfour%20Declaration (accessed on November 30, 2011).

Brown, Nathan J. "U.S. Policy and the Muslim Brotherhood." *Carnegie Endowment for International Peace* (April 13, 2011). http://carnegieendowment.org/2011/04/13/u.s.-policy-and-muslim-brotherhood/i6 (accessed on November 30, 2011).

Dalacoura, Katerina. "The Middle East and the West: Misunderstandings and Stereotypes." *Fathom* (2001). http://www.fathom.com/course/21701764/index.html (accessed on November 30, 2011).

El Mansour, Mohammed. "The U.S.-Middle East Connection: Interests, Attitudes, and Images." *Teach Mideast* (2004). http://teachmideast.org/essays/28-history/110-the-us-middle-east-connectioninterests-attitudes-and-images (accessed on November 30, 2011).

"Islamophobia." *Council on American-Islamic Relations (CAIR).* http://www.cair.com/Issues/Islamophobia/Islamophobia.aspx (accessed on November 30, 2011).

"Modern History Sourcebook: Rudyard Kipling, The White Man's Burden 1899." *Fordham University.* http://www.fordham.edu/halsall/mod/kipling.asp (accessed on November 30, 2011).

"Text: Obama's Speech in Cairo." *New York Times* (June 4, 2009). http://www.nytimes.com/2009/06/04/us/politics/04obama.text.html?pagewanted=all (accessed on November 30, 2011).

Shaheen, Jack G. "Reel Bad Arabs: How Hollywood Vilifies a People." *Institute of Communication Studies* (July 2003). http://ics.leeds.ac.uk/papers/pmt/exhibits/2501/shaheen.pdf (accessed on November 30, 2011).

"Views of Middle East Unchanged by Recent Events: Public Remains Wary of Global Engagement." *Pew Research Center* (June 10, 2011). http://www.people-press.org/2011/06/10/views-of-middle-east-unchanged-by-recent-events/ (accessed on November 30, 2011).

Wingfield, Marvin, and Bushman Karaman. "Arab Stereotypes and American Educators." *American-Arab Anti-Discrimination Committee* (March 1995). http://www.adc.org/index.php?id=283 (accessed on November 30, 2011).

Where to Learn More

Books

Al Aswany, Alaa. *On the State of Egypt: What Made the Revolution Inevitable.* New York: Vintage Books, 2011.

Anderson, Sean, and Stephen Sloan. *Historical Dictionary of Terrorism.* Lanham, MD: Scarecrow Press, 2002.

Barr, James. *A Line in the Sand: Anglo-French Struggle for the Middle East.* New York: W.W. Norton and Co., 2012.

Brown, Nathan J. *Palestinian Politics after the Oslo Accords: Resuming Arab Palestine.* Berkeley: University of California Press, 2003.

Carew-Miller, Anna. *Palestinians.* Philadelphia: Mason Crest, 2010.

Cleveland, William L. *A History of the Modern Middle East.* Boulder, CO: Westview Press, 2004.

Council on Foreign Relations/Foreign Affairs. *New Arab Revolt: What Happened, What It Means, and What Comes Next .* New York: Council on Foreign Relations, 2011.

Currie, Stephen. *Terrorists and Terrorist Groups.* San Diego, CA: Lucent Books, 2002.

DeFronzo, James. *The Iraq War: Origins and Consequences.* Boulder, CO: Westview Press, 2009.

Drummond, Dorothy. *Holy Land Whose Land: Modern Dilemma Ancient Roots.* Seattle, WA: Educare Press, 2002.

Encyclopedia of the Modern Middle East and North Africa. 4 vols. New York: Macmillan Reference USA, 2004.

Engel, David. *Zionism.* Harlow: Pearson/Longman, 2009.

Etheredge, Laura S., ed. *Persian Gulf States: Kuwait, Qatar, Bahrain, Oman, and the United Arab Emirates.* New York: Rosen/Britannica Educational Publishing, 2011.

Farsoun, Samih K., with Christina E. Zacharia. *Palestine and the Palestinians*. Boulder, CO: Westview Press, 1997.

Finkel, Caroline. *Osman's Dream: The History of the Ottoman Empire*. New York: Basic Books, 2007.

Gelvin, James L. *The Modern Middle East: A History*, 3rd ed. New York: Oxford University Press, 2011.

Gunderson, Cory Gideon. *The Israeli-Palestinian Conflict*. Edina, MN: Abdo, 2004.

Hirst, David. *Beware of Small States: Lebanon, Battleground of the Middle East*. New York: Nation Books, 2010.

Hourani, Albert. *A History of the Arab Peoples*. Cambridge, MA: Belknap, 1991.

Kalin, Ibrahim. "Roots of Misconception: Euro-American Perceptions of Islam before and after September 11." In *Islam, Fundamentalism, and the Betrayal of Tradition: Essays by Western Muslim Scholars*. Edited by Joseph E.B. Lumbard. Bloomington, IN: World Wisdom, 2004, pp. 144–187. Available online at http://www.worldwisdom.com/uploads/pdfs/58.pdf (accessed on November 30, 2011).

Karsh, Efraim. *The Arab-Israeli Conflict: The 1948 War*. New York: Rosen Publishing, 2008.

———. *The Iran-Iraq War: 1980–1988*. Oxford, UK: Osprey, 2002.

Kennedy, Hugh. *The Great Arab Conquests: How the Spread of Islam Changed the World We Live In*. Cambridge, MA: Da Capo Press, 2008.

Khalidi, Rashid. *The Iron Cage: The Story of the Palestinian Struggle for Statehood*. Boston, MA: Beacon, 2006.

Kherdian, David. *The Road from Home: The Story of an Armenian Girl*. New York: Greenwillow Books, 1979.

Kinross, Lord. *The Ottoman Centuries: The Rise and Fall of the Turkish Empire*. New York: Morrow Quill Paperbacks, 1979.

Kort, Michael. *The Handbook of the Middle East*. Brookfield, CT: Twenty-First Century Books, 2002.

Lewis, Bernard. *The Middle East: A Brief History of the Last 2,000 Years*. New York: Scribner, 1995.

Mackey, Sandra. *Mirror of the Arab World: Lebanon in Conflict*. New York: W.W. Norton, 2009.

Miller, Debra A. *The Arab-Israeli Conflict*. San Diego, CA: Lucent Books, 2005.

Milton-Edwards, Beverly, and Stephen Farrell. *Hamas: The Islamic Resistance Movement*. Cambridge, England: Polity Press, 2010.

Myre, Greg, and Jennifer Griffin. *This Burning Land: Lessons from the Front Lines of the Transformed Israeli-Palestinian Conflict*. Hoboken, NJ: Wiley, 2010.

Nardo, Don. *The Islamic Empire*. Detroit, MI: Lucent Books, 2011.

Polk, William R. *Understanding Iran: Everything You Need to Know, from Persia to the Islamic Republic, from Cyrus to Ahmadinejad.* Basingstoke, United Kingdom: Palgrave Macmillan, 2011.

Ra'ad, Basem L. *Hidden Histories: Palestine and the Eastern Mediterranean.* London: Pluto Press, 2010.

Rabinovich, Itamar. *The Lingering Conflict: Israel, Arabs, and the Middle East, 1948–2011.* Washington, DC: Brookings Institution Press, 2011.

Rapoport, David C. "Terrorism." In *Encyclopedia of Violence, Peace, & Conflict.* Vol. 3. 2nd ed. Edited by Lester Kurtz. San Diego, CA: Academic Press, 2008.

Shindler, Colin. *A History of Modern Israel.* Cambridge: Cambridge University Press, 2008.

Schneer, Jonathan. *The Balfour Declaration: The Origins of the Arab-Israeli Conflict.* New York: Random House, 2010.

Shlaim, Avi. *Israel and Palestine: Reappraisals, Revisions, Refutations.* London and New York: Verso, 2010.

Slavicek, Louise Chipley. *Israel.* New York: Chelsea House, 2008.

Smith, Charles D., ed. *Palestine and the Arab-Israeli Conflict: A History with Documents,* 7th ed. Boston MA: Bedford/St. Martin's, 2009.

Taheri, Amir. *The Persian Night: Iran Under the Khomeinist Revolution.* New York: Encounter Books, 2010.

Wingate, Katherine. *The Intifadas.* New York: Rosen, 2004.

Wright, Robin. *Dreams and Shadows: The Future of the Middle East.* New York: Penguin, 2008.

Young, Michael. *The Ghosts of Martyrs Square: An Eyewitness Account of Lebanon's Life Struggle.* New York: Simon and Schuster, 2010.

Periodicals

Anderson, Jon Lee. "Who Are the Rebels?" *New Yorker* (April 4, 2011). Available online at http://www.newyorker.com/talk/comment/2011/04/04/110404taco_talk_anderson (accessed on November 30, 2011).

Beinin, Joel. "Is Terrorism a Useful Term in Understanding the Middle East and the Palestinian-Israeli Conflict?" *Radical History Review* no. 85 (Winter 2003): 12–23. Available online at http://www.why-war.com/files/85.1 beinin.pdf (accessed on November 30, 2011).

"A Bitter Stalemate." *Economist* (September 24, 2011): 58.

Diamond, Larry. "Why Are There No Arab Democracies?" *Journal of Democracy* 21, no. 1 (January 2010).

"Gaza Strip," *New York Times* (August 11, 2011). Available online at http://topics.nytimes.com/top/news/international/countriesandterritories/gaza_strip/index.html (accessed on November 30, 2011).

Ghosh, Bobby. "Islamophobia: Does America Have a Muslim Problem?" *Time* (August 19, 2010). Available online at http://www.time.com/time/print out/0,8816,2011936,00.html (accessed on November 30, 2011).

Hogan, Matthew. "The 1948 Massacre at Deir Yassin Revisited." *Historian* 63, no. 2 (Winter 2001).

Huntington, Samuel P. "The Clash of Civilizations?" *Foreign Affairs* 72, no. 3 (Summer 1993). Available online at http://www.polsci.wvu.edu/faculty/ hauser/PS103/Readings/HuntingtonClashOfCivilizationsForAffSummer 93.pdf (accessed on November 30, 2011).

Khouri, Rami G. "Drop the Orientalist Term 'Arab Spring.'" *Daily Star* (August 17, 2011). Available online at http://www.dailystar.com.lb/ Opinion/Columnist/2011/Aug-17/Drop-the-Orientalist-term-Arab-Spring. ashx#axzz1ZMX0FZfe (accessed on November 30, 2011).

Lebanon: The Israel-Hamas-Hezbollah Conflict. CRS Report for Congress. U.S. Library of Congress, Congressional Research Service (September 15, 2006). Available online at http://www.fas.org/sgp/crs/mideast/RL33566.pdf (accessed on November 30, 2011).

Masoud, Tarek. "The Upheavals in Egypt and Tunisia: The Road to (and from) Liberation Square." *Journal of Democracy* Vol. 22, No. 3 (July 2011). Available online at http://www.journalofdemocracy.org/articles/gratis/ Masoud-22-3.pdf (accessed on November 30, 2011.

Shapiro, Samantha. "Revolution, Facebook Style." *New York Times* (January 22, 2009). Available online at http://www.nytimes.com/2009/01/25/magazine/ 25bloggers-t.html (accessed on November 30, 2011).

Steavenson, Wendell. "Roads to Freedom: The View from within the Syrian Crackdown." *New Yorker* (August 29, 2011): 26–32.

Web Sites

"Al-Qaeda (a.k.a. al-Qaida, al-Qa'ida)." *Council on Foreign Relations* (June 17, 2011). http://www.cfr.org/terrorist-organizations/al-qaeda-k-al-qaida-al-qaida/ p9126 (accessed on November 30, 2011).

Asser, Martin. "The Muammar Gaddafi Story." *BBC News* (October 21, 2011). http://www.bbc.co.uk/news/world-africa-12688033 (accessed on November 30, 2011).

"Background Note: Lebanon." *U.S. Department of State* (May 23, 2011). http:// www.state.gov/r/pa/ei/bgn/35833.htm#history (accessed on November 30, 2011).

"Bahrain News: The Protests (2011)." *New York Times* (September 26, 2011). http://topics.nytimes.com/top/news/international/countriesandterritories/ bahrain/index.html (accessed on November 30, 2011).

"The Battle for Libya: Killings, Disappearances, and Torture." *Amnesty International* (September 2011). http://www.amnesty.org/en/library/asset/MDE19/025/ 2011/en/8f2e1c49-8f43-46d3-917d-383c17d36377/mde190252011en.pdf (accessed on November 30, 2011).

Beinin, Joel, and Lisa Jajjar. "Palestine, Israel and the Arab-Israeli Conflict: A Primer." *Middle East Research and Information Project.* http://www. merip.org/palestine-israel_primer/intro-pal-isr-primer.html (accessed on November 30, 2011).

Brown, Nathan J. "U.S. Policy and the Muslim Brotherhood." *Carnegie Endowment for International Peace* (April 13, 2011). http://carnegieendow ment.org/2011/04/13/u.s.-policy-and-muslim-brotherhood/i6 (accessed on November 30, 2011).

"Bullets to Ballet Box: A History of Hezbollah." *Frontline World.* www.pbs.org/ frontlineworld/stories/lebanon/history.html (accessed on November 30, 2011).

Collelo, Thomas, ed. "Syria." *Country Studies.* (1987). http://countrystudies.us/ syria/ (accessed on November 30, 2011).

El Mansour, Mohammed. "The U.S.-Middle East Connection: Interests, Attitudes, and Images." *Teach Mideast* (2004). http://teachmideast.org/ essays/28-history/110-the-us-middle-east-connectioninterests-attitudes-and-images (accessed on November 30, 2011)

"Foreign Terrorist Organizations." *U.S. Department of State.* (May 19, 2011). http://www.state.gov/s/ct/rls/other/des/123085.htm (accessed on November 30, 2011).

Grace, Francie. "Munich Massacre Remembered." *CBS News.* (February 11, 2009). http://www.cbsnews.com/stories/2002/09/05/world/main520865.shtml (accessed on November 30, 2011).

"The Gulf War." *Harper's Magazine.* http://www.harpers.org/GulfWar.html (accessed on November 30, 2011).

"The Gulf War: an In-Depth Examination of the 1990–1991 Persian Gulf Crisis." *PBS Frontline.* http://www.pbs.org/wgbh/pages/frontline/gulf/ (accessed on November 30, 2011).

"A History of Conflict—Israel and the Palestinians: A Timeline." *BBC News.* http://news.bbc.co.uk/2/shared/spl/hi/middle_east/03/v3_ip_timeline/html/ (accessed on November 30, 2011).

"Hunting Bin Laden." *PBS Frontline.*. http://www.pbs.org/wgbh/pages/front line/shows/binladen/ (accessed on November 30, 2011).

Internet Islamic History Sourcebook. Fordham University, http://www.fordham. edu/halsall/islam/islamsbook.html#Islamic%20Nationalism (accessed on November 30, 2011).

"Iran: A Brief History." *MidEast Web.*. http://www.mideastweb.org/iranhistory. htm (accessed on November 30, 2011).

"Guide to the Middle East Peace Process." *Israeli Ministry of Foreign Affairs.* http://www.mfa.gov.il/MFA/Peace+Process/Guide+to+the+Peace+Process/ (accessed on November 30, 2011).

The Islamic World to 1600. Applied History Research Group, University of Calgary. http://www.ucalgary.ca/applied_history/tutor/islam/ (accessed on November 30, 2011).

"Islamophobia." *Council on American-Islamic Relations (CAIR)*. http://www. cair.com/Issues/Islamophobia/Islamophobia.aspx (accessed on November 30, 2011).

The Ottomans.org. http://www.theottomans.org/english/history/index.asp (accessed on November 30, 2011).

"Profile: Egypt's Muslim Brotherhood." *BBC News Middle East*. http://www. bbc.co.uk/news/world-middle-east-12313405 (accessed on November 2, 2011).

The Question of Palestine and the United Nations. United Nations Department of Public Information (March 2003). http://www.un.org/Depts/dpi/ palestine/ (accessed on September 16, 2011).

Slim, Randa. "Hezbollah's Most Serious Challenge." *Foreign Policy* (August 5, 2011). http://mideast.foreignpolicy.com/posts/2011/05/03/hezbollah_s_most_ serious_challenge (accessed on November 30, 2011).

"The Suez Crisis: An Affair to Remember." *Economist* (July 27, 2006). http:// www.economist.com/node/7218678 (accessed on November 30, 2011).

"Zionism and the Creation of Israel." *MidEast Web*. http://www.mideastweb. org/zionism.htm (accessed November 3, 2011).

Index

Illustrations are marked by (ill.).

H

I

O

P

U

Y

Z